Services
rough Council

Public Procurement in the European Union

Public Procurement in the European Union

By Christopher Bovis

palgrave
macmillan

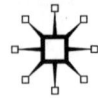

© Christopher Bovis 2005

All rights reserved. No reproduction, copy or transmission of this publication may be made without written permission.

No paragraph of this publication may be reproduced, copied or transmitted save with written permission or in accordance with the provisions of the Copyright, Designs and Patents Act 1988, or under the terms of any licence permitting limited copying issued by the Copyright Licensing Agency, 90 Tottenham Court Road, London W1T 4LP.

Any person who does any unauthorised act in relation to this publication may be liable to criminal prosecution and civil claims for damages.

The author has asserted his right to be identified as the author of this work in accordance with the Copyright, Designs and Patents Act 1988.

First published 2005 by
PALGRAVE MACMILLAN
Houndmills, Basingstoke, Hampshire RG21 6XS and
175 Fifth Avenue, New York, N. Y. 10010
Companies and representatives throughout the world

PALGRAVE MACMILLAN is the global academic imprint of the Palgrave Macmillan division of St. Martin's Press, LLC and of Palgrave Macmillan Ltd. Macmillan® is a registered trademark in the United States, United Kingdom and other countries. Palgrave is a registered trademark in the European Union and other countries.

ISBN-13: 978–1–4039–3607–3 hardback
ISBN-10: 1–4039–3607–2   hardback

This book is printed on paper suitable for recycling and made from fully managed and sustained forest sources.

A catalogue record for this book is available from the British Library.

Library of Congress Cataloging-in-Publication Data
Bovis, Christopher.
  Public procurement in the European Union / by Christopher Bovis.
    p. cm.
  Includes bibliographical references and index.
  ISBN 1–4039–3607–2 (hardback)
    1. Government purchasing–Law and legislation–European Union countries. 2. Public contracts–European Union countries. I. Title.
KJE5632.B687 2005
346.2402'3–dc22   2005042933

10 9 8 7 6 5 4 3 2 1
14 13 12 11 10 09 08 07 06 05

Printed and bound in Great Britain by
Antony Rowe Ltd, Chippenham and Eastbourne

to Pine
for taking care of business

Contents

Cases before the European Court of Justice	xiii
Foreword	xix

Introduction	**1**
The emergence of public markets and their interface with the common market	1
The public policy dimension in public procurement	5
Regionalism and public procurement	6
The industrial policy potential in public procurement	9
Public procurement and defence	10
Chapter 1 European Integration and Public Procurement	**14**
Introduction	14
Public procurement as a component of the common market	14
The conceptual elements of public procurement regulation	17
The evolution of public procurement regulation	23
Chapter 2 Public Procurement Regulation	**33**
Introduction	33
Part 1 The legal regime on public procurement	**33**
The supplies procurement	33
The works procurement	35
Utilities procurement	38
Procurement of services	42
Enforcement and compliance: The Compliance Directives	45
The WTO Government Procurement Agreement	46
Part 2 Definitions and the mechanics of public procurement regulation	**49**
The concept of contracting authorities	49
The principle mandatory advertisement and publication of public contracts	50
The monetary applicability of the Public Procurement Directives	52
Selection and qualification criteria	54

Legal requirements for the qualification of contractors 56
The list of recognised contractors 56

Part 3 The award of public contracts 58
Tendering procedures 58
The award criteria 61
Framework agreements 64
In-house contracts and contracts to affiliated undertakings 65
Design contests 65
Concession contracts 66
The award of public housing schemes 66
Socio-economic considerations 67
Employee protection and transfer of undertakings 68
Environmental considerations as award criteria 69

Chapter 3 Lessons from Jurisprudence 71
Introduction 71

Part 1 The European Court of Justice and Public Procurement 72
The principle of non-discrimination 72
Technical standards 72
Selection and qualification 73
Preference purchasing schemes 76
The principle of objectivity 78
Award procedures 78
Award criteria 79

Part 2 The emerging themes 82
The public nature of public procurement 82
The functional dimension of contracting authorities 83
Bodies governed by public law 85
The dependency test 85
Commerciality and needs in the general interest 88
The dual capacity of contracting authorities 91
The connection of contracting authorities with private undertakings 92
Procurement as a policy instrument 95
Social considerations as award criteria 95
Transfer of undertakings and public procurement 98
Environmental considerations as award criteria 99

Chapter 4 Public Procurement as Economic and Policy Exercise 100
Introduction 100

The new approach towards the integration of public markets   101
A neo-classical perspective to public procurement regulation   106
The distinctiveness of public markets   106
Procurement regulation as an economic exercise   107
Anti-trust and public procurement regulation   111
The ordo-liberal approach to public procurement regulation   112
Public procurement as part of the European Integration   113
Contract compliance and public procurement   115
A rule of reason   117
Inherent dangers in the regulation of public procurement   121

Chapter 5   A Critical Assessment of Public Procurement   124
Introduction   124
Inherent shortcomings in the public procurement rules   125
The dimensionality of public procurement   125
The effects of the principle of transparency   128
The abuse of award procedures which may restrict competition   130
Public monopolies   134
Standardisation and specification   136
Reluctance in initiating litigation   137
Public procurement and the sustainability of certain industries   139

Chapter 6   The New Public Procurement Regime   145
Introduction   145

Part 1   The new concepts in public procurement regulation   146
The Codified Public Supplies, Works and Services Directive   146
A thematic analysis of the new concepts in procurement   148
Eligibility of bodies governed by public law to tender   148
Joint and centralised procurement   149
A new award procedure: the competitive dialogue   150
Framework procurement   153
Electronic procurement   155
Electronic auctions   157
The use of electronic signatures   160
Public procurement and the environment   160
Procurement and employment   162
Public procurement and WTO   163
Procurement and culture   164
Procurement, small and medium enterprises and subcontracting   164
Contractual performance and public procurement   164
Procurement and probity   165

The award criteria	166
Exclusive rights in the utilities	168
Postal utilities	169
Competitive markets in utilities	169
Part 2 Future developments	**170**
Public procurement and Public-Private Partnerships	170
Revision of remedies in public procurement	173
Chapter 7 Public-Private Partnerships	**175**
Introduction	175
From corporatism to contractualised governance	177
Part 1 The emergence of the Private Finance Initiative	**179**
The intellectual origins of the Private Finance Initiative	182
The procedural delivery of the Private Finance Initiative	187
The contractual nature of a PFI project	187
The services/works dilemma	188
The case of mixed contracts	189
The case of concession contracts	191
The award procedures for PFI	193
Publicity requirements	196
Part 2 The development of public-private partnerships at European level	**196**
The contractual public-private partnership	198
The institutional public-private partnership	200
Chapter 8 The Procurement of Services of General Interest	**205**
Introduction	205
Part 1 The services of general interest under EU law	**206**
The services of general interest through public procurement	208
The non-commercial character of services of general interest have	209
Services of general interest and contracting authorities	211
Links between contracting authorities and private undertakings	213
Procurement, contractualised governance and services of general interest	216
The "public" nature of public procurement	218
Part 2 How are public services financed?	**220**
The ECJ and its approach to the financing of services of general interest	221

Public service obligations	224
The role of public procurement in the assessment of state aids	226
The interaction of public procurement with the three approaches of state aids assessment	228
Part 3 Market forces and services of general interest	**232**
A new approach	234
Conclusions	**237**
Notes	241
Index	287

Cases before the European Court of Justice

C-13/61, *Kledingverkoopbedrijf de Geus en Uitdenbogerd v. Robert Bosch GmbH* [1962] ECR 45.

C-26/62, *NV Algemene Transporten Expeditie Onderneming Van Gend en Loos v. Nederlandse Administrtie der Belastigen* [1963] ECR 1.

C-6/64, *Costa v. ENEL* [1964] ECR 585.

C-48/65, *Alfons Luttucke GmbH v. Commission* [1966] ECR 19.

C-57/65, *Alfons Luttucke GmbH v. Haupzollampt Saarlouis* [1966] ECR 205.

C-27/67, *Firma Fink-Frucht GmbH v. Haupzollamt Munchen Landsbergerstrasse* [1968] ECR 223.

C-28/67, *Firma Molkerei Zentrale Westfalen/Lippe GmbH v. Haupzollampt Paderborn* [1968] ECR 143.

C-13/68, *SpA Salgoil v. Italian Ministry for Foreign Trade* [1968] ECR 453.

C-14/68, *Wilhem v. Bundeskartellampt* [1969] ECR 1 at 27.

C-78/70, *Deutche Grammophon GmbH v. Metro-SB Grossmarkte GmbH* [1971] ECR 1 at 31.

C-21-24/72, *International Fruit Co NV v. Produktschap voor Groenten en Fruit* [1972] ECR 1236.

C-127/73, *BRT v. SABAM* [1974] ECR 313.

C-167/73, *Commission v. France* [1974] ECR 359.

C-173/73, *Italy v. Commission* [1974] ECR 709.

C-40-48, 50, 54-56, 111, 113-114/73, *Cooperative Vereniging "Suiker Unie" UA v. Commission* [1975] ECR 1663.

C-2/74, *Reyners v. Belgian State* [1974] ECR 631.

C-33/74, *Van Bisbergen v. Bestuur van de Bedrijfsvereninging voor de Metaalinijverheid* [1974] ECR 1299.

C-41/74, *Van Duyn v. Home Office* [1974] ECR 1337.

C-36/74, *Walrave and Koch v. Association Union Cycliste International et al.* (1974) ECR 1423.

C-43/75, *Drefenne v. SABENA* (1976) ECR 473.

C-74/76, *Ianelli & Volpi Spa v. Ditta Paola Meroni* [1977] 2 CMLR 688.

C-38/77, *ENKA BV v. Inspecteur der Invoerrecht en Accijnzen* [1977] ECR 2203.

C-61/77R, *Commission v. Ireland* [1977] ECR 1411.

C-156/77, *Commission v. Belgium* [1978] ECR 1881.

C-102/79, *Commission v. Belgium* [1980] ECR 1489.

C-300/81, *Commission v. Italy* [1983] ECR 449.

C-314-316/81&82, *Procureur de la Republique et al. v. Waterkeyn* [1982] ECR 4337.

C-249/81, *Commission v. Ireland* [1982] ECR 4005.

244/81, *Commission v. Ireland* [1982] ECR 4005.

C-76/81, *SA Transporoute et Travaux v. Minister of Public Works* [1982] ECR 457.

C-283/81, *Srl CILFIT v. Minisrty of Health* [1982] ECR 3415.

C-323/82, *Intermills v. Commission* [1984] ECR 3809.

C-286/82 & 26/83, *Luisi & Carbone v. Ministero del Tesoro* [1984] ECR 377.

C-240/83, *Procureur de la République v. ADBHU* [1985] ECR 531.

C-247/83, *Commission v. Italy* [1985] ECR 1077.

C-118/83R, *CMC Co-operativa Muratori e Cementisti v. Commission* [1983] ECR 2583.

C-44/84, *Hurd v. Jones* [1986] ECR 29.

C-152/84, *Marshall v. Southampton and South West Hampshire Area Health Authority* [1986] ECR 723.

C-18/84, *Commission v. France* [1985] ECR 1339.

C-03/84, *Commission v. Italy* [1986] ECR 1759.

C-234/84, *Belgium v. Commission* [1986] ECR 2263.

C-24/85, *Spijkers v. Gebroders Benedik Abbatoir CV* [1986] ECR 1, 1123.

C-40/85, *Belgium v. Commission* [1986] ECR I-2321.

C-67/85, 68/85 and 70/85, *Van der Kooy and Others v. Commission* [1988] ECR 219.

C-118/85, *Commission v. Italy* [1987] ECR 2599.

C-199/85, *Commission v. Italy* [1987] ECR 1039.

C-239/85, *Commission v. Belgium* [1986] ECR 1473.

C-310/85, *Deufil v. Commission* [1987] ECR 901.

C-66/86, *Ahmed Saeed Flugreisen v. Commerssion* [1989] ECR 803.

C-147/86, *Commission v. Hellenic Republic* [1988] ECR 765.

C-308/86, *Ministere Public v. Lambert* [1988] ECR 478.
C-27/86, 28/86, 29/86, *Constructions et Enterprises Indusrtielles S.A. (CEI) v. Association Intercommunale pour les Autoroutes des Ardennes, CEI and Bellini* [1987] ECR 3347.
C-84/86, *Commission v. Hellenic Republic*, not reported.
C-27/86, *Constructions et Enterprises Indusrtielles S.A. (CEI) v. Association Intercommunale pour les Autoroutes des Ardennes,* C-28/86, *Ing.A. Bellini & Co. S.p.A. v. Regie de Betiments,* C-29/86, *Ing.A. Bellini & Co. S.p.A. v. Belgian State* [1987] ECR 3347.

C-45/87, *Commission v. Ireland* [1988] ECR 4929.
C-31/87, *Gebroeders Beenjes B.V v. The Netherlands* [1989] ECR 4365.
C-45/87, *Commission v. Ireland* [1988] ECR 4929.
C-45/87R, *Commission v. Ireland* [1987] ECR 1369.
C-301/87, *France v. Commission* [1990] ECR I, p. 307.
C-3/88, *Commission v. Italy* [1989] ECR 4035.

C-21/88, *Du Pont de Nemours Italiana SpA v. Unita Sanitaria Locale N.2 di Carrara* [1990] ECR 889.
C-103/88, *Fratelli Costanzo S.p.A. v. Comune di Milano* [1989] ECR 1839.
C-351/88, *Lavatori Bruneau Slr. v. Unita Sanitaria Locale RM/24 di Monterotondo*.
C-194/88R, *Commission v. Italy* [1988] ECR 5647.
C-303/88, *Italy v. Commission* [1991] ECR I-1433.

C-188/89, *Foster v. British Gas* [1990] ECR-1313.
C-213/89, *The Queen v. Minister of Agriculture Fisheries and Food* [1990] ECR I-2433.
C-247/89, *Commission v. Portugal* [1991] ECR I-3659.
C-261/89, *Italy v. Commission* [1991] ECR I-4437.
C-305/89, *Italy v. Commission ('Alfa Romeo')* [1991] ECR I-1603.
C-360/89, *Commission v. Italy* [1992] ECR I-3401.
C-179/89, *Farmaindusrtia v. Consejeria de salud de la Junta de Andalucia* [1989] O.J. C 160/10.
296/89, *Impresa Dona Alfonso di Dona Alfonso & Figli s.n.c. v. Consorzio per lo Sviluppo Industriale del Comune di Monfalcone*, judgement of June 18, 1991.

C-6/90 and 9/90, *Francovich and Bonifaci v. Italian Republic* [1993] ECR 61.
C-179/90, *Merci Convenzionali Porto di Gevova* [1991] ECR 1-5889.
C-362/90, *Commission v. Italy*, judgement of March 31, 1992.

C-24/91, *Commission v. Kingdom of Spain* [1994] CMLR 621.

C-29/91, *Dr Sophie Redmond Stichting v. Bartol*, IRLR 369.
C-209/91, *Rask v. ISS Kantinservice*, [1993] ECR 1.
C-272/91R, *Commission v. Italian Republic*, order of June 12, 1992.
C-389/92, *Ballast Nedam Groep NV v. Belgische Staat* [1994] 2 CMLR.
C-107/92, *Commission v. Italy*, judgement of August 2, 1993.
C-296/92, *Commission v. Italy*, judgement of January 12, 1994.
C-71/92, *Commission v. Spain*, judgement of June 30, 1993.
C-89/92, *Ballast Nedam Groep NV v. Belgische Staat* [1994] 2 CMLR.
C-278/92 to C-280/92, *Spain v. Commission* [1994] ECR I-4103.
C-296/92, *Commission v. Italy*, judgement of January 12, 1994.
C-343/95, *Diego Cali et Figli* [1997] ECR 1-1547.
C-364/92, *SAT Fluggesellschafeten* [1994] ECR 1-43.
C-382/92, *Commission v. United Kingdom* [1994] ECR 1.
C-387/92, *Banco Exterior* [1994] ECR I-877.
C-392/92, *Schmidt v. Spar und Leihkasse der fruherer Amter Bordersholm, Kiel und Cronshagen* [1994] ECR 1, 1320.

C-46 & 48/93, *Brasserie du Pecheur SA v. Germany, Regina v. Secretary of State for Transoprt, ex parte Factortame LTD*, 5 March 1996: [1996] 1 CMLR 889.
C-56/93, *Belgium v. Commission* [1996] ECR I-723.
C-359/93, *Commission v. The Netherlands*, judgement of January 24, 1995.
C-280/93, *Germany v. Council*, judgement of 5 October 1994.
C-324/93, *R. v. The Secretary of State for the Home Department, ex parte Evans Medical Ltd and Macfarlan Smith Ltd*, judgement of 28 March 1995.
C-382/92, *Commission v. United Kingdom* [1994] ECR 1.
C-392/93, *The Queen and H.M. Treasury, ex parte British Telecommunications PLC*, O.J. 1993, C 287/6.

C-39/94 *SFEI and Others* [1996] ECR I-3547.
C-48/94, *Rygaard v. Stro Molle Akustik*, judgement of 19/9/1995.
C-57/94, *Commission v. Italy*, judgement of May 18, 1995.
T-67/94, *Ladbroke Racing v. Commission* [1998] ECR II-1.
C-79/94, *Commission v. Greece*, judgement of May 4, 1995.
C-87/94R, *Commission v. Belgium*, order of April 22, 1994.
C-157/94, *Commission v. Netherlands* [1997] ECR I-5699.
C-158/94, *Commission v. Italy* [1997] ECR I-5789.
C-159/94, *Commission v. France* [1997] ECR I-5815.
C-160/94, *Commission v. Spain* [1997] ECR I-5851.
C-241/94, *France v. Commission* [1996] ECR I-4551.
T-358/94, *Air France v. Commission* [1996] ECR II-2109.

T-106/95, *FFSA and Others v. Commission* [1997] ECR II-229.
C-343/95, *Diego Cali et Figli* [1997] ECR 1-1547.
C-44/96, *Mannesmann Anlangenbau Austria AG et al. v. Strohal Rotationsdurck GesmbH*, judgement of 15 January 1998.
T-16/96, *Cityflyer Express v. Commission* [1998] ECR II- 757).
C-44/96, *Mannesmann Anlangenbau Austria AG et al. v. Strohal Rotationsdurck GesmbH* [1998] ECR 73.
C-323/96, *Commission v. Kingdom of Belgium* [1998] ECR I-5063.
C-342/96, *Spain v. Commission* [1999] ECR I-2459.
C-353/96, *Commission v. Ireland* and C-306/97, *Connemara Machine Turf Co Ltd v. Coillte Teoranta* [1998] ECR I-8565.
C-360/96, *Gemeente Arnhem Gemeente Rheden v. BFI Holding BV* [1998] ECR 6821.
C-44/96, *Mannesmann Anlangenbau Austria AG et al. v. Strohal Rotationsdurck GesmbH* [1998] ECR 73.

C-5/97, *Ballast Nedam Groep NV v. Belgische Staat*, judgement of 18 December 1997.
C-6/97, *Italy v. Commission* [1999] ECR I-2981.
T-46/97, [2000] ECR II-2125.
C-75/97, *Belgium v. Commission* [1999] ECR I-3671.

C-107/98, *Teckal Slr v. Comune di Viano*, judgement of 18 November 1999.
C-144/97, *Commission v. France* [1998] ECR 1-613.
C-174/97 P, [1998] ECR I-1303.
T-204/97 and T-270/97, *EPAC v. Commission* [2000] ECR II-2267.
C-256/97, *DM Transport* [1999] ECR I-3913.
T-613/97, *Ufex and Others v. Commission* [2000] ECR II-4055.
C-107/98, *Teckal Slr. v. Comune di Viano* [1999] ECR I-8121.
C-156/98, *Germany v. Commission* [2000] ECR I-6857.
C-176/98, *Holst Italia v. Comune di Cagliari*, judgement of 2 December 1999.
C-380/98, *The Queen and H.M. Treasury, ex parte University of Cambridge* [2000] ECR 8035.

C-94/99, *ARGE Gewässerschutzt v. Bundesministerium für Land-und Forstwirtschaft*, judgement of 7 December 2000.
C-223/99, *Agora Srl v. Ente Autonomo Fiera Internazionale di Milano* and C-260/99 *Excelsior Snc di Pedrotti Runa & C v. Ente Autonomo Fiera Internazionale di Milano* [2001] ECR 3605.
C-237/99, *Commission v. France* [2001] ECR 934.

C-285/99 & 286/99, *Impresa Lombardini SpA v. ANAS*, judgement of 27 November 2001.

C-513/99, *Concordia Bus Filandia v. Helsingin Kaupunki et HKL-Bussiliikenne* [2002] ECR 7213.

C-53/00, *Ferring SA v. Agence centrale des organismes de sıcuritı sociale (ACOSS)* [2001] ECR I-09067.

C-280/00, *Altmark Trans GmbH and Regierungsprdsidium Magdeburg v. Nahverkehrsgesellschaft Altmark GmbH and Oberbundesanwalt beim Bundesverwaltungsgericht* [2003] ECR 1432.

C-280/00, *Altmark Trans GmbH, Regierungsprdsidium Magdeburg et Nahverkehrsgesellschaft Altmark GmbH, Oberbundesanwalt beim Bundesverwaltungsgericht* (third party), judgement of 24 July 2003.

C-5/01, *Belgium v. Commission* [2002] ECR I-3452.

C-83/01 P, C-93/01 P and C-94/01, *Chronopost and Others* [2003], not yet reported.

C-126/01, *Ministre de l'economie, des finances et de l'industrie v. GEMO SA* [2003] ECR 3454.

Foreword

Public procurement is a specialist subject. It has many dimensions and many facets emerge in its regulation. It reflects on the need to liberalise the relevant markets to achieve competitiveness and efficiencies. It also retrieves many links with national policies. It provides a platform for businesses to expand within the European Union and beyond. It is a key element of the European integration process. It interfaces with other Community Policies. It represents one of the last remaining non-tariff barriers for the completion of the common market. Finally, it plays an important role in international trade liberalisation under the auspices of the WTO.

This book approaches the subject of public procurement in the European Union from a multi-discipline stance. The legal framework of public procurement has been examined in such a way as to reveal its policy interplay and provide for a clear landscape of the side-effects of its regulation.

The recent enlargement of the European Union has placed the concept of the common market at the heart of the European integration process. New members have to adapt the public procurement *acquis communautaire* and existing ones must improve on the quality of its implementation. The challenge is on for member states and European institutions to provide the public markets of the European Union with a regulatory system of multi-focal attributes. The success of such an exercise will be measured by reference to market access for companies supplying the public sector, the quality of services provided, value-for-money considerations and finally the degree of complementarity of public purchasing with socio-economic policies of the European Union and its member states.

It would have been difficult to complete this project without the involvement of a number of people to whom here I record my great indebtedness. First of all, my thanks go to the Publishers for their professionalism and the assistance they provided. It is also with deep appreciation that I express my gratitude to Dr Christine Cnossen, for reading the manuscript and discussing numerous concepts which I have developed, particularly in the light of the recent jurisprudential and policy developments.

xx *Foreword*

Finally, I am indebted to Peter Cnossen for his guidance and his insights into business strategies and government practices relevant to public procurement. He gave me an inspiration to approach the public procurement regime critically and assess its relationship with main anti-trust principles. His support has been invaluable.

Introduction

The regulation of public procurement in the European Union has been the cinderella of the European integration. Often neglected as a discipline of European law and policy, although directly relevant to the fundamental principles of the common market, public procurement has not received equal priority to other regulatory regimes by the Member States of the European Union.

As one of the major subject areas of the common market, public procurement exhibits the symptoms of regime rejection. For almost three decades, the implementation of the European *acquis* has been slow and at rather irritatingly procrastinated pace, particularly when compared to other legal and policy regimes which are carried through the European Union principles of free movement of goods, services and the right of establishment. The implementation of the public procurement regime by the EU Member States reflects on something peculiar: either the deliberate opposition of Member States with the principles enshrined in the relevant legal framework or the impossibility of providing an *umbrella* legal regime which can embrace a plethora of multi-policy orientations and domestic considerations arising from the award of public contracts.

Procurement, public or private, is a powerful exercise. It carries the aptitude of acquisition; it epitomises economic freedom; it depicts the nexus of trade relations amongst economic operators; it represents the necessary process to deliver public services; it demonstrates strategic policy options.

The emergence of public markets and their interface with the common market

Why regulate public procurement? The main reason for regulating public sector and utilities procurement is to bring their respective markets parallel to the operation of private markets. European policy makers have recognised the distinctive character of *public markets* and focused on establishing conditions similar to those that control the operation of private markets. The public markets reflect an economic equation where the demand side is represented by the public sector and its contracting authorities and the supply side covers the industry.

The intellectual support of public procurement regulation in the European Union rests with liberal economic theories, where enhanced competition in public markets could bring about beneficial effects for the supply side. It is envisaged that optimal allocation of resources within the European industries, rationalisation of production and supply, promotion of mergers and acquisitions and elimination of sub-optimal firms and creation of globally competitive industries will transform the European industrial base. It seems that public procurement regulation transmits from the start signals of industrial policy, a policy that is desperately needed in the European Union. Although the regulation of public procurement aims primarily at the purchasing patterns of the demand side, its surrogate effects on the supply side have been also deemed to yield substantial purchasing savings for the public sector. Public procurement has cyclical dynamics. It purports to change both behavioural and structural perceptions and applies its effects to both the demand and supply sides.

The European institutions envisaged the creation of such a competitive regime in public markets through the establishment of a legal framework which aims at eliminating preferential public procurement practices which favour *national champions*. Legally, the existence of *national champions* falls foul of the principle of non-discrimination laid down in the European Treaties, but also on policy grounds combating discrimination on grounds of nationality in public procurement and eliminating domestic preferential purchasing schemes could result in efficiency gains at European and national levels. When the demand side is viewed as a conglomerate of purchasing entities at European level, the efficiency gains represent a challenge too good to miss.

Public procurement regulation will set in motion three major effects which would primarily influence the supply side, but have a phenomenal impact on the demand side as well. These include a *trade effect*, a *competition effect* and a *restructuring effect*.

The trade effect represents the actual and potential savings that the public sector will be able to achieve through lower cost purchasing. The trade effect emanates as a result of the principle of transparency in public markets (compulsory advertisement of public contracts above certain thresholds). However, the principle of transparency and the associated trade effect in public markets do not in themselves guarantee the establishment of competitive conditions in the relevant markets, as market access – a structural element in the process of integration of public markets in Europe – could be hindered by the discriminatory behaviour of contracting authorities in the selection stages and the award stages of public procurement. The trade effect has a static dimension, since it emerges as a consequence of enhanced market access in the relevant sector or industry.

The competition effect relates to the changes of industrial performance as a result of changes in the price behaviour of national firms which had previously been protected from competition by means of preferential and discriminatory procurement practices. The competition effect derives also from the principle of transparency and appears to possess rather static characteristics. Transparency in public procurement breaks information and awareness barriers in public markets, and as mentioned above brings a trade effect in the relevant sectors or industries by means of price competitiveness. The competition effect comes as a natural sequence to price competitiveness and inserts an element of long-term competitiveness in the relevant industries in aspects other than price (e.g. research and development, innovation, customer care). The competition effect would materialise in the form of *price convergence* of goods, works and services destined for the public sector. Price convergence could take place both nationally and Community-wide, in as much as competition in the relevant market would equalise the prices of similar products.

Finally, the restructuring effect reveals the restructuring dimension and the re-organisational dynamics in the supply side, as a result of increased competition in the relevant markets. The restructuring effect is a dynamic one and refers to the long-term industrial and sectoral adjustment within industries that supply the public sector. The restructuring effect attempts to encapsulate the reaction of the relevant sector or industry to the competitive regime imposed upon the demand and supply sides, as a result of openness and transparency and the sequential trade and competition effects. The response of the relevant sector or industry and the restructuring effect itself would depend on the efficiency of the industry to merge, diversify, convert or abort the relevant competitive markets and would also reflect contemporary national industrial policies.

The above scenario represents the model envisaged by European Institutions on a macro-perspective and depicts the orientation of policy-making towards the formation of a coherent industrial policy at European level. The regulation of the purchasing behaviour of the demand side in public markets seems to constitute an effective way of introducing competitive elements to the European industries, which apparently suffer from overcapacity and excessive compartmentalisation. In addition, the cost of research and development in such a market structure builds up and it is reflected in pricing, particularly in high-tech products. Industrial restructuring and adjustment has been a priority for the European Commission for a long time.

The regulation of public procurement in the European Union received priority as a result of the policy and legal momentum which influenced the whole European integration process in the eighties (The White Paper for the Completion of the Internal Market and the Single European Act). The inefficiency of the relevant primary legal provisions to combat discriminatory practices and preferential public purchases was disclosed, as statistical results revealed considerably low cross-border import penetration in public contracts. A disturbing picture emerged revealing the extent of differentiation between the structures of private and public markets within the Member States. Public markets appear as closed and protected offering very little access to intra-community trade patterns.

Public procurement has served well in the national governments' armory of industrial policies. In the past many of the advantages offered to *national champions* and locally operating firms in public markets had discouraged the tradability of public contracts amongst European industries. Persistence in low import penetration in protected public procurement sectors exposes often a type of strategy applicable to the relevant industries. Before the opening-up of the public procurement in Europe, the typical strategic choice was low on integration and high on responsiveness, including the replication of all major corporate functions such as production, research and development, and marketing in Member State. The functioning of the common market and the regulation of public procurement in the European Union has been forcing firms to revise those strategies and to build up *network organisations*, which combine local responsiveness with a high degree of centralisation and co-ordination of major supporting activities. The new strategy has the characteristics of a multi-focal strategy for the supply side.

The adoption of multi-focal strategies or global integration strategies involves a major shift in location patterns of key functions within firms. The old decentralised multinational organisations which duplicated major functions in each country in which they operated need to transform into an integrated system of which the key elements show a different degree of regional concentration. As a consequence of the new organisational structure, different types of international transactions are expected to occur. Specialisation and concentration of activities in certain regions will lead to more trade between Member States. In addition, as a result of the corporate network system, trade will increasingly develop into intra firm trade and intra-industry trade with greater exchange of intermediary products. The organisational rationalisation following the development of network organisations poses the problem of ownership and location of the corporate headquarters. Some Member States fear that they relinquish strategic control in the restructuring process and therefore may resist the rationalisation process that the industry has been undergoing, by imposing various restrictions in terms of ownership or control structures of locally operating firms.

The public policy dimension in public procurement

Policy makers should not overlook the effects of public procurement on the formulation of the industrial policy of the European Union. The aim and objective of its regulation has to a large extent acquired an industrial policy background, which mainly focuses on the achievement of savings for the public sector and the much desired restructuring and adjustment of the European industrial base. However, public spending in the form of procurement is indissolubly linked with adjacent policies and agendas in all Member States. The most important policy associated with public purchasing is social policy. Such an argument finds justification in two reasons: the first relates to the optimal utilisation of human resources in industries supplying the public sector; the second reason acquires a strategic dimension, in the sense that public purchasing serves aims and objectives stipulated in the European Treaties, such as social cohesion, combating of long-term unemployment, and finally the achievement of acceptable standards of living. The underlying objectives of the European regime on public procurement relating to enhanced competition and unobstructed market access in the public sector at first sight appear incompatible with the social dimension of European integration, particularly in an era where recession and economic stagnation have revealed the combating of unemployment as a main theme of European governance.

The award of public contracts can be based on two criteria: i) the lowest price or ii) the most economically advantageous offer. Contracting authorities have absolute discretion in adopting the award criterion under which they wish to award their public contracts. The lowest price award criterion is mostly used when the procurement process is relatively straightforward. On the other hand, the most economically advantageous offer award criterion is suited for more complex procurement schemes.

The most economically advantageous offer as an award criterion represents a flexible framework for contracting authorities wishing to insert a qualitative parameter in the award process of a public contract. Needless to say, price, as a quantitative parameter plays an important role in the evaluation stage of tenders, as the meaning of "economically advantageous" could well embrace financial considerations in the long run. So, if the qualitative criteria of a particular bid compensate for its more expensive price, potential savings in the long run could not be precluded. It is not clear whether the choice of the two above mentioned award criteria has been intentional with a view to providing contracting authorities a margin of discretion to take into account social policy objectives when awarding their public contracts, or if it merely reflects an element of flexibility which is considered necessary in modern purchasing transactions. If the most economically advantageous offer represents elements relating to quality of public purchasing other than price, an argument arises here supporting the fact that the enhancement of the socio-economic fabric is a "qualitative" element which can fall into the framework of the above criterion. This argument would take away the assumption that the award of public contracts is a pure *economic exercise*. On the other hand, if one is to insist that public procurement should reflect only *economic choices*, the social policy considerations that may arise from the award of public contracts would certainly have an economic dimension attached to them, often in public service activities which are parallel to public procurement. To what extent contracting authorities should contemplate such elements remains unclear.

Regionalism and public procurement

A possible way of combating recession and its side effects (industrial decline, unemployment, social exclusion) is the enhancement of regionalism and the development of decentralised policies that can boost peripheral growth in the economy. A scenario like the above will need to incorporate not only the commitment of a central government towards regional economic development but also the participation of local and regional authorities in implementing the strategic plan.

Regionalism and spatial economic development should focus on incentives aimed at growth, optimal allocation of resources, operating as much as possible within a regime of workable and effective competition. Regional development policies, centralised or decentralised, should have as their priority small and medium sized enterprises which are often located in less favoured regions, or regions of economic decline and industrial restructuring. The idea behind the above policies is to promote and enhance the market performance and participation of small and medium firms in order to achieve economic growth within a region. The concentration of policy makers on small and medium sized firms could also be justified by the fact that in real terms they represent the vast majority of businesses within European economies. Large firms often lack flexibility in adapting their strategies to new market requirements, where industrial restructure in most cases has been materialised by taking the form of voluntary or compulsory redundancies and workforce cuts. On the other hand, small firms appear more flexible in changes as they diversify their activities more effectively than large firms, without the need to have necessary recourse to labour cuts. It has been suggested that economic recovery from the present recession will emerge from the small enterprises which will first detect the signals of growth.

The policies which aim to assist small and medium sized enterprises focus on participation incentives in the market, which could then be defined as private or public markets. These policies adopt regionalism as their objective and endeavour to promote a decentralised economic growth through the periphery. Regional policies are sophisticated measures aiming at optimal allocation of resources throughout a state and equal distribution of income amongst its citizens. Small and medium sized enterprises occupy a large share in European economies and should be considered as one of the most important factors of Europe's industrial policy. The economic importance of small and medium sized enterprises in the market could be attributed to their ability to increase efficiency and enhance macroeconomic growth, promote industrial re-structuring and adjustment, create the opportunity for industrial and sectoral exploitation of particular skills and advantages and facilitate better allocation of resources and more equal income distribution

Although the opening up of protected public procurement markets and the liberalisation of the public sector of the European Member States have been defined as priority objectives not only for the completion of the common market but also for the proper functioning of global markets, they pose serious obstacles and to some extent threats for small and medium sized firms. Small and medium sized firms have often relied on regional preferences or other types of protectionism; they have developed long-standing dependency relations with a very limited number of buyers and their low competitiveness and quality augmented by the lack of economies of scale and the inefficient mobility of labour, capital and know-how constitute a real threat. Small and medium sized firms need extensive preparation in order to enter public markets. They need to adapt to high technical standards rather than depend on traditional relationships with established purchasers, which then will open their horizons to larger geographical markets. They have to familiarise themselves with the procedural requirements stipulated by European legislation and ensure that they meet quality assurance standards. Finally, they have to adopt and develop sophisticated marketing and management structures specifically designed for public sector contracts, a strategy which will be of substantial assistance to their future competitiveness.

Policy makers at both domestic and European level face a dilemma in their attempts to promote the participation of small and medium sized firms in public procurement. The dilemma lies in the choice of the most appropriate framework for the promotion of SMEs participation in tendering procedures and the award of public contracts. The principal factors which have been claimed to inhibit small and medium sized enterprises in public procurement include the relatively large size of the contracts, the difficulty in obtaining adequate information on forthcoming contracts, the shortage of language skills particularly in technical areas, the availability of time and the costs involved in preparing bids, the scarce management resources, problems relating to specification of standards, difficulties in certification in other Member States and obtaining quality assurance in other Member States, difficulties in achieving credibility in other Member States and finally delays in payment. The most effective way to stimulate SMEs participation in public procurement and ensure for them a fair share of the awarded public contracts has been achieved through the operation of preference schemes. So far, these schemes have been indissolubly linked with regional development policies, but since the completion of the Single Market project in 1992 they have been abolished, as they are deemed to contravene directly or indirectly the basic principle of non-discrimination on grounds of nationality stipulated in the European Treaties.

The industrial policy potential in public procurement

The implementation of industrial policies through public purchasing focuses on either the sustainability of strategic national industries, or the development of infant industries. In both cases, preferential purchasing patterns can provide the economic and financial framework for the development of such industries, at the expense of competition and free trade. Although the utilisation of public procurement as a means of industrial policy in Member States may breach directly or indirectly primary Treaty provisions on free movement of goods and the right of establishment and the freedom to provide services, it is far from clear whether the European Commission and the European Court of Justice could accept public procurement as legitimate state aids.

The industrial policy dimension of public procurement is also reflected in the form of strategic purchasing by public utilities. Public utilities in the European Union, which in the majority are monopolies, are accountable for a substantial magnitude of procurement, in terms of volume and in terms of price. Responsible for this are the expensive infrastructure and high technology products that are necessary to procure in order to deliver their services to the public. Given the fact that most of the suppliers to public utilities depend almost entirely on their procurement and that, even when some degree of privatisation has been achieved, the actual control of the utilities is still vested in the state, the first constraint in liberalising public procurement in the European Union is apparent. Utilities, in the form of public monopolies or semi-private enterprises appear prone to perpetuate long standing over-dependency purchasing patterns with certain domestic suppliers. Reflecting the above observations, the reader should bear in mind that until 1991, utilities were not covered by European legislation on procurement. The delay of their regulation can be attributed to the resistance from Member States in privatising their monopolies and the uncertainty of the legal regime that will follow their privatisation.

The industrial policy dimension of public procurement evolves around public monopolies in the Member States which predominately operate in the utilities sectors (energy, transport, water and telecommunications) and have been assigned with the exclusive exploitation of the relevant services in their respective Member States. The legal status of these entities varies from legal monopolies (where they are constitutionally guaranteed) to delegated monopolies (where the state confers certain rights on them) and during the last decade they have been the target of a sweeping process of transformation from monolithic and sub-optimal public corporations to competitive enterprises. Public monopolies very often possess a monopsony position. As they are state controlled enterprises, they tend to perform under different management patterns than private firms. Their decision making responds not only to market forces but mainly to political pressure. Understandably, their purchasing behaviour follows, to a large extent, parameters reflecting current trends of domestic industrial policies. Public monopolies in the utilities sector have sustained national industries in Member States through exclusive or preferential procurement. The sustainability of *national champions*, or in other terms, strategically perceived enterprises, could only be achieved through discriminatory purchasing patterns. The privatisation of public monopolies, which absorb the output of such industries, will discontinue such dependency patterns and will result in industrial policy imbalances. It could be difficult for the *national champions* to secure new markets to replace the traditional long dependency on public monopolies and at the same time it would take time and effort to diversify their activities or to convert to alternative industrial sectors.

The protected and preferential purchasing frameworks between monopolies and *national champions* and the output dependency patterns and secured markets of the latter have attracted considerable foreign direct investment, to the extent that European Union institutions face the dilemma of threatening to discontinue the investment flow when liberalising public procurement in the common market. However, it could be argued that the industrial restructuring following the opening-up of the procurement practices of public monopolies would possibly attract similar levels of foreign direct investment, which would be directed towards supporting the new structure. The liberalisation of public procurement in the European Union has as one of its main aims the restructuring of industries suffering from overcapacity and sub-optimal performance. However, the industries supplying public monopolies and utilities are themselves, quite often, public corporations. In such cases, procurement dependency patterns between state outfits when disrupted can result in massive unemployment attributed to the supply side's inadequacy to secure new customers. The monopsony position when abolished could often bring about the collapse of the relevant sector.

Public procurement and defence

Industrial policies through public procurement can also be implemented with reference to defence industries, particularly for procurement of military equipment. The Procurement Directives cover equipment of dual-use purchased by the armed forces, but explicitly exclude from their ambit the procurement of military equipment. It should be also mentioned here that every Member State in the European Union pursues its own military procurement policy by virtue of Article 223. In the light of the Maastricht Treaty on European Union, there is a need for a centralised mechanism to take over independent military procurement practices, establish a common European Defence Policy and harmonise and regulate defence contracts and procurement of military equipment by Member States.

Attempts have been made to liberalise, to a limited extent, the procurement of military equipment at European level under the auspices of European Defence Equipment Market (EDEM). This initiative is a programme of gradual liberalisation of defence industries in the relevant countries and has arisen through the operation of the Independent European Programme Group, which has been a forum of industrial co-operation in defence industry matters amongst European NATO members. The programme has envisaged, apart from collaborative research and development in defence technology, the introduction of a competitive regime in defence procurement and a modest degree of transparency, subject to the draconian primary Treaty provisions of Article 223. Award of defence procurement contracts, under the EDEM should follow a similar rationale with civilian procurement, particularly in the introduction of award criteria based on economic and financial considerations and a minimum degree of publicity for contracts in excess of 1 million EURO.

The establishment of a Common European Defence Policy could possibly bring about the integration of defence industries in the European Union and this will inevitably require a change in governments' policies and practices. Competitiveness, public savings considerations, value for money, transparency and non-discrimination should be the principles of the centralised mechanism regulating defence procurement in Europe. The establishment of a centralised defence agency with specific tasks of *contractorisation, facilities management* and *market testing* represent examples of new procurement policies which would give an opportunity to the defence industry to adopt its practices in the light of the challenges, risks, policy priorities and directions of the modern era. In particular, risk management and contracting arrangements measuring reliability of deliveries and cost compliance, without penalising the supply side are themes which could revolutionise defence procurement and play a significant role in linking such strategic industries with national and European-wide industrial policies.

Public procurement as a discipline expands from a simple internal market topic, to a multi-faceted tool of European regulation and governance covering policy choices and revealing an interesting interface between centralised and national governance systems. This is where the legal effects of public procurement regulations will be felt most; in its neighboring disciplines, such as public policy, management and economic theory.

This book aims to provide the reader with a comprehensive analysis of the policy and legal landscape of the regulation of public procurement in the European Union. The main objective of the author is to introduce the concept of public procurement as an integral part of the emerging European economic law, as well as to introduce the regulation of public procurement from a *macro-policy* perspective. The legal and economic dynamics of the European integration process have revealed a series of dramatic changes in the interaction amongst Member States of the European Union which has taken many by surprise. The culture and ethos of public sector management has been the subject of fundamental transformation as a result of efficiency related objectives in the delivery of public service. Efficiency gains and cost savings in the public sector of the European Union could amount to a phenomenal sum equal, according to some calculations, to the budget attached to the Common Agricultural Policy. These gains could be attributed to a liberalised public purchasing regime, where supply from a pan-European market will result in better prices for the public sector. The book also endeavors to familiarise its reader with the mechanisms and practices of achieving the desirable effects of integration of public markets in the European Union by assessing the impact of the regime on the common market.

Chapter 1 assesses the intellectual approach to the regulation of public procurement. It attempts to define the parameters of the European integration process which are relevant to the public sector of the Member States and their subsequent interaction with public procurement. In Chapter 2, a detailed analysis is provided covering the public purchasing regime, the legal and socio-economic background of the reform of the public sector in the Member States, the method of legal integration of public markets, the motives and objectives of the process and the anticipated enhancement of competitiveness in the relevant markets through efficiency gains, the threats and dangers of the process, the principles of European Public Procurement Law, as well as the extra-territorial application and effects of the legal regime in its relation with other international agreements in which the European

Union is signatory. Chapter 3 presents and analyses the developments from the case-law of the European Court of Justice, the inferences of the judgements and the thematic evolution of concepts and notions emerging from the application of the legal framework. In Chapter 4, the regulation of public procurement is viewed through the prism of economic exercise as well as that of policy choice. The analysis reflects on two major theories which underpin such perceptions of public procurement regulation: the neo-classical approach and the ordo-liberal interpretation respectively. In Chapter 5, the author seeks to evaluate the impact of the public procurement regime and assess its strengths and weaknesses by reference to five concepts: inherent constraints in the legislation, the existence of public monopolies and the process of their privatisation in the Member States, harmonisation of standards and specifications, the reluctance of the supply side in initiating litigation and finally the need to sustain certain industries through public procurement. Chapter 6 presents the new public procurement regime which will become operational from 2006. The new Directives proclaim to modernise the public markets of the European Union by means of simplification. In Chapter 7 the author presents the public-private partnership phenomenon and its interaction with the public procurement framework. The evolution of privately financed projects and institutionalised partnerships between the public and private sectors has revealed a new dimension of European governance. Finally, in Chapter 8 the author presents the interplay of public procurement with the delivery of services of general interest and significance of the regime as a conceptual justification instrument in state aids policy and jurisprudence.

1
European Integration and Public Procurement

Introduction

The definition of public procurement is a complex one. It depicts a series of practices and government actions interacting with public policy. Public procurement could be best described as the supply chain system for the acquisition of all necessary goods, works and services by the state and its organs when acting in pursuit of public interest. Public procurement constitutes a significant *modus operandi* in the public sector arena and it stands as the procedural prerequisite for the delivery of public services. Apart from reasons relating to accountability in public expenditure, avoidance of corruption and political manipulation, the regulation of public procurement within the European legal and political systems has acquired a multi-disciplined dimension. The regulation of public procurement, does not only represent a best practice in the delivery of public service by the state and its organs, it most importantly qualifies as an instrument of policy. The spill-over effects from the deployment of a particular strategy relevant to the procurement practices of the public sector will have significant implications for national and international trade patterns as it can be detrimental to any economic and political integration process a European Union state is committed to.

Public procurement as a component of the common market

The establishment of the *common market*, as the core objective envisaged by the Treaty of Rome (the treaty creating the European Economic Communities) and reinforced by the Treaty of Maastricht (the treaty creating the European Union) is to be achieved through the progressive approximation of the economic policies of Member States.[1] The concept of the *common market* embraces legal and economic dynamics of the European integration process, with clear political effects from its accomplishment, and unfolds the characteristics of a genuine integral market, where unobstructed mobility of factors of production[2] is guaranteed and a regime of effective and undistorted competition regulates its operation. These characteristics embrace the four basic freedoms of a customs union (free movement of goods, persons, capital and services)[3] and, to the extent that the customs union tends to become an economic and a monetary one,[4] the adoption of a common economic policy and the introduction of a single currency. Adherence by Member States to the above-mentioned fundamental principles of economic integration would ensure the abolition of any restriction, protection or obstacle to interstate trade. The level of success of economic integration in Europe would determine the level of success in political integration, as the ultimate objective stipulated in the Treaties.

The law of the European Union has conceived the creation of a legal supranational system alongside existing domestic ones, where the supremacy of the former over national laws has been declared by the European Court of Justice.[5] The economic integration of the European Union requires the assistance of a legal order that can facilitate and observe its development with a view to achieving the ultimate aim which is the establishment of a political union. The *new legal order* is a conglomerate of mutual rights and duties between the European Union and its subjects, both Member States and private persons, and also amongst these subjects themselves and provides for the procedures which are necessary for determining and adjudicating infringements of law. The *new legal order* does confer rights and obligations not only to Member States but also to individuals (physical or legal persons). Both Member States and individuals are the subjects of European law, with respect to compliance and observance, and in as much as Member States participate in market activities, they have the same rights and obligations as those of individuals.

Two strategic plans have facilitated the economic integration of the Member States. These plans were enacted by European institutions and have been subsequently transposed into national laws and policies by Member States. The first plan has comprised a series of actions, measures and mechanisms aiming at the abolition of all *tariff* and *non-tariff barriers* to intra-community trade (trade amongst Member States). The second plan has focused on the establishment of an effective, workable and undistorted regime of competition within the common market, in order to prevent possible abuse of market dominance and cartelisation, factors which could have serious economic implications in its functioning. The first plan, the abolition of all *tariff* and *non-tariff barriers* to intra-community trade, appears to have a static effect aimed at eliminating all administrative and legal obstacles to free trade and has as its focal point Member States and their national administrations, whereas the second plan, the establishment of an effective, workable and undistorted regime of competition within the common market, has been addressed at industry level and has a more on-going and dynamic effect.

All tariff barriers appear to have been abolished by the end of the first transitional period,[6] so customs duties, quotas and other forms of quantitative restrictions can no longer hinder the free flow of trade amongst Member States. Non-tariff barriers, however, have proved more difficult to eliminate, as they involve long-established market practices and patterns that cannot change overnight. Non-tariff protection represents a disguised form of discrimination and can take place through a wide spectrum of administrative or legislative frameworks relating to public monopolies, fiscal factors such as indirect taxation, state aids and subsidisation, technical standards and last but not least public procurement. Non-tariff barriers are by no means confined to the European Integration process only. The existence of non-tariff barriers is a common phenomenon in world markets and the main objective of regulatory instruments of international trade is their elimination. However, non-tariff barriers could seriously distort the operation of the common market and its fundamental freedoms and derail the process of European integration.

The European Commission's White Paper for the Completion of the Internal Market[7] identified existing non-tariff protection and provided the framework for specific legislative measures[8] in order to address the issue at national level. A set of Directives have been deemed necessary for the completion of the internal market by the end of 1992, and the time table was set out in the Single European Act, which in fact amended the Treaty of Rome by introducing *inter alia* the concept of the *internal market*. The internal market, in quantifiable terms, could be considered as something less than the common market but, perhaps the first and most important part of the latter, as it "...... *would provide the economic context for the regeneration of the European industry in both goods and services and it would give a permanent boost to the prosperity of the people of Europe and indeed the world as a whole*".[9]

The internal market, as an economic concept could be described as an area without internal frontiers, where the free circulation of goods and the unhindered provision of services in conjunction with the unobstructed mobility of factors of production are ensured. Literally speaking the concept of the internal market is a reinforcement of the customs union principle as the foundation stone of the common market. The internal market embraces, obviously, less than the common market to the extent that the economic and monetary integration elements are missing. The whole Single European Act, as an instrument amending the Treaties, revealed strong public law characteristics. The regulatory and interventionist feature of its provisions indicate the importance of certain fields that had been overlooked in the past. There has been both centralised and decentralised regulatory control by Community Institutions over environmental policy, industrial policy, regional policy and the regulation of public procurement. These areas represented the priority objectives in the process of completing the internal market. Public procurement was pointed out as a significant non-tariff barrier and action was scheduled to address the issue. The European Commission based its momentum on two notable studies,[10] where empirical proof of the distorted market situation in the public sector was highlighted and the benefits of the regulation of public procurement were emphasised.

The conceptual elements of public procurement regulation

State participation in free markets would normally take place on behalf or in pursuit of public interest.[11] The concept of the state embraces an entrepreneurial dimension to the extent that it exercises *dominium*.[12] Where state participation in the market place exists, the relevant markets can be described as public markets. Although the state as entrepreneur enters into transactions with a view to providing goods, services and works for the public, this kind of action does not resemble the commercial characteristics of entrepreneurship, in as much as the aim of the state's activities is not the maximisation of profits but the observance of public interest. In contrast, private markets comprise undertakings whose only reason for staying in the market place is profit maximisation. *Public interest* substitutes *profit maximisation* and can justify state participation in public markets.

Apart from the above fundamental differentiating factor, a number of striking variances distinguish private from public markets. These variances focus on structural elements of the market place, competitiveness, demand conditions, supply conditions, the production process, and finally pricing and risk. They also provide for an indication as to the different methods and approaches employed in their regulation.

Private markets are generally structured as a result of competitive pressures originating in the buyer/supplier interaction and their configuration can vary from monopoly/oligopoly to almost perfect competition models. Demand in private markets arises from heterogeneous buyers with a variety of specific needs. It is based on expectations and is multiple for each product. Supply, on the other hand, is offered through various product ranges, where products are standardised using known technology, but constantly improved through research and development processes. The production process is based on mass-production patterns and the product range represents a large choice including substitutes, whereas the critical production factor is cost level. The development cycle appears to be short to medium-term and finally, the technology of products destined for the private markets is evolutionary. Purchases are made when an acceptable balance between price and quality is achieved. Purchase orders are multiple and at limited intervals. Pricing policy in private markets is determined by competitive forces and the purchasing decision is focused on the price-quality relation. The risk factor is highly present.

On the other hand, public markets appear to function in a different way. The market structure often reveals a monopsony/oligopsony character. In terms of its origins, demand in public markets is institutionalised (*viz.* susceptible to legal and policy formalities) and operates mainly under budgetary considerations rather than price mechanisms. It is also based on fulfilment of tasks (pursuit of public interest) and it is single for many products. Supply also has limited origins, in terms of the establishment of close ties between the public sector and industries supplying it and there is often a limited product range. Products are rarely innovative and technologically advanced and pricing is determined through tendering and negotiations. The purchasing decision is primarily based upon the life-time cycle, reliability, price and political considerations. Purchasing patterns follow tendering and negotiations and often purchases are dictated by policy rather than price/quality considerations.

Whereas the regulatory weaponry for private markets is dominated by anti-trust law and policy, public markets are *fora* where the structural and behavioural remedial tools of competition law emerge as a rather inappropriate regulatory framework. The applicability of competition law is limited, mainly due to the fact that anti-trust often clashes with monopolistic structures which exist in public markets. State participation in market activities is regularly assisted through exclusive exploitation of a product or a service within a geographical market. The market activities of the state are protected from competition by virtue of laws on trading and production or by virtue of delegated monopolies. Another reason for the limited applicability of anti-trust law and policy in public markets is the fact that conceptual differences appear between the two categories of markets – private and public – in the eyes of anti-trust, which could be attributed to their different nature. In private markets, anti-trust law and policy seek to punish cartels and abusive dominance of undertakings. The focus of the remedial instruments is the supply side, which is conceived as the commanding part in the supply/demand equation due to the fact that it instigates and controls demand for a product. In private markets, the demand side of the equation (the consumers in general) are susceptible to exploitation and the market equilibria are prone to distortion as a result of collusive behaviour of undertakings or abusive monopoly position. On the other hand, the structure of public markets reveals a different picture. In the supply/demand equation, the predominant part appears to be the demand side (the state and its organs as purchasers), which initialises demand through purchasing, whereas the supply side (the industry) fights for access to the relevant markets. Although this is normally the case, one should not exclude the possibility of market oligopolisation and the potential manipulation of the demand side.[13] These advanced market structures can occur more often in the future, as a result of well established trends of industrial concentration.

Another argument which has relevance to the different regulatory approach of public and private markets reflects on the methods of possible market segmentation and abuse. It is maintained that the segmentation of private markets appears different than the partitioning of public ones. In private markets, market segmentation occurs as a result of cartels and collusive behaviour, which would lead to abuse of dominance, with a view to driving competitors out of the relevant market, increasing market shares and ultimately increasing profits. Private markets can be segmented both geographically and by reference to product or service, whereas public ones can only be geographically segmented. This assumption leads to the argument that the partition of the public markets would be probably the result of concerted practices attributed to the demand side. As such concerted practices focus on the origin of a product or a service or the nationality of a contractor, and then the only way to effectively partition the relevant market would be by reference to its geographical remit. In contrast, as far as private markets are concerned, the segmentation of the relevant market (either product or geographical) can only be attributed to the supply side. The argument goes further to reveal the fact that the balance of powers between the supply and the demand side are reversed when superimposed on private or public markets. In the latter, it is the demand side that has the dominant role in the equation by dictating terms and conditions in purchases, initiation of transactions, as well as by influencing production trends (supplies, works and services destined for the public sector tend to shift from the traditional *inventory pattern* of production to *a custom made/built by order* one).[14]

In public markets, concerted practices of the demand side (e.g. excluding foreign competition, application of buy-national policies, and application of national standards policies) represent geographical market segmentation, as they result in the division of the European public markets into different national public markets. It could also be maintained that public markets are subject to protection rather than restriction from competition, to the extent that the latter are quasi-monopolistic and monopsonistic in their structure. Indeed, the state and its organs, as contractors possess a monopoly position in the sense that no one competes against them in their market activities.[15] Even in cases of privatisation, the monopoly position is shifted from the public to private hands. The situation is slightly different in cases of an open privatised regime pursuing an operation of public interest. In that case, it would be more appropriate to refer to oligopolistic competition in the relevant market. Also in privatised regimes, interchangeability of supply is very limited, to an extent that monopoly position characteristics survive the transfer of ownership from public to private hands. The state and its organs also possess a monopsony position, as firms engaged in transactions with them have no alternatives to pursue business. Access barriers to geographical public markets are erected by states by means of exercising their discretion to conclude contracts with national undertakings. This sort of activity constitutes the partition of public markets in the Community, whereas, apparently, undertakings operating in private markets must enter into a restrictive agreement between themselves in order to split up the relevant markets. Due to their different integral nature, private and public markets require different control. The control in both cases has a strong public law character, but while anti-trust regulates private markets, it appears rather inappropriate for public ones. Anti-trust law and policy is a set of rules of a negative nature; undertakings must *restrain* their activities to an acceptable range pre-determined in due course by the competent authorities. On the other hand, public markets require a set of rules that have positive character. It should be recalled that the integration of public markets is based on the abolition of barriers and obstacles to national markets; it then follows that the sort of competition envisaged for their regulation is mainly *market access competition*. This primarily indicates that price competition is expected to emerge in Community public markets, only after their integration.

It appears, however, that in both private and public markets, two elements have relevance when attempting their regulation. The first element is the *price differentiation* of similar products; the second element is *access* to the relevant markets. As the European integration is an economic process which aims at dismantling barriers to trade and approximating national economies, the need to create acceptable levels of competition in both public and private markets becomes more demanding. In fact, a regime of genuine competition in public markets would benefit the public interest as it will lower the price of goods and services for the public, as well as achieve substantial savings for the public purse.

If one accepts as point of departure the fact that the introduction of elements of competition in public markets would have desirable effects, a question which might arise is if, by dismantling public markets and entrusting private markets for the provision of goods and services destined for the public, the above desirable effects can be accomplished. As mentioned previously, private markets operate under the laws of demand and supply and the private sector is profit orientated. Privatisation, as a process of transfer of public assets and operations to private hands, on grounds of market efficiency and competition, as well as responsiveness to customer demand and quality considerations is often accompanied by simultaneous regulation by the state, in the form of a legal framework within which privatised industries will pursue public interest functions. It is not entirely clear that the process of privatisation would reclaim public markets and transform them to private ones. We should never underestimate the fact that the control of undertakings' operations relevant to public interest remain within the competence of the state in the form of the regulatory regime, thus maintaining strong public market characteristics. To what extent the market freedom of a privatised entity can be curtailed by regulatory frameworks deserves a complex and thorough analysis which exceeds the thrust of this work. However, it can be maintained that through the privatisation process, the previously clear-cut distinction between public and private markets becomes blur, as a new market place emerges. This type of market embraces strong public law elements to the extent that it is regulated by the state with a view to observing public interest in the relevant operations. The economic freedom and the risks associated with such operations are also subject to sector-specific regulation; this implies that any regulatory framework incorporates much more than mere procedural rules. This type of market place reveals a transformation from traditional *corporatism* to a public management system where *governance is dispersed through contract* under terms and conditions determined by the state. It very much resembles the *principle of outsourcing* which is often utilised in restructuring exercises in the private sector. Outsourcing introduces elements of contractualisation in the production process, as sub-contracting takes over from the in-house operation in the production chain. Government by contract, along the same lines, introduces the principle of outsourcing in the dispersement of public service, but the *contractualised governance* appears far more stringent than outsourcing by virtue of regulation. Furthermore, apart from operational savings, outsourcing in the private sector would normally spread the risk factor amongst the operations in the production chain. If the sub-contractor cannot deliver according to expectations, the main operator can switch to an alternative with no major implications. Outsourcing, therefore, introduces an element of flexibility in the production process. It remains to be seen whether contractualised governance or government by contract conforms to the same parameters (savings, risk sharing, and flexibility) as private sector outsourcing.

In addition to the above remarks, one should expect that the introduction of competitive forces in public markets through privatisation would result in a shift of the relevant regulatory instruments for these markets. However, within the European Union, the process of privatisation has not been approached in a uniform manner by the Member States. Although the element of competition in the relevant public markets, as well as the potential effects on public savings remains undisputed, the process and methods of privatisation have faced considerable criticism from the stakeholders of the European Community. Despite the fact that European institutions have in principle endorsed the process of privatisation as a means to reduce public debt and achieve a harmonious economic and budgetary policy throughout the common market,[16] industrial relations in the Member States often have diluted both the principle and the effects of such transformation.

Attempts to privatise state-controlled enterprises may have resulted in the regulation of their corporate performance through anti-trust, but apparently the purchasing relations are subject to the same regime as those of public sector bodies. The privatised utility, for example, although a private entity, has to comply with a rigorous purchasing system for its supply chain requirements.

The evolution of public procurement regulation

In the history of European economic integration, public procurement has been an important part of the Member States' industrial policy. Procurement has been utilised as a tool with a view to supporting domestic policy considerations.[17] Protectionism from competition in public procurement and preferential award of public contracts to indigenous suppliers and contractors has reflected mainly a concern of Member States for the preservation of national industries and the related workforce. The regulation of public procurement in the early days clearly allowed for "preference schemes" in less favoured regions of the European common market which were experiencing industrial decline.[18] Such schemes required the application of award criteria based on considerations other than the lowest price or qualitative criteria reflecting on elements of works or services to be delivered. Preference schemes challenged the compatibility of public procurement with regimes such as those covering the free movement of goods and services, the competition law regime of the common market and finally the rules governing state aids. Preference schemes have been indissolubly linked with regional development policies, as they sought to guarantee a certain percentage of public contracts to local firms. Traditionally, this link has indicated the close interplay between public purchasing and state aids.[19] However, protectionist public procurement practices, when strategically exercised, resulted in the evolution of vital industries for the state in question. The sustainability of *national champions* has brought about benefits for a sector or an industry, which, when protected from competition in the short-run, managed to achieve specialisation and internationalisation. Nevertheless, since the completion of the internal market in 1992 preference schemes have been abolished, as they have been deemed capable in contravening directly or indirectly the basic principle of non-discrimination on grounds of nationality stipulated in the European treaties.

It would be interesting to reflect on the potential role of preferential public procurement in a state's economy. First, it appears in the form of an exercise which aims at preserving some domestic sectors or industries at the expense of the principles of the European integration process. In such a form, there is obviously no exit plan. Impact assessment studies undertaken by the European Commission showed that the operation of preference schemes had a minimal effect on the economies of the regions where they had been applied, both in terms of the volume of procurement contracts, as well as in terms of real economic growth attributed to the operation of such schemes.[20] Thus, in that form, preferential public procurement perpetuates the sub-optimal allocation of resources and represents a welfare loss for the economy of the relevant state. On the other hand, preferential purchasing in the form of strategic sustainability of selected industries might represent a viable instrument of industrial policy, to the extent that the infant industry, when specialised and internationalised, would be in a position to counterbalance any welfare losses during its protected period. In the above form, preferential public procurement, as an integral part of industrial policy could possibly represent welfare gains.[21]

Irrespective of the dimension which preferential public procurement is looked at, its regulation requires a balancing exercise between related economic policies and the objectives stipulated in the European treaties. Public procurement, as a discipline involving legal, economic and public policy considerations has acquired a significant role within the context of the European integration, but more importantly at domestic level, where national administrations have been required to implement and comply with a legal regime which aims at integrating the public markets of the European Union and at establishing a competitive regime similar to that envisaged for the private markets. The latter regime, the competition law and policy of the European Union has introduced a framework of effective and workable competition in the common market and has resulted in a market structure which reveals strong trends of industrial concentration through mergers and acquisitions, restructuring, outsourcing and optimisation of human and capital resources within the sectors of the European industries.

Public procurement in the European Union amounts to 1 trillion EURO and represents a staggering 12 per cent of the EU GDP. Its regulation does not only reflect upon the conceptualisation of public procurement as an important component of the common market, but it also reveals the parallel and complementary relationship of public procurement with the four freedoms and related community policies. In budgetary terms, public procurement represents a significant amount of the Member States' gross domestic product, a fact that has been seen as very important by European institutions for the process of European integration. Given the amount and level, and transnational dimension of the infrastructure required to deliver public services in the European Union as well as the expenditure earmarked every financial year by public authorities to procure goods, works and services in pursuit of public interest, the public sector procurement has revealed a significant dimension within the European Integration process. Such revelation necessitates the regulation of the procurement practices of Member States in order to eliminate market distortions. Public procurement, as the procedural blueprint of the delivery of public services by the state and its organs does not only represent a substantial proportion of the European Union's economy but, when viewed in the context of domestic budgetary frameworks, it can easily qualify as an instrument with which governments can support national conjunctural (short-term economic policies) or even long-term economic policies relating to employment, regional development, industrial adjustment and performance. Such application of public procurement practices by Member States in the direction of promoting domestic policies should always be weighted against the process of the completion of the common market through the progressive abolition of all existing non-tariff barriers which are deemed to inhibit the functioning of a genuinely integrated market in the Community. The regulation of public markets aims primarily at combating discrimination on grounds of nationality and also at the achievement of efficiency and optimal allocation of resources destined for the public sector Community wide, under a more competitive regime. The motive is again the pursuit of public interest, but through the regulation of public procurement public interest acquires a Community dimension with mainly economic characteristics.

The European Commission's White Paper for the Completion of the Internal Market has pointed out that public procurement in the Member States represented a serious threat to the process of economic integration of the European Community and could possibly derail the outcome of the common market. It should be mentioned that amongst the areas identified as actual or potential non-tariff barriers, public procurement was the most substantive and urgent discipline to be tackled by European institutions and the Member States. The European Commission formulated a strategy for eliminating discriminatory public procurement amongst Member States which have posed significant obstacles to the fundamental principles of free movement of goods, the right of establishment and the freedom to provide services.

That strategy was based on two principal assumptions: the first assumption acknowledged the fact that in order to eliminate preferential and discriminatory purchasing practices in European public markets, a great deal of *transparency* and *openness* was needed; the second assumption rested on the premise that the only way to regulate public procurement in the Member States in an effective manner was through the process of *harmonisation* of existing laws and administrative practices which had been in operation, and not through a *uniform* regulatory pattern which would replace all existing laws and administrative practices throughout the Community. The latter assumption indirectly recognised the need for a decentralised system of regulation for public procurement in the Community, well ahead of the pronouncement of the principle of *subsidiarity*, which was introduced in the European law jargon some years later by virtue of the Maastricht Treaty on European Union.

Since harmonisation was adopted as the most appropriate method of regulation of public procurement in the common market, and the decentralised character of the regime was reinforced through legislation, the onus then was shifted to the national administrations of the Member States, which had to implement the Community principles into domestic law and give a certain degree of clarity and legitimate expectation to interested parties. Occasionally, the European Commission is criticised for not having central powers in order to enforce public procurement rules, in addition to those already available to it as the guardian of the Treaty. The critics often refer to the applicability of competition law and policy of the European Community and the regime which legally implements it through specific Regulations. However, although in principle competition law of the European Community may apply to the award of public contracts,[22] the *effectiveness* and *efficiency* of a regulatory regime in the public markets through basic anti-trust remedies remains a challenge for the law and policy maker. A rigid regime which is applied through a uniform way across the common market cannot take into account national particularities in public procurement. It would probably eliminate any elements of *flexibility* envisaged to compensate for the sensitivities arising out of national legal and policy orders. Public procurement, as the *nexus* of transactions in the supply chain of the public sector, does not differ in principle with the management of purchasing practices in the private sector, which remains unregulated.

The legal instruments opted for by European institutions to achieve the objective of flexibility are Directives. Public markets and their regulation are dominated by different legal regimes and legal approaches that diverge to a considerable extent from each other. Directives, as flexible legal instruments, leaving a great deal of discretion in the hands of Member States with respect to the forms and the methods of their implementation, can harmonise public markets taking into account existing divergences in domestic legal systems. The appropriateness of Directives to achieve the desired degree of competition in public markets and establish a regime where optimal resource allocation benefits the public interest is unquestionable. The nature and character of Directives, as *"framework"* legal instruments aim at harmonising existing legal systems, bringing them in conformity with Community envisaged objectives. Directives attempt to approximate different national laws and achieve a similar legal regime throughout the common market based on the lowest common denominator amongst the systems of the Member States. Divergences will inevitably remain, as the European Union lacks the powers to abolish existing domestic legal regimes and impose *ab initio* a different one.[23] On the other hand, it should be pointed out that Regulations aim at unification of the regimes governing the Member States' legal orders and have been exclusively used in the anti-trust field. It could be further argued that Regulations reveal all the characteristics of instruments of public law, in particular to the extent that they are directly applicable and produce vertical and horizontal direct effectiveness. Apart from the creation of a uniform system common to the internal legal orders of the Member States, other notable advantages by having recourse to Regulations instead of Directives would be the fact that individuals could directly rely on their provisions not only against the state but also against other individuals before domestic courts.

Directives, on the other hand, appear to have strong characteristics of instruments of public law, in as much as they constitute the legal framework within which the state must enact rules that regulate the relevant sector. Directives, unlike Regulations lay down duties and obligations addressed only to Member States. Regulations, in addition, introduce rights of individuals to be respected by Member States and also other individuals. Directives resemble circulars at domestic administrative level, to the extent that the latter provide the framework for action by central government to the competent decentralised authority. The difference is that Directives are binding legal instruments and may be relied upon before national courts by individuals under certain circumstances restrictively interpreted by the European

Court of Justice (the case of direct effectiveness), whereas administrative circulars produce no binding effects. Directives, as Community legal instruments were thought to be the most appropriate method to regulate public markets in the European Community. As mentioned above, fundamental differences in existing national legal systems dictated the continuation of domestic public market regimes, but the main concern was their enforcement at national level. In fact, it was the range of procedural and substantive sensibilities and peculiarities found in the judicial infrastructure of the Member States, especially the system through which judicial review of public procurement is channelled, that prevented legal unification at Community level by means of Regulations.

Treaty provisions on non-discrimination, on the prohibition to barriers to intra-community trade, on the freedom to provide services and on the right of establishment, on public undertakings and undertakings to which Member States grant special or exclusive rights and on state monopolies providing services of general economic interest, seemed insufficient on their own in eliminating protection afforded to domestic undertakings through preferential public procurement. These provisions are capable of embracing the basic legal relations between the demand and supply sides of the public procurement equation according to the principles stipulated in the Treaties, but their effect on award of public contracts is minimal. The diversity of legal systems within the Member States of the European Union and the differences in existing domestic public procurement rules would have rendered the regulation of public markets ineffective, if recourse solely to primary Community legislation was sought. The negative character of the primary Community provisions which may apply to public procurement could be seen as the main reason for the need by Community Institutions to introduce rules which have a positive character, in the sense that they allow a margin of discretion in their implementation. Due to the decentralised nature of any regulatory form of public procurement in the common market, the normative character of the primary Community rules was diluted in favour of a process of harmonisation of existing laws and practices in the Member States.

The existence of Community legislation in the form of Directives which aimed to co-ordinate the award of public contracts at national level,[24] as well as the application of primary Treaty provisions to public procurement within the European Community appeared inadequate for the abolition of non-tariff barriers posed by preferential purchasing patterns of Member States and their organs.[25] That particular inadequacy could be attributed to the fact that the secondary legislation (Directives) on public procurement mainly focused on procedural, and to some extent bureaucratic matters in the award of public contracts in the Member States, while the substantive elements of the regulation of intra-community trade through public purchasing were left in the hands of national administrations, which, by exercising a great deal of discretion in selection and award procedures, discriminated against firms established in other Member States and instead favoured domestic suppliers. The main factors responsible for the lack of success of the first generation of Public Procurement Directives according to the Commission's Communication to the Council[26] included *inter alia*: i) failure to advertise contracts above certain thresholds in the Official Journal, as a result of intentional splitting-up of contracts in order to avoid the mandatory advertisement requirement, although improvements had been made in the retrieval of information by the establishment of the Tenders Electronic Daily (TED) Data Bank; (however, the introduction of information technology to public procurement should be regarded as a means to facilitate the supply side (the industry) in determining the purchasing intentions of the demand side and not as a *panacea* in improving transparency ratios of contracting authorities); ii) ignorance of the relevant rules on the part of contracting authorities or deliberate omission of these rules; iii) excessive use of the exceptions permitting non-competitive tendering (negotiated procedures) instead of open or restricted procedures; iv) discriminatory requirements imposed by contracting authorities upon tenderers demanding compliance with national technical standards, to the exclusion of European standards or equivalent standards of other countries; and v) unlawful disqualification of suppliers or contractors or discriminatory use of the award criteria (either the lowest price or the most economically advantageous offer). Moreover, the Directives were inappropriately transposed into domestic legal systems, thus not conferring the envisaged access to justice and rights to individuals. Member States are obliged to implement Directives in a manner that satisfies the requirements of clarity, legal certainty and legitimate expectation, thus transposing their provisions into national ones by virtue of laws which have binding force.[27] Administrative circulars or administrative practices and official instructions, which by their nature can always be changed as and when the authorities please and which do not confer rights to individuals, are not considered sufficient to constitute proper fulfilment of the obligation to implement Directives. Even the direct effectiveness of the provisions of Directives does not exempt a Member State from the obligation to adopt the appropriate implementing measures within the period prescribed therein.[28] The inadequacy of primary Community law to regulate public procurement within the common market was clearly augmented with the complexity of the legal regimes in operation in the Member States, as well as their polarised nature and the character of national regulatory powers in relation to public purchasing. Thus, harmonisation and not uniformity was deemed to be the appropriate approach towards the integration of public markets in the European Community and the elimination of actual and potential non-tariff barriers arising therein.

If public markets are considered as a major component of the common market, the regulation of public procurement, as an essential feature for their implementation, obtains a crucial role for the whole European integration process. Public markets comprise different geographical and product/services markets, but also embrace national ones. Thus, a possible public market segmentation acquires a separate dimension – that of the national/domestic public market – as states often define their geographical public markets in accordance with their borders. It follows that the regulation of public procurement aims at dismantling national public markets and creating a Community wide public market for products, works and services destined for the European public. It is useful here to explain the logic behind the tendency of Member States to partition public markets according to physical/geographical borders. The public sector in each Member State represents transactions in excess of 10 per cent of the gross domestic product. That reveals the fact that public expenditure in the relevant markets is a powerful tool of policy making. If public expenditure relating to procurement in a Member State is diverted back to the domestic economy, then the state in question enjoys relatively strong and predictable industrial bases, which in the short-run can attract foreign investment. In addition to that, in the long-run and if properly managed through the promotion of research and development and product innovation, public markets segmentation through "buy-national" policies can lead to industrial specialisation and competitiveness of strategic industries, thus leaving the state in a position to plan not only conjectural but also long term economic policies. Another effect which emerges out of partitioning public markets and protecting them from outside competition is a control over domestic unemployment. If construction, supplies and services contracts are allocated to domestic contractors, the rate of production in the relevant sectors would be considerably high. Balancing the above effect, a number of secondary effects appear as a result of a state protecting its public markets. Economies of transport indicate better and more efficient delivery of products and after-sales services, as well as more efficient completion of construction projects or service contracts if the contractor is a domestic one. It could be argued that public markets segmentation often results in promoting firms engaged in transactions with the public sector and in supporting domestic economy as part of a carefully orchestrated industrial policy.

Public procurement has been considered the most important non-tariff barrier for the completion of the common market by the Commission's White Paper[29] and its regulation received priority by the European Union Institutions and the Member States. The liberalisation of public markets reflects the attempts of the European institutions to enhance competitiveness in the public sector and industrial efficiency in order to achieve a uniform pattern of industrial policy at centralised level. Priority has been given by the European Community to the fact that Member States must embark upon a process of changing their public sector management ethos and adopting more market-oriented parameters in the delivery of public service. The objectives of such processes include: value for money (efficiency, risk management, savings, and quality), transparency and competitiveness in public purchasing.

Public procurement has been elevated as a key parameter for an integrated market in the European Union and at the same time as an important policy tool at domestic level. This appears, at first sight, contradictory, as the regulation of public procurement obeys two diametrically opposite dynamics: one of a community-wide orientation and one of national priorities. As the market structure of the European Community reveals strong tendencies towards industrial concentration through mergers and acquisitions, rationalisation and restructuring of firms, downsizing, outsourcing and optimisation of human and capital resources within the sectors of the European industries,[30] the integration of public markets has threatened to bring about an end to long-standing dependency purchasing patterns which have undoubtedly sustained certain industries in the Member States of the European Community.[31]

The set of the Directives enacted by European institutions as the result of the internal market programme and subsequently amended after its completion by the end of 1992 introduce a new regime that attempts to establish gradually[32] a public market in the Community without frontiers. This regime seeks to accomplish unobstructed access to public markets through transparency of public expenditure relating to procurement, improved market information, elimination of technical standards capable of discriminating against potential contractors and uniform application of objective criteria of participation in tendering and award procedures.

Public procurement has been considered one of the last obstacles – non tariff barriers – for the establishment and proper functioning of the common market. Whether it still remains as the most substantial one should be rather the subject of exposure of the regime to empirical criticism.[33] Many commentators have attempted to describe how the regime works in practice.[34] In this book, the author aims to provide a comprehensive background of the evolution of the regime and its interplay with public policy agendas within the European integration process. It is envisaged that such approach, will expose the impact of the public procurement regime on both the industry and government and ascertain the degree of progress in the integration of the public markets of the European Union.

2
Public Procurement Regulation

Introduction

The regulation of public procurement in the European Union intends to insert a regime of competitiveness in the relevant markets and eliminate all non-tariff barriers to intra-community trade that emanate from preferential purchasing practices favouring national undertakings. Apart from the obvious reasons relating to accountability in public expenditure, avoidance of corruption and political manipulation, the regulation of public procurement does not only represent a best practice in the delivery of public service by the state and its organs, it most importantly qualifies as an instrument of policy.

The existing public procurement regime can be classified into the public supplies sector,[1] the public works sector,[2] the public utilities sector[3] (entities operating in the water, energy, transport and telecommunications sectors) and the public services sector.[4] Alongside the substantive regime, two Compliance Directives provide for review procedures at domestic levels in relation to public and utilities procurement respectively.

Part 1 The legal regime on public procurement

The supplies procurement

The Public Supplies Directive 93/36 covers contracts between a supplier (natural or legal persons) and a contracting authority, having as their objective the purchase and hire of goods. The supplies regime appears as the most straightforward. Directive 70/32 attempted to integrate markets relating to the supply of goods destined for the public sector from within and from outside the

Community. It indirectly made clear to national administration and law and policy makers that public supplies markets could not be confined within the geographical territory of the Community, or the national borders of Member States, but encompass a broader field of sourcing of goods, a fact that cultivated the ground for the introduction of common commercial policy consideration in public procurement. Indeed, ten years later the European Commission was concluding on behalf of the Member States the Agreement on Government Procurement during the GATT Tokyo Round, thus expanding the territorial application of the EC internal regime to members/signatories to the Agreement.

In 1977, the Council adopted Directive 77/62[5] pursuant to Articles 30 and 100 EC. This instrument was designed to ensure a more effective supervision of compliance with the negative obligations of Article 30 EC and Directive 70/32 by means of imposing a number of positive obligations on purchasing bodies [article 1(b): contracting authorities specified in Annex I]. However, the scope of the Directive was rather limited. It explicitly excluded from its coverage public supplies contracts by public utilities (authorities in the transport, energy water and telecommunications sectors). The Directive was also inapplicable to public supplies contracts awarded i) pursuant to an international agreement between a Member Sate and one or more non-Member countries; ii) pursuant to an international agreement relating to the stationing of troops between undertakings in a Member State or a non-Member country and iii) pursuant to a particular procedure of an international agreement.

In 1980 Directive 77/62 was amended by Directive 80/767[6] in order to take account of the 1979 GATT Agreement on Government Procurement.[7] The Agreement, through the application of lower thresholds, committed the Community and its Member States in providing to suppliers from third countries access to central government purchasing and to some defence procurement, access which was better than that afforded to European suppliers enjoyed under Directive 77/62. Clearly, Directive 80/767 instituted an element of multilaterality in access to international public markets based on the principle of *reciprocity*. That Agreement became part of Community law as it was approved by Council Decision 80/271.[8]

The Commission's White Paper on the Completion of the internal market[9] reiterated that there was a serious and urgent need for improvement and clarification of the relevant Public Procurement Directives. In accordance with the Commission's action programme,

Directive 88/295[10] amending all previous Supplies Directives was adopted. The main improvements were:

- with open tendering procedures as the norm, negotiated ones were allowed in exceptional circumstances;[11]
- the definition of the types of supplies contracts was widened[12] and the method of calculation of the thresholds was clarified;[13]
- the exempted sectors were more strictly defined;[14]
- purchasing authorities had to publish in advance information on their annual procurement programmes and their timetable, as well as a notice giving details of the outcome of each decision of award.[15]
- the rules on technical standards were brought in line with the new policy on standards which were based on the mutual recognition of national requirements, where the objectives of national legislation were essentially equivalent, and on the process of legislative harmonisation of technical standards through non-governmental standardisation organisations (CEPT, CEN, CENELEC).[16]

Finally, Directive 93/36[17] consolidated all previous legislation relating to public supplies and aligned it in conformity with the relevant Directives on Public Works[18] and Public Services[19] and the Utilities Sectors.[20]

The works procurement

The Public Works Directive 93/37 covers contracts between a contractor (natural or legal persons) and a contracting authority, having as their objective the completion of works/construction projects.

The concept of public works contracts under the first Works Directive was very extensive[21] and covered those contracts concluded in writing between a contractor and a contracting authority for pecuniary interest concerning either the execution or both the execution and design of works related to building or civil engineering activities listed in class 50 of the NACE Classification,[22] or the execution by whatever means of a work corresponding to the requirements specified by the contracting authority. The above formula was wide enough to embrace modern forms of works contracts such as project developing contracts, management contracts and concession contracts.[23] With reference to the latter type of contracts, a public works concession is defined by the Works Directive[24] as a written contract between a contractor and a contracting authority concerning either the execution or both the execution and design of a work and for which remunerative considerations consist, at least partly, in the right of the *concessionaire* to exploit exclusively the finished construction works for a period of time. The initial Works Directive 71/305 did not apply to concession contracts, except in the case that the concessionaire was a public authority covered by the Directive. In such situations, only the works subcontracted to third parties would be fully subject to its provisions. In any other case, the only provision of the Directive applicable to works concessions was that the *concessionaire* should not discriminate on grounds of nationality when it awarded contracts to third parties.[25] The regulation of concession contracts was introduced to the *aquis communautaire* almost two decades later by virtue of Directive 89/440 which amended Directive 71/305. In fact, it incorporated the Voluntary Code of Practice, which was adopted by the Representatives of Member States meeting within the Council in 1971.[26] The Code was a non-binding instrument and contained rules on the advertising of contracts and the principle that contracting authorities awarding the principal contract to a concessionaire were to require him to subcontract to third parties at least 30 per cent of the total work provided for by the principal contract. Obviously, these requirements could not easily be incorporated in a binding instrument such as Directive 89/440, thus a more relaxed regime occurred. As a result, the co-ordination rules of the Directive applied to concession contracts only in respect of their advertising. The Directive's rules on tendering procedures, suitability criteria, selection and qualification, technical specifications and award procedures and criteria were inapplicable.

The amended Works Directive has adopted a special, mitigated regime for the award of concession contracts.[27] The provisions of the Directive only apply to concession contracts when the value is at least 5 million EURO. No rules are given as to the way in which the contract value must be calculated. For the award of concession contracts, contracting authorities must apply similar rules on advertising as the advertising rules concerning open and restricted procedures for the award of every works contract. Also, the provisions on technical standards and on criteria for qualitative selection of candidates and tenderers do apply to the award of concession contracts. The Directive does not prescribe the use of specific award procedures for concession contracts. The Directive presupposes that concession contracts should be awarded in two rounds, such as in the case of restricted procedures or negotiated procedures for ordinary works contracts. Nothing, however, prevents contracting authorities from applying one-round open procedures. The Directive contains no rules on the minimum number of candidates which have to be invited to negotiate or to submit a tender. It would seem that a contracting authority may limit itself to selecting only one single candidate, provided the intention to award a concession contract has been adequately published. A contracting authority may under no circumstances refrain from publicising a notice to the Official Journal indicating its intention to proceed with the award of a concession works contract.

As far as contracting authorities are concerned, their definition is very wide and covers bodies governed by public law which is defined as being any body *established for the specific purpose of meeting needs in the general interest and not having an industrial or commercial character, which has legal personality and is financed for the most part by the State or is subject to management supervision by the latter.*[28] There is a list of such bodies in Annex I of Directive 71/305, which is not an exhaustive one like that in the Supplies Directive, and Member States were under an obligation to notify the Commission of any changes in that list.

Works contracts in the utilities and defence sectors and those contracts awarded in pursuance of certain international agreements were explicitly excluded by virtue of Articles 4 and 5 of the Directive. These provisions are identical in effect to the corresponding ones of the Supplies Directive.[29] This revealed the fact that public contracts under the framework of the Works Directive covered mainly construction projects in the education, health, sports and leisure facilities sectors, in as much as the State or regional or local authorities undertake such projects. In cases that entities involved in this sort of activity (e.g. a hospital or a University) enjoyed considerable independence from the State or local government, as to the undertaking of works contracts, Directive 71/305 was inapplicable, since they were not included in its Annex I as bodies governed by public law for the purposes of the Directive in question. This seems to have limited the scope of the Directive only to cases where the State or local government had direct control over the above mentioned entities. Given the fact that works contracts in the utilities sectors were also excluded from the framework of the Directive, its applicability covered a rather modest portion of the construction sector. In order to moderate this apparently undesirable result, the amending Directive 89/440[30] provides for an obligation upon Member States to ensure compliance with its provisions when they subsidise directly by more than 50 per cent, a works contract awarded by an entity involved in activities relating to certain civil engineering works and to the building of hospitals, sports recreation and leisure facilities, schools and university buildings and buildings used for administrative purposes. These conditions seem not to impose a heavy duty on Member States, as only direct subsidies trigger the applicability of the Directive. Indirect ways of subsidising the entities in question, such as tax exemptions, guaranteed loans, or provision of land free of charge, render it inapplicable.

It should be noted that under both the original Supplies and Works Directives, preference schemes in the award of contracts were allowed. Such schemes required the application of award criteria based on considerations other than the lowest price or the most economically advantageous tender, which are common in both regimes.[31] However, preferences could only be compatible with Community Law in as much they did not run contrary to the principle of free movement of goods (Article 30 EC *et seq.*) and to competition law considerations in respect of state aids.[32] Preference schemes have been abolished since the completion of the internal market at the end of 1992.

Works contracts which are subsidised directly by more than 50 per cent by the States, can still fall within the scope of the Directive.[33] Works which are not subsidised directly, or for less than 50 per cent, fall outside this anti-circumvention provision. Not all subsidised works fall within the scope of the Directive: only civil engineering works, such as the construction of roads, bridges and railways, as well as building work for hospitals, facilities intended for sports, recreation and leisure and university buildings and buildings used for administrative purposes are referred to as subsidised works contracts.[34] This list is exhaustive. The Works Directive does not apply to works contracts which are declared secret or the execution of which must be accompanied by special security measures[35] in accordance with the laws, regulations or administrative provisions in force in the Member State concerned; nor does the Directive apply to works contracts when the protection of the basic interests of the Member States' security so requires. Finally, the Works Directive does not apply to public works contracts awarded in pursuance of certain international agreements;[36] nor does the Directive apply to public works contracts awarded pursuant to the particular procedure of an international organisation.[37] Several international organisations, such as NATO, have their own rules on the award of public works contracts.

Utilities procurement

The Utilities Directive 93/38 covers supplies, works and services contracts between a supplier, contractor or service provider and a public utility (an entity operating in the water, energy, telecommunications and transport sectors).

The Utilities Directive has been the most radical approach to the public sector integration in Europe and its enactment coincided with the envisaged international liberalisation of public procurement during the Uruguay GATT negotiations. One could question such a strategy by European Institutions, particularly bearing in mind the vulnerability of Europe's high-tech industry in comparison with that in the USA and Japan. However, the GATT regime has introduced a new era in the accessibility of international public markets, to the extent that highly protectionist countries like the USA and Japan must, under the new regime, abolish their buy-national laws and policies and open, on a reciprocal basis, their public markets to international competition.

The ambit of the Utilities Directive and its field of application appear more complicated than those in the Supplies and Works Directives, although the internal legal structure among the three Directives is very similar. The Utilities Directive devotes a substantial amount of provisions in an attempt to exempt from its application certain contracts or activities that have been deemed ineligible for community-wide regulation.

Apart from the normal exemptions under the grounds of defence and security and confidentiality, the major exemptions are provided for under Articles 1 and 2. Radio and television broadcasting have not been classified as telecommunication activities and have been specifically excluded from the ambit of the Directive by virtue of Article 2. Also, bus transport services to the public are excluded on condition that their providers operate under a regime of competitive conditions, which means that other potential contractors or suppliers of similar services are allowed to enter the relevant geographical and product markets and compete against the existing utilities provider (Article 2 (4). A similar rule applies to telecommunication services which operate within a competitive market.[38]

Under the same Article (2) special exemptions are also provided to private entities supplying gas, heat, drinking water and electricity. Although the wording and spirit of the Directive cover private entities operating under exclusive and special rights in the utilities sectors, nevertheless under certain conditions, these entities can be exempted from the application of the rules of the Directive. In the case of the production of drinking water and electricity, if a private entity is able to show that it does so for its own purposes, which are not related to the provision of drinking water or electricity to the public, it is exempt.

Similarly, if a private entity is able to show that it supplies to the public network drinking water or electricity which is destined for its own consumption, and that the total so supplied to the network is not more than 30 per cent of the total produced by that network in any one year over a three year period, it is also exempt.[39]

In the case of gas and heat supplies, if the production by a private entity is related to an activity other than the supply to a network for public consumption, then these entities are also exempt. In the same line, if the supply of gas and heat by a private entity to a public network relates to economic exploitation only and does not exceed 20 per cent of the firms turnover in any one year, taking an average of the preceding three years and the current year, then such an entity is also exempt.[40] These exemptions predominantly cover entities which have research and development as their main objective in the relevant utilities sector, or do not play a major role in supplying public networks with water or energy.

There are also exemptions for entities exploring for gas, oil, coal and other solid fuels under Article 3. Entities operating in these sectors will not be regarded as having an exclusive right provided certain conditions are fulfilled. These conditions are cumulative and stipulate that, when an exploitation right is granted to the entity in question, the latter is exempt from the Utilities Directives provided other bodies are able to compete for the same exclusive rights under free competition; that the financial and technical criteria to be used in awarding rights are clearly spelt out before the award is made; that the objective criteria are specified as to the way in which exploitation is to be carried out; that these criteria are published before requests for tenders are made and applied in a non-discriminatory way; that all operating obligations, royalty and capital and revenue participation agreements are being published in advance; and finally, that contracting authorities are not required to provide information on their intentions about procurement except at the request of national authorities.[41] Furthermore, Member States have to ensure that these exempted bodies apply, at least, the principles of non-discrimination and competition. They are obliged to provide a report to the EC on request about such contracts. However, this requirement is less stringent than the mandatory reporting rules in the Supply and Works Directives. It should be mentioned that the Utilities Directive does not apply to concession contracts granted to entities operating in utilities sectors, awarded prior to the coming into force of the Directive. All exemption provisions within the Utilities Directive are subject to assessment in the light of the four year overall review of the process.[42]

Other exemptions cover entities in the relevant sectors which can demonstrate that their service and network associated contracts are not related to the specific supply and works functions specified in the Directive, or if they are related, they take place in a non-Member State and they are not using a European public network or physical area.[43] The Member States are under an obligation to inform the European Commission, on request, of the cases when these exemptions have been allowed. There are also provisions which allow for resale and hire contracts to third parties to be exempt when the awarding body does not possess an exclusive or special right to hire or sell the subject of the contract, and there is competition already in the market from other suppliers or producers to provide the commodity or service to third parties.[44] Similar relaxed reporting and monitoring requirements are found in Article 8 which applies to telecommunications exemptions.[45]

Another set of significant exemptions is provided for water authorities under Article 9. Under this provision water authorities specified in Annex 1 are specifically exempt from the rules when they purchase water. They are however covered by the Directive when they purchase other supply and construction products.[46] Similarly, there are specific exemptions for the electricity, gas and heat, oil and gas and coal and other solid fuels entities outlined in Annex II, III, IV and V, but only when they award contracts for the supply of energy or for fuels for the production of energy. For all other relevant contracts these bodies are included in the rules. These exemptions were provided because of the need to allow contracting authorities to buy from local sources of supply, which may not always be the cheapest, but which are important on the basis of regional development policies or environmental grounds, and because these purchases are central to the entities' operations and not part of normal supply and works procurement process.[47]

Finally, specific exemptions under the Utilities Directive are provided for those carriers of passengers and providers of transport services by air and by sea. In the preamble of the Directive it is stated that, under a series of measures adopted in 1987 with a view to introducing more competition between firms providing public air services, it was decided to exempt such carriers from the scope of the legislation. Similarly, because shipping has been subject to severe competitive pressures, it was decided to exempt certain types of contracts from the Directive.[48]

The Utilities Directive intends to open up procurement practices in the four previously excluded sectors mainly to EC-wide competition.

With respect to goods (and services) originating in third countries, things are more complicated. A product outside the Community, in order to be subject to a public contract regulated by one of the EC Public Procurement Directives, must lawfully be put in free circulation in at least one Member State.[49] Except where there has been an international agreement which grants comparable and effective access for Community undertakings to public markets of a third country (reciprocity principle), Article 29 renders possible for European contracting authorities in the utilities sector to reject offers from outside the Community and practise Community preference where Community offers are equivalent to offers from third countries (where the price difference does not exceed 3 per cent). With reference to an international agreement granting access to public markets, the Utilities Directive opens the door for the application of the GATT Agreement on Government Procurement in the utilities sector.

Procurement of services

The Public Services 92/50 covers contracts between a service provider (natural or legal persons) and a contracting authority, having as their objective the provision of services, as defined in the United Nations Nomenclature of Product and Service Classification.

Under the Services Directive, public services contracts are contracts which have as their object the provision of services classified in the Common Product Classification (CPC) Nomenclature of the United Nations, as a Nomenclature for Classification of Services at Community level is lacking. The United Nations Common Product Classification covers almost every conceivable service an undertaking may provide, although the services description is rather plain.

The Services Directive is the first legal instrument which attempts to open the increasingly important public services sector to intra-community competition. It should be mentioned that the Directives on Public Supplies, Public Works and Utilities contain provisions where the provision of services is regarded as ancillary to the main contract under their regime, provided the value of the services are less than the value of the supplies or works. Such services are covered by the relevant Directive.

Specific services contracts are excluded from the scope of the Services Directive. It should be mentioned that not all of these specific exclusions are listed in the amended Utilities Directive 93/38, because they would not, in any event, fall within the ambit of a defined activity.

Apart from those contracts which are covered by the relevant provisions of the Works, Supplies and Utilities Directives, and therefore not considered as services, the other contracts excluded from the Services Directive and amended Utilities Directive 93/38 are:

(i) contracts for the acquisition or rental, by whatever financial means, of land, existing buildings, or other immovable property or concerning rights thereon. (However, financial service contracts concluded at the same time as, before or after the contract of acquisition or rental, in whatever form, will be subject to the Directive);
(ii) contracts for the acquisition, development, production or joint production of programme material by broadcasters and contracts for broadcasting time;[50]
(iii) contracts for voice telephony, telex, radiotelephony, paging and satellite services;[51]
(iv) contracts for arbitration and conciliation services;
(v) contracts for financial services in connection with the issue, sale, purchase or transfer of securities or other financial instruments, and central bank services;[52]
(vi) employment contracts;
(vii) research and development service contracts other than those where the benefits accrue exclusively to the contracting authority for its use in the conduct of its own affairs, on condition that the service provided is mostly remunerated by the contracting authority.

Research and development services contracts are covered in identical terms in both. The exclusion of such contracts under both the Services and the Utilities Directives lies in the assumption that research and development projects should not be financed by public funds. However, where research and development contracts are covered by the procurement rules, a provision in the Utilities Directive allows a contracting entity to award a contract without a prior call for competition where it is purely for the purpose of research, experiment, study or development and not for the purpose of ensuring profit or of recovering research and development costs and in so far as the award of such contract does not prejudice the competitive award of subsequent contracts which have in particular these purposes.[53]

Interestingly, service concessions, although included in the draft Directive,[54] have been excluded from the provisions of Directive 92/50.

The exclusion of service concessions falls short of the aspirations to regulate concession contracts for the public sector under the Works Directive and breaks the consistency in the two legal instruments. The reasons for the exclusion of service concessions from the regulatory regime of public procurement could be attributed to the different legal requirements in Member States to delegate powers to concessionaires. The delegation of services by public authorities to private undertakings in some Member States runs contrary to constitutional provisions.

The Directive adopts a two-tier approach in classifying services procured by contracting authorities. This classification is based on a "priority" and a "non-priority" list of services, according to the relative value of such services in intra-community trade. *Priority services* include: Maintenance and repair services, Land transport services (except for rail transport services), including armoured car services and courier services, except transport of mail, Air transport services of passengers and freight, except transport of mail, Transport of mail by land and by air, Telecommunications services (except voice telephony, telex, radiotelephony, paging and satellite services), Financial services including *(a)* Insurance services, *(b)* Banking and investment services (except contracts for financial services in connection with the issue, sale, purchase or transfer of securities or other financial instruments, and central bank services), Computer and related services, Research and development services, Accounting, auditing and bookkeeping services, Market research and public opinion polling services, Management consultant services (except arbitration and conciliation services) and related services, Architectural services, Engineering services and integrated engineering services, Urban planning and landscape architectural services, related scientific and technical consulting services, technical testing and analysis services, Advertising services, Building-cleaning services on a fee or contract basis, Publishing and printing services on a fee or contract basis, Sewage and refuse disposal services, Sanitation and similar services. *Non-Priority services* include: Hotel and restaurant services, Rail transport services, Water transport services, Supporting and auxiliary transport services, Legal services, Personnel placement and supply services, Investigation and security services, Education and vocational education services, Health and social services and Recreational, cultural and sporting services.

The division is not permanent and the European Commission has the situation under constant review by assessing the performance of "*non-priority*" services sectors. The two-tier approach, in practical terms, means that the award of *priority* services contracts are subject to the rigorous regime of the Public Procurement Directives (advertisement, selection of tenderers, award procedures, award criteria), whereas the award of *non-priority services* contracts must follow the basic rules of non-discrimination and publicity of the results of the award.

Article 6 of the Services Directive provides that the Directive does not apply service contracts which are awarded to an entity which is itself a contracting authority within the meaning of the Directive on the basis of an exclusive right which is granted to the contracting authority by a law, regulation or administrative provision of the Member State in question.[55] Article 1(3) of the Utilities Directive provides for the exclusion of certain contracts between contracting authorities and affiliated undertakings.[56] These are service contracts which are awarded to a service-provider which is affiliated to the contracting entity and participating in a joint venture formed for the purpose of carrying out an activity covered by the Directive.[57] The exclusion from the provisions of the Directive is subject, however, to two conditions: the service-provider must be an undertaking affiliated to the contracting authority and, at least 80 per cent of its average turnover arising within the European Community for the preceding three years, derives from the provision of the same or similar services to undertakings with which it is affiliated. The Commission is empowered to monitor the application of this Article and to request the notification of the names of the undertakings concerned and the nature and value of the service contracts involved.

Enforcement and compliance: The Compliance Directives

In an attempt to complement the substantive Procurement rules enacted by virtue of the Supplies, Works and Services Directives and to provide a system of effective protection of individuals in cases of infringements of their provisions, European Institutions enacted the Compliance Directive 89/665 EC[58] on the harmonisation of laws, regulations and administrative provisions relating to the application of review procedures in the award of public works and public supply contracts. To encompass the Utilities procurement rules, the Utilities Compliance Directive 92/13[59] extends the remedies and review procedures covered by Directive 89/665 to the water, energy, transport and telecommunications sectors.

The scope and thrust of the Compliance Directives focuses on the obligation of Member States to ensure effective and rapid review of decisions taken by contracting authorities which infringe public procurement provisions. Undertakings seeking relief from damages in the context of a procedure for the award of a contract should not be treated differently under national rules implementing European public procurement laws and under other national rules. This means that the measures to be taken concerning the review procedures should be similar to national review proceedings, without any discriminatory character. Any person having or having had an interest in obtaining a particular public supply or public works contract and who has been or risks being harmed by an alleged infringement of public procurement provision must be entitled to seek review before national courts. This particular obligation is followed by a stand-still provision concerning the prior notification by the person seeking review to the contracting authority of the alleged infringement and of his intention to seek review. However, with respect to admissibility aspects, there is no qualitative or quantitative definition of the interest of a person in obtaining a public contract. As to the element of potential harm by an infringement of public procurement provisions, it should be cumulative with the first element, that of interest. The prior notification should intend to exhaust any possibility of amicable settlement before the parties have recourse to national courts. A novelty in the Compliance Directive of the Utilities sectors[60] is the introduction of the *attestation procedure*. Member States are required to give the contracting entities the possibility of having their purchasing procedures and practices *attested* by persons authorised by law to exercise this function. Indeed, this attestation mechanism may investigate in advance possible irregularities identified in the award of a public contract and allow the contracting authorities to correct them. The latter may include the attestation statement in the notice inviting tenders published in the Official Journal. The system appears flexible and cost-efficient and may prevent wasteful litigation. Quite promisingly, the attestation procedure under Directive 92/13 will be the essential requirement for the development of European standards of attestation.[61]

The WTO Government Procurement Agreement

The Government Procurement Agreement (GPA) is based on a number of general principles, which depict the principles of the old AGP regime. The most important of them is the principle of *national treatment*. Under this principle, the parties to the GPA must give the same treatment afforded to national providers and products to providers and products of other signatory states. Reinforcing the principle of national treatment, the *most favoured nation* (MFN) principle guarantees treatment no less favourable than that afforded to other parties. In addition to the above principles, the principle of *non-discrimination* prohibits discrimination against local firms on grounds of the degree of their foreign affiliation or ownership, or on the grounds of origin of the goods or services where these have been produced in one of the states which is party to the Agreement.

The GPA stipulates a set of procedures for contracting authorities in the signatory parties which must be followed when awarding contracts within its scope. These procedures aim to ensure transparency and openness as well as objectivity and legitimacy in the award of public contracts and to facilitate cross-border trade between the signatories. The influence of the European Community on the GPA regime is apparent, an indication of the maturity and validity of the regulatory process of the European public markets integration. The procedures are, however, less strict than those applicable for the award of public sector contracts under the Community regime, and depict the integral flexibility envisaged by the regulatory regime for utilities procurement.

The GPA intends to regulate access specifically to the government procurement markets. General market access between the signatories is in principle dealt with under other agreements, notably the GATT (on the import of goods) and the GATS (on access to services markets). The detailed scope and coverage of the GPA with regard to the entities covered, the type of procurement and monetary thresholds is set out in Appendix I of the Agreement. The Agreement applies in principle to all bodies which are deemed as "contracting authorities" for the purposes of the European Public Sector Directives. With reference to utilities, the GPA applies to entities which carry out one or more of certain listed "utility" activities, where these entities are either "public authorities" or "public undertakings", in the sense of the Utilities Directive. However, the GPA does not cover entities operating in the utilities sector on the basis of *special and exclusive rights*. The utility activities which are covered include (i) activities connected with the provision of water through fixed networks; (ii) activities concerned with the provision of electricity through fixed networks; (iii) the provision of terminal facilities to carriers by sea or inland waterway; and (iv) the operation of public services in the field of transport by automated systems, tramway, trolley bus, or bus or cable. The provision of public transport services by rail is included in principle, but there is exclusion for entities listed in Annex VI of the European Utilities Directive, designed to exclude non-urban transport services. However, the trust of the applicability of the

GPA in relation to utilities activities appears short in comparison with that under the European regime. Activities connected with the distribution of gas or heat, the exploration or extraction of fuel are notable exceptions from the GPA's ambit.

The thresholds for the applicability of the GPA regime to public contracts of signatories are as follows: For supplies and services it is SDR 130,000 for central government; 200,000 for local government; and 400,000 for all contracts in the utilities sectors (including those awarded by central and local government). For works contracts, the threshold is SDR 5 m, for all entities.

Although in principle the GPA regime represents a significant improvement in relation to the old AGP regime in terms of coverage and thrust, certain important derogations from its applicability would result in diluting the principal aims and objectives envisaged by the signatories. As far as central or federal government works and supply contracts are concerned, the Agreement is expected to facilitate market access and enhance cross-border trade patterns in public contracts. However, for contracts relating to services and for certain contracts in the utilities sector, as well as for contracts awarded by local, municipal or regional authorities, the effect of the Agreement appears considerably moderate. A number of signatories have been unable, or unwilling, to offer for coverage all of their entities or contracts in the above categories. Political and legal particularities in the systems of the signatories have prevented similar coverage between the parties. In addition, by applying the principle of *reciprocity* in negotiating the GPA, the result would probably have been very similar to the old AGP regime in covering central or federal public contracts. The solution to this fundamental apparently deadlock was to be found in a rather peculiar method. Each signatory should effectively negotiate with each other and to come to a satisfactory agreement on coverage based on reciprocity on a bilateral basis. This approach constitutes a significant departure from the premise of the MFN and has resulted in some considerable divergence in the applicability of the GPA by virtue of derogations and limitations imposed by signatories on access to their public markets. Thus, for example, coverage in the utilities sector does not apply to Canada, since that country did not commit itself to opening its own markets to the European Community. When the Agreement was first concluded in December 1993 there was also no coverage for utilities with respect to the United States, but there have since been modifications to the EC-US coverage as a result of subsequent EC–US bilateral agreements. Also outside the coverage of the

Agreement in the utilities sector is, in relation to Japan, urban transport and electricity; in relation to South Korea, urban transport and airports; and in relation to Israel, urban transport. There are also significant derogations for certain categories of services and for specified types of equipment.

The scope and coverage the GPA, as well as the structure of its applicability present a unique instrument of international law which is based on a series of bilateral agreements rather than a multilateral arrangement. This represents a significant compromise of the most favoured nation principle, which is a fundamental premise of the majority of international trade agreements. Members to the World Trade Organisation joining the GPA, at their discretion, need to reach separate agreements on the scope of coverage with all existing parties to the Agreement. The GPA thus, has acquired a *plurilaterality* status, a fact that weakens its thrust and complicates its applicability.

Part 2   Definitions and the mechanics of public procurement regulation

The concept of contracting authorities

The structure of the Directives is such as to embrace the purchasing behaviour of all entities, which have a close connection with the state. These entities, although not formally part of the state, disperse public funds in pursuit or on behalf of public interest. The Directives describe as contracting authorities the *state*, which covers central, regional, municipal and local government departments, as well as *bodies governed by public law*. Provision has been also made to cover entities, which receive more than 50 per cent subsidies by the state or other contracting authorities.

However, that connection might be weak to cover entities which operate in the utilities sector and have been privatised. The *Foster* principle[62] established that state accountability could not embrace privatised enterprises.[63] The enactment of the Utilities Directives[64] brought under the procurement framework entities operating in the water, energy, transport and telecommunications sectors. A wide range of these entities are covered by the term *bodies governed by public law*, which is used by the Utilities Directives for the contracting entities operating in the relevant sectors.[65] Interestingly, another category of contracting authorities under the Utilities Directives includes *public undertakings*.[66] The term indicates any undertaking over which the state may exercise direct or indirect dominant influence by means of ownership, or by means of financial participation, or by means of laws and regulations which govern the public undertaking's operation. Dominant influence can be exercised in the form of a majority holding of the undertaking's subscribed capital, in the form of majority controlling of the undertaking's issued shares, or, finally in the form of the right to appoint the majority of the undertaking's management board. Public undertakings cover utilities operators, which have been granted exclusive rights of exploitation of a service. Irrespective of their ownership, they are subject to the Utilities Directive in as much as the *exclusivity* of their operation precludes other entities from entering the relevant market under substantially the same competitive conditions. Privatised utilities could be, in principle, excluded from the procurement rules when a genuinely competitive regime[67] within the relevant market structure would rule out purchasing patterns based on non-economic considerations.

The principle mandatory advertisement and publication of public contracts

One of the most important principles of the Public Procurement Directives is the principle of transparency. The principle of transparency serves two main objectives: the first is to introduce a system of openness in public purchasing of the Member States, so a greater degree of accountability is established and potential direct discrimination on grounds of nationality is eliminated. The second objective aims at ensuring that transparency in public procurement represents a substantial basis for a system of best practice for both parts of the equation, but of particular relevance to the supply side, so that it has a more *proactive* role in determining the needs of the demand side. Transparency in public procurement is achieved through community-wide publicity and advertisement of public procurement contracts over certain thresholds by means of publication of three types of notices in the Official Journal of the European Communities:

i) Periodic Indicative Notices (PIN). Every contracting authority must notify its intentions for public procurement contracts within the forthcoming financial year.[68] By doing so, it provides for an estimate intention of its purchasing and gives the supply side the necessary time for planning and response to future contract opportunities. The publication of Periodic Indicative Notices, if properly observed, also serves as a useful indicator in determining the relevant market size for the supply side, as well as the relevant procurement magnitude for a type of contracting authorities on an annual basis. The fact that through PIN notices contracting authorities produce only an estimated figure for forthcoming contracts they intend to award, does not absolve them from their responsibilities in strictly adhering to their publication.[69]

ii) Invitations to tender. All contracts above the relevant thresholds should be tendered and the notice containing the invitation to tender must include the award procedures and the award criteria for the contract in question.[70] The Invitation to tender is the most important publicity and advertisement requirement for the creation of transparent and open public markets in the European Community. The publication of the invitation to tender refers only to a particular contract or a range of similar contracts of repetitive nature and provides the supply side with the opportunity to respond and make an offer in order to meet the needs and requirements of the demand side. The invitation to tender is part of the contractual nexus in the public procurement process between the relevant contracting authority and the tenderers/candidates competing for the award of the contract in question. It is through the invitation to tender that the supply side has a clear view as to the award procedures and the award criteria contracting authorities intend to utilise, thus being able to respond accordingly. The invitation to tender represents the first step towards the award of public contracts and failure by contracting authorities to adhere to the minimum requirements specified in the Directives could invalidate the whole process.

iii) Contract Award Notices (CAN). This is a form of notification after the award of the contract of the successful tenderer and the price of its offer, as well as the reasons for its selection by the contracting authority.[71] In principle, Contract Award Notices publicise the reasoning of contracting authorities during the selection and award stages of the process, but quite often price information of the successful tenderers and other candidates is withheld for reasons of commercial confidentiality. The publication of CAN notices can be used as an effective indicator in monitoring the purchasing patterns of contracting authorities, as well as in providing a picture relevant to the tradability of public contracts.

All types of notices are published by the Publications Office of the European Communities. Within twelve days (or five days in the case of the accelerated form of restricted or negotiated procedures), the Publications Office publishes the notices in the Supplement to the Official Journal and via the TED (Tenders Electronic Daily) database. Two notices are published in full in their original language only and in summary form in the other Community languages. The Publications Office takes responsibility for the necessary translations and summaries. The costs of publishing notices in the Supplement to the Official Journal are borne by the Community.

The monetary applicability of the Public Procurement Directives

The European rules of public procurement and all the requirements and procedures laid down therein are triggered only if certain value thresholds are met. The application of the Directives is subject to monetary considerations in relation to the value of the relevant contracts. There is a clear-cut distinction of coverage of the public procurement rules upon contracts representing transactions between the public sector and the industry of a certain economic substance and volume. Contracts below the required thresholds are not subject to the rigorous regime envisaged by the Directives. However, contracting authorities are under the explicit obligation to avoid discrimination on nationality grounds and apply all the provisions related to the fundamental principles of the Treaties of Rome and Maastricht. The thresholds laid down are as follows:

- 5 million EURO for all work and construction projects[72]
- 200,000 EURO for supplies contracts within the European Union[73] and 136,000 EURO for supplies contracts from third countries[74] which participate in the WTO Government Procurement Agreement.
- 600,000 EURO for supplies of telecommunication equipment under the Utilities Directive[75] and 400,000 EURO for all other supplies contracts awarded by public utilities.[76]
- 200,000 EURO for services contracts.[77]

The way in which the value of a contract is calculated is crucial for the application of the relevant Directive. To ensure that identical calculation methods are used throughout the Member States of the European Community and to prevent intentional avoidance of the Procurement Directives by artificially low contract valuations, the Directives lay down specific rules.[78] Where the contract is to be concluded in the form of a lease, rental or hire-purchase agreement, the calculation method varies according to the duration of the contract. The estimated value is to be calculated on the basis of the following requirements:

- where its term is 12 months or less, the total value for the contract's duration;
- where its term exceeds 12 months, the total value for the contract's duration, including the estimated residual value of the products;
- where the contract is concluded for an indefinite period or where its term cannot be defined, the monthly value multiplied by 48.
- where contracts are of a regular nature or are to be renewed over a given period, the following must be taken into account:
  – either the actual aggregate value of similar successive contracts awarded over the previous 12 months or accounting period, adjusted where possible for anticipated changes in quantity or value over the subsequent 12 months;
  – or the estimated aggregate value of the successive contracts concluded during the 12 months following the initial delivery or accounting periods where this exceeds 12 months. In any event, the choice between these two valuation methods must not be made with the intention of keeping contracts outside the scope of the Directive.

If a proposed procurement of supplies of the same type may lead to contracts being awarded at the same time in separate lots, the estimated value of all the lots must be taken into account. If it reaches the relevant threshold, all the lots must be awarded in compliance with the Directive. The same rules apply when estimating the value of leasing, rental or hire-purchase contracts. Where provision is explicitly made for options, the basis for calculating the estimated contract value must be the highest possible total permitted for the purchase, lease, rental or hire options included.

When calculating the value of a public works contract, account has to be taken of the estimated value of the works and of the estimated value of the supplies needed to carry out the works, even if these supplies are made available to the contractor by the contracting authorities. The estimated value of work which the contracting authority intends to have carried out later by the contractor awarded the current contract and which consists in a repetition of the work to be carried out under the current contract, must be included in the contract value.

The Works Directive provides for special rules when a contract is subdivided into several lots. When the aggregate value of the lots is over 5 million EURO, the provisions of the Directive apply to all lots. A work or a contract may not be split up with the intention of avoiding the applicability of the Directive. However, lots of a value, net of VAT, less than 1 million EURO may be exempted from the scope of the Directive, provided that the total estimated value of all the lots exempted does not exceed 20 per cent of the total estimated value of all lots.

Selection and qualification criteria

After the advertisement and publicity requirements the next phase in the public procurement process is the selection and qualification of the tenderers. At this stage, contracting authorities vet all the responses received and determine the suitability of the candidates according to objectively defined criteria which aim at eliminating arbitrariness and discrimination. The selection criteria are determined through two major categories of qualification requirements; i) legal, and ii) technical/economic. Contracting authorities must strictly follow the homogeneously specified selection criteria for enterprises participating in the award procedures of public procurement contracts in an attempt to abolish potential grounds for discrimination on grounds of nationality and exclude technical specifications which are capable of favouring national undertakings.

The relevant provisions of the Procurement Directives relating to the criteria of a tenderer's good standing and qualification are directly effective.[79] These criteria comprise of grounds for exclusion from participation in the award of public contracts, such as bankruptcy, professional misconduct, failure to fulfil social security obligations and obligations relating to taxes. They also refer to the technical ability and knowledge of the contractor, where proof of them may be furnished by educational or professional qualifications, previous experience in performing public contracts and statements on the contractor's expertise. In construction projects, the references which the contractor may be required to produce must be specified in the notice or invitation to tender.[80] They include: the contractor's educational and professional qualifications or those of the firm's managerial staff, and, in particular, those of the person or persons responsible for carrying out the works; a list of the works carried out over the past five years, accompanied by certificates of satisfactory execution for the most important works. These certificates must indicate the value, date and site of the works and must specify whether they were carried out according to the rules of the trade and properly completed. Where necessary, the competent authority must submit these certificates direct to the authority awarding the contracts; a statement of the tools, plant and technical equipment available to the contractor for carrying out the work; a statement of the firm's average annual manpower and number of managerial staff for the last three years; a statement of the technicians or technical divisions which the contractor can call upon for carrying out the work, whether or not they belong to the firm.

On the other hand, in supplies contracts, the references which may be requested[81] must be mentioned in the invitation to tender and are the following: a list of the principal deliveries effected in the past three years, with the sums, dates and recipients, public or private, involved in the form of certificates issued or countersigned by the competent authority; a description of the undertaking's technical facilities, its measures for ensuring quality and its study and research facilities; indication of the technicians or technical bodies involved, whether or not belonging directly to the undertaking, especially those responsible for quality control; samples, descriptions or photographs of the products to be supplied, the authenticity of which must be certified if the contracting authority so requests; certificates drawn up by official quality-control institutes or agencies of recognised competence attesting conformity to certain specifications or standards of goods clearly identified by references to specifications or standards; where the goods to be supplied are complex or, exceptionally, are required for a special purpose, a check carried out by the contracting authorities (or on their behalf by a competent official body of the country in which the supplier is established, subject to that body's agreement) on the production capacities of the supplier and, if necessary, on his study and research facilities and quality control measures. The provisions covering the contractors' eligibility and technical capacity constitute an exhaustive list.

In principle, there are automatic grounds for exclusion,[82] when a contractor, supplier or service provider; i) is bankrupt or is being wound up; ii) is the subject of proceedings for a declaration of bankruptcy or for an order for compulsory winding up; iii) has been convicted for an offence concerning his professional conduct; iv) has been guilty of grave professional misconduct; v) has not fulfilled obligations relating to social security contributions; and vi) has not fulfilled obligations relating to the payment of taxes.

However, for the purposes of assessing the financial and economic standing of contractors, an exception to the exhaustive list covering the contractors' eligibility and technical capacity is provided for,[83] where, in particular, contracting entities may request references other than those expressly mentioned therein. Evidence of financial and economic standing may be provided[84] by means of references including: i) appropriate statements from bankers; ii) the presentation of the firm's balance sheets or extracts from the balance sheets where these are published under company law provisions; and iii) a statement of the firm's annual turnover and the turnover on construction works for the three previous financial years.

Legal requirements for the qualification of contractors

The definition of a contractor wishing to submit a tender for the award of a public contract comprises any legal or natural person involved in supplies, construction or services activities. It also includes private consortia, as well as joint ventures or groupings. Contracting authorities may impose a requirement as to the form and legal status of the contractor that wins the award.[85] This requirement focuses only on the post selection stage, after the award of the contract and indicates the need for legal certainty. Specific legal form and status required by contracting entities facilitates monitoring of the performance of the contract and allows better access to justice in case of a dispute between the contracting entity and the undertaking in question. The successful contractor should also fulfil certain qualitative requirements concerning his eligibility and technical capacity[86] and his financial and economic standing.

The list of recognised contractors

Registration in lists of recognised contractors that exist in various Member States may be used by contractors as an alternative means of proving their suitability, also before contracting authorities of other Member States.[87] Information deduced from registration in an official list may not be questioned by contracting authorities. Nonetheless, the actual level of financial and economic standing and technical knowledge or ability required of contractors is determined by the contracting authorities. Consequently, contracting authorities are required to accept that a contractor's financial and economic standing and technical knowledge and ability are sufficient for works corresponding to his classification only in so far as that classification is based on equivalent criteria with respect to the capacities required.

The relevant provisions of the Procurement Directives relating to the qualitative selection and qualification criteria refer to the technical ability and knowledge of tenderers, where proof may be furnished by evidence of educational or professional qualifications, previous experience in performing public contracts and statements on the contractor's expertise.[88] The references, which the tenderers may be required to produce, must be specified in the notice or invitation to tender. The rules relating to technical capacity and eligibility of tenderers represent an exhaustive list and are capable of producing direct effect.[89] The *Transporoute* legacy paved the way for the Court to elaborate on forms of selection and qualification, such as registration in lists of recognised contractors. Such lists exist in Member States and tenderers may use their registration in them as an alternative means of proving their technical suitability, also before contracting authorities of other Member States. *CEI-Bellini* followed the same line[90] although it conferred discretion to contracting authorities to request further evidence of technical capacity, other than the mere certificate of registration in official lists of approved contractors, on the grounds that such lists might not be referring to uniform classifications.

Ballast Nedam I[91] took qualitative selection and qualification criteria a step further. The Court ruled that a holding company which does not itself carry out works may not be precluded from registration on an official list of approved contractors, and consequently, from participating in tendering procedures, if it shows that it actually has available to it the resources of its subsidiaries necessary to carry out the contracts, unless the references of those subsidiaries do not themselves satisfy the qualitative selection criteria specified in the Directives. *Ballast Nedam II*[92] conferred an obligation to the authorities of Member States which are responsible for the compilation of lists of approved contractors to take into account evidence of the technical capacity of companies belonging to the same group, when assessing the parent company's technical capacity for inclusion in the list, provided the holding company establishes that it has available to it the resources of the companies belonging to the group that are necessary to carry out public contracts. *Holst Italia*,[93] by analogy applied the *Ballast* principle to undertakings that belong to the same group structure but do not have the status of a holding company and the requisite availability of the technical expertise of its subsidiaries. The Court held that with regard to the qualitative criteria relevant to the economic, financial and technical standing, a tenderer may rely on the standing of other entities, regardless of the legal nature of the links which it has with them, provided that it is able to show that it actually has at its disposal the resources of those entities which are necessary for performance of a public contract.

However, for the purposes of assessing the financial and economic standing of contractors,[94] an exception to the exhaustive (and directly applicable) nature of technical capacity and qualification rules has been made. The non-exhaustive character of the list of references in relation to the contractors' economic and financial standing was recognised by Court in the *CEI-Bellini* case, where the value of the works which may be carried out at any one time may constitute a proof of the contractors' economic and financial standing. The contracting authorities are allowed to fix such a limit, as the provisions of the Public Procurement Directives do not aim at delimiting the powers of Member States, but at determining the references or evidence which may be furnished in order to establish the contractors' financial and economic standing. Of interest is the recent case ARGE,[95] where even the receipt of aid or subsidies incompatible with the Treaty by an entity may be a reason for disqualification from the selection process, as an obligation to repay an illegal aid would threaten the financial stability of the tenderer in question.

The Court also maintained[96] that the examination of a contractor's suitability based on its technical capacity and qualifications and its financial and economic standing may take place simultaneously with the award procedures of a contract.[97] However, the two procedures (the suitability evaluation and bid evaluation) are totally distinct processes, which must not be confused.[98]

Part 3   The award of public contracts

Tendering procedures

Participation in tendering procedures is channelled through open, negotiated or restricted procedures.

- Open procedures are those where every interested supplier, contractor or service provider may submit an offer.[99]
- Negotiated procedures[100] are such procedures for the award of public contracts whereby contracting authorities consult contractors of their choice and negotiate the terms of the contract with one or more of them. In most cases they follow restricted procedures and they

are heavily utilised under framework agreements in the Utilities sectors.[101] There are two different kinds of negotiated procedures: i) negotiated procedures with prior notification and ii) negotiated procedures without prior notification.
- Negotiated procedures with prior notification[102] provide for selection of candidates in two rounds. In the first round, all interested contractors may submit their tenders and the contracting authority selects, from the candidates, those who will be invited to negotiate. In the second round, negotiations with various candidates take place and the successful tender is selected. In principle, the minimum number of candidates to be selected is three, provided that there are a sufficient number of suitable candidates.
- Negotiated procedures without prior notification[103] are the least restrictive of the various award procedures laid down in the Directive and may be conducted in one single round. Contracting authorities are allowed to choose whichever contractor they want, begin negotiations directly with this contractor and award the contract to him. The Directive provides for only a few rules with which this procedure must comply. A prior notice in the Official Journal is not required.
- Finally, restricted procedures[104] are those procedures for the award of public contracts whereby only those contractors invited by the contracting authority may submit tenders. The selection of the winning tender usually takes place in two rounds. In the first round, all interested contractors may submit their interest and the contracting authority selects, from the candidates, those who will be invited to tender. In principle, the minimum number of candidates to be selected is five. In the second round, bids are submitted and the successful tender is selected.

An accelerated form of restricted or negotiated procedure may be used[105] where, for reasons of urgency, the periods normally required under the normal procedures cannot be met. In such cases, contracting authorities are required to indicate in the tender notice published in the Official Journal the grounds for using the accelerated form of the procedure. The use of an accelerated procedure must be limited to the types and quantities of products or services which can be shown to be urgently required. Other products or services must be supplied or provided under open or restricted procedures.

The Directives stipulate that open procedures, where possible should constitute the norm. Open procedures increase competition without doubt and can achieve better prices for the contracting authorities when purchasing goods in large volumes. Price reduction based on economies of scale can bring about substantial cost savings for the public sector. Open procedures are mostly utilised when the procurement process is relatively straightforward and are combined with the lowest price award criterion. On the other hand, competition in tendering procedures is limited by using the restricted and negotiated procedures. By definition, the number of candidates that are allowed to tender is limited (5 in restricted 3 in negotiated procedures respectively), therefore the Directives have attached a number of conditions for the contracting authorities to justify when they intend to award their contracts through restricted or negotiated procedure. Restricted and negotiated procedures are utilised in relation to the most economically advantageous offer award criterion and suited for more complex procurement schemes. Although contracting authorities can freely opt for open or restricted procedures, the latter should be justified by reference to the nature of the products or services to be procured and the balance between contract value and administrative costs associated with tender evaluation. A more rigorous set of conditions apply for the use of negotiated procedures. When negotiated procedures with prior notification are used, they must be justified on grounds of irregular or unacceptable tenders received as a result of a previous call. Negotiated procedures without prior notification are restrictively permitted in absence of tenders, when the procurement involves manufactured products or construction works purely for research and development, when for technical or artistic reasons or reasons connected with the protection of exclusive rights a particular supplier or contractor is selected, in cases of extreme urgency brought by unforseeable events not attributable to the contracting authorities or when additional deliveries and supplies or works would cause disproportionate technical, operational and maintenance difficulties.

All negotiations with candidates or tenderers on fundamental aspects of contracts, in particular on prices, are prohibited in open and restricted procedures; discussions with candidates or tenderers may be held, but only for the purpose of clarifying or supplementing the content of their tenders or the requirements of the contracting authorities and provided this does not involve discriminatory practices.[106] The need for such a prohibition is clear, since the possibility to negotiate may allow the contracting authority to introduce subjective appraisal criteria.

According to the Procurement Directives, negotiated procedures without prior notification must be used restrictively *inter alia...when for technical or artistic reasons or reasons connected with the protection of exclusive rights the services could only be procured by a particular provider ... and ...in cases of extreme urgency brought about by events unforeseeable by the contracting authority.*

The Court reinforced its restrictive interpretation of the above two reasons to which contracting authorities might be allowed to have recourse to, and maintained their exceptional character rather than their prohibitive use, and the onerous obligation of contracting authorities to justify them.

The alleged existence of technical or artistic reasons or reasons connected with the protection of exclusive rights which reveal a particular contractor or service provider for a contracting authority to negotiate without prior advertisement attracted the attention of the Court in two instances.[107] The Court rejected the existence of exclusive rights in both cases and regarded the abuse of this provision as contrary to the right of establishment and freedom to provide services which are based on the principle of equal treatment and prohibit not only overt discrimination on grounds of nationality, but also all covert forms of discrimination, which, by the application of other criteria of differentiation, lead to the same result. Interestingly, the Court elucidated that exclusive rights might include contractual arrangements such as know-how and intellectual property rights (case 199/85, *Commission v. Italy*).

Urgency reasons brought by unforeseen events to contracting authorities received similarly restrictive interpretation.[108] The Court maintained the need for a justification test based on the proportionality principle (case 199/85, *Commission v. Italy*), as well as the existence of a causal link between the alleged urgency and the unforeseen events.[109]

The award criteria

In principle, there are two criteria laid down in the Public Procurement Directives for awarding public contracts:

- the lowest price
- the most economically advantageous offer

The lowest price criterion is self-explanatory.[110] The tenderer who submits the cheapest offer must be awarded the contract. Subject to the qualitative criteria and financial and economic standing, contracting authorities do not rely on any other factor than the price quoted to complete the contract. The reasons for utilising the lowest price criterion are: simplicity, speed and less qualitative consideration during the evaluation of tenders.

The appreciation of what is the most economically advantageous tender offer[111] is to be made on a series of factors and determinants chosen by the contracting entity for the particular contract in question. These factors include: price, delivery or completion date, running costs, cost-effectiveness, profitability, technical merit, product or work quality, aesthetic and functional characteristics, after-sales service and technical assistance, commitments with regard to spare parts and components and maintenance costs, security of supplies. The above list is not exhaustive and the factors listed therein serve as a guideline for contracting authorities in the weighted evaluation process of the contract award. The order of appearance of these factors in the invitation to tender or in the contract documents is of paramount importance for the whole process of evaluation of the tenders and award of the contract. The most economically advantageous factors must be in hierarchical or descending sequence so tenderers and interested parties can clearly ascertain the relative weight of factors other than price for the evaluation process. However, factors which have no strict relevance to the particular contract in question or factors which are irrelevant in economic terms are classified as subjective.

Two criteria laid down in the Public Procurement Directives provide the conditions under which contracting authorities award public contracts: the lowest price or the most economically advantageous offer.[112] It should be mentioned that the Directives provide for an automatic disqualification of an "obviously abnormally low offer". The term has not been interpreted in detail by the Court and serves rather as an indication of a "lower bottom limit".[113] The Court, however, pronounced on the direct effect of the relevant provision requiring contracting authorities to examine the details of the tender before deciding the award of the contract. The contracting authorities are under duty to seek from the tenderer an explanation for the price submitted or to inform him that his tender appears to be abnormally low and to allow a reasonable time within which to submit further details, before making any decision as to the award of the contract.

The debate over the terminology of "obviously abnormally low" tenders surfaced when the Court held[114] that rejection of a contract based on mathematical criteria without giving the tenderer an opportunity to furnish information is inconsistent with the spirit of the Public Procurement Directives. The Court following previous case-law,[115] ruled that the contracting authorities must give an opportunity to tenderers to furnish explanations regarding the genuine nature of their tenders, when those tenders appear to be abnormally low. Unfortunately, the Court did not proceed to an analysis of the wording "obviously". It rather seems that the term "obviously" indicates the existence of precise and concrete evidence as to the abnormality of the low tender. On the other hand, the wording "abnormally" implies a quantitative criterion left to the discretion of the contracting authority. However, if the tender is just "abnormally" low, it could be argued that it is within the discretion of the contracting authority to investigate the genuine offer of a tender. *Impresa Lombardini*,[116] followed the precedence established by *Transporoute* and maintained the unlawfulness of mathematical criteria used as an exclusion of a tender which appears abnormally low. Nevertheless, it held that such criteria may be lawful if used for determining the abnormality of a low tender, provided an *inter partes* procedure between the contracting authority and the tenderer that submitted the alleged abnormal low offer, offers the opportunity to clarify the genuine nature of that offer. Contracting authorities must take into account all reasonable explanations furnished and avoid limiting the grounds on which justification of the genuine nature of a tender should be made. Explicitly, the provisions of the Public Procurement Directives direct contracting authorities to seek explanation and reject unrealistic offers, informing the Advisory Committee.[117] In ARGE,[118] the rejection of a tender based on the abnormally low pricing attached to it got a different twist in its interpretation. Although the Court ruled that directly or indirectly subsidised tenders by the state or other contracting authorities or even by the contracting authority itself can be legitimately part of the evaluation process, it did not elaborate on the possibility of rejection of an offer, which is appreciably lower than those of unsubsidised tenderers by reference to the disqualification ground based on abnormally low offers.[119]

On the other hand, the meaning of the most economically advantageous offer includes a series of factors chosen by the contracting authority, including price, delivery or completion date, running costs, cost-effectiveness, profitability, technical merit, product or work quality, aesthetic and functional characteristics, after-sales service and technical assistance, commitments with regard to spare parts and components and maintenance costs, security of supplies.

The above list is not exhaustive and the factors listed therein serve as a guideline for contracting authorities in the weighted evaluation process of the contract award. The Court reiterated the flexible and wide interpretation of the relevant award criterion[120] and had no difficulty in declaring that contracting authorities may use the most economically advantageous offer as award criterion by choosing the factors which they want to apply in evaluating tenders,[121] provided these factors are mentioned, in hierarchical order or descending sequence in the invitation to tender or the contract documents, so tenderers and interested parties can clearly ascertain the relative weight of factors other than price for the evaluation process. However, factors, which have no strict relevance in determining the most economically advantageous offer by reference to objective criteria do involve an element of arbitrary choice and therefore should be considered as incompatible with the Directives.

Framework agreements

The Utilities Directives have introduced a new selection and tendering procedure, namely framework agreements which is influenced to a large extent by the benefits of chain supply management and partnership schemes. The Supplies, Works and Services Directives do not refer to framework agreements. A framework agreement is an agreement between a contracting authority and one or more suppliers, contractors or service-providers the purpose of which is to establish the terms, in particular with regard to prices and, where appropriate, the quantity envisaged, governing the contracts to be awarded during a given period. A framework agreement does not possess binding character and should not be considered as a contract between the relevant parties.[122] In practical terms it represents a sort of a standing offer which remains valid during its time-span. Within the provisions of the Utilities Directive, when a contracting authority awards a framework agreement under the relevant procedures which are common to other public contracts covered therein, subsequent individual contracts concluded under the framework agreement may be awarded without having recourse to a call for competition. Individual contracts which have been awarded under a framework agreement are subject to the requirement of the publication of a contract-award notice in the Official Journal. The Directive specifically stipulates that misuse of framework agreements may distort competition and trigger the application of the relevant rules, particularly with reference to concerted practices which lead to collusive tendering.

In-house contracts and contracts to affiliated undertakings

Article 6 of the Services Directive provides for the inapplicability of the Directive to service contracts which are awarded to an entity which is itself a contracting authority within the meaning of the Directive on the basis of an exclusive right which is granted to the contracting authority by a law, regulation or administrative provision of the Member State in question. Article 13 of the Utilities Directive provides for the exclusion of certain contracts between contracting authorities and affiliated undertakings. An affiliated undertaking, for the purposes of the Utilities Directive, is one the annual accounts of which are consolidated with those of the contracting entity in accordance with the requirements of the seventh Company Law Directive [Council Directive 83/349 (OJ 1983 L193/1)]. These are service contracts which are awarded to a service-provider which is affiliated to the contracting entity and service contracts which are awarded to a service-provider which is affiliated to a contracting entity participating in a joint venture formed for the purpose of carrying out an activity covered by the Directive. The explanatory memorandum accompanying the text amending the Utilities Directive (COM (91) 347-SYN 36 1) states that this provision relates to three types of service provision. These categories, which may or may not be distinct, are: the provision of common services such as accounting, recruitment and management; the provision of specialised services embodying the know how of the group; the provision of a specialised service to a joint venture. The exclusion from the provisions of the Directive is subject, however, to two conditions: the service-provider must be an undertaking affiliated to the contracting authority and, at least 80 per cent of its average turnover arising within the European Community for the preceding three years, derives from the provision of the same or similar services to undertakings with which it is affiliated. The Commission is empowered to monitor the application of this Article and require the notification of the names of the undertakings concerned and the nature and value of the service contracts involved.

Design contests

Under the Services Directive, provision has been made for a fourth type of award procedure, namely *design contests*, with particular reference to planning projects. According to the Services Directive, *design contests* are those national procedures which enable the contracting authority to acquire in the fields of area planning, town planning, architecture and civil engineering, a plan or a design selected by a jury, after being put out to competition with or without the award of prizes. The award of *design contests*, according to the Services Directive must follow specific rules. The admission of participants to the contest must not be limited either by reference to the territory or part of a Member State, or on the grounds that under the law of the Member State in which the contest is organised, participants would have been required to be either natural or legal persons. Furthermore, where design contests are restricted to a limited number of participants, the contracting authorities must lay down clear and non-discriminatory selection criteria which ensure sufficient and genuine competition among the participants. The jury must be composed exclusively of natural persons who are independent. The award criteria for design contests remain the same with other public contracts (the lowest price or the most economically advantageous offer)

Concession contracts

The Public Works Directive has adopted a special, mitigated regime for the award of concession contracts the value of which is 5 million EURO or more. There are no specific rules as to the way the value of the contract must be calculated or rules referring to aggregation. For the award of concession contracts, contracting authorities are obliged to follow the advertising rules concerning open and restricted procedures for the award of ordinary works contracts. Also, the provisions on technical standards and on criteria for qualitative selection of candidates and tenderers do apply. However, the Works Directive does not prescribe the use of specific award procedures for concession contracts. The Directive presupposes the concession contracts are awarded in two rounds, such as in the case of restricted procedures or negotiated procedures for works contracts. Nothing, however, prevents contracting authorities from applying a one-round open procedure. The Directive contains no rules on the minimum number of candidates who have to be invited to negotiate or to submit a tender. It would seem that a contracting authority may limit itself to selecting only one single candidate, provided the intention to award a concession contract has been adequately published. A contracting authority may under no circumstances refrain from publishing a notice.

The award of public housing schemes

The award of public housing contracts[123] may deviate from the normal regime of the Directive for the purpose of selecting a contractor who meets the requirements specified by the public authority. The design and construction of a public housing scheme, as well as the size and complexity of the project, as well as the estimated duration of the work involved, require that planning be based from the outset on close collaboration within a team comprising representatives of the contracting authorities, experts and the contractor to be responsible for carrying out the works. In these cases, the contracting authorities have to apply the advertising rules and the criteria for qualitative selection relating to the restricted procedure. Moreover, the contracting authorities have to include in the contract notice as accurately as possible, a description of the works to be carried out. With respect to quantitative selection, no restrictions apply. Hence, there is no obligation for the contracting authorities to select more that one single contractor to negotiate admission to the building team.

Socio-economic considerations

In *Beentjes*,[124] the Court ruled that social policy considerations and in particular measures aiming at the combating of long term unemployment could only be part of the award criteria of public contracts, especially in cases where the most economically advantageous offer is selected. The Court accepted that the latter award criterion contains features that are not exhaustively defined in the Directives, therefore there is discretion conferred on contracting authorities to specify what would the most economically advantageous offer for them. However, contracting authorities cannot refer to such measures as a selection criterion and disqualify candidates who could not meet the relevant requirements. The selection of tenderers is a process which is based on an exhaustive list of technical and financial requirements expressly stipulated in the relevant Directives and the insertion of contract compliance as a selection and qualification requirement would be considered *ultra vires*. The Court held that a contractual condition relating to the employment of long term unemployed persons is compatible with the Public Procurement Directives, if it has no direct or indirect discriminatory effect on tenders from other Member States. Furthermore, such a contractual condition must be mentioned in the tender notice.[125] Rejection of a contract on the grounds of a contractor's inability to employ long-term unemployed persons has no relation to the checking of the contractor's suitability on the basis of his economic and financial standing and his technical knowledge and ability. The Court maintained that measures relating to employment could be utilised as a feature of the award criteria, only when they are part of a contractual obligation of the public contract in question and on condition that they do not run contrary to the fundamental principles of the Treaty. The significance of that qualification has revealed the Court's potential stance over the issue of contract compliance in public procurement.

In the recent case *Nord-pas-de-Calais*, the Court considered whether a condition linked to a local project to combat unemployment could be considered as an award criterion of the relevant contract. The Commission alleged that the French Republic has infringed Article 30(1) of Directive 93/37 purely and simply by referring to the criterion linked to the campaign against unemployment as an award criterion in some of the disputed contract notices. Under Article 30(1) of Directive 93/37, the criteria on which contracting authorities are to base the award of contracts are the lowest price only or, when the award is made to the most economically advantageous tender, various criteria according to the contract, such as price, period for completion, running costs, profitability, and technical merit.

The Court held that the most economically advantageous offer does not preclude all possibility for the contracting authorities to use as a criterion a condition linked to the campaign against unemployment provided that that condition is consistent with all the fundamental principles of Community law, in particular the principle of non-discrimination deriving from the provisions of the Treaty on the right of establishment and the freedom to provide services. Furthermore, even if such a criterion is not in itself incompatible with Directive 93/37, it must be applied in conformity with all the procedural rules laid down in that Directive, in particular the rules on advertising.[126] The Court therefore accepted the employment considerations as an award criterion, part of the most economically advantageous offer, provided it is consistent with the fundamental principles of Community law, in particular the principle of non-discrimination and it is advertised in the contract notice.

Employee protection and transfer of undertakings

The relevance of the Acquired Rights Directive[127] with the public procurement regime became clear when contracting authorities started *testing the market* in an attempt to define whether the provision of works or services from a commercial operator could be cheaper than that from the in-house team. This is the notion of *contracting out*, an exercise which aims at achieving potential savings and efficiency gains for contracting authorities. The application of the transfer of undertakings rules in contracting out cases has the important consequence that the external bidder (if successful) must engage the authority's former employees on the same conditions as they enjoyed under the authority itself.

The initial Directive proclaimed its inapplicability in cases where the undertaking was not in the nature of a commercial venture; this proviso was interpreted as exclusive of contracting out by government. The impact of the transfer of undertakings Directive in the context of public procurement was felt in a landmark decision of the Court,[128] which maintained that the Directive does not permit such a limitation. Thus it became apparent that contracting out by government and other public authorities was covered, and a transfer of an undertaking may take place where the government contracts out to the private sector a function previously carried out in-house[129] and *vice versa*, *viz.* where the contracting authority takes back in-house a service formerly contracted out. The exact circumstance in which a transfer of an undertaking through contracting out occurs depends upon the transfer retaining its identity.[130] However, the "retention of identity" test can only be satisfied when the undertaking transferred represents *substantially the same* or *similar activities*,[131] as well as it relates to a *stable economic entity*.[132] The existence of a contractual link or relation between the parties to a transfer of an undertaking is not a decisive criterion to establish the applicability of the Directive.[133]

Serious concerns have been raised over the compatibility of the public procurement and the transfer of undertakings regimes. It appeared that there was a clear antithesis between the drivers of two regimes in achieving savings on the one hand, whilst protecting employees on the other. However, the *Liikenne*[134] case confirmed the compatibility of the two regimes.[135] The Court's jurisprudence relating to the applicability of transfer of undertakings to public procurement has positioned transfers amongst contractual terms and conditions of a contract, thus obliging contracting authorities to inform tenderers appropriately, so the latter can factor all relevant financial consequences to their bid.

Environmental considerations as award criteria

In *Concordia*,[136] the Court was asked *inter alia* whether environmental considerations such as low emissions and noise levels of vehicles could be included amongst the factors of the most economically advantageous criterion, in order to promote certain types of vehicles that meet or exceed certain emission and noise levels. The Advocate-General in his opinion[137] followed the *Beentjes* principle and established that contracting authorities are free to determine the factors under which the most economically advantageous offer is to be assessed and that environmental considerations could be part of the award criteria, provided they do not discriminate over alternative offers, as well as they have been clearly publicised in the tender or contract documents. However, the inclusion of such factors in the award criteria should not prevent alternative offers that satisfy the contract specifications being taken into consideration by contracting authorities.[138]

Criteria relating to the environment, in order to be permissible as additional criteria under the most economically advantageous offer must satisfy a number of conditions, namely they must be objective, universally applicable, strictly relevant to the contract in question, and clearly contribute an economic advantage to the contracting authority.

The line of argument adopted in *Beentjes* and followed up in *Nord-pas-de-Calais* with reference to social considerations could apply *mutatis mutandis* for environmental considerations. The inclusion of such considerations amongst the factors of the most economically advantageous offer is clearly subject to the caveat of conformity with the fundamental principles of the Treaty, in particular the non-discrimination principle and the attainment of the four freedoms, as well as the procedural requirements (advertisement and publicity) stipulated in the Public Procurement Directives. The Court followed the Advocate General's opinion, and reiterated that the flexibility of the most economically advantageous offer as an award criterion of public contracts could embrace environmental considerations by analogy to the inclusion of social considerations to the award criteria of public contracts.

3
Lessons from Jurisprudence

Introduction

Subjecting the public procurement legal framework to the scrutiny of the European Court of Justice has revealed a distinctive pattern. This pattern is reflected in the Court's judgements and embraces two approaches: a positive and at the same time a restrictive interpretation of the regime. Although at first sight the stance taken by the European judiciary may seem contradictory, the Court's bi-focal approach, serves the European institution's efforts to strengthen the three principles (non-discrimination, objectivity and transparency) underlying the regulation of public procurement.[1] It is worth mentioning the emphasis that the legal regime has placed in pursuing these principles in the preamble of the Works Directive ...*it is necessary to improve and extend the safeguards in the directives that are designed to introduce transparency into the procedures and practices for the award of such contracts, in order to be able to monitor compliance with the prohibition of restrictions more closely and at the same time to reduce disparities in the competitive conditions faced by nationals of different Member States.*

The positive approach of the Court comprises its attempts to eliminate discrimination and non-tariff barriers in the fields of technical standards (product specification and standardisation) and the selection procedures (quantitative and qualitative suitability criteria). The Court's jurisprudential positivism through the observance of non-discrimination and objectivity principles epitomises the integral role of public procurement in the attainment of the fundamental principles of the Treaty, specifically the right of establishment and the freedom to provide services. On the other hand, the Court's restrictive approach serves the principle of objectivity, with particular reference to the use of the award procedures.

The above pattern which is revealed through the jurisprudence of the Court also reflects on a strategic goal of the European judiciary: to vest the regime wherever possible with direct effect. Arming the public procurement rules with direct effect will enhance access to justice at national level, improve compliance, increase the quality of the regulatory regime and finally streamline the public procurement process across the common market by introducing an element of uniformity. By conferring direct effect upon the Public Procurement Directives and inviting national courts to play prominent role in future public procurement litigation, the Court has hinted towards its preference for a decentralised enforcement of the public procurement regime. However, the most important lesson law and policy makers have learnt from the Court's approaches to public procurement is the potential of its regulation with regard to policy formulation at national and European levels.

Part 1   The European Court of Justice and Public Procurement

The principle of non-discrimination

Technical standards

The influence of the 1986 White Paper[2] upon the European integration process epitomises the need to abolish all forms of covert or overt discrimination on grounds of nationality which have a detrimental effect in intra-community trade. The 1986 White Paper for the Competition of the Internal Market could be viewed as the foundation stone of many legislative initiatives relating to the accomplishment of the four freedoms guaranteed in the Treaties. Technical standards and specifications, despite previous attempts to harmonise at Community level were identified as serious non-tariff barriers because Member States' regulatory competence in this field had been consistently used to discriminate against foreign products or services.

The Court seized every opportunity to condemn discriminatory use of specification requirements and standards.[3] It established the "equivalent standard" doctrine, where contracting authorities are prohibited from introducing technical specifications or trade marks which mention products of a certain make or source, or a particular process which favour or eliminate certain undertakings, unless these specifications are justified by the subject and nature of the contract and on condition that they are only permitted if they are accompanied by the words "or equivalent".

The procurement of goods, works and services based on discriminatory practices relevant to standards and specifications was a serious obstacle for the functioning of the internal market. Protectionist devices such as national technical standards and tender participation requirements have created artificial blockages for the free movement of goods, works and services destined for the public sector across the Community. There are two ways that standardisation and specification can be used as a non-tariff barrier in public procurement: first, contracting authorities may use certain (national) systems of standards and specifications as an excuse for disqualification of tenderers. That was the scenario in the *Dundalk*[4] case, where Irish authorities specified a certain standard for pipelines. Secondly, standardisation and specification requirements can be restrictively defined in order to exclude products or services of a particular origin, or narrow the field of competition amongst tenderers. To that extent, the *Neerlands Inkoopcentrum*[5] case concerned with the use of trade marks as compulsory specifications for the purchase of meteorological equipment.

In both cases the use of specifications was contrary to the principle of non-discrimination, as it precluded other interested tenderers whose bids could not meet the contracting authority's perceived technical standards. The Court has followed a strict approach for technical standards, similar to that relating to the technical ability and capacity of undertakings in public procurement. That similarity of approach evolves around two themes: first, the requirement that certain procedural logistics relating to the publicity and the advertisement of the technical standards as well as the means of proof of the technical capacity must be met; secondly, specifications and technical capacity must not refer to national laws in an attempt to narrow the field of competition or exclude certain tenderers.

One of the most significant, yet judicially unresolved aspects of standardisation and specification appears to be the operation of voluntary standards, which are mainly specified at industry level. Voluntary standards and specifications are used quite often in the Utilities sector, where the relevant procurement requirements are complex and cannot be specified solely by reference to "statutory" standards, thus leaving a considerable margin of discretion in the hands of the contracting authorities, which may abuse it during the selection and qualification stages of the procurement process.

Selection and qualification

The relevant provisions of the Procurement Directives relating to the qualitative selection and qualification criteria refer to the technical ability and knowledge of tenderers, where proof may be furnished by evidence of educational or professional qualifications, previous experience in performing public contracts and statements on the contractor's expertise.[6] The references, which the tenderers may be required to produce, must be specified in the notice or invitation to tender. The rules relating to technical capacity and eligibility of tenderers represent an exhaustive list and are capable of producing direct effect.[7] The *Transporoute* legacy paved the way for the Court to elaborate on forms of selection and qualification, such as registration in lists of recognised contractors. Such lists exist in Member States and tenderers may use their registration in them as an alternative means of proving their technical suitability, also before contracting authorities of other Member States. *CEI-Bellini* followed the same line,[8] although it conferred discretion to contracting authorities to request further evidence of technical capacity other than the mere certificate of registration in official lists of approved contractors, on the grounds that such lists might not be referring to uniform classifications.

Ballast Nedam I[9] took qualitative selection and qualification criteria a step further. The Court ruled that a holding company which does not itself carry out works may not be precluded from registration on an official list of approved contractors, and consequently, from participating in tendering procedures, if it shows that it actually has available to it the resources of its subsidiaries necessary to carry out the contracts, unless the references of those subsidiaries do not themselves satisfy the qualitative selection criteria specified in the Directives. *Ballast Nedam II*[10] conferred an obligation to the authorities of Member States which are responsible for the compilation of lists of approved contractors to take into account evidence of the technical capacity of companies belonging to the same group, when assessing the parent company's technical capacity for inclusion into the list, provided the holding company establishes that it has available to it the resources of the companies belonging to the group that are necessary to carry out public contracts. *Holst Italia*,[11] by analogy applied the *Ballast* principle to undertakings that belong to the same group structure but do not have the status of a holding company and the requisite availability of the technical expertise of its subsidiaries. The Court held that with regard to the qualitative criteria relevant to the economic, financial and technical standing, a tenderer may rely on the standing of other entities, regardless of the legal nature of the links which it has with them, provided that it is able to show that it actually has at its disposal the resources of those entities which are necessary for performance of a public contract.

However, for the purposes of assessing the financial and economic standing of contractors, an exception to the exhaustive (and directly applicable) nature of technical capacity and qualification rules has been made. Evidence of financial and economic standing may be provided by means of references including: i) appropriate statements from bankers; ii) the presentation of the firm's balance sheets or extracts from the balance sheets where these are published under company law provisions; and iii) a statement of the firm's annual turnover and the turnover on construction works for the three previous financial years. The non-exhaustive character of the list of references in relation to the contractors' economic and financial standing was recognised by Court in the *CEI-Bellini* case,[12] where the value of the works which may be carried out at any one time may constitute a proof of the contractors' economic and financial standing. The contracting authorities are allowed to fix such a limit, as the provisions of the Public Procurement Directives do not aim at delimiting the powers of Member States, but at determining the references or evidence which may be furnished in order to establish the contractors' financial and economic standing. Of interest is the recent case *ARGE*,[13] where even the receipt of aid or subsidies incompatible with the Treaty by an entity may be a reason for disqualification from the selection process, as an obligation to repay an illegal aid would threaten the financial stability of the tenderer in question.

The Court also maintained[14] that the examination of a contractor's suitability based on his technical capacity and qualifications and his financial and economic standing may take place simultaneously with the award procedures of a contract.[15] However, the two procedures (the suitability evaluation and bid evaluation) are totally distinct processes, which shall not be confused.[16]

Clearly the selection and qualification criteria relating to the financial standing of tenderers are not capable of producing direct effect. The Court has allowed for a significant margin of discretion to contracting authorities to assess the financial standing of undertakings participating in tendering procedures. Although the broad rules are carefully circumscribed as to avoid discrimination and arbitrariness, the selection and qualification of tenderers with reference to their financial standing and capacity reflect a type of risk management on the part of contracting authorities at a given time and for a given project, thus a uniform and directly applicable rule could not be the most optimum medium.

Preference purchasing schemes

Preference schemes have been indissolubly linked with regional development policies, but since the completion of the single market they have been abolished, as they are deemed to contravene directly or indirectly the basic principle of non-discrimination on grounds of nationality stipulated in the Treaties establishing the European Community. Preference schemes guaranteed a certain percentage of public procurement to local firms, a fact that has indicated the close interplay between public purchasing and state aids.[17] Impact assessment studies undertaken by the European Commission[18] showed that the operation of preference schemes had a minimal effect on the economies of the regions where they had been applied, both in terms of the volume of procurement contracts, as well as in terms of real economic growth attributed to the operation of such schemes.

The interpretation of preference schemes by the Court has always been restrictive. The Commission brought Greece before the Court,[19] where a circular of the Minister of National Economy, which favoured domestic products in case of public, supplies contracts was deemed to breach both Article 30 EC and the Public Supplies Directive 77/62. The circular imposed a co-efficient of 21 per cent on prices of imported products. The Court declared the failure of the Greek State to fulfil its obligations under the Treaty and condemned the relevant preference scheme as restrictive for the unobstructed access to public supply contracts envisaged by the Directives

Italian courts sought a preliminary ruling from the Court in two cases. Both concerned supply of pharmaceutical products to local health authorities. In the *Dupont de Nemours*,[20] the Court determined the effect which a preferential system reserving to undertakings established in certain regions of a national territory a proportion of public supplies contracts is likely to have on the free movement of goods. The Court held that the system of the reserved quota of public supply contracts fell foul of Article 30 EC. It could not be justified under the rule of reason under Article 36 EC, nor under Article 26 of Directive 77/62, which governed technical and financial capacity requirements. It also stated that it is inconsistent with Article 30, even if it is considered as state aid within the meaning of Article 92 EC. The second case, the *Lavatori Bruneau*,[21] concerned whether the reservation of a percentage of public supplies contracts (30%) to undertakings located in a specific area is incompatible with Article 30 EC, even if the measures fall under Article 92 EC. The Court followed the same logic as in

Dupont de Nemours and condemned the preferential purchasing scheme in question.

The Commission also brought an action against Italy[22] for a declaration that domestic law, which reserved a proportion of public works to sub-contractors whose registered offices were in the region where the works were to be carried out, was incompatible with Article 59 EC and the Public Works Directives.[23] The Court ruled that such provision had an actual or potential discriminatory effect on undertakings outside that particular region and other undertakings from Member States, thus being inconsistent with Article 59 EC. Furthermore, it represents a criterion of selection that is not mentioned in the Works Directives[24] and in particular does not reflect any of the requirements of an economic or technical nature provided for in Articles 25 and 26 of the Public Works Directive 71/305.

Italy was again brought before the Court in a case[25] which concerned the compatibility of preference schemes with public procurement rules. The *Unita Sanitaria Locale XI Genoa* (health authority) stipulated that, in order to enable tenderers to participate in a public supply contract, 50 per cent of the minimum amount of supplies required to have been made over the preceding three years should have been supplies to public administration authorities. Although such a condition appears as obviously inconsistent with the Supplies Directives, the Court did not proceed on the substance of the case and declared the action inadmissible, as the Commission did not observe the proceedings laid down in Article 169 EC.

There has been a great deal of controversy over the issue of the compatibility of preference schemes with Community law at large and in particular with the Public Procurement Directives. Although the utilisation of public procurement as a tool of regional development policy in the form of state aids may not breach directly or indirectly primary Treaty provisions on free movement of goods, the right of establishment and the freedom to provide services, it is far from clear whether the European Commission or the Court could accept the legitimate use of public procurement as a means of state aids. Prior notification of the measures or policies intended to be used as state aid to the European Commission, does not apparently legitimise such measures and absolve them from the draconian framework of the four freedoms. The parallel applicability of Articles 92 EC and 30 EC, in the sense that national measures conceived as state aids must not violate the principle of free movement of goods, render the thrust of regional policies through state aids practically ineffective. The Court of Justice seemed to have experimented with the question of the compatibility of Article 92 EC (state aids) with Article 30 (free movement of goods) in a number of cases where, initially, it was held that the two regimes are mutually exclusive, to the extent that the principle of free movement of goods could not apply to measures relating to state aids.[26] The acid test for such mutual exclusivity was the prior notification of such measures to the European Commission. However, the Court apparently departed from such a position, when it applied Article 30 EC to a number of cases concerning state aids, which had not been notified to the Commission.[27] Quite surprisingly, the Court brought notified state aids measures under the remit of the provision of free movement of goods in the *Du Pont de Nemours* case and reconsidered the whole framework of the mutual exclusivity of Articles 92 EC and 30 EC.

The principle of objectivity

Award procedures

The process of liberalising public procurement relies to a great extent on the principle of objectivity in the award of public contracts. The Court had the opportunity to reflect on award procedures under the relevant Directives and subject the negotiated procedures, particularly those without prior advertisement to a restrictive interpretation. According to the Procurement Directives, negotiated procedures without prior notification shall be used restrictively *inter alia...when for technical or artistic reasons or reasons connected with the protection of exclusive rights the services could only be procured by a particular provider ...* and *...in cases of extreme urgency brought about by events unforeseeable by the contracting authority.*

The Court reinforced its restrictive interpretation of the above two reasons to which contracting authorities might be allowed to have recourse and maintained their exceptional character rather than their prohibitive use, and the onerous obligation of contracting authorities to justify them.

The alleged existence of technical or artistic reasons or reasons connected with the protection of exclusive rights which reveal a particular contractor or service provider for a contracting authority to negotiate without prior advertisement attracted the attention of the Court in two instances.[28] The Court rejected the existence of exclusive rights in both cases and regarded the abuse of this provision as contrary to the right of establishment and freedom to provide services which are based on the principle of equal treatment and prohibit not only overt discrimination on grounds of nationality, but also all covert forms of discrimination, which, by the application of other criteria of differentiation, lead to the same result. Interestingly, the Court elucidated that exclusive rights might include contractual arrangements such as know-how and intellectual property rights (case 199/85, *Commission v. Italy*).

Urgency reasons brought by unforeseen events to contracting authorities received similarly restrictive interpretation.[29] The Court maintained the need of a justification test based on the proportionality principle (case 199/85, *Commission v. Italy*), as well as the existence of a causal link between the alleged urgency and the unforeseen events.[30]

Award criteria

Two criteria laid down in the Public Procurement Directives provide the conditions under which contracting authorities award public contracts: the lowest price or the most economically advantageous offer.[31]

The first criterion indicates that, subject to the qualitative criteria and financial and economic standing, contracting authorities do not rely on any other factor than the price quoted to complete the contract. The tenderer who submits the cheapest offer must be awarded the contract. It should be mentioned that the Directives provide for an automatic disqualification of an "obviously abnormally low offer". The term has not been interpreted in detail by the Court and serves rather as an indication of a "lower bottom limit".[32] The Court, however, pronounced on the direct effect of the relevant provision requiring contracting authorities to examine the details of the tender before deciding the award of the contract. The contracting authorities are under duty to seek from the tenderer an explanation for the price submitted or to inform him that his tender appears to be abnormally low and to allow a reasonable time within which to submit further details, before making any decision as to the award of the contract.

The debate over the terminology of "obviously abnormally low" tenders surfaced when the Court held[33] that rejection of a contract based on mathematical criteria without giving the tenderer an opportunity to furnish information is inconsistent with spirit of the Public Procurement Directives. The Court following previous case-law,[34] ruled that the contracting authorities must give an opportunity to tenderers to furnish explanations regarding the genuine nature of their tenders, when those tenders appear to be abnormally low. Unfortunately, the Court did not proceed to an analysis of the wording "obviously". It rather seems that the term "obviously" indicates the existence of precise and concrete evidence as to the abnormality of the low tender. On the other hand, the wording "abnormally" implies a quantitative criterion left to the discretion of the contracting authority. However, if the tender is just "abnormally" low, it could be argued that it is within the discretion of the contracting authority to investigate the genuine offer of a tender. *Impresa Lombardini*,[35] followed the precedence established by *Transporoute* and maintained the unlawfulness of mathematical criteria used as an exclusion of a tender which appears abnormally low. Nevertheless, it held that such criteria may be lawful if used for determining the abnormality of a low tender, provided an *inter partes* procedure between the contracting authority and the tenderer that submitted the alleged abnormal low offer offers the opportunity to clarify the genuine nature of that offer. Contracting authorities must take into account all reasonable explanations furnished and avoid limiting the grounds on which justification of the genuine nature of a tender should be made. Both the wording and the aim of the Public Procurement Directives direct contracting authorities to seek explanation and reject unrealistic offers, informing the Advisory Committee.[36] In *ARGE*,[37] the rejection of a tender based on the abnormally low pricing attached to it got a different twist in its interpretation. Although the Court ruled that directly or indirectly subsidised tenders by the state or other contracting authorities or even by the contracting authority itself can be legitimately part of the evaluation process, it did not elaborate on the possibility of rejection of an offer, which is appreciably lower than those of unsubsidised tenderers by reference to the abnormally low disqualification ground. In *ARGE* the Court adopted a literal interpretation of the Directives and concluded that if the legislature wanted to preclude subsidised entities from participating in tendering procedures for public contracts, it should have said so explicitly in the relevant Directives.[38] Although the case has relevance in the fields of selection and qualification procedures and award criteria, the Court made no references to previous case-law regarding state aids in public procurement, presumably because the *Dupont de Nemours* precedence is still highly relevant.

On the other hand, the meaning of the most economically advantageous offer includes a series of factors chosen by the contracting authority, including price, delivery or completion date, running costs, cost-effectiveness, profitability, technical merit, product or work quality, aesthetic and functional characteristics, after-sales service and technical assistance, commitments with regard to spare parts and components and maintenance costs and security of supplies. The above list is not exhaustive and the factors listed therein serve as a guideline for contracting authorities in the weighted evaluation process of the contract award. The Court reiterated the flexible and wide interpretation of the relevant award criterion[39] and had no difficulty in declaring that contracting authorities may use the most economically advantageous offer as award criterion by choosing the factors which they want to apply in evaluating tenders,[40] provided these factors are mentioned, in hierarchical order or descending sequence in the invitation to tender or the contract documents,[41] so tenderers and interested parties can clearly ascertain the relative weight of factors other than price for the evaluation process. However, factors, which have no strict relevance in determining the most economically advantageous offer by reference to objective criteria do involve an element of arbitrary choice and therefore should be considered as incompatible with the Directives.[42]

A question whether, under the most economically advantageous offer, each individual award factor has to provide an economic advantage which directly benefits the contracting authority, or it is sufficient that each individual factor has to be measurable in economic terms, without the requirement that it directly provides an economic advantage for the contracting authority in the given contract was put before the Court in *Concordia*.[43] Through the second interpretation, the discretion conferred to contracting authorities would permit a wide range of factors to feature as part of award criteria in public contracts, without the need to demonstrate a direct economic advantage to a contracting authority which is attributable to each of these factors. On the contrary, if each individual factor has to establish a measurable (in quantifiable terms) economic advantage to the contracting authority, which is directly attributed to its inclusion as part of the award criterion, the discretion of contracting authorities is curtailed, since they would be required to undertake and publicise in the tender or contract documents a clear cost-benefit analysis of the relevant factors that comprise in their view the most economically advantageous offer.

This question intended to provide guidance in order to assess the integral function of the factors that comprise the most economically advantageous offer for contracting authorities. Although there is wide discretion conferred to them in compiling the relevant factors, subject to the requirements of relevance to the contract in question and their publicity, their relative importance, in economic terms, remains somehow unknown. Unfortunately, the Court did not clarify the relevant points.

Part 2 The emerging themes

The public nature of public procurement

The remit and thrust of public procurement legislation relies heavily on the connection between contracting authorities and the state. Compliance procedures brought by the European Commission against Member States are a good indication of determining contracting authorities under public procurement law. If the State can be held responsible under Article 169 EC (now Article 226 EC) for breaches of EC law committed by the central or local government, and also for breaches by other public entities and bodies over which it exercises a certain degree of control, that responsibility denotes a degree of connection between the state and the entities in question sufficient enough to characterise these entities as contracting authorities for the purposes of the Public Procurement Directives.[44] A comprehensive and clear definition of the term *contracting authorities*, a factor that determines the applicability of the relevant rules is probably the most important element of the public procurement legal framework. The structure of the Directives is such as to embrace the purchasing behaviour of all entities which have a close connection with the state. These entities, although not formally part of the state, disperse public funds in pursuit or on behalf of public interest. The Directives describe as contracting authorities the *state*, which covers central, regional, municipal and local government departments, as well as *bodies governed by public law*. Provision has been also made to cover entities, which receive more than 50 per cent subsidies by the state or other contracting authorities.

However, that connection might be weak to cover entities which operate in the utilities sector and have been privatised. The *Foster* principle[45] established that state accountability could not embrace privatised enterprises.[46] The enactment of the Utilities Directives[47] brought under the procurement framework entities operating in the water, energy, transport and telecommunications sectors. A wide range of these entities are covered by the term *bodies governed by public law*, which is used by the Utilities Directives for the contracting entities operating in the relevant sectors.[48] Interestingly, another category of contracting authorities under the Utilities Directives includes *public undertakings*.[49] The term indicates any undertaking over which the state may exercise direct or indirect dominant influence by means of ownership, or by means of financial participation, or by means of laws and regulations which govern the public undertaking's operation. Dominant influence can be exercised in the form of a majority holding of the undertaking's subscribed capital, in the form of the majority controlling of the undertaking's issued shares, or, finally in the form of the right to appoint the majority of the undertaking's management board. Public undertakings cover utilities operators which have been granted exclusive rights of exploitation of a service. Irrespective of their ownership, they are subject to the Utilities Directive in as much as the *exclusivity* of their operation precludes other entities from entering the relevant market under substantially the same competitive conditions. Privatised utilities could be, in principle, excluded from the procurement rules when a genuinely competitive regime within the relevant market structure would rule out purchasing patterns based on non-economic considerations. The determination of a genuinely competitive regime is left to the utilities operators themselves. This is perhaps a first step towards self-regulation which could lead to the disengagement of the relevant contracting authorities from the public procurement regime.[50]

Also, under the Tokyo Round GATT Agreement on Government Procurement, the term public authorities confined itself to central governments and their agencies only.[51] The new World Trade Organisation Government Procurement Agreement (GPA) applies in principle to all bodies which are deemed as "contracting authorities" for the purposes of the Public Supplies and Public Works Directives. As far as utilities are concerned, the GPA applies to entities which carry out one or more of certain listed "utility" activities, where these entities are either "public authorities" or "public undertakings", in the sense of the Utilities Directive. The listed utility activities which are covered under the new GPA include (i) activities connected with the provision of water through fixed networks; (ii) activities concerned with the provision of electricity through fixed networks; (iii) the provision of terminal facilities to carriers by sea or inland waterway; and (iv) the operation of public services in the field of transport by automated systems, tramway, trolley bus, or cable bus. However, the GPA does not cover entities operating in the utilities sector on the basis of *special and exclusive rights*.

The functional dimension of contracting authorities

Although the term contracting authorities appears rigorous and well defined, public interest functions are dispersed through a range of organisations which *stricto sensu* could not fall under the ambit of the term contracting authorities, since they are not formally part of the state, nor all criteria for the definition of bodies governed by public law are present. This is particularly the case of non-governmental organisations (NGOs) which operate under the auspices of the central or local government and are responsible for public interest functions.[52] The Court addressed the *lex lacuna* through its landmark case *Beentjes*.[53] The Court diluted the rigorous definition of contracting authorities for the purposes of public procurement law, by introducing a *functional dimension* of the state and its organs. In particular, it considered that a *local land consolidation committee* with no legal personality, but with its functions and compositions specifically governed by legislation, part of the state. The Court interpreted the term contracting authorities in *functional terms* and considered the local land consolidation committee, falling within the notion of state, even though it was not part of the state administration in *formal terms*.[54] The committee in question depended on the relevant public authorities for the appointment of its members and its operations were subject to their supervision and it had as its main task the financing and award of public works contracts.

The Court in two recent cases applied the functionality test when requested to determine the nature of entities which could not meet the criteria of bodies governed by public law, but had a distinctive public interest remit. In *Teoranta*,[55] a private company established according to national legislation to carry out business of forestry and related activities was deemed as falling within the notion of the state. The company was set up by the state and was entrusted with specific tasks of public interest, such as managing national forests and woodland industries, as well as providing recreation, sporting, educational, scientific and cultural facilities. It was also under decisive administrative, financial and management control by the state, although the day-to-day operations were left entirely to its board. The Court accepted that since the state had at least indirect control over the *Teoranta's* policies, in functional terms the latter was part of the state. In the *Vlaamese Raad*,[56] the Flemish parliament of the Belgian federal system was considered part of the "federal" state. The Court held that the definition of the state encompasses all bodies, which exercise legislative, executive and judicial powers, at both regional and federal levels. The Raad, as a legislative body of the Belgian state, although under no direct control by it, was held as falling within the definition of the state and thus being regarded as a contracting authority. The fact that the Belgian Government did not, at the time, exercise any direct or indirect control relating to procurement policies the Vlaamese Raad was considered immaterial on the grounds that a state cannot rely on its own legal system to justify non-compliance with EC law and particular Directives.[57]

The functional dimension of contracting authorities has exposed the Court's departure from the formality test, which has rigidly positioned an entity under state control on *stricto sensu* traditional public law grounds. Functionality, as an ingredient of assessing the relationship between an entity and the state demonstrates, in addition to the elements of management or financial control, the importance of constituent factors such as the intention and purpose of establishment of the entity in question. Functionality depicts a flexible approach in the applicability of the Procurement Directives, in a way that the Court through its precedence established a pragmatic approach as to the nature of the demand side of the public procurement equation.

Bodies governed by public law

The latter category is subject to a set of cumulative criteria[58] in order to be classified as contracting authorities for the purposes of the Directives. In particular, *bodies governed by public law* i) must be established for the specific purpose of meeting needs in the general public interest not having an industrial or commercial character; ii) they must have legal personality; and iii) they must be financed, for the most part, by either the state, or regional or local authorities, or other bodies governed by public law; or subject to management supervision by these bodies, or having an administrative or supervisory board, more than half of whose members are appointed by the state, regional or local authorities or by other bodies governed by public law. There is a list of such bodies in Annex I of Directive 93/37 which is not an exhaustive one, in the sense that Member States are under an obligation to notify the Commission of any changes to that list. The term bodies governed by public law provided the opportunity to the Court to elaborate on each of the cumulative criteria and shed light on their constituent elements. The Court's jurisprudence has revealed the following thematic areas:

The dependency test

To assess the existence of the third criterion of bodies governed by public law, the Court assumed that there is a close dependency of these bodies on the State, in terms of corporate governance, management supervision and financing.[59] These dependency features are alternative, thus the existence of one satisfies the third criterion. The Court held in *OPAC*[60] that management supervision by the state or other contracting authorities entails not only administrative verification of legality or appropriate use of funds or exceptional control measures, but the conferring of significant influence over management policy, such as the narrowly circumscribed remit of activities, the supervision of compliance, as well as the overall administrative supervision. Of interest and high relevance is the Court's analysis and argumentation relating to the requirements of management supervision by the state and other public bodies, where it maintained that entities entrusted to provide social housing in France are deemed to be bodies governed by public law, thus covered by the Public Procurement Directives.

The Court (and the Advocate General) drew an analogy amongst the dependency features of bodies governed by public law on the state. Although the corporate governance and financing feature are quantitative (the state must appoint more than half of the members of the managerial or supervisory board or it must finance for the most part the entity in question), the exercise of management supervision is a qualitative one. The Court held that management supervision by the state denotes dependency ties similar to the financing or governance control of the entity concerned.

Receiving public funds from the state or a contracting authority is an indication that an entity could be a body governed by public law. However, this indication is not an absolute one. The Court, in the *University of Cambridge* case[61] was asked whether i) awards or grants paid by one or more contracting authorities for the support of research work; ii) consideration paid by one or more contracting authorities for the supply of services comprising research work; iii) consideration paid by one or more contracting authorities for the supply of other services, such as consultancy or the organisation of conferences; and iv) student grants paid by local education authorities to universities in respect of tuition for named students constitute public financing for the University.

The Court held that only specific payments made to an entity by the state of other public authorities have the effect of creating or reinforcing a specific relationship or subordination and dependency. The funding of an entity within a framework of general considerations indicates that the entity has close dependency links with the state of other contracting authorities. Thus, funding received in the form of grants or awards paid by the state or other contracting authorities, as well as in the form of student grants for tuition fees for named students, constitutes public financing. The rationale for such approach lies in the lack of any contractual consideration between the entity receiving the funding and the state or other contracting authorities, which provide it in the context of the entity's public interest activities. The Court drew an analogy of public financing received by an entity with the receipt of subsidies.[62] However, if there is a specific consideration for the state to finance an entity, such as a contractual nexus, the Court suggested that the dependency ties are not sufficiently close to merit the entity financed by the state meeting the third criterion of the term bodies governed by public law. Such a relationship is analogous to the dependency that exists in normal commercial relations formed by reciprocal contracts, which have been negotiated freely between the parties. Therefore, funding received by Cambridge University for the supply of services for research work, or consultancies, or conference organisations cannot be deemed as public financing. The existence of a contract between the parties, apart from the specific considerations for funding, indicates strongly supply substitutability, in the sense that the entity receiving the funding faces competition in the relevant markets.

The Court stipulated that the proportion of public finances received by an entity, as one of the alternative features of the third criterion of the term bodies governed by public law must exceed 50 per cent to enable it meeting that criterion. For assessment purposes of this feature, there must be an annual evaluation of the (financial) status of an entity for the purposes of being regarded as a contracting authority.

Dependency, in terms of overall control of an entity by the state or another contracting authority presupposes a control similar to that which the state of another contracting authority exercises over its own departments. The "similarity" of control denotes lack of independence with regard to decision-making. The Court in *Teckal*,[63] concluded that when a contracting authority exercises control over an entity, which could be a contracting authority itself or a private undertaking, similar to that which exercises over its own departments and at the same time that entity carries out the essential part of its activities with that contracting authority, any contract between them is not a public contract. The similarity of control as a reflection of dependency reveals another facet of the thrust of contracting authorities: the non-applicability of the public procurement rules for in-house relationships.

In-house contracts and contracts to affiliated undertakings escape the clutches of the Directives. Article 6 of the Services Directive provides for the inapplicability of the Directive to service contracts which are awarded to an entity which is itself a contracting authority within the meaning of the Directive on the basis of an exclusive right which is granted to the contracting authority by a law, regulation or administrative provision of the Member State in question. Article 13 of the Utilities Directive provides for the exclusion of certain contracts between contracting authorities and affiliated undertakings. For the purposes of Article 1(3) of the Utilities Directive, an affiliated undertaking is one the annual accounts of which are consolidated with those of the contracting entity in accordance with the requirements of the seventh company law Directive.[64] These are service contracts, which are awarded to a service-provider, which is affiliated to the contracting entity, and service contracts, which are awarded, to a service-provider, which is affiliated, to a contracting entity participating in a joint venture formed for the purpose of carrying out an activity covered by the Directive. The explanatory memorandum accompanying the text amending the Utilities Directive (COM (91) 347-SYN 36 1) states that this provision relates, in particular, to three types of service provision within groups. These categories, which may or may not be distinct, are: the provision of common services such as accounting, recruitment and management; the provision of specialised services embodying the know-how of the group; the provision of a specialised service to a joint venture. The exclusion from the provisions of the Directive is subject, however, to two conditions: the service-provider must be an undertaking affiliated to the contracting authority and, at least 80 per cent of its average turnover arising within the European Community for the preceding three years, derives from the provision of the same or similar services to undertakings with which it is affiliated. The Commission is empowered to monitor the application of this Article and require the notification of the names of the undertakings concerned and the nature and value of the service contracts involved.

Commerciality and needs in the general interest

Commerciality and its relationship with needs in the general interest is perhaps the most important theme that has emerged from the Court's jurisprudence in relation to the remit of bodies governed by public law as contracting authorities. In fact the theme sets to explore the interface between profit-making and public interest, as features which underpin the activities of bodies governed by public law.

The criterion of specific establishment of an entity to meet needs in the general interest having non-commercial or industrial character has attracted the attention of the Court is some landmark cases.[65] The above criterion appears as the first of the three cumulative criteria for bodies governed by public law. The Court drew its experience from jurisprudence in the public undertakings field as well as case-law relating to public order to define the term *needs in the general interest*.[66] The Court approached the above concept by a direct analogy of the concept "general economic interest", as defined in Article 90(2) EC.[67] The concept "general interest" denotes the requirements of a community (local or national) in its entirety, which should not overlap with the specific or exclusive interest of a clearly determined person or group of persons.[68] However, the problematic concept of the *specificity* of the establishment of the body in question was approached by reference to the reasons and the objectives behind its establishment. Specificity of the purpose of an establishment does not mean exclusivity, in the sense that other types of activities can be carried out without escaping classification as a body governed by public law.[69]

On the other hand, the requirement of non-commercial or industrial character of needs in the general interest has raised some difficulties. The Court had recourse to case-law and legal precedence relating to public undertakings, where the nature of industrial and commercial activities of private or public undertakings was defined.[70] The industrial or commercial character of an organisation depends much upon a number of criteria that reveal the thrust behind the organisation's participation in the relevant market. The state and its organs may act either by exercising public powers or by carrying economic activities of an industrial or commercial nature by offering goods and services on the market. The key issue is the organisation's intention to achieve profitability and pursue its objectives through a spectrum of commercially motivated decisions. The distinction between the range of activities which relate to public authority and those which, although carried out by public persons, fall within the private domain is drawn most clearly from case-law and judicial precedence of the Court concerning the applicability of competition rules of the Treaty to the given activities.[71]

The Court in *BFI*[72] had the opportunity to clarify the element of non-commercial or industrial character. It considered that the relationship of the first criterion of bodies governed by public law is an integral one. The non-commercial or industrial character is a criterion intended to clarify the term needs in the general interest. In fact, it is regarded as a category of needs of general interest. The Court recognised that there might be needs of general interest, which have an industrial and commercial character and it is possible that private undertakings can meet needs of general interest which do not have industrial and commercial character. The acid test for needs in the general interest not having an industrial or commercial character is that the state or other contracting authorities choose themselves to meet these needs or to have a decisive influence over their provision.

In the *Agora* case[73] the Court indicated that if an activity which meets general needs is pursued in a competitive environment, there is a strong indication that the entity which pursues it is not a body governed by public law. The reason can be found in the relationship between competitiveness and commerciality. Market forces reveal the commercial or industrial character of an activity, irrespective the latter meeting the needs of general interest or not. However, market competitiveness as well as profitability cannot be absolute determining factors for the commerciality or the industrial nature of an activity, as they are not sufficient to exclude the possibility that a body governed by public law may choose to be guided by considerations other that economic ones. The absence of competition is not a condition necessarily to be taken into account in order to define a body governed by public law, although the existence of significant competition in the market place may be indicative of the absence of a need in the general interest, which does not carry commercial or industrial elements. The Court reached this conclusion by analysing the nature of the bodies governed by public law contained in Annex 1 of the Works Directive 93/37 and verifying that the intention of the state to establish such bodies has been to retain decisive influence over the provision of the needs in question.

Certain activities, which by their nature fall within the fundamental tasks of the public authorities, cannot be subject to a requirement of profitability and therefore are not meant to generate profits. It is possible, therefore, that the reason, in drawing a distinction between bodies whose activity is subject to the public procurement legislation and other bodies, could be attributed to the fact that the criterion of "needs in the general interest not having an industrial or commercial character" indicates the lack of competitive forces in the relevant marketplace. The concept of the state encapsulates an entrepreneurial dimension to the extent that it exercises *dominium*. Although the state as entrepreneur enters into transactions with a view to providing goods, services and works for the public, this type of activities do not resemble the characteristics of entrepreneurship, in as much as the aim of the state's activities is not the maximisation of profits but the observance of public interest. The relevant markets where the state enters can be described as public markets. Public markets are the *fora* where *public interest* substitutes *profit maximisation*.[74]

The dual capacity of contracting authorities

The dual capacity of an entity as a public service provider and a commercial undertaking respectively, and the weighting of the relevant activity in relation to the proportion of its output, should be the decisive factor in determining whether an entity is a body governed by public law. This argument appeared for the first time before the Court in the *Strohal*[75] case. The Austrian Government suggested that only if the activities in pursuit of the "public services obligations" of an entity supersede its commercial thrust, the latter could be considered as a body covered by public law and a contracting authority. In support of its argument that the relevant entity (*Österreichische Staatsdruckerei*) is not a body governed by public law, the Austrian Government maintained that the proportion of public interest activities represents no more than 15–20 per cent of its overall activities.[76]

In practice, the argument put forward implied a selective application of the Public Procurement Directives in the event of dual capacity entities. This sort of application is not entirely unjustified as, on a number of occasions,[77] the Public Procurement Directives themselves utilise thresholds or proportions considerations in order to include or exclude certain contracts from their ambit. Examples of such selective application of the regime include, the relevant provisions stipulating the thresholds for the applicability of the public procurement rules as well as the provisions relating to the so-called "mixed contracts", where the proportion of the value of the works or the supplies element in a public contract determines the applicability of the relevant Directive and finally the relevant provisions which embrace the award of works contracts subsidised *directly* by more than 50 per cent by the state within the scope of the Directive.

However, the Court ruled out a selective application of the Directives in the case of dual capacity contracting authorities based on the principle of legal certainty. It substantiated its position on the fact that only the purpose for which an entity is established is relevant in order to classify it as body governed by public law and not the division between public and private activities. Thus, the pursuit of commercial activities by contracting authorities is incorporated with their public interest orientation aims and objectives, without taking into account their proportion and weighting in relation to the total activities dispersed, and contracts awarded in pursuit of commercial purposes fall under the remit of the Public Procurement Directives. The Court recognised the fact that by extending the application of public procurement rules to activities of a purely industrial or commercial character, an onerous constraint would be probably imposed upon the relevant contracting authorities, which may also seem unjustified on the grounds that public procurement law, in principle, does not apply to private bodies, which carry out identical activities.[78] The above situation represents a considerable disadvantage in delineating the distinction between private and public sector activities and their regulation, to the extent that the only determining factor appears to be the nature of the organisation in question. The Court suggested that that disadvantage could be avoided by selecting the appropriate legal instrument for the objectives pursued by public authorities. As the reasons for the creation of a body governed by public law would determine the legal framework which would apply to its contractual relations, those responsible for establishing it must restrict its thrust in order to avoid the undesirable effects of that legal framework on activities outside their scope.

The Court in *Strohal* established dualism, to the extent that it specifically implied that contracting authorities may pursue a dual range of activities; to procure goods, works and services destined for the public, as well as participate in commercial activities. They can pursue other activities in addition to those which meet needs of general interest not having an industrial and commercial character. The proportion between activities pursued by an entity, which on the one hand aim to meet needs of general interest not having an industrial or commercial character, and commercial activities on the other is irrelevant for the characterisation of that entity as a body governed by public law. What is relevant is the intention of establishment of the entity in question, which reflects on the "specificity" requirement. Also, specificity does not mean exclusivity of purpose. Specificity indicates the intention of establishment to meet general needs. Along theses lines, ownership or financing of an entity by a contracting authority does not guarantee the condition of establishment of that entity to meet needs of general interest not having industrial and commercial character.

The connection of contracting authorities with private undertakings

There is considerable risk of circumventing the Public Procurement Directives, if contracting authorities award their public contracts via private undertakings under their control, which cannot be covered by the framework of the Directives. Under the domestic laws of the Member States, there is little to prevent contracting authorities from acquiring private undertakings in an attempt to participate in market activities. In fact, in many jurisdictions the socio-economic climate is very much in favour towards public-private sector partnerships, in the form of joint-ventures or in the form of private financing of public projects. A classic example of such an approach is the views of the UK Government in relation to the involvement of the private sector in delivering public services. A number of government documents have eulogised the so-called *Private Finance Initiative (PFI)*, which attempts to create a framework between the public and private sectors working together in delivering public services.[79]

Unfortunately, the Public Procurement Directives have not envisaged such a scenario, where avoidance of the rules could be based on the fact that the entities which award the relevant contracts cannot be classified as contracting authorities within the meaning of the Directives.

The Court, prior to the *Strohal* case, did not have the opportunity to examine such corporate relationships and the effect that public procurement law has upon them. Even in *Strohal*, the Court did not rule directly on the subject, but instead it provided the necessary inferences for national courts, in order to ascertain whether such relations between public and private undertakings aim at avoiding the application of the Public Procurement Directives. Indeed, national courts, in litigation before them, must establish *in concreto* whether a contracting authority has established an undertaking in order to enter into contracts for the sole purpose of avoiding the requirements specified in public procurement law. Such conclusions must be beyond doubt based on the examination of the actual purpose for which the undertaking in question has been established. The rule of thumb is the connection between the nature of a project and the aims and objectives of the undertaking which awards it. If the realisation of a project does not contribute to the aims and objectives of an undertaking, then it is assumed that the project in question is awarded "on behalf" of another undertaking, and if the latter beneficiary is a contracting authority under the framework of public procurement law, then the relevant Directives should apply. The Court followed the *Strohal* lines to *Teckal*,[80] where the exercise of a similar control over the management of an entity by a contracting authority prevents the applicability of the Directives.

The above inferences from the Court, although useful in terms of guidance and general reference, could prove problematic in their actual application at domestic level for a number of reasons. First, the examination of any relation between contracting authorities and private undertakings presupposes litigation before national courts. Questions over legal competence, *locus standi* and accessibility to justice at domestic level arise, when a dispute over the award of a contract by a private undertaking is the subject of litigation. In contrast to domestic litigation relating to public procurement disputes, where there are detailed rules which provide for remedies and access to justice before national courts,[81] in a situation where a contract has been awarded by a private undertaking on behalf of a contracting authority with a view to avoiding the relevant Directives, it is unclear where an aggrieved party or contractor should address its complaints. Secondly, even in the event that the relationship between a private undertaking and a contracting authority represents a coherent framework in the dispersement of public service, it appears that there might be a lack of uniform evaluation patterns of the actual purpose of an undertaking controlled by a contracting authority, as Member States (and their judiciaries) tend to view in a different way aspects of *contractualised governance*. In various jurisdictions within the common market, it would be difficult, in legal and political terms, to justify the empowerment of the private sector in as much as it could assume the role of service deliverer alongside the public sector. Constitutional provisions could nullify such attempts and often a number of socio-economic factors would collide with the idea of private delivery of public services. The evolution of public/private sector relations has arrived in times when the role and the responsibilities of the state are in the process of being redefined. Constitutionally, the state and its organs are under obligation to provide a range of services to the public in the form of e.g. healthcare, education, transport, energy, defence, social security and policing. The state and its organs then enter the market place and procure goods, works and services in pursuit of the above objective, on behalf of the public.[82] The state in its own capacity or through delegated or legal monopolies and publicly controlled enterprises has engaged in market activities in order to serve public interest. Traditionally, the function of the state as a public service provider has been linked with ownership of the relevant assets. The integral characteristics of privately financed projects reveal the degree that the state and its organs are prepared to drift away from *traditional corporatism* towards *contractualised governance*. Departure from traditional corporatism also reflects the state's perception *vis-à-vis* its responsibilities towards the public. A shift towards contractualised governance would indicate the departure from the assumption that the state embraces both roles of asset owner and service deliverer. It should also insinuate the shrinkage of the state and its organs and the need to define a range of core activities that are not to be contractualised. Finally, in practical terms, it would be very difficult to prove the intention of a contracting authority to circumvent the public procurement rules and enforce their application on private undertakings.

The dual capacity of contracting authorities is irrelevant to the applicability of public procurement rules. If an entity is a contracting authority, it must apply public procurement rules irrespective of the pursuit of general interest needs or the pursuit of commercial activities. Also, if a contracting authority assigns the rights and obligations of a public contract to an entity, which is not a contracting authority, that entity must follow public procurement rules. The contrary would be acceptable if the contract fell within the remit of the entity, which is not a contracting authority, and the contract was entered into on its behalf by a contracting authority.

The irrelevance of dualism for the applicability of public procurement represents a safeguard for the *acquis communautaire*. Dualism could be viewed as recognition of contractualised governance, where the demarcation between public and private activities of the public sector has become difficult to define, as well as a counterbalance of commerciality. If commercialism might shield the activities of a contracting authority from the application of public procurement rules, dualism provides for the necessary inferences to subject dual capacity entities to the *acquis communautaire*.

Procurement as a policy instrument

The most economically advantageous offer as an award criterion has provided the Court for the opportunity to balance the economic considerations of public procurement with policy choices. Although in numerous instances the Court has maintained the importance of the economic approach[83] to the regulation of public sector contracts, it has also recognised the relative discretion of contracting authorities to utilise non-economic considerations as award criteria.

Social considerations as award criteria

In *Beentjes*,[84] the Court ruled that social policy considerations and in particular measures aiming at the combating of long term unemployment could only be part of the award criteria of public contracts, especially in cases where the most economically advantageous offer is selected. The Court accepted that the latter award criterion contains features that are not exhaustively defined in the Directives, therefore there is discretion conferred on contracting authorities to specify what would the most economically advantageous offer for them. However, contracting authorities cannot refer to such measures as a selection criterion and disqualify candidates which could not meet the relevant requirements. The selection of tenderers is a process, which is based on an exhaustive list of technical and financial requirements expressly stipulated in the relevant Directives and the insertion of contract compliance as a selection and qualification requirement would be considered *ultra vires*. The Court held that a contractual condition relating to the employment of long term unemployed persons is compatible with the Public Procurement Directives, if it has no direct or indirect discriminatory effect on tenders from other Member States. Furthermore, such a contractual condition must be mentioned in the tender notice.[85] Rejection of a contract on the grounds of a contractor's inability to employ long-term unemployed persons has no relation to the checking of the contractors' suitability on the basis of their economic and financial standing and their technical knowledge and ability. The Court maintained that measures relating to employment could be utilised as a feature of the award criteria, only when they are part of a contractual obligation of the public contract in question and on condition that they do not run contrary to the fundamental principles of the Treaty. The significance of that qualification has revealed the Court's potential stance over the issue of contract compliance in public procurement.

In the recent case *Nord-pas-de-Calais*,[86] the Court considered whether a condition linked to a local project to combat unemployment could be considered as an award criterion of the relevant contract. The Commission alleged that the French Republic has infringed Article 30(1) of Directive 93/37 purely and simply by referring to the criterion linked to the campaign against unemployment as an award criterion in some of the disputed contract notices. Under Article 30(1) of Directive 93/37, the criteria on which contracting authorities are to base the award of contracts are either the lowest price only or, when the award is made to the most economically advantageous tender, various other criteria according to the contract, such as price, period for completion, running costs, profitability, technical merit are taken into consideration.

The Court held that the most economically advantageous offer does not preclude all possibility for the contracting authorities to use as a criterion a condition linked to the campaign against unemployment provided that that condition is consistent with all the fundamental principles of Community law, in particular the principle of non-discrimination deriving from the provisions of the Treaty on the right of establishment and the freedom to provide services.[87] Furthermore, even if such a criterion is not in itself incompatible with Directive 93/37, it must be applied in conformity with all the procedural rules laid down in that directive, in particular the rules on advertising.[88] The Court therefore accepted the employment considerations as an award criterion, part of the most economically advantageous offer, provided it is consistent with the fundamental principles of Community law, in particular the principle of non-discrimination and it is advertised in the contract notice.

The Commission adopted a myopic view repeating previous arguments that *Beentjes* concerned a condition of performance of the contract and not a criterion for the award of the contract. The Court had the opportunity to correct the Commission's interpretation of the *Beentjes* case and point to the right direction of its judgement,[89] where the condition relating to the employment of long-term unemployed persons, which was at issue in that case, had been used as the basis for rejecting a tender and therefore necessarily constituted a criterion for the award of the contract.

The Court's rulings in *Beentjes* and *Nord-pas-de-Calais* have opened an interesting chapter in public procurement jurisprudence. *Beentjes* started a debate on the integral dimensions of contract compliance and differentiated between the *positive* and *negative* approaches. A positive approach within contract compliance encompasses all measures and policies imposed by contracting authorities on tenderers as suitability criteria for their selection in public procurement contracts. Such positive action measures and policies intend to complement the actual objectives of public procurement, which are confined in economic and financial parameters and are based on a transparent and predictable legal background. Although the complementarity of contract compliance with the actual aims and objectives of the public procurement regime was acknowledged, the Court has been reluctant in accepting such a flexible interpretation of the Directives and based on the literal interpretation of the relevant provisions disallowed positive actions of a social policy dimension as part of the selection criteria for tendering procedures in public procurement. However, it should be mentioned that contract compliance could incorporate not only unemployment considerations, but also promote equality of opportunities and eliminate sex or race discrimination in the relevant market.[90] Indeed, the Directives on public procurement stipulate that the contracting authority may require tenderers to observe national provisions of employment legislation when they submit their offers. The ability to observe and conform to national employment laws in a Member State may constitute a ground of disqualification and exclusion of the defaulting firm from public procurement contracts. In fact, under such interpretation, contract compliance may be a factor of selection criteria specified in the Directives, as it contains a *negative approach* (obey otherwise excluded) to legislation and measures relating to social policy. It should be mentioned that adherence to health and safety laws have been considered by a British court as part of the technical requirements specified in the Works Directive for the process of selection of tenderers.[91]

Transfer of undertakings and public procurement

The relevance of the Acquired Rights Directive,[92] with the public procurement regime became clear when contracting authorities started *testing the market* in an attempt to define whether the provision of works or services from a commercial operator could be cheaper than that from the in-house team. This is the notion of *contracting out*, an exercise which aims at achieving potential savings and efficiency gains for contracting authorities. The application of the transfer of undertakings rules in contracting out cases has the important consequence that the external bidder (if successful) must engage the authority's former employees on the same conditions as they enjoyed under the authority itself.

The initial Directive proclaimed its inapplicability in cases where the undertaking was not in the nature of a commercial venture; this proviso was interpreted as exclusive of contracting out by government. The impact of the transfer of undertakings Directive in the context of public procurement was felt in a landmark decision of the Court,[93] which maintained that the Directive does not permit such a limitation. Thus it became apparent that contracting out by government and other public authorities was covered, and a transfer of an undertaking may take place where the government contracts out to the private sector a function previously carried out in-house[94] and *vice versa*, viz. where the contracting authority takes back in-house a service formerly contracted out. The exact circumstances in which a transfer of an undertaking through contracting out occurs depends upon the transfer retaining its identity.[95] However, the "retention of identity" test can only be satisfied when the undertaking transferred represents *substantially the same* or *similar activities*,[96] as well as it relates to a *stable economic entity*.[97] The existence of a contractual link or relation between the parties to a transfer of an undertaking is not a decisive criterion to establish the applicability of the Directive.[98]

Serious concerns have been raised over the compatibility of the public procurement and the transfer of undertakings regimes.[99] It appeared that there was a clear antithesis between the drivers of two regimes in achieving savings on the one hand, whilst protecting employees on the other. However, the *Liikenne*[100] case, confirmed the compatibility of the two regimes.[101] The Court's jurisprudence relating to the applicability of transfer of undertakings to public procurement has positioned transfers amongst contractual terms and conditions of a contract, thus obliging contracting authorities to inform tenderers appropriately, so the latter can factor all relevant financial consequences to their bid.

Environmental considerations as award criteria

In *Concordia*,[102] the Court was asked *inter alia* whether environmental considerations such as low emissions and noise levels of vehicles could be included amongst the factors of the most economically advantageous criterion, in order to promote certain types of vehicles that meet or exceed certain emission and noise levels. The Advocate-General in his opinion[103] followed the *Beentjes* principle and established that contracting authorities are free to determine the factors under which the most economically advantageous offer is to be assessed and that environmental considerations could be part of the award criteria, provided they do not discriminate over alternative offers, as well as they have been clearly publicised in the tender or contract documents. However, the inclusion of such factors in the award criteria should not prevent alternative offers that satisfy the contract specifications being taken into consideration by contracting authorities. Clearly the Advocate General wanted to exclude any possibility of environmental considerations being part of selection criteria or disguised as technical specifications, capable of discriminating against tenderers that could not meet them.[104]

Criteria relating to the environment, in order to be permissible as additional criteria under the most economically advantageous offer must satisfy a number of conditions, namely they must be objective, universally applicable, strictly relevant to the contract in question, and clearly contribute an economic advantage to the contracting authority.[105]

The line of argument adopted in *Beentjes* and followed up in *Nord-pas-de-Calais* with reference to social considerations could apply *mutatis mutandis* for environmental considerations. The inclusion of such considerations amongst the factors of the most economically advantageous offer is clearly subject to the caveat of conformity with the fundamental principles of the Treaty, in particular the non-discrimination principle and the attainment of the four freedoms, as well as the procedural requirements (advertisement and publicity) stipulated in the Public Procurement Directives.

4
Public Procurement as Economic and Policy Exercise

Introduction

The regulation of public procurement in the European Union has been significantly influenced by the internal market project. The White Paper for the Completion of the Internal Market[1] and the Single European Act represent the conceptual foundations of the regulation of public markets of the Member States. The identification of public procurement as a major non-tariff barrier has revealed the economic importance of its regulation.[2] Savings and price convergence appeared as the main arguments for liberalising the trade patterns of the demand (the public and utilities sectors) and supply (the industry) side of the public procurement equation.[3] The economic approach to the regulation of public procurement aims at the integration of public markets across the EU. Through the principles of transparency, non-discrimination and objectivity in the award of public contracts, it is envisaged that the regulatory system will bring about competitiveness in the relevant product and geographical markets, will increase import penetration of products and services destined for the public sector, will enhance the tradability of public contracts across the common market, will result in significant price convergence and finally it will be the catalyst for the needed rationalisation and industrial restructuring of the European industrial base.[4]

Parallel with the economic arguments, legal arguments emerged supporting the regulation of public procurement as a necessary ingredient of the fundamental principles of the Treaties such as the free movement of goods and services, the right of establishment and the prohibition of discrimination on nationality grounds.[5] The legal significance of the regulation of public procurement in the common market has been well documented. Public procurement liberalisation reflects the wish of European institutions to eliminate preferential and discriminatory purchasing patterns by the public sector and create seamless intra-community trade patterns between the public and private sectors. Procurement by Member States and their contracting authorities is often susceptible to a rationale and policy that favours indigenous undertakings and *national champions*[6] at the expense of more efficient competitors (domestic or Community-wide). As the relevant markets (product and geographical) have been sheltered from competition, distorted patterns emerge in the trade of goods, works and services destined for the pubic sector. These trade patterns represent a serious impediment in the functioning of the common market and inhibit the fulfilment of the principles enshrined in the Treaties.[7]

Legislation, policy guidelines and jurisprudence have all played their role in determining the need for integrated public markets in the European Union, where sufficient levels of competition influence the most optimal patterns in resource allocation for supplying the public sector as well as the public utilities with goods, works and services. Public procurement has now been elevated as a key objective of the EU's vision in becoming the most competitive economy in the world by 2010.[8]

The new approach towards the integration of public markets

The rationale behind the whole process of the integration of public markets of the Member States has been the establishment of an effectively competitive regime, similar to that envisaged for the operation of private markets.[9] European Institutions have intellectually supported such an attempt by reference to liberal economic theories,[10] where a regime of enhanced competition in public markets could bring about beneficial effects for the supply side of the equation (the industry), by means of optimal allocation of resources within the European industries, rationalisation of production and supply, promotion of mergers and acquisitions and elimination of sub-optimal firms and creation of globally competitive industries. These effects have been also deemed to yield substantial purchasing savings for the public sector.[11] The European institutions envisaged the creation of such a competitive regime in public markets through the establishment of a legal framework which aims at abolishing discrimination on grounds of nationality and at eliminating preferential public procurement practices which favour *national champions*.

The above regime intends to introduce a strict regulatory framework of operations related to the supply chain of contracting authorities in the public sector. This indicates the fact that the demand side in the supply/demand equation of public procurement is the dominant part and its regulation would materialise the objectives of the process.

However, the attempts to integrate the public markets of the European Community solely by reference to the regulation of the purchasing behaviour of the demand side (the contracting authorities) appear to have left the supply side of public procurement unaffected by the above regulatory framework. The behaviour of the supply side is not the subject of public procurement legislation, although its regulation appears equally important with reference to the integration of public markets in Europe. Theoretically speaking, the supply side in the public procurement equation is subject to the competition law and policy of the Treaties, but it is evident that there is lack of an integral mechanism in public procurement legislation capable of incorporating the results of the anti-trust rules when applied to the supply side. *Stricto sensu*, anti-competitive behaviour of undertakings or collusive tendering does not appear to be reasons for disqualification from the selection and award processes of public contracts. It seems that the assumptions of European Institutions concentrate on the fact that by forcing contracting authorities throughout the Community into a common purchasing behaviour which is based on the principles of openness, transparency and non-discrimination, industrial restructuring (in the supply side) will follow as a result of such a stimulant and therefore all the above-mentioned desirable effects concerning efficiency gains and public sector savings will occur.

The European Commission has claimed that the regulation of public procurement throughout the Community and the resulting elimination of non-tariff barriers arising from discriminatory and preferential purchasing patterns of Member Sates could bring about substantial savings of ECU 20 bn or 0.5 per cent of GDP to the (European) public sector. Combating discrimination on grounds of nationality in public procurement and eliminating domestic preferential purchasing schemes could result in efficiency gains at European and national levels through the emergence of three major effects which would primarily influence the supply side.[12] These include a *trade effect*, a *competition effect* and a *restructuring effect*.

The trade effect is associated with the actual and potential savings that the public sector will be able to achieve through lower cost purchasing. This effect appears to have a static dimension, since it emerges as a consequence of enhanced market access in the relevant sector or industry. The trade effect emanates as a result of the principle of transparency in public markets (compulsory advertisement of public contracts above certain thresholds), a fact that constitutes an improvement from previously closed preferential regimes. However, the principle of transparency and the associated trade effect in public markets do not in themselves guarantee the establishment of competitive conditions in the relevant markets, as market access – a structural element in the process of integration of public markets in Europe – could be hindered by discriminatory behaviour of contracting authorities in the selection stages and the award stages of public procurement.

On the other hand, the competition effect relates to the changes of industrial performance as a result of changes in the price behaviour of national firms which had previously been protected from competition by means of preferential and discriminatory procurement practices. The competition effect derives also from the principle of transparency and appears to possess rather static characteristics. Transparency in public procurement breaks information and awareness barriers in public markets, and as mentioned above brings a trade effect in the relevant sectors or industries by means of price competitiveness. The competition effect comes as a natural sequence to price competitiveness and inserts an element of long-term competitiveness in the relevant industries in aspects other than price (e.g. research and development, innovation, customer care). The competition effect would materialise in the form of *price convergence* of goods, works and services destined for the public sector. Price convergence could take place both nationally and Community-wide, in as much as competition in the relevant market would equalise the prices of similar products.

Finally, the third effect (the restructuring effect) reflects the restructuring dimension in the supply side as a result of increased competition in the relevant markets. The restructuring effect is a dynamic one and refers to the long-term industrial and sectoral adjustment of industries that supply the public sector. The restructuring effect attempts to capture the reaction of the relevant sector or industry to the competitive regime imposed upon the demand and supply sides, as a result of openness and transparency and the sequential trade and competition effects. The response of the relevant sector or industry and the restructuring effect itself would depend on the efficiency of the industry to merge, diversify, convert or abort the relevant competitive markets and would also reflect contemporary national industrial policies.[13]

The above scenario represents the model envisaged by European Institutions on a macro-perspective and depicts the orientation of policy making towards the formation of a coherent industrial policy at European level. The regulation of the purchasing behaviour of the demand side in public markets seems to constitute an effective way of introducing competitive elements to the European industries, which apparently suffer from overcapacity and excessive compartmentalisation, when compared to rival industries in North America and Japan.[14] In addition, the cost of research and development in such a market structure builds up and it is reflected in pricing, particularly in high-tech products. Industrial restructuring and adjustment has been a priority for the European Commission for a long time, and attempts to control the structure of the European industrial base have been witnessed during the eighties with the introduction of the merger control regulation[15] and a number of regulations which provide for block exemptions from Article 85 EC of otherwise anti-competitive behaviour.[16] It is submitted that by the introduction of a regulatory regime for the public markets in Europe, a coherent policy towards industrial restructuring and adjustment has been put in place covering both private and public markets, with a view to establishing a more competitive interface amongst industries in the common market and *vis-à-vis* rivals in non-Member States.[17]

As a result of the momentum gathered in the mid-eighties, the regulation of public procurement in the European Community became a priority overnight and the inefficiency of the relevant primary and secondary Community provisions to combat discriminatory practices and preferential public purchases of contracting authorities throughout the common market was disclosed as statistical results revealed considerably low cross-border import penetration in public contracts. Furthermore, a disturbing picture emerged as to the extent of differentiation between a key element in the structures of private and public markets within the European Member States. Although it is correct to maintain that there are striking differences between demand and supply structures in private and public markets, one particular market structure element that had an interestingly low presence in public markets was the element of *market access*. Market access reflects the effectiveness of import penetration strategies (marketing, predatory pricing, venture alliances) of an undertaking and very much depends upon the regime of competition reigning in the relevant market place. Public markets differ considerably from private ones in terms of structure, demand and supply conditions as well as in terms of competitiveness.

If scale economies were important in defining the most desirable purchasing pattern for the public sector and competition increases amongst industries which supply the latter, an efficient European industrial structure would support less firms operating at full capacity.[18] Strategic mergers and cross-border investments would reshape the industries and reorganise the operation of firms. Within this reorganisation process, the structural adjustment would constantly change in order to adopt to the new market environment introduced by the legal regime on public procurement. In the process of developing new industrial strategies, two factors appear essential: the need for integration of industrial activities[19] and the need to meet local demands.

In the past many of the advantages offered to *national champions* and locally operating firms in public procurement markets had discouraged the tradability of public contracts[20] amongst European industries.[21] Persistently low import penetration in protected public procurement sectors dictated a corporate strategy to the relevant industries. Before the opening up of the public procurement in Europe, the typical strategic choice was low on integration and high on responsiveness, including the replication of all major corporate functions (production, R&D, marketing) in each Member State. The on-going realisation of the common market and the regulation of public procurement in the European Community have been forcing undertakings to revise their strategies and to build-up *network organisations*, which combine local responsiveness with a high degree of centralisation and co-ordination of major supporting activities. The new strategy has the characteristics of a multi-focal strategy.

The adoption of multi-focal strategies or global integration strategies involves a major shift in location patterns of key functions within firms.[22] The old decentralised multinational organisations which duplicated major functions in each country which they operated need to transform into an integrated system of which the key elements show a different degree of regional concentration.[23] As a consequence of the new organisational structure, different types of international transactions are expected to occur.[24] Specialisation and concentration of activities in certain regions will lead to more trade between certain Member States. In addition, as a result of the corporate network system, trade will increasingly develop into intra-firm trade and intra-industry trade with greater exchange of intermediary products.[25] The organisational rationalisation following the development of network organisations poses the problem of ownership and location of the corporate headquarters. Some Member States may fear losing strategic control in the restructuring process[26] and therefore may resist the rationalisation process that the industry has been undergoing, by imposing various restrictions in terms of ownership or control structures of locally operating firms.

A neo-classical perspective to public procurement regulation

The distinctiveness of public markets

From an economic perspective, the state and its organs would enter the market in pursuit of public interest.[27] Such activity does not resemble the commercial characteristics of private entrepreneurship, in as much as the aim of the public sector is not the maximisation of profits but the observance of public interest.[28] This fundamental factor provides the differential ground for the creation of *public markets* where public interest substitutes profit maximisation.[29] Further variances distinguish private from public markets. These focus on structural elements of the market place, competitiveness, demand conditions, supply conditions, the production process, and finally pricing and risk. They also provide for an indication as to the different methods and approaches employed in their regulation.[30]

Private markets are generally structured as a result of competitive pressures originating in the buyer/supplier interaction and their configuration can vary from monopoly/oligopoly to perfect competition. Demand arises from heterogeneous buyers with a variety of specific needs. It is based on expectations and is multiple for each product. Supply, on the other hand, is offered through various product ranges, where products are standardised using known technology, but constantly improved through research and development processes. The production process is based on mass-production patterns and the product range represents a large choice including substitutes, whereas the critical production factor is cost level. The development cycle appears to be short to medium-term and finally, the technology of products destined for the private markets is evolutionary. Purchases are made when an acceptable balance between price and quality is achieved. Purchase orders are multitude and at limited intervals. Pricing policy in private markets is determined by competitive forces and the purchasing decision is focused on the price-quality relation. The risk factor is highly present.

On the other hand, public markets tend to be structured and function in a different way. The market structure often reveals monopsonistic characteristics.[31] In terms of its origins, demand in public markets is institutionalised and operates mainly under budgetary considerations rather than price mechanisms. It is also based on fulfillment of tasks (pursuit of public interest) and it is single for many products. Supply also has limited origins, in terms of the establishment of close ties between the public sector and industries supplying it and there is often a limited product range. Products are rarely innovative and technologically advanced and pricing is determined through tendering and negotiations. The purchasing decision is primarily based upon the life-time cycle, reliability, price and political considerations. Purchasing patterns follow tendering and negotiations and often purchases are dictated by policy rather than price/quality considerations.

Procurement regulation as an economic exercise

Viewing public procurement from the prism of an economic exercise, its regulation displays strong neo-classical influences. Such influences embrace the merit of efficiency in the relevant market and the presence of competition, mainly price competition, which would create optimal conditions for welfare gains. The connection between public procurement regulation and the neo-classical approach to economic integration in the common market is reflected upon the criterion for awarding public contracts based on the lowest offer.[32] This feature of the legal framework focuses on price competition being inserted into the relevant markets and, assisted by the transparency requirement to advertise public contracts above certain thresholds[33] would result in production and distribution efficiencies and drive the market towards an optimal allocation of resources.

Removing protectionism and preferential treatment and inserting an environment of competition in public markets will bring about allocative efficiencies, which in turn will result in social welfare gains at European and national levels through the emergence of three major effects that would primarily influence the supply side.[34] These gains include a *trade effect*, a *competition effect* and a *restructuring effect*.

The trade effect is associated with the actual and potential savings that the public sector would be able to achieve through lower cost purchasing. This effect appears to have a static dimension, since it emerges as a consequence of enhanced market access of the relevant sectors or industries. The trade effect emanates from the principle of transparency[35] in public markets (compulsory advertisement of public contracts above certain thresholds). On the other hand, the competition effect relates to the changes of industrial performance as a result of changes in the price behaviour of national firms which had previously been protected from competition by means of preferential and discriminatory procurement practices. The competition effect derives also from the principle of transparency and appears to possess dynamic characteristics. The competition effect comes as a natural sequence to price competitiveness and inserts an element of long-term competitiveness in the relevant sectors or industries in aspects other than price (e.g. research and development, innovation, customer care). The competition effect would materialise in the form of *price convergence,* at both national and Community-wide levels, of goods, works and services destined for the public sector. Finally, the third effect (the restructuring effect) reflects upon the restructuring dimension of the supply side as a result of increased competition in the relevant markets. The restructuring effect possesses dynamic characteristics and refers to the long-term industrial and sectoral adjustment through strategic investment, takeovers and mergers and acquisitions. The restructuring effect attempts to capture the reaction of the relevant sector or industry *vis-à-vis* the competitive regime imposed upon the demand and supply sides, as a result of openness and transparency and the sequential trade and competition effects.

The lowest offer as an award criterion of public contracts is a quantitative method of achieving market equilibrium between the demand and supply sides. The supply side competes in cost terms to deliver standardised (at least in theory) works, services and goods to the public sector. Price competition is bound to result in innovation in the relevant industries, where through investment and technological improvements, firms could reduce production and/or distribution costs. The lowest offer criterion could be seen as the necessary stimulus in the relevant market participants in order to improve their competitive advantages.

The lowest offer award criterion reflects on, and presupposes low barriers to entry in a market and provides for a type of predictable accessibility for product or geographical markets. This is a desirable characteristic in a system such as public procurement regulation which is charged with integrating national markets and creating a homogenous and transparent common market for public contracts. In addition, the low barriers to enter a market, together with the transparent price benchmarking for awarding public contracts through the lowest offer criterion would inevitably attract new undertakings in public procurement markets. This can be seen as an increase of the supply-side pool, a fact which would provide the comfort and the confidence to the demand side (the public sector) in relation to the competitive structure of an industry. Nevertheless, the increased number of participants in public tenders could have adverse effects. Assuming that the financial and technical capacity of firms is not an issue,[36] the demand side (the public sector) will have to bear the cost of tendering and in particular the costs relating to the evaluation of offers. The more participants enter the market for the award of public contracts, the bigger the costs attributed to the tendering process that would have to be borne by the public sector.

However, competitiveness in an industry is not reflected solely by reference to low production costs.[37] Efficiencies which might result through production or distribution innovations are bound to have a short term effect on the market for two reasons: if the market is bound to clear with reference to the lowest price, there would be a point where the quality of deliverables is compromised (assuming a product or service remains standardised). Secondly, the viability of industries which tend to compete primarily on cost basis is questionable. Corporate mortality will increase and the market could revert to oligopolistic structures.

The welfare gains emanating from a neo-classical approach of public procurement regulation encapsulate the actual and potential savings the public sector (and consumers of public services at large) would enjoy through a system that forces the supply side to compete on cost (and price). These gains, however, must be counterbalanced with the costs of tendering (administrative and evaluative costs borne by the public sector), the costs of competition (costs related to the preparation and submission of tender offers borne by the private sector) and litigation costs (costs relevant to prospective litigation borne by both aggrieved tenderers and the public sector). If the cumulative costs exceed any savings attributed to lowest offer criterion, the welfare gains are negative.

A neo-classical perspective of public procurement regulation reveals the zest of policy makers to establish conditions which calibrate market clearance on price grounds. Price competitiveness in public procurement raises a number of issues with anti-trust law and policy. If the maximisation of savings is the only (or the primary) achievable objective for the demand side in the public procurement process, the transparent/competitive pattern cannot provide any safeguards in relation to underpriced (and anti-competitive) offers.

The price competitive tendering reflects on the dimension of public procurement regulation as an economic exercise. On the one hand, when the supply side responds to the perpetually competitive purchasing patterns by lowering prices, the public sector could face a dilemma: *what would be the lowest offer it can accept.* The public sector faces a considerable challenge in evaluating and assessing low offers other than "abnormally low" ones.[38] It is difficult to identify dumping or predatory pricing disguised behind a low offer for a public contract. On the other hand, even if there is an indication of anti-competitive price fixing, the European public procurement rules do not provide for any kind of procedure to address the problem. The anti-trust rules take over and the suspension of the award procedures (or even the suspension of the contract itself) would be subject to a thorough and exhaustive investigation by the competent anti-trust authorities.

Evidence of the neo-classical approach in public procurement regulation can be found in Guidelines[39] issued by the European Commission. The Commission adopted a strict interpretation of the rules and focused Member States on an economic approach in the application of the Public Procurement Directives. The Commission has championed the neo-classical approach for two reasons: first, to bring an acceptable level of compliance of Member States with the public procurement regime and secondly, to follow the assumptions made through the internal market process that procurement represents a significant non-tariff barrier and its regulation can result in substantial savings for the public sector.

It is interesting to follow the Commission's approach[40] in litigation before the European Court of Justice, where as an applicant in compliance procedures, or as an intervening party in reference procedures, it consistently regarded public procurement regulation as an economic exercise. The backbone of such an approach has been the price approach to the award of public contracts, predominately through the lowest offer award criterion, but also through the most economically advantageous offer criterion, where factors other than price can play a role in the award process. Even in the latter category, where some degree of flexibility is envisaged by the legal regime, the Commission has been sceptical of any attempts to apply the so-called "qualitative" factors in the award process.

Along these lines, the European Court of Justice pursued a neo-classical approach of public procurement regulation through its rulings relating to i) compliance procedures against Member States for not observing the publicity and mandatory advertisement requirements, ii) procedures concerning standardisation and technical specifications[41] and iii) procedures relating to the notion of abnormally low offers.[42]

Anti-trust and public procurement regulation

The regulatory weaponry for private markets evolves around anti-trust law and policy, where the influence of the neo-classical economic approach has been evident.[43] Public markets are *fora* where the structural and behavioural remedial tools of competition law also apply. However, they focus on the supply side (the industry) which *ipso facto* is subject to the relevant rules relating to cartels and abusive dominance.

There is a conceptual difference relating to the application of anti-trust in public markets. The demand side (the public sector and its organs) can hardly be embraced by its remit, except in the case of state aids and illegal subsidies. In private markets, anti-trust law and policy seek to punish cartels and the abusive dominance of undertakings. The focus of the remedial instruments is the supply side, which is conceived as the commanding part in the supply/demand equation due to the fact that it instigates and often controls demand for a product. In private markets, the demand side of the equation (the consumers at large) is susceptible to exploitation and the market equilibria are prone to distortion as a result of collusive behaviour of undertakings or abusive monopoly position. On the other hand, the structure of public markets reveals a different picture. In the supply/demand equation, the dominant part appears to be the demand side (the state and its organs as purchasers), which initialises demand through purchasing, where the supply side (the industry) fights for access to the relevant markets.

In public markets, market segmentation occurs as a result of concerted practices attributed to the demand side. Since such concerted practices of Member States and their contracting authorities (e.g. excluding foreign competition, application of buy-national policies, and application of national standards policies) focus on the origin of a product or a service or the nationality of a contractor, market segmentation in public markets tends to have geographical characteristics and results in the division of the European public market into different national public markets.

The regulation of public markets requires more than the control of the supply side through anti-trust. The primary objective is *market access* and the abolition of barriers and obstacles to trade. Therefore, the regulation aims at the demand side, which effectively controls access and can segment the relevant market. Whereas price competition is the main characteristic of anti-trust,[44] public procurement regulation pursues firstly market access. This perspective reflects on the *sui generis* nature of public markets and has provided ground for developing a regulatory system which is strongly influenced by neo-classical economics, whilst at the same time integrating the relevant market. Such a system has also strong public law characteristics, to the extent that it has been branded as *droit public de la concurrence*.[45]

The ordo-liberal approach to public procurement regulation

The vehicle of harmonisation has been entrusted to carry the progress of public procurement regulation. Directives, as legal instruments, have been utilised to provide the framework of the *acquis communautaire*, but at the same time afford the necessary discretion to the Member States as to the forms and methods of their implementation. This is where the first deviation from the traditional economic approach of public procurement occurs. Anti-trust law and policy is enacted through the principle of uniformity across the common market, utilising directly applicable regulations. By allowing for discretion to the Member States, an element of public policy is inserted in the equation, which often has decentralised features. Traditionally, discretion afforded by Directives takes into account national particularities and sensitivities as well as the readiness of domestic administrations to implement *acquis* within a certain deadline. In addition, individuals, who are also subjects of the rights and duties envisaged by the Directives, do not have access to justices, unless provisions of Directives produce direct effect.

However, the public policy dimension of public procurement regulation is not exhausted in the nature of the legal instruments of the regime. The genuine connection of an ordo-liberal perspective[46] with public procurement regulation in reflected in the award criterion relating to the most economically advantageous offer. The public sector can award contracts by reference to "qualitative" criteria, in conjunction with price, and thus can legitimately deviate from the strict price competition environment set by the lowest offer criterion.[47] There are three themes emanating from such an approach: one reflects on public procurement as a complimentary tool of the European Integration process; the second regards public procurement as an instrument of contract compliance; last, the ordo-liberal perspective can reveal a rule of reason in public procurement, where the integration of public markets in the European Union serves as a conveyor belt of common policies, such as environmental policy, consumer policy, social policy, industrial policy and takes into account a flexible and wider view of national and community priorities, and a type of "European public policy".

Public procurement as part of the European Integration

Procurement rules and the public markets do not operate in a vacuum. Irrespective of the often publicised nature of public procurement as the most significant non-tariff barrier for the functioning of the common market and the clinical presentation of the arguments in favour of an integrated public market across the EU,[48] public purchasing is indissolubly linked with national policies and priorities.[49] In the history of European economic integration, public procurement has been an important part of the Member States' industrial policies. It has been utilised as a policy tool[50] in order to support indigenous suppliers and contractors and preserve national industries and the related workforce.

There has been a great deal of controversy over the issue of the compatibility of preferential procurement with EU law. Preference schemes have been linked with regional development policies, a fact that indicates the close interplay between public procurement and state aids.[51] Protectionist public procurement practices, when strategically exercised has resulted in the evolution of vital industries for the state in question.[52] The sustainability of *national champions* has brought about benefits for a sector or an industry, which, when protected from competition in the short-run, managed to achieve specialisation and internationalisation.

Preferential public procurement reveals a double dimension. First, it appears in the form of an exercise which aims at preserving some domestic sectors or industries at the expense of the principles of the European integration process. In such a format, there is obviously no exit plan. Impact assessment studies undertaken by the European Commission showed that the operation of preference schemes had a minimal effect on the economies of the regions where they had been applied, both in terms of the volume of procurement contracts, as well as in terms of real economic growth attributed to the operation of such schemes.[53] Thus, in such a format, preferential public procurement perpetuates the sub-optimal allocation of resources and represents a welfare loss for the economy of the relevant state. On the other hand, preferential purchasing in the format of strategic investment to the sustainability of selected industries might represent a viable instrument of industrial policy, to the extent that the infant industry, when specialised and internationalised, would be in a position to counterbalance any welfare losses during its protected period. In the above form, preferential public procurement, as an integral part of industrial policy could possibly result in welfare gains.[54]

Although the utilisation of public procurement as a tool of regional development policy in the form of state aids may breach directly or indirectly primary Treaty provisions on free movement of goods, the right of establishment and the freedom to provide services, it is far from clear whether the European Commission or the Court could accept the legitimate use of public procurement as a means of state aids. Prior notification to the European Commission of the measures or policies intended to be used as state aid does not, apparently, legitimise such measures and absolve them from the well-established framework of the four freedoms. The parallel applicability of rules relating to state aids and the free movement of goods, in the sense that national measures conceived as state aids must not violate the principle of free movement of goods, renders the thrust of regional policies through state aids practically ineffective. It appears that the Court of Justice has experimented with the question of the compatibility between state aids and free movement of goods in a number of cases where, initially, it was held that the two regimes are mutually exclusive, to the extent that the principle of free movement of goods could not apply to measures relating to state aids.[55] The acid test for such mutual exclusivity was the prior notification of such measures to the European Commission. However, the Court departed from such a position, when it applied free movement of goods provisions to a number of cases concerning state aids, which had not been notified to the Commission.[56] Surprisingly, the Court also brought notified state aids measures under the remit of the provision of free movement of goods and reconsidered the whole framework of the mutual exclusivity of states aids and free movement of goods.[57]

Preferential procurement does contradict directly the fundamental principles of free movement of goods and services. However, the notification of Member States' intention to utilise it as a form of state aids, aims at moving the focus of potential disputes towards the anti-trust remit of the *acquis*. Two reasons seem to support the above assumption. First, the public procurement legal framework is positively in favour of strategic subcontracting.[58] The nomination of regional or national firms in the award process of public contracts under such premises could, legitimately, elevate preferential procurement as an instrument of industrial policy. This might shift the debate from the potential violation of internal market provisions towards the overall compatibility of the regime with national or common market-wide industrial policies, thus positioning preferential public procurement in the remit of anti-trust. Secondly, there is a fundamental change in perceptions about the role and responsibilities expected from governments in delivering public services. The public sector not only initiates and facilitates the delivery of public services but also can actively be involved in the actual delivery process. Such changes, in practical terms viewed through the evolution of public-private partnerships,[59] are translated into a new contractual interface between public and private sectors,[60] which in turn encapsulate an era of *contractualised governance.*

Contract compliance and public procurement

The most economically advantageous offer as an award criterion has provided the Court with the opportunity to balance the economic considerations of public procurement with policy choices. Although in numerous instances the Court has maintained the importance of the economic approach[61] to the regulation of public sector contracts, it has also recognised the relative discretion of contracting authorities to utilise non-economic considerations as award criteria.

The term *contract compliance*[62] could be best defined as the range of secondary policies relevant to public procurement, which aim at combating discrimination on grounds of sex, race, religion or disability.[63] When utilised in public contracts, contract compliance is a system whereby, unless the supply side (the industry) complies with certain conditions relating to social policy measures, contracting authorities can lawfully exclude tenderers from selection, qualification and award procedures. The concept is well-known and practiced in North American jurisdictions and in particular in the United States,[64] as it has been in operation for some time in an attempt to reduce racial and ethnic minority inequalities in the market and to achieve equilibrium in the workforce market.

Apparently, the potential of public purchasing as a tool capable of promoting social policies has been met with considerable scepticism. Policies relevant to affirmative action or positive discrimination have caused a great deal of controversy, as they practically accomplish very little in rectifying labour market equilibria. In addition to the practicality and effectiveness of such policies, serious reservations have been expressed with regard to their constitutionality,[65] since they could limit, actually and potentially, the principles of economic freedom and freedom of transactions.[66]

Contract compliance legislation and policy is familiar to most European Member States, although the enactment of Public Procurement

Directives has changed the situation dramatically.[67] The position of European Institutions on contract compliance has been addressed in three instances before the European Court of Justice.[68] The Court maintained that contract compliance with reference to domestic or local employment cannot be used as a selection criterion in tendering procedures for the award of public contracts. The selection of tenderers is a process which is based on an exhaustive list of technical and financial requirements expressly stipulated in the relevant Directives and the insertion of contract compliance as a selection and qualification requirement would be considered *ultra vires*. The Court ruled that social policy considerations can only be part of award criteria in public procurement, and especially in cases where the most economically advantageous offer is selected, provided that they do not run contrary to the basic principles of the Treaty and that they have been mentioned in the tender notice.

The Court's approach has also opened an interesting debate on the integral dimensions of contract compliance and the differentiation between the *positive* and *negative* approaches. The concept of positive approach within contract compliance encompasses all measures and policies imposed by contracting authorities on tenderers as suitability criteria for their selection in public procurement contracts. Such positive action, measures and policies intend to complement the actual objectives of public procurement which are confined in economic and financial parameters and are based on a transparent and predictable legal background. Although the complementarity of contract compliance with the actual aims and objectives of the public procurement regime was acknowledged, the Court (and the European Commission) were reluctant in accepting such an over-flexible interpretation of the Directives and based on the literal interpretation of the relevant provisions disallowed positive actions of a social policy dimension as part of the selection criteria for tendering procedures in public procurement.

However, contract compliance can incorporate not only unemployment considerations, but also promote equality of opportunities and eliminate sex or race discrimination in the relevant market.[69] Indeed, the Directives on public procurement stipulate that the contracting authority may require tenderers to observe national provisions of employment legislation when they submit their offers. The ability to observe and conform to national employment laws in a Member State may constitute a ground of disqualification and exclusion of the defaulting firm from public procurement contracts.[70] In fact, under such interpretation, contract compliance may be a factor of selection criteria specified in the directives, as it contains a *negative approach* to legislation and measures relating to social policy.

There are arguments in favour and against incorporating social policy considerations in public procurement.[71] The most important argument in favour focuses on the ability of public procurement to promote parts of the Member States' social policy, with particular reference to long-term unemployment, equal distribution of income, social exclusion and the protection of minorities. Under such a positively oriented approach, public purchasing could be regarded as an instrument of policy in the hands of national administrations with a view to rectifying social equilibria. Contract compliance in public procurement could also cancel the stipulated aims and objectives of the liberalisation of the public sector. The regulation of public markets focuses on economic considerations and competition. Adherence to social policy factors could derail the whole process, as the public sector will pay more for its procurement by extra or hidden cost for the implementation of contract compliance in purchasing policies.[72]

A rule of reason

In European Union law, the rule of reason serves as an expansion of the determined exemptions from a prohibition principle.[73] The rule of reason is a juridical development where the Court interprets the margins of discretion allotted to an executive authority (Member States and/or the Commission), as well as the grounds, the limits and the levels of deviation from a prohibition's exemptions. For public procurement, a rule of reason has emerged through the application of the most economically advantageous offer criterion. The Court, through a steady accumulation of case-law adopted a bi-focal stance: positive yet restrictive. Where the rules allow for discretion, the Court did not claw back any margin of appreciation from Member States and their contracting authorities; in fact, in many instances, it gradually expanded the grounds of flexibility in the award procedures.

The meaning of the most economically advantageous offer includes a series of factors chosen by the contracting authority, including price, delivery or completion date, running costs, cost-effectiveness, profitability, technical merit, product or work quality, aesthetic and functional characteristics, after-sales service and technical assistance, commitment with regard to spare parts and components and maintenance costs, security of supplies. The above list is not exhaustive and the factors listed therein serve as a guideline for contracting authorities in the weighted evaluation process of the contract award.

The Court reiterated the flexible and wide interpretation of the relevant award criterion[74] and had no difficulty in declaring that contracting authorities may use the most economically advantageous offer as award criterion by choosing the factors which they want to apply in evaluating tenders,[75] provided these factors are mentioned, in hierarchical order or descending sequence in the invitation to tender or the contract documents,[76] so tenderers and interested parties can clearly ascertain the relative weight of factors other than price for the evaluation process. However, factors, which have no strict relevance in determining the most economically advantageous offer by reference to objective criteria do involve an element of arbitrary choice and therefore should be considered as incompatible with the Public Procurement Directives.[77]

A question arises whether, under the most economically advantageous offer, each individual award factor has to provide an economic advantage which directly benefits the contracting authority, or it is sufficient that each individual factor has to be measurable in economic terms, without the requirement that it directly provides an economic advantage for the contracting authority in the given contract. This question intends to assess the integral function of the factors that comprise the most economically advantageous offer for contracting authorities. Although there is wide discretion conferred to them in compiling the relevant factors, subject to the requirements of relevance to the contract in question and their publicity, their relative importance, in economic terms, remains somehow unknown.

If the second interpretation were accepted, the discretion conferred to contracting authorities would permit a wide range of factors to feature as part of award criteria in public contracts, without the need to demonstrate a direct economic advantage to a contracting authority which is attributable to each of these factors. On the contrary, if each individual factor has to establish a measurable (in quantifiable terms) economic advantage to the contracting authority, which is directly attributed to its inclusion as part of the award criterion, the discretion of contracting authorities is curtailed, since they would be required to undertake and publicise in the tender or contract documents a clear cost-benefit analysis of the relevant factors that comprise in their view the most economically advantageous offer.

There are two instances where the rule of reason as applied in public procurement brought the relevant regime in line with European policy.

The first is the case of transfer of undertakings, where the Court expanded the remit of the Acquired Rights Directive to the public procurement contractual relations.[78] The second instance is the permissibility of environmental factors[79] as part of the award criteria for public contract and the explicit recognition of the environmental policy of the European Union as being complimentary to all legal and policy activities of the common market.

The latter development reveals also the importance of public procurement in relation to harmonisation and even standardisation of national policies. Public procurement in such cases serves as a conveyor belt for transferring homogenous legal or policy standards across the common market. The protection of the environment as an award criterion in public contracts is a classic example of the potential of public procurement regulation as an instrument of public policy. There will be instances in the future where positive integration will be required by European Institutions and Member States equally in areas such as social security, business ethics and anti-corruption policies. Harmonisation of laws and policies within the common market has traditionally sought a common denominator amongst divergences and differences of national administrations. Under an ordo-liberal approach, the rule of reason seems an essential tool to convey effectively rights and obligations of Community law.

There is no attempt yet to instill a type of European public policy across the common market. Not only have the legal and political differences of Member States dictated that such approach would face considerable resistance, the very need for a common denominator of public policy in the European Union has been questionable. However, if the European Union is to become a serious competitor to major trading forces in the world, perhaps the introduction of such a common denominator is something that requires further consideration. Productivity rises, competitiveness, industrial restructuring exercises, privatisation, employment relations, taxation, and corporate governance are mere examples of the features which the European Union and its Member States will be facing in a post-enlargement era. Public procurement could play a role in carrying over the European legal and policy standards into national systems.

The influence of neo-classical economic theory on public procurement regulation has taken the relevant regime through the paces of the liberalisation of public markets within the European Union and with reference to the World Trade Organisation. Anti-trust and its remedies have played a seemingly important role in determining the necessary competitive conditions for the supply side to service the public sector. However, we have seen the emergence of a *sui generis* market place where the mere existence and functioning of anti-trust is not sufficient to achieve the envisaged objectives. Public markets require a positive regulatory approach in order to enhance market access. Whereas anti-trust and the neo-classical approach to economic integration depend heavily on price competition, public procurement regulation requires a system which primarily safeguards market access. Such a regulatory system could be described as public competition law.

The above represents the first departure from the *stricto sensu* neo-classical perspective of public procurement. A policy orientation has emerged mainly through the jurisprudential approach of the regime and the willingness of the Court to expand on the element of flexibility that is inherent in the Public Procurement Directives.

The neo-classical versus the ordo-liberal approach reflects the frequently rehearsed debate about the origins of anti-trust law and policy *per se*. The European integration has benefited from a system where the neo-classical approach has contributed to the functioning of an environment of workable competition. However, consistently the rigidity of the neo-classical influence has been diluted with policy considerations, often attributed to national policy requirements. The reflection of the above picture is presented in public procurement regulation, although there are certain differences: the Court has allowed for a flexible policy-oriented application of public procurement, where in anti-trust the Commission has eroded the strict neo-classical approach of Article 81(1) EC with the plethora of policy considerations under 81(3) EC. Nevertheless, the similarity of balancing an economic exercise with policy choice is remarkable.

Public procurement regulation is an essential instrument of the internal market. With the European Union in an expansion mode, European Institutions need to provide for a hint as to what public procurement stands for. There is a new generation of legal instruments currently through the legislative process which intend to simplify and modernise the regime. In addition, there is strong evidence that the existence of competitive conditions within public markets would disengage the applicability of the relevant Directives. This development indicates the referral of public markets to anti-trust, perhaps as the ultimate regulatory regime. Public procurement remains one of the most influential instruments of policy choice in the hands of Member States and also the European Commission. Its complementarity and compatibility with common policies is recognised and accepted by European Institutions and Member States. Public procurement in the common market of the 21st century could embrace more public policy considerations and depart from the premises of being a mere economic exercise.

Inherent dangers in the regulation of public procurement

The process of the integration of public markets in Europe and the integral mechanism of dismantling national borders in intra-community public trade have revealed a number of considerable threats amongst the potential benefits of the exercise. Firstly, the integration of public markets and the opening-up of public procurement in the Member States do not seem to take fully into account the inherent danger of market concentration. As a result of such a stimulant to the demand side, sub-optimal firms would be forced to leave the market and the volume of industrial concentration through mergers and acquisitions of less competitive firms would inevitably grow, the danger of market oligopolisation becomes eminent.[80] The adverse effects of market concentration as a result of the oligopolistic structure of the relevant markets could seriously hinder the objectives of the exercise. It was mentioned previously that the restructuring effect would facilitate the clearing of the relevant markets of any sub-optimal firm or industry. However, there is no indication as to the market structure after the impact of the restructuring effect, and given the fact that the above effect has a dynamic character, the relevant market would present trends of continuous adjustment. Industrial adjustment and restructuring would inevitably lead to a more concentrated structure of the market place as a result of predation, take-overs and amalgamation of rival firms. The potential threats of market oligopolisation should be counterbalanced with the long-awaited desirable effects on the structure of the European industrial base. If the results of the market oligopolisation were translated to a more innovative and specialised production output along the supply chain system and if the expected industrial competitiveness across a European-wide basis could put firms in a position to compete directly with rival industries in other parts of the world, then the dangers arising from market concentration would be minimal. However, one should never underestimate the threats of collusive behaviour and the pricing policies that could emerge from oligopolistic structure.[81] Conspiratorial practices of oligopolists which supply the public sector could possibly lead to high prices, perhaps higher than those prior to the restructuring and adjustment exercise. Furthermore, even if prices of goods, works and services destined for the public sector would converge and settle at a higher level, this could result in supra-competitive profits for the oligopolists at the expense of the demand side. Another dimension of the concentration and oligopolisation of public markets reflects considerable socio-economic considerations. If one is to accept that industrial restructuring and adjustment emanate from the need to eliminate sub-optimal overcapacity, the factor of production which would be affected most is labour. Redundancies and reduction of workforce often follow market concentration in an attempt to minimise duplication, or to achieve rationalisation.

It is important here to distinguish high technology industries supplying public procurement markets from more "traditional" ones. The high-tech group of industries is characterised by strong technological developments and reinvestment of a considerable amount on research and development. Such industries include telecommunications, data-processing equipment, medical equipment, bio-tech and pharmaceutical products and aerospace. These industries have been demarcated by high cross-country investment patterns, with an important presence of Japanese and American interests.[82] The group of traditional industries supplying public procurement markets includes industries dealing with railway equipment, heavy steel structures, shipbuilding, vehicles and textiles. Most of these industries have been *national champions*[83] and heavily protected from competition and sustained through public sector purchasing.[84] The high-tech public procurement industry has a tendency to operate in several national public procurement markets, thus having a large share of European production. This could be explained by the high levels of concentration observed for such industries over the last decade.[85] On the other hand, traditional public procurement industries have a strong tendency to operate at national level and enjoy the advantages of being *national champions*.

The second inherent threat of the process of integrating the public markets of the European Community reveals the vulnerable position of small and medium size firms as a consequence of their exposure to the new regime. Small and medium firms would find it difficult to sustain existing market shares or penetrate product or geographical markets as a result of either collusive tendering of oligopolists suppliers, or inefficient own resources which cannot be compared with those of large firms (volume production and economies of scale, financial and economic standing). Arguably, if the enhanced competitive regime in public markets results in industrial concentration which could bring about efficiency gains for public sector purchasing, then there is little complaint about market inequalities concerning access and opportunities for small and medium firms. This, however, runs contrary to the declarations and undertakings[86] by European Institutions on the role of SMEs for the completion of the common market and its importance for regional and economic development, social cohesion and industrial adjustment. The fears of oligopolisation of public markets and its subsequent effect of marginalisation of SMEs have been confirmed.[87] Market access for SMEs in public procurement is limited and disproportionately low in relation to their numbers throughout the European Union.

In addition to the internal effects of the public procurement regulatory regime, the integration of public markets has acquired an external dimension through the GATT/WTO Agreement on Government Procurement.[88] Exposure of the supply side to competitive forces from both within and outside the common market has intensified the impact and the effect of the new regime. Market access is guaranteed to firms established in signatories to the Agreement in an attempt to liberalise globally public procurement, although it was not until recently that contracting entities, other than central authorities, as well as construction procurement and procurement of services and telecommunications equipment were included in the Agreement during the GATT/WTO Uruguay Round. Despite the fact that the GATT Agreement on Government Procurement has been in existence since the Tokyo Round (1980), the tradability of public contracts *vis-à-vis* member-signatories to the Agreement has been rather limited. Import penetration for the public sector has been marginal and, again, large conglomerates appear to be the beneficiaries.[89] European SMEs, particularly those in highly specialised industries, have been the target of US or Japanese takeovers, as the flow of direct investment within the European Union has been increased over the last years. Interestingly enough, the vulnerability of SMEs, as a result of the global integration of public markets follows similar patterns with those on internal public sector integration.

5
A Critical Assessment of Public Procurement

Introduction

The process of the liberalisation of public procurement in the European Union has two primary objectives: i) to achieve an open and competitive regime of public purchasing which would yield substantial savings to the public sector and ii) to act as a stimulant for the much needed restructuring and adjustment of the European industrial base. When compared with other advanced integrated economic or political systems, the regulation of public procurement in the European Union has no precedence. It is not only the aspiration for the creation of a genuinely integrated public sector market within the Community, but to a large extent it is the impact of such a regime upon the overall process of European Integration that deserves further attention. The mechanism of the public purchasing regulation has revealed a considerable range of socio-economic considerations which interact with the envisaged aims and objectives of the regime. The public procurement sector in the European Union is by no means readily receptive to the parameters of any legislative framework. Rather, it is a *forum* of well-established socio-economic and legal patterns which for a long time have served national interests.

One should not expect a dramatic and unprecedented transformation of the way public procurement has been conducted in the Member States of the European Union, for two main reasons. Firstly, what has been asked by European law and policy on public procurement represents a significant change of the *modus operandi* of contracting authorities, which quite often have regarded the European rules as a burden. The unwillingness of public authorities to change well established public purchasing patterns and practices not only does reflect their reservations over the financial implications of such an exercise, but mostly their concern over domestic policy considerations which are closely associated with public procurement. The second reason for the modest progress in adapting to the new regime can be attributed to a number of factors which may not only slow the progress of public sector integration but also hinder the delivery of the envisaged results and the accomplishment of the objectives under the relevant framework. The primary concern of European institutions over the progress of public procurement regulation is the simple assumption that the Member States and their contracting authorities do indeed comply with the stipulated requirements of the Public Procurement Directives. However, the integration the public markets in the European Union could encounter problems which focus on five main areas: a) inherent constraints in the legislation, b) the existence of public monopolies and the process of their privatisation in the Member States, c) harmonisation of standards and specifications, d) the reluctance of the supply side in initiating litigation, and e) the need to sustain certain industries through public procurement.

Inherent shortcomings in the public procurement rules

The legislation on public procurement is far from perfect. It has envisaged the creation of a framework which will enhance competition in public markets, but the actual mechanism in delivering the objectives has revealed a number of limitations with its impact on the demand and supply sides. The most significant danger in the legislative framework of public procurement in the Community is the potential elements of non-tariff protection which might arise from its application. Indeed, inherent shortcomings in the legislation could pose considerable obstacles to the integration of the public sector in Europe. The impact of the law and policy of public purchasing upon the demand side in particular has exposed two fundamental limitations which are integral to the legislative framework. The first limitation refers to the quantitative division of public markets in dimensional (above certain thresholds) and sub-dimensional ones (below the thresholds which trigger the applicability of the Directives). The second limitation is concerned with the potential adverse effects of the principle of transparency upon the public procurement process.

The dimensionality of public procurement

The main objective of the European rules on public procurement, as implemented by Member States in the form of domestic laws is the establishment of the principle of transparency in the award of public contracts. The rules stipulate that public contracts of estimated value which exceed certain thresholds shall be advertised in the Official Journal of the European Communities.[1] The legislation on public procurement has put much faith on the principle of transparency. Transparency and openness in the public sector in Europe represent prerequisites for its integration. The principle of transparency encompasses the principle of accountability in the public sector and is materialised through the advertisement and publicity of procurement requirements of contracting authorities. However, the ambit of the law does not encapsulate all public procurement contracts awarded by contracting authorities. It rather introduces *a de minimis rule*, where certain thresholds in relation to the value of the contracts are utilised for the applicability of the Directives. The dimensional public procurement should, in principle, encompass the majority of procurement requirements of Member States and their contracting authorities. However, the legislation on public procurement has had little effect on the principle of transparency, as empirical investigation of the patterns of contracting authorities of Member States concerning their publication record in relation to their contracts reveals a rather gloomy picture. The volume of public purchasing which is advertised and tendered according to the requirements of the relevant Directives in comparison with the total volume of public procurement of the Member States appears disproportionate and beyond expectation, bearing in mind the vital importance that has been given to the principle of transparency for the opening-up of the public markets in the European Union. The percentages of public contracts advertised in the Official Journal by Member States reveal the relatively low impact of the public procurement legislation on the principle and objectives of transparency in European public markets (see Table 5.1). Clarification of the above impact of the law upon the transparency patterns which contracting authorities have established should be sought by exploring three scenarios.

The first scenario is based on the distinction between dimensional and sub-dimensional public procurement in the Member States. The European Directives allow the division of public contracts into lots[2] without any justification from contracting authorities. This in most cases may result in intentional contravention of the Directives, as sub-dimensional (below certain thresholds) public contracts escape their applicability. As sub-dimensional public procurement escapes from the mandatory publication requirement, contracting authorities tend to divide contracts into separate lots. It should be mentioned

A Critical Assessment of Public Procurement   127

Table 5.1   Transparency Rates by Member States (%)

	1995	1996	1997	1998	1999	2000	2001	2002
Belgium	6.9	7.6	10.9	13.8	15.6	15.6	18.6	15.8
Denmark	16.4	13.4	13.4	13.5	14.3	20.9	15.8	14.5
Germany	5.1	5.6	6.3	6.5	5.2	5.6	5.7	7.5
Greece	34.1	37.7	42.9	45.1	39.9	31.9	35.3	45.7
Spain	8.5	11.0	11.5	11.5	16.8	25.4	23.4	23.6
France	5.5	6.8	8.4	11.0	11.7	14.6	16.8	17.7
Ireland	11.4	16.3	19.3	16.1	16.8	21.4	19.3	18.0
Italy	9.8	9.9	11.3	10.7	13.2	17.5	15.3	20.3
Luxembourg	5.2	7.0	9.2	14.3	12.9	12.3	10.7	13.3
Netherlands	4.8	5.1	5.5	5.2	5.9	10.8	12.5	8.9
Austria	4.5	7.5	7.5	8.3	7.0	13.5	14.6	15.5
Portugal	15.5	17.7	15.1	15.5	14.6	15.0	17.7	19.4
Finland	8.0	9.2	8.2	9.2	9.8	13.2	15.1	13.9
Sweden	10.5	10.6	11.5	11.6	12.5	17.9	23.4	19.3
UK	15.0	15.6	17.9	16.9	15.1	21.5	21.5	21.1
EU 15	**8.4**	**9.2**	**10.7**	**11.1**	**11.2**	**14.9**	**15.4**	**16.2**

Source: Internal Market Directorate General

that the Directives stipulate the prohibition of intentional division of contracts into lots with a view to avoiding the relevant thresholds, but the provision presents practical difficulties in its observance and enforcement. Until the time of writing, there is no case or complaint before national courts or before the European Court of Justice relating to the intentional division of contracts into lots with lower thresholds in order to avoid the application of the Directives. The relevant thresholds which require the mandatory publication requirement clearly result in a segmentation of the public markets in quantitative terms by creating a *dimensional forum* which is subject to the rigorous legal regime. A *de minimis* rule applies to contracts below the thresholds, which exempts them from the provisions of the Directives. The sub-dimensional public procurement is only subject to the principle of non-discrimination at European level, whereas at domestic level, national tendering rules regulate the award of these contracts.

The second scenario is based on the excessive utilisation of award procedures without prior publication. Indeed, the Directives allow, under certain circumstances the award of contracts through direct negotiations with a contractor. Although the European Court of Justice condemned the above practice in a number of cases before it, the actual utilisation of negotiated procedures without prior publication is widespread. Finally, the third scenario implies the blunt violation of Community Law by Member States by avoiding the publication of tender notices in the Official Journal of the European Communities.

Bearing in mind the relative absence of complaints and subsequent litigation concerning non-advertisement of public contracts before national courts or the European Court of Justice, the third scenario reflects to a large extent the underlying reason for the lack of transparency in public procurement. In fact, intentional division of contracts into lots with a view to avoiding the Directives and excessive and unjustified recourse to award procedures without prior publication amounts to a blunt violation of Member States' obligations arising from the relevant Directives and also form primary Treaty provisions.

The effects of the principle of transparency

Transparency, as a principle in public purchasing has an obvious trade effect, that of price competitiveness. If more interested suppliers are aware of a contracting authority's determination to procure, automatically an element of competition occurs. This sort of competitive pattern would probably be reflected in the prices received by the contracting authority, when it evaluates the offers. The fact that more suppliers are aware of a forthcoming public contract and the fact that interested suppliers are aware that their rivals are informed about it, indicates two distinctive parameters which are relevant to savings and value for money. The first parameter focuses on value for money for the demand side of the equation of public purchasing and reveals the possibility for contracting authorities to compare prices (and quality). The second parameter has an effect on the supply side of the equation (the suppliers) which amongst other things can no longer rely on the lack of price comparisons when serving the public sector. Openness in public procurement, by definition, results in price competition and the benefits for contracting authorities appear achievable.

However, transparency and openness in public purchasing pose a question over long-term savings and value for money considerations. Price competition, as a result of the awareness of forthcoming public contracts, represents a rather static effect in the value for money process. The fact that more and more interested suppliers are aware and do submit tenders in the long run, appears rather as a burden. If transparency and the resulting price competitiveness are based on a *win-to-win* process, the potential benefits for contracting authorities could easily be counterbalanced by the administrative costs in tender evaluation and replies to unsuccessful tenders. Furthermore, the risk management factor is much higher in a win-to-win purchasing scenario. Price competitiveness represents also some threats for contracting authorities, to the extent that quality of deliverables as well as the delivery process itself could be jeopardised, if contracting authorities deal with different and unknown contractors. It could thus be argued here that price competitiveness, as a trade effect potentially beneficial for the demand side of the public purchasing equation, has a static character. It seems that it does not take into account medium or long-term purchasing patterns, as well as counter effects of competition. Two elements deserve further analysis here:

The first raises questions over the aggregate loss of the economy through transparent competitive purchasing patterns. For example, if a large number of interested suppliers submit their offer to a particular contracting authority, two types of costs should be examined. Firstly, the cost which is attributed to the response and tendering stage of the procurement process should not be underestimated. Human and capital resources are directed by the suppliers towards the preparation of documents and the submission of the offers. If one of these suppliers wins the contract, the remaining would have suffered an unrecoverable loss. If that aggregate loss exceeds the benefit/saving accomplished by the contracting authority by following transparent and competitive purchasing patterns, value for money has not been achieved. Secondly, along the same lines, the evaluation and selection process during tendering represents a considerable administrative cost for the contracting authorities. If the principle of transparency complements the principle of equal treatment, contracting authorities should give the same attention to all interested suppliers that have submitted a response. Downsizing the list through evaluation and assessment based on stipulated criteria is by no means an inexpensive exercise. Human and capital resources have to be directed by contracting authorities towards meeting that cost. If the latter exceeds the potential savings achieved through the competitive tendering route, then value for money is unaccomplished.

The second element that deserves attention relates to the definition of price competitiveness in public purchasing as well as its interrelation with anti-trust law and policy. A question which arises in price competitive tendering patterns is *what would be the lowest offer contracting authorities can accept*. If the maximisation of savings is the only achievable objective in the public procurement process, the transparent/competitive pattern cannot guarantee and evaluate safeguards in relation to underpriced offers. If the supply side responds to the perpetuated competitive purchasing pattern by lowering prices, contracting authorities could face a dilemma: where to stop. It should be mentioned here that the European rules provide for an automatic disqualification of an "abnormally low offer".[3] The term has not been interpreted in detail by the judiciary at European and domestic levels and serves rather as a "lower bottom limit".[4] Also, when an offer appears low, contracting authorities may request clarifications from the tenderer in question. Contracting authorities face a dilemma in evaluating and assessing low offers other than abnormal ones. It is difficult for them to identify dumping or predatory pricing disguised behind a low offer for a public contract. In addition, even if there is an indication of anti-competitive price fixing, the European public procurement rules do not provide for any kind of procedure. The suspension of the award procedures (or even the suspension of the conclusion of the contract itself) would be unlikely without a thorough and exhaustive investigation by the competent anti-trust authorities.

The abuse of award procedures which may restrict competition

The participation of the supply side of the public procurement equation in the tendering process is channelled through open, negotiated or restricted procedures. Open procedures are those where every interested supplier, contractor or service provider may submit an offer.[5] Negotiated procedures[6] are such procedures for the award of public contracts whereby contracting authorities consult contractors of their choice and negotiate the terms of the contract with one or more of them. Finally, restricted procedures[7] are those procedures for the award of public contracts whereby only those contractors invited by the contracting authority may submit tenders. The selection of the winning tender takes place in two rounds. In the first round, all interested contractors may submit their tenders and the contracting authority selects, from the candidates, those who will be invited to tender. In principle, the minimum number of candidates to be selected is five. In the second round, bids are submitted and the successful tenderer is selected.

The Utilities Directives have introduced a new selection and tendering procedure, namely framework agreements, which was influenced to a large extent by the benefits of chain supply management and partnership schemes. The Supplies, Works and Services Directives do not refer to framework agreements. A framework agreement is an agreement between a contracting authority and one or more suppliers, contractors or service-providers the purpose of which is to establish the terms, in particular with regard to price and, where appropriate, the quantity envisaged which govern the contracts to be awarded during a given period.[8] A framework agreement does not possess a binding character and should not be considered as a contract between the relevant parties. In practical terms it represents a sort of a standing offer which remains valid during its time-span. Within the provisions of the Utilities Directive, when a contracting authority awards a framework agreement under the relevant procedures which are common to other public contracts covered therein, subsequent individual contracts concluded under the framework agreement may be awarded without having recourse to a call for competition.[9] Individual contracts which have been awarded under a framework agreement are subject to the requirement of the publication of a contract-award notice in the Official Journal. The Directive specifically stipulates that misuse of framework agreements may distort competition and trigger the application of the relevant rules, particularly with reference to concerted practices which lead to collusive tendering.

Certain types of award procedures (particularly negotiated with or without prior publication in the Official Journal) are prone to abuse by contracting authorities in order to avoid the publicity requirement in advertising public contracts and in order to favour certain suppliers or contractors. Negotiated procedures[10] are such procedures for the award of public contracts whereby contracting authorities consult contractors of their choice and negotiate the terms of the contract with one or more of them. In most cases they follow restricted procedures and they are heavily utilised under framework agreements in the Utilities sectors. There are two different types of negotiated procedures: i) negotiated procedures with prior notification and ii) negotiated procedures without prior notification.

- Negotiated procedures with prior notification[11] provide for selection of candidates in two rounds. In the first round, all interested

contractors may submit their tenders and the contracting authority selects, from the candidates, those who will be invited to negotiate. In the second round, negotiations with various candidates take place and the successful tenderer is selected. In principle, the minimum number of candidates to be selected is three, provided that there are a sufficient number of suitable candidates.
- Negotiated procedures without prior notification[12] are the least restrictive of the various award procedures laid down in the Directive and may be conducted in one single round. Contracting authorities are allowed to choose whichever contractor they want, begin negotiations directly with this contractor and award the contract to him. The Directive provides for only a few rules with which this procedure must comply. A prior notice in the Official Journal is not required.

An accelerated form of negotiated procedures may be used[13] where, for reasons of urgency, the periods normally required under the normal procedures cannot be met. In such cases, contracting authorities are required to indicate in the tender notice published in the Official Journal the grounds for using the accelerated form of the procedure. The use of an accelerated procedure must be limited to the types and quantities of products or services which can be shown to be urgently required. Other products or services must be supplied or provided under open or restricted procedures.

The Public Procurement Directives stipulate that open procedures, where possible should constitute the norm. Open procedures increase competition without doubt and can achieve better prices for the contracting authorities when the latter purchase goods in large volumes. Price reduction based on economies of scale can bring about substantial cost savings for the public sector. Open procedures are mostly utilised when the procurement process is relatively straightforward and are combined with the lowest price award criterion. On the other hand, competition in tendering procedures is limited by using the restricted and negotiated procedures. By definition, the number of candidates that are allowed to tender is limited (5 in restricted, 3 in negotiated procedures respectively), therefore the Directives have attached a number of conditions for the contracting authorities to justify when they intend to award their contracts through restricted or negotiated procedure. Restricted and negotiated procedures are utilised in relation with the most economically advantageous offer award criterion and suited for more complex procurement schemes. Although contracting authorities can freely opt for open or restricted procedures, the latter should be justified by reference to the nature of the products or services to be procured and the balance between contract value and administrative costs associated with tender evaluation. A more rigorous set of conditions apply for the use of negotiated procedures. When negotiated procedures with prior notification are used, they must be justified on grounds of irregular or unacceptable tenders received as a result of a previous call. Negotiated procedures without prior notification are restrictively permitted in absence of tenders, when the procurement involves manufactured products or construction work purely for research and development, when for technical or artistic reasons or reasons connected with the protection of exclusive rights a particular supplier or contractor is selected, in cases of extreme urgency brought by unforeseeable events not attributable to the contracting authorities, when additional deliveries and supplies or works would cause disproportionate technical, operational and maintenance difficulties.

Negotiated procedures with prior publication, since they restrict the number of tenderers may constitute an element of non-tariff protection and may encourage practices which appear to run counter to effective competition. If they are being employed as a non-tariff barrier, negotiated procedures may give rise to discrimination on grounds of nationality, preference and support of domestic uncompetitive suppliers, all of which would or could be detrimental to the position of foreign firms which will be placed at a competitive disadvantage. However, negotiated procedures may have certain positive effects in public procurement, as they may reduce the economic costs of the contracting entities, particularly in cases where product complexity which requires negotiations for the quality of procurement, or a large number of tenderers makes tender evaluation relatively expensive. Contracting authorities have also abusive recourse to award procedures without prior notification and claim a number of reasons varying from extreme urgency to the protection of industrial or commercial property rights and the need to guarantee the flow of supplies or works and award public contracts through direct negotiations with the contractor(s) of their choice. They also claim (particularly the Utilities) that the utilisation of framework agreements or list of approved vendors has resulted in cost-efficiency gains of administrative costs relating to the evaluation of tenders.

The European Court of Justice has always been very reluctant in accepting the use of negotiated procedures, particularly without prior advertisement. In a number of notable cases before it relating to improper use of the award procedures, the Court has maintained the exceptional character of negotiated procedures and the extremely onerous obligation of contracting authorities to justify them. It might be construed from the case law of the Court of Justice that the particular procedure stipulated by the rules requires some sort of clearance prior to its utilisation. This is not however the case, as the only form of official notification by contracting authorities which use negotiated procedures takes place after the award of the contract in question, when a notice containing the reasons for having recourse to negotiation should be communicated to the European Commission. This rather reinforces the exceptional character of the negotiated procedures rather than their prohibitive use. A number of cases before the European Court of Justice have clarified the position of European Institutions *vis-à-vis* the use of negotiated procedures.

Public monopolies

Public monopolies in the European Union, which in the majority are utilities, are accountable for a substantial magnitude of procurement, in terms of volume and in terms of price. Responsible for this are the expensive infrastructure and high technology products which are necessary to procure in order to deliver their services to the public. Given the fact that most of the suppliers to public utilities depend almost entirely on their procurement and that, even when some degree of privatisation has been achieved, the actual control of the utilities is still vested in the state, the first constraint in liberalising public procurement in the European Union is apparent. Utilities, in the form of public monopolies or semi-private enterprises appear prone to perpetuate long standing over dependency purchasing patterns with certain domestic suppliers. Reflecting the above observations, the reader should bear in mind that until 1991, utilities were not covered by European legislation on procurement.[14] The delay of their regulation can be attributed to the resistance from Member States in privatising their monopolies and the uncertainty of the legal regime that will follow their privatisation.

Public monopolies[15] operating in the utilities sector (energy, transport, water, telecommunications) have been the target of a sweeping process of transformation from monolithic and sub-optimal public corporations to competitive enterprises. These legal or delegated monopolies have been assigned with the exclusive exploitation of the relevant services in their respective Member States (production, distribution of water and any form of energy and the provision of telecommunications and transport) and very often possess a monopsonistic position. State controlled enterprises perform a different management pattern than private ones in their market activities. Profit maximisation is not their main objective and decision making responds not only to market forces but mainly to political pressure. Understandably, their purchasing behaviour follows, to a large extent, parameters reflecting current trends of the industrial policy of the government in power. It has become apparent that public monopolies in the utilities sector have sustained industries in Member States through exclusive or preferential procurement. Preferential and protectionist purchasing behaviour could not easily withstand the competitive forces under which private firms are exposed. One of the most important elements of corporate performance is sourcing and the associated costs. The private firm which is exposed to competitive forces for its deliverables would be certainly compelled to have recourse to the most cost-efficient sources. This covers not only procurement but also extends to a wide range of legal and corporate activities such as sub-contracting, research and development, maintenance services. Sustainability of *national champions*, or in other terms, strategically perceived enterprises, could only be achieved through discriminatory purchasing patterns. The privatisation of public monopolies, which absorb, to a large extent or even entirely, the output of such industries will most probably discontinue such patterns and will result in industrial policy imbalances as it would be difficult for the *national champions* to secure new markets to replace the traditional long dependency on public monopolies and it would take time and effort to diversify their activities or to convert to alternative industrial sectors. Imbalances in social policy (unemployment) will also occur, as a result of the restructuring of the public monopoly and also the industries which are dependent on it.

The protected and preferential purchasing frameworks between monopolies and *national champions* and the output dependency patterns and secured markets of the latter have attracted considerable foreign direct investment, to the extent that Community Institutions face the dilemma of threatening to discontinue the investment flow when liberalising public procurement in the common market. However, it could be argued that the industrial restructuring following the opening-up of the procurement practices of public monopolies would possibly attract similar levels of foreign direct investment, which would be directed towards supporting the new structure.

As mentioned above, the liberalisation of public purchasing aims *inter alia* at achieving a restructuring effect in the common market, particularly in industries suffering from overcapacity and sub-optimal performance. However, the industries supplying public monopolies and utilities are themselves quite often public corporations. In such cases, procurement dependency patterns between state outfits, when disrupted can result in massive unemployment attributed to the supply side's inadequacy to secure new customers. The monopsony position when abolished could often bring about the collapse of the relevant sector.

Standardisation and specification

National technical standards, industrial product and service specifications and their harmonisation were considered priority areas for the internal market programme. The European Commission's White Paper for the Completion of the Internal Market stipulated for a number of Directives to be adopted and implemented with a view to eliminating discrimination based on the description of national standards. The rules on technical standards and specifications have been brought in line with the new policy which is based on the mutual recognition of national requirements, where the objectives of national legislation are essentially equivalent, and on the process of legislative harmonisation of technical standards through non-governmental standardisation organisations (CEPT, CEN, CENELEC).[16] However, persistence of contracting authorities to specify their procurement requirements by reference to national standards poses obstacles in the public sector integration.[17] The European Commission has been for some time aware of the most notable examples of circumvention of the policy on standards and specifications.[18] These include the exclusive familiarity of national suppliers with technical data existing in a particular Member State, over-specification by contracting authorities in order to exclude potential bidders and finally favouritism and discrimination by contracting authorities as a result of the availability of technical standards and specifications to certain suppliers only.

Standardisation and specification can act as a non-tariff barrier in public procurement contracts in two ways. Firstly, contracting authorities may use apparently different systems of standards and specifications as an excuse for disqualification of tenderers. It should be maintained here that the description of the intended supplies, works or services to be procured is made by reference to the Common Product

Classification, the NACE (General Industrial Classification of Economic Activities within the European Communities) and the Common Procurement Vocabulary (CPV), however, this type of description is of generic nature and does not cover industrial specifications and standardisation requirements. Secondly, standardisation and specification requirements can be restrictively defined in order to exclude products or services of a particular origin, or narrow the field of competition amongst tenderers. National standards are not only the subject of domestic legislation, which, of course, need to be harmonised and mutually recognised across the common market. One of the most significant aspects of standardisation and specification appears to be the operation of voluntary standards, which are mainly specified at industry level. The above category is rather difficult to harmonise, as any approximation and mutual recognition relies on the willingness of the industry in question. Voluntary standards and specifications are used quite often in the Utilities sector, where the relevant procurement requirements are complex and cannot be specified solely by reference to "statutory" standards, thus leaving a considerable margin of discretion in the hands of the contracting authorities, which may abuse it during the selection and qualification stages of the procurement process.

Reluctance in initiating litigation

The litigation before the European Court of Justice and national courts in relation to public procurement contracts has pointed out the areas of contention between defaulting contracting authorities and the Commission or aggrieved contractors. The most common disputes subject to centralised or decentralised judicial control include the following:

- advertisement and publicity of contracts
- selection procedures (quantitative and qualitative suitability criteria)
- technical standards (product specification and standardisation)
- award procedures
- award criteria

Interestingly, all the relevant provisions of the Directives covering the above areas are capable of producing direct effect, thus maximising the opportunities for access to justice for aggrieved contractors. The impact of public procurement legislation on the demand and supply sides identified certain areas which represent obstacles to public market integration. Although the relevant legislation has provided for a great deal of flexibility, in terms of implementing methods and time, national legal systems responded slowly to the envisaged regime. The limited number of cases relating to public procurement, in contrast with its volume and the economic importance for Member States reflects a false picture. One may assume that because of the relatively disproportionate number of cases before the European Court of Justice or before national courts, the integration of public markets is on good course and has progressed satisfactorily.

However, examination and analysis of the case-law on public procurement as the impact of the relevant legislation on the demand and supply sides reveals the nature of public procurement as a *nexus* of transaction activities between the state and its organs on the one hand and the private sector on the other. Such a nature appears to have strong *endocentric* characteristics, in terms of the reluctance in initiating litigation, the secrecy and confidentiality of the dispute itself, and finally the belief that litigation represents the *ultium refugium* in resolving the dispute. Furthermore, the contractual relation between the supply and the demand side after the litigation of a dispute between them appears to be irretrievably broken. This means that prior to having recourse to legal proceedings, parties in a public procurement dispute appear to have comprehensively exhausted all the routes in resolving the issue in an amicable way. Therefore, the relevant litigation and its outcome serve as the epitaph in a rather unclear nexus of legal relations. The supply side appears reluctant in taking contracting authorities to court for a number of reasons: psychological, legal and financial.

The psychology behind enforcement and compliance with public procurement legislation is the key point for understanding the behaviour of the supply side. The supply side is often afraid of the vindictive behaviour of the contracting authorities. A contractor who initiates litigation (or some form of official complaint) against a contracting authority would find himself on a "black list" and would not continue doing business with the latter. Even in the unlikely event that a contract is awarded to a supplier that had previously created some form of trouble for the contracting authority, the latter could make the performance of the contract intolerable, ensuring minimisation of margins of profit and delaying payments. The psychology in public procurement enforcement and compliance works against the supply side, as the latter initiates the majority of litigation against contracting authorities. Even in the case of the European Commission taking the defaulting Member State before the European Court of Justice, there is a complaint from an aggrieved contractor who has identified himself.

The supply side also appears reluctant in initiating litigation against contracting authorities because of financial reasons. If the court finds that the contracting authority breached the law, the damages that could be awarded would be disproportionate to the legal costs. The extent to which compensation is awarded varies among legal orders. Compensation for loss of incurred expenses, for loss of profits and for loss of opportunity is theoretically available in all Member States, in accordance with the Compliance Directives. However, in practice the only relatively certain heading of damages an aggrieved contractor may count on is that of out-of-pocket expenses, *viz.* the cost of preparing the bid. Forgone profits and losses of opportunities would be deemed as elements of speculative litigation by the courts and would probably be rejected. It is worth mentioning that in Italy, due to the very strict requirement that only successful tenderers that have been awarded the contract may lodge an action for damages against the contracting authority, losses of profits are not easily granted. On the other hand, under the relevant arbitration proceedings for public contracts in the Netherlands, compensation is available for injury to a firm's commercial reputation. Direct compensation from administrative bodies, without judicial interference, is theoretically available in Denmark and Spain. These examples demonstrate the diversity of national systems as far as enforcement of public procurement law is concerned.

Finally, legal obstacles appear to have constrained the supply side in its attempts to enforce its rights under public procurement law. These obstacles act as non-tariff barriers, particularly in cases of cross-country litigation, where the nature of the competent *forum*, the cost of initiating a suit, legal and expert fees, translation costs and the chances of a favourable outcome deter aggrieved contractors from taking defaulting contracting authorities to court. The complexity of domestic legal regimes relating to public procurement disputes, in conjunction with the uncertainties arising from the parallel application of public and private law remedies in some Member States, appear a major deterrent for initiating litigation against contracting authorities.

Public procurement and the sustainability of certain industries

The low transparency levels and the low *tradability* of public contracts within the European Union have been particularly intriguing (see Table 5.2). The term *tradability,* refers to the cross-border import

Table 5.2   Import Penetration in Public Procurement (selected Member States)

MS	t	i
Belgium	67.9	17.7
Denmark	58.1	9.2
France	54.7	9.3
Germany	66.8	7.1
Greece	78.2	19.1
Ireland	81.5	20.4
Italy	60.6	8.6
Luxembourg	77.5	24.2
Netherlands	76.5	11.6
Portugal	65.4	17.6
Spain	68.4	15.7
United Kingdom	76.4	14.4

MS: Member State
t: private markets penetration levels (%)
i: public procurement import penetration levels (%)

penetration of public procurement contracts within the common market. Although it is very difficult to measure direct cross-border public procurement activities, information available from statistical data bases of the European Union suggest very weak trade patterns.

For example, in a selection of Member States, the import penetration in public procurement markets is rather low, when compared with that in private markets for the same or similar products.

The effectiveness of the public procurement legislation relies mainly on its decentralised application by the Member States and its enforcement by the competent *fora*. The greater the regime of transparency Member States provide for their public markets, the more efficient the level of competition that occurs and the more enhanced the cross-frontier trade with the public sector that emerges, facts that will result in their full integration. Empirical results have revealed that contracting authorities award the majority of public contracts without recourse to the advertisement and publicity provisions of the relevant Directives. This finding discloses the size of dimensional and sub-dimensional procurement in Member States and brings into play questions concerning the utilisation of sub-dimensional public procurement as a tool for policy implementation in Member States. The percentages of public contracts advertised in the Official Journal by Member States justify also the concerns that the results of these efforts will not change the ingrained habits of nationalistic procurement overnight.

The above background concerning transparency and openness in the public markets brings into play questions relating to the impact of competitiveness on the public procurement markets of the Member States. Does low transparency in public markets imply low competitiveness and what is the interplay between protectionist public purchasing patterns and *national champions*? As already indicated above, the majority of public procurement contracts are awarded without prior advertisement, and if one is prepared to accept the argument of excessive bureaucracy and the implied costs in transparent public procurement procedures, the question that follows is *who is awarded those contracts*? If competitive indigenous suppliers were awarded the majority of public contracts, then the failure of the principle of transparency has had minimal effect on purchasing patterns. On the other hand if uncompetitive indigenous suppliers were awarded the majority of public contracts, then the protectionist procurement pattern would provide evidence of existing discriminatory industrial sustainability attributable to long-dependency relations between the industries concerned and the contracting authorities in question.

In order to establish the interrelation between low transparency in public procurement and industrial competitiveness in a Member State, a number of industries/sectors representing more than 80 per cent of the total industrial output of the Member States have been under investigation by the European Commission.[19] The investigation of these industries revealed that a number of industrial sectors enjoy protection by contracting authorities in the sense that the relevant public procurement import penetration ratios are relatively low. It was also revealed that the sectors in question were not internationalised, in the sense that they showed low export to production ratios and were relatively uncompetitive, in the sense that they presented low specialisation ratios.

When sectoral public procurement import penetration is low and the volume of public purchasing is met from domestic output, then the domestic industry in question would most probably be sustained through public procurement, if its competitiveness is low. It follows that public purchasing patterns, which survived the enactment of public procurement legislation may have sustained certain industries in the Member States and are responsible for perpetuating price discrepancies, attributed to factors other than quality, for public procurement within the European Union. Sectoral import penetration in public procurement denotes the amount of imports destined for the public markets. It also reveals the relative openness of the public market in question and it is useful to compare with the volume of public procurement which is met from domestic output. In theory, import penetration and public procurement met from domestic sources should cover the total volume of sectoral public procurement in a Member State.

On the other hand, the competitiveness of an industrial sector in a Member State can be determined by reference to the balance between export and production, which determines the degree of internationalisation of the sector in question as well as the production specialisation, which determines competitive and comparative advantages of the sector within the European Union. If a substantial proportion of sectoral public procurement is met from domestic output and the sectoral import penetration appears low, the sectoral public procurement market can be identified as protectionist. Moreover, when the industry in question has low export to production ratio, this might indicate its lack of internationalisation. However, the export to production ratio in itself cannot sufficiently support the argument of low competitiveness in an industry. For this purpose, the specialisation index, which measures the competitive advantage of an industry within the whole European Union, indicates whether the industry in question has competitive advantages over rival industries. When an industry has low internationalisation and low specialisation levels, there is a strong indication that it is sub-optimal (uncompetitive). When the above pattern is combined with high levels of domestic public purchasing, then the picture of sustainable trends through public procurement emerges.

Apparently, the relatively uncompetitive industries (mainly *national champions*) have been sustained over the years through public purchasing patterns which have survived the public procurement legislation. These patterns represent the most important non-tariff barrier for the integration of the public markets in the European Union. The findings run parallel with the relevant theories which investigate public procurement as an instrument of industrial policy of Member States.

In December 1996, the European Commission published the *Green Paper on Public Procurement: Exploring the Way Forward*. In this document the Commission has reflected on the law and policy of public procurement particularly since the completion of the internal market. The Green Paper does not proclaim a huge success by the regime or any unprecedented impact upon the demand and supply sides of the public purchasing equation. It rather acknowledges the modest effect of the law and policy on the principles envisaged in the opening up of the public sector markets in the European Community. It invited all interested parties to submit written evidence on the effect of the regime upon them and possible suggestions as to future improvements.

The Green Paper has recognised the complementarity of public procurement with other Community and national policies. Because of the economic importance of public procurement, an effective regulatory regime on the law and policy of public purchasing in the European Community is considered as fundamental to the success of the common market. The effectiveness of the public procurement regime would bring about cost-efficiency gains for the public sector, which could consequently affect the success of fiscal deficit reduction policies imposed by the Maastricht convergence criteria. Thus, the European Commission has made clear the possible links between public sector savings and convergence criteria of the European Monetary Union. However, to what extent the success of monetary integration in the European Community would be affected by the outcome of the public sector integration process of the common market deserves thorough and in-depth quantitative and qualitative research for the years to come.

Although the Commission acknowledged some improvements in the transparency of the public procurement process as a result of the obligatory publicity and advertisement requirements, substantial progress in the implementation of the Directives within domestic systems has not been recorded. The Green Paper raised the thorny question of *qualitative implementation* of the public procurement regime into national legal orders. To what extent the Member States have failed to meet the expectations of European Institutions and share their aspirations for an integrated procurement system in the common market, is a matter for the European Court of Justice to decide. The reservations of the successful implementation of the regime expressed by the author in relation to the limited amount of litigation and the relatively low number of complaints in public procurement could perhaps trigger the need for a new approach to Member States' obligations arising from Directives. The acid test for the *qualitative implementation* of the Public Procurement Directives is *access to justice* at national level. Moreover, the expectations of the new regime in relation to the actual or potential savings for the public sector have not been fully materialised. The author has pointed out the relatively limited economic impact of the public procurement law and policy on the demand and supply side respectively and in particular the effects on price convergence and the public sector import penetration.

The 1996 Commission's Green Paper on Public Procurement[20] paved the way for the 1998 Commission's Communication, in which European institutions attempted to assess the progress of the regime in the common market. The Public Procurement Directives have been seen as an instrument of economic reform. As a consequence they are an integral part of the Commission's 2000 Work Programme, which pledges to modernise the relevant legislation for the completion of the internal market and at the same time implement the Lisbon European Council's call for economic reform within the internal market.

The Green Paper on Public Procurement and the subsequent policy developments adopted by the European Commission called for a modernisation of the public procurement regime. The previous legal framework of public sector procurement separated supplies, works and services, as well as the utilities procurement into different legal instruments. The jurisprudence of the European Court of Justice has been the main influence of the need to codify the public procurement regime into two mainstream Directives: the Public Sector Directive and the Utilities Directive.

The codification of the Supplies, Works and Services Directives into a single legal instrument is intended to simplify the public procurement framework and enhance legal certainty. In addition, it is expected to facilitate legal efficiency and compliance in the sense that it could streamline its implementation process by national governments and provide for a one-stop shop reference point in national legal orders. On the other hand, the utilities procurement remains a separate regime due to complexity of the regulatory regimes applicable by Member States to utilities undertakings and their respective markets. It should be noted that the character of the utilities markets reflects a quasi-oligopolistic environment, as the existence of special or exclusive rights granted by the Member States for the supply, provision or operation of networks for providing the service concerned, necessitates a special regulatory regime for the procurement requirements of these undertakings. Such regime must be compatible with the principles of transparency and competitiveness, which underpin the public sector procurement and, more important, adhere to the fundamental principles of EU Law.

6
The New Public Procurement Regime

Introduction

The European Union has finally adopted a new set of rules which govern the award of public contracts in the supplies, works and services sectors, as well as in the public utilities[1] after a considerable amount of debate and consultation.[2] The new Directives reflect on the 1996 Commission's Green Paper on Public Procurement[3] and subsequently the 1998 Commission's Communication. The Directives have been seen as an integral part of the Commission's 2000 Work Programme, which pledges to modernise the relevant legislation for the completion of the internal market and at the same time implement the Lisbon European Council's call for economic reform within the internal market. The new Public Procurement regime will become operational by January 31, 2006, when Member States are expected to transpose the Directives into national law.[4] Currently the previous regime is still applicable.[5]

The Directives have been based upon two basic premises: *simplification* and *modernisation*. Drawing on the wealth of experience from three previous generations of legal instruments, and the Court's jurisprudential inferences to public procurement regulation, the new Directives are set to achieve what is perhaps the most challenging objective of the internal market: fully integrate its public sector and abolish any remaining non-tariff barriers. The new regime maps also a clear-cut *dichotomy* between the public and the utilities sectors respectively. Although the same fundamental principles underlie the liberalisation of procurement in government and public utilities, their separate regulation reveals a diametrically opposed nature of the contracting authorities/entities under these sectors. Over the past two decades, public utilities in the EU Member States have been undergoing a process of transformation. Their change in ownership from public to private has stimulated commercialism and competitiveness and provided for the justification of a more relaxed regime and the acceptance that utilities, in some form or another represent a *sui generis* contracting authorities not in need of a rigorous and detailed regulation of their procurement. The above dichotomy reflects an insight of current market conditions and political priorities across the European Union, as well as an indication that the main emphasis should be placed on attempts to open up the public sector.

The intellectual paternity of the reasons behind past and current efforts to *"...co-ordinate the procedures for the award of public contracts...."*[6] could be traced in a neo-classical economic approach to market integration.[7] Public procurement has been identified as a serious non-tariff barrier and a hindering factor for the functioning of a genuinely competitive common market. Its regulation, apart from seeking an endorsement of the *acquis communautaire* by Member States of the fundamental principles of the common market, aims, primarily, at introducing radical changes in the industrial base of the European Union. Integration of public markets will bring substantial savings to the public sector, rationalise an over-capacity ridden industry, and allocate more efficiently resources (human and capital) and increase productivity and competitiveness of European firms to provide them a fair chance in the global arena.

Part 1 The new concepts in public procurement regulation

The Codified Public Supplies, Works and Services Directive

The Green Paper on Public Procurement prompted a modest modernisation of the existing Directives and as a consequence of industry pressure, minor amendments were made to the Public Services Directive,[8] the Public Supplies Directive[9] and the Public Works Directive.[10] Previous regimes on the public sector procurement (public supplies, works and services for central and local governments and bodies governed by public law) were segmented for two main reasons: first, the applicability thresholds for the relevant public contracts were, and still are, different; this feature gave apparently a false perception that the thrust of the rules would be applied better if procurement of works, supplies and services is regulated through different regimes. It should be maintained that apart from the differential applicability thresholds, every other aspect of the previous regime (advertisement and publicity, selection and qualification, award procedures, award criteria) was virtually identical, or replicated *verbatim* throughout the Directives. In numerous instances the ECJ applied its reasoning by analogous interpretation to all three Directives, perhaps hinting the case of consistency and the future need for rationalising the unnecessary plethora of the legal instruments on public procurement.

Secondly, the timing of the introduction of rules governing the award of public contracts was diachronically spread over three decades. Whilst supplies and works contracts were the subject of the first generation of Public Procurement Directives, the regulation of the award of public services contracts coincided with the completion of the internal market and appeared as a recognition of an evolution of the procurement needs of contracting authorities and the pragmatic acceptance that services contracts, alongside works and supplies play an important part in the procurement remit of contracting authorities of Member States.

The codification of the provisions of the Supplies, Works and Services Directives into a single legal instrument, apart from the obvious benefits of simplification and legal certainty, has further important implications: legal efficiency and compliance discipline. As far as legal efficiency is concerned, the new codified Directive will speed up and streamline its implementation process by Member States and provide for a one-stop shop reference point in national legal orders, augmented by the Court's vesting of direct effectiveness upon the Directive's predecessors in numerous occasions. On the other hand, codification will enhance compliance, as it will remove any remaining uncertainties over the applicability of the previously fragmented regime and afford contracting authorities a disciple method in dispersing their procurement functions.

Case-law from the European Court of Justice[11] has been the main influence of the codified Directive, in particular case-law on award criteria, which clarifies the possibilities for the contracting authorities to utilise criteria relating to environmental and social considerations to meet the needs of the general public. Such criteria can be used by contracting authorities provided that they are linked to the subject-matter of the contract, that they do not confer an unrestricted freedom of choice on the contracting authority and they are expressly mentioned in the tender documents. Finally, environmental and social considerations as award criteria of public contracts must comply with the fundamental principles of EU Law such as the principle of freedom of movement of goods, the principle of freedom of establishment, the principle of freedom to provide services and the surrogate principles deriving from them, such as the principle of equal treatment, the principle of non-discrimination, the principle of mutual recognition, the principle of proportionality and the principle of transparency.[12]

As far as the utilities procurement is concerned, there are two main reasons for the introduction of rules co-ordinating procedures for the award of contracts in the utilities sectors. Firstly, is the variety of ways in which national authorities can influence the behaviour of these entities, including participation in their capital and representation in the administrative, managerial or supervisory bodies of these entities. Secondly, the closed nature of the markets in which utilities operate, due to the existence of special or exclusive rights granted by the Member States concerning the supply, provision or operation of networks for providing the service concerned necessitates a special regulatory regime which ensures transparency and competitiveness alongside adherence to the fundamental principles of the EU Treaty.

A thematic analysis of the new concepts in procurement

The codified Public Sector Directive has introduced a series of new concepts in its regulatory framework. These concepts are the product of jurisprudential inferences and policy refining of the previous regime. They intend to modernise public purchasing and align the procurement of government and its agencies with that of utilities and entities operating in a more commercially oriented environment.

Eligibility of bodies governed by public law to tender

The new Public Sector Directive clearly accepts that entities which are covered by its rules, can participate in the award of public contracts, alongside private sector undertakings. Member States should ensure that the participation of a body governed by public law as a tenderer in a procedure for the award of a public contract does not cause any distortion of competition in relation to private tenderers. The eligibility of bodies governed by public law to participate in tendering procedures has been influenced by case-law.[13] There is a protection mechanism built in the above liberty of contracting authorities. Article 55(e) of the Public Sector Directive specifies that in the case of abnormally low tenders, in relation to the goods, works or services, the contracting authority may reject those tenders, if there is a possibility of the tenderer obtaining State aid. Where a contracting authority establishes that a tender is abnormally low because the tenderer has obtained State aid, his tender can be rejected on that ground alone only after consultation with the tenderer where the latter is unable to prove, within a sufficient time limit fixed by the contracting authority that the aid in question was granted legally. Where the contracting authority rejects a tender in these circumstances, it must inform the Commission.

According to Article 1.8 of the Public Sector Directive, the term economic operator covers equally the concepts of contractor, supplier and service provider. It is used merely in the interest of simplification. An economic operator who has submitted a tender is designated as a "tenderer". One who has sought an invitation to take part in a restricted or negotiated procedure or a competitive dialogue is designated as a "candidate".

Interestingly, the new utilities regime excludes from its remit contracts awarded to affiliated undertakings. The new Utilities Directive does not apply to contracts awarded: (a) by a contracting entity to an affiliated undertaking, or (b) by a joint venture, formed exclusively by a number of contracting entities for the purpose of carrying out activities which are covered by the Utilities Directive to an undertaking which is affiliated with one of these contracting entities. Article 23 of the new Utilities Directive excludes contracts awarded to an affiliated undertaking, to a joint venture or to a contracting entity forming part of a joint venture from the remit of the Directive. Under the utilities procurement regime, the term affiliated undertaking means any undertaking the annual accounts of which are consolidated with those of the contracting entity in accordance with the requirements of the Seventh Council Directive 83/349/EEC on consolidated accounts[14] based on the Article 44(2)(g) of the EU Treaty. In cases of entities which are not subject to that Directive, affiliated undertaking means any undertaking over which the contracting entity may exercise, directly or indirectly, a dominant influence within the meaning of Article 2(1)(b), or any undertaking over which the contracting entity may exercise a dominant influence by virtue of ownership, financial participation, or the rules which govern it.

Joint and centralised procurement

In view of the diversity of public works contracts, contracting authorities should be given the freedom to make provision for contracts for the design and execution of work to be awarded either separately or jointly. The decision to award contracts separately or jointly must be determined by qualitative and economic criteria, which may be defined by national law. According to Article 1.10 of the Public Sector

Directive, a central purchasing body is a contracting authority which: i) acquires supplies and/or services intended for contracting authorities, or ii) awards public contracts or concludes framework agreements for works, supplies or services intended for contracting authorities.

The Public Sector Directive allows Member States to establish official lists of contractors, suppliers or service providers or a system of certification by public or private bodies, and makes provision for the effects of such registration or such certification in a contract award procedure in another Member State. As regards official lists of approved economic operators, it is important to take into account Court of Justice case-law[15] in cases where an economic operator belonging to a group claims the economic, financial or technical capabilities of other companies in the group in support of its application for registration. In this case, it is for the economic operator to prove that those resources will actually be available to it throughout the period of validity of the registration. For the purposes of that registration, a Member State may therefore determine the level of requirements to be met and in particular, for example where the operator lays claim to the financial standing of another company in the group, it may require that that company be held liable, if necessary jointly and severally.

Certain centralised purchasing techniques have been developed in Member States. Several contracting authorities are responsible for making acquisitions or awarding public contracts/framework agreements for other contracting authorities. In view of the large volumes purchased, those techniques help increase competition and streamline public purchasing. The terms and conditions which cover the procurement of works, supplies and services through a central purchasing body must observe the principles of non-discrimination and equal treatment. According to Article 11, which lays down the provisions of public contracts and framework agreements awarded by central purchasing bodies, Member States may stipulate that contracting authorities may purchase works, supplies and/or services from or through a central purchasing body. In addition, contracting authorities which purchase works, supplies and/or services from or through a central purchasing body in the cases set out in Article 1(10) must comply with the Public Sector Directive insofar as the central purchasing body has complied with it.

A new award procedure: the competitive dialogue

According to Article 1.11(c) of the Public Sector Directive, competitive dialogue is a procedure in which any economic operator may request to participate and where the contracting authority conducts a dialogue with the candidates admitted to that procedure, with the aim of developing one or more suitable alternatives capable of meeting its requirements, and on the basis of which the candidates chosen are invited to tender. Contracting authorities which carry out particularly complex projects may, without any fault on their part, find it objectively impossible to define the means of satisfying their needs or of assessing what the market can offer in the way of technical solutions and/or financial/legal solutions. This situation may arise in particular with the implementation of important integrated transport infrastructure projects, large computer networks or projects involving complex and structured financing, the financial and legal make-up of which cannot be defined in advance. To the extent that use of open or restricted procedures does not allow the award of such contracts, a flexible procedure should be provided which preserves not only competition between economic operators but also the need for the contracting authorities to discuss all aspects of the contract with each candidate. However, this procedure must not be used in such a way as to restrict or distort competition, particularly by altering any fundamental aspects of the offers, or by imposing substantial new requirements on the successful tenderer, or by involving any tenderer other than the one selected as the most economically advantageous.

For clarification purposes, a public contract is considered to be "particularly complex" where the contracting authorities: are not objectively able to define the technical means in accordance with Article 23(3)(b), (c) or (d), not capable of satisfying their needs or objectives, and/or are not objectively able to specify the legal and/or financial make-up of a project. Before launching a competitive dialogue for the award of a contract, contracting authorities may, using a technical dialogue, seek or accept advice which may be used in the preparation of the specifications provided, however, that such advice does not have the effect of precluding competition.

Article 29 of the Public Sector Directive regulates the use of the competitive dialogue as an award procedure. In the case of particularly complex contracts, Member States may provide that where contracting authorities consider that the use of the open or restricted procedure will not allow the award of the contract, the latter may make use of the competitive dialogue in accordance with this Article. A public contract must be awarded on the sole basis of the award criterion for the most economically advantageous tender. Contracting authorities are obliged to publish a contract notice setting out their needs and requirements, which they must define in that notice and/or in a descriptive document.

Contracting authorities must open, with the candidates selected in accordance with the relevant provisions of Articles 44 to 52 of the Public Sector Directive,[16] a dialogue the aim of which is to identify and define the means best suited to satisfying their needs. They may discuss all aspects of the contract with the chosen candidates during this dialogue. During the dialogue, contracting authorities must ensure equality of treatment among all tenderers. In particular, they must not provide information in a discriminatory manner which may give some tenderers an advantage over others. Contracting authorities may not reveal to the other participants solutions proposed or other confidential information communicated by a candidate participating in the dialogue without his/her agreement.

Contracting authorities may provide for the procedure to take place in successive stages in order to reduce the number of solutions to be discussed during the dialogue stage by applying the award criteria in the contract notice or the descriptive document. The contract notice or the descriptive document must indicate that recourse may be had to this option. The contracting authority must continue such dialogue until it can identify the solution or solutions, if necessary after comparing them, which are capable of meeting its needs. Having declared that the dialogue is concluded and having so informed the participants, contracting authorities must ask them to submit their final tenders on the basis of the solution or solutions presented and specified during the dialogue.

These tenders must contain all the elements required and necessary for the performance of the project. These tenders may be clarified, specified and fine-tuned at the request of the contracting authority. However, such clarification, specification, fine-tuning or additional information may not involve changes to the basic features of the tender or the call for tender, variations in which are likely to distort competition or have a discriminatory effect.

Contracting authorities must assess the tenders received on the basis of the award criteria laid down in the contract notice or the descriptive document and must choose the most economically advantageous tender in accordance with Article 53. At the request of the contracting authority, the tenderer identified as having submitted the most economically advantageous tender may be asked to clarify aspects of the tender or confirm commitments contained in the tender provided this does not have the effect of modifying substantial aspects of the tender or of the call for tender and does not risk distorting competition or causing discrimination. The contracting authorities may specify prices or payments to the participants in the dialogue.

Framework procurement

According to Article 1.5 of the Public Sector Directive, a framework agreement is an agreement between one or more contracting authorities and one or more economic operators, the purpose of which is to establish the terms governing contracts to be awarded during a given period, in particular with regard to price and, where appropriate, the quantity envisaged.

A Community definition of framework agreements, together with specific rules on framework agreements concluded for contracts falling within the scope of the Public Sector Directive, is provided in Article 32. Under these rules, when a contracting authority enters into a framework agreement in accordance with the provisions of the Public Sector Directive relating, in particular, to advertising, time limits and conditions for the submission of tenders, it may enter into contracts based on such a framework agreement during its term of validity either by applying the terms set forth in the framework agreement or, if all terms have not been fixed in advance in the framework agreement, by reopening competition between the parties to the framework agreement in relation to those terms. The reopening of competition should comply with certain rules the aim of which is to guarantee the required flexibility and to guarantee respect for the general principles, in particular the principle of equal treatment. For the same reasons, the term of the framework agreements should not exceed four years, except in cases duly justified by the contracting authorities.

Article 32 is the institutional foundation of framework agreements. Member States may provide that contracting authorities may conclude framework agreements. For the purpose of concluding a framework agreement, contracting authorities must follow the rules of procedure referred to in the Public Sector Directive for all phases up to the award of contracts based on that framework agreement. The parties to the framework agreement must be chosen by applying the award criteria set in accordance with Article 53.[17]

Contracts based on a framework agreement must be awarded in accordance with the procedures laid down in paragraphs 3 and 4 of Article 32. Those procedures may be applied only between the contracting authorities and the economic operators originally party to the framework agreement. When awarding contracts based on a framework agreement, the parties may under no circumstances make substantial amendments to the terms laid down in that framework agreement, in particular in the case referred to in paragraph 3. The term of a framework agreement may not exceed four years, save in exceptional cases duly justified, in particular by the subject of the framework agreement. Contracting authorities may not use framework agreements improperly or in such a way as to prevent, restrict or distort competition.

Article 32(3) stipulates that where a framework agreement is concluded with a single economic operator, contracts based on that agreement must be awarded within the limits of the terms laid down in the framework agreement. For the award of those contracts, contracting authorities may consult the operator party to the framework agreement in writing, requesting it to supplement its tender as necessary.

Article 32(4) stipulates that where a framework agreement is concluded with several economic operators, the latter must be at least three in number, insofar as there is a sufficient number of economic operators to satisfy the selection criteria and/or of admissible tenders which meet the award criteria. Contracts based on framework agreements concluded with several economic operators may be awarded either: i) by application of the terms laid down in the framework agreement without reopening competition, or ii) where not all the terms are laid down in the framework agreement, when the parties are again in competition on the basis of the same and, if necessary, more precisely formulated terms, and, where appropriate, other terms referred to in the specifications of the framework agreement, in accordance with a specific procedure which provides the following:

(a) for every contract to be awarded, contracting authorities must consult in writing the economic operators capable of performing the contract;
(b) contracting authorities must fix a time limit which is sufficiently long to allow tenders for each specific contract to be submitted, taking into account factors such as the complexity of the subject-matter of the contract and the time needed to send in tenders;
(c) tenders must be submitted in writing, and their content must remain confidential until the stipulated time limit for reply has expired;
(d) contracting authorities must award each contract to the tenderer who has submitted the best tender on the basis of the award criteria set out in the specifications of the framework agreement.

Electronic procurement

New electronic purchasing techniques are continually being developed. Such techniques help to increase competition and streamline public purchasing, particularly in terms of the savings in time and money which their use will allow. Contracting authorities may make use of electronic purchasing techniques, provided such use complies with the rules drawn up under the Public Sector Directive and the principles of equal treatment, nondiscrimination and transparency. To that extent, a tender submitted by a tenderer, in particular where competition has been reopened under a framework agreement or where a dynamic purchasing system is being used, may take the form of that tenderer's electronic catalogue.

According to Article 1.6 of the Public Sector Directive, a dynamic purchasing system is a completely electronic process for making commonly used purchases, the characteristics of which, as generally available on the market, meet the requirements of the contracting authority, which is limited in duration and open throughout its validity to any economic operator which satisfies the selection criteria and has submitted an indicative tender that complies with the specification. In view of the rapid expansion of electronic purchasing systems, appropriate rules should now be introduced to enable contracting authorities to take full advantage of the possibilities afforded by these systems. Against this background, it is necessary to define a completely electronic dynamic purchasing system for commonly used purchases, and lay down specific rules for setting up and operating such a system in order to ensure the fair treatment of any economic operator who wishes to take part therein. Any economic operator which submits an indicative tender in accordance with the specification and meets the selection criteria should be allowed to join such a system. This purchasing technique allows the contracting authority, through the establishment of a list of tenderers already selected and the opportunity given to new tenderers to take part, to have a particularly broad range of tenderers as a result of the electronic facilities available, and hence to ensure optimum use of public funds through broad competition.

The use of dynamic purchasing systems is described in Article 33. Member States may provide that contracting authorities may use dynamic purchasing systems. In order to set up a dynamic purchasing system, contracting authorities must follow the rules of the open procedure in all its phases up to the award of the contracts to be concluded under this system. All the tenderers satisfying the selection criteria and having submitted an indicative tender which complies with the specification and any possible additional documents, must be admitted to the system. Indicative tenders may be improved at any time provided that they continue to comply with the specification.

With a view to setting up the system and to the award of contracts under that system, contracting authorities must use solely electronic means in accordance with Article 42(2) to (5). For the purposes of setting up the dynamic purchasing system, contracting authorities must:

(a) publish a contract notice making it clear that a dynamic purchasing system is involved;
(b) indicate in the specification, amongst other matters, the nature of the purchases envisaged under that system, as well as all the necessary information concerning the purchasing system, the electronic equipment used and the technical connection arrangements and specifications;
(c) offer by electronic means, on publication of the notice and up to the expiry of the system, unrestricted, direct and full access to the specification and to any additional documents and must indicate in the notice the internet address at which such documents may be consulted.

Contracting authorities must give any economic operator, throughout the entire period of the dynamic purchasing system, the possibility of submitting an indicative tender and of being admitted to the system. They must complete evaluation within a maximum of 15 days from the date of submission of the indicative tender. However, they may extend the evaluation period provided that no invitation to tender is issued in the meantime. The contracting authority must inform the tenderer referred to in the first subparagraph at the earliest possible opportunity, of its admittance to the dynamic purchasing system or of the rejection of its indicative tender.

Each specific contract must be the subject of an invitation to tender. Before issuing the invitation to tender, contracting authorities must publish a simplified contract notice inviting all interested economic operators to submit an indicative tender within a time limit that may not be less than 15 days from the date on which the simplified notice was sent. Contracting authorities may not proceed with tendering until they have completed evaluation of all the indicative tenders received by that deadline.

Contracting authorities must invite all tenderers admitted to the system to submit a tender for each specific contract to be awarded under the system. To that end they must set a time limit for the submission of tenders. They must award the contract to the tenderer which submitted the best tender on the basis of the award criteria set out in the contract notice for the establishment of the dynamic purchasing system. A dynamic purchasing system may not last for more than four years, except in duly justified exceptional cases. Contracting authorities may not resort to this system to prevent, restrict or distort competition. No charges may be billed to the interested economic operators or to parties to the system.

Electronic auctions

According to Article 1.7 of the Public Sector Directive an electronic auction is a repetitive process involving an electronic device for the presentation of new prices, revised downwards, and/or new values concerning certain elements of tenders, which occurs after an initial full evaluation of the tenders, enabling them to be ranked using automatic evaluation methods. Consequently, certain service contracts and certain works contracts having as their subject-matter intellectual performances, such as the design of works, may not be the object of electronic auctions.

Since use of the technique of electronic auctions is likely to increase, such auctions should be given a Community definition and governed by specific rules in order to ensure that they operate in full accordance with the principles of equal treatment, non-discrimination and transparency. To that end, provision should be made for such electronic auctions to deal only with contracts for works, supplies or services for which the specifications can be determined with precision. Such may in particular be the case for recurring supplies, works and service contracts. With the same objective, it must also to be possible to establish the respective ranking of the tenderers at any stage of the electronic auction. Recourse to electronic auctions enables contracting authorities to ask tenderers to submit new prices, revised downwards, and when the contract is awarded to the most economically advantageous tender, also to improve elements of the tenders other than prices. In order to guarantee compliance with the principle of transparency, only the elements suitable for automatic evaluation by electronic means, without any intervention and/or appreciation by the contracting authority, that is, only the elements which are quantifiable so that they can be expressed in figures or percentages, may be the object of electronic auctions. On the other hand, those aspects of the tenders which imply an appreciation of non-quantifiable elements should not be the object of electronic auctions. Consequently, certain works contracts and certain service contracts having as their subject matter intellectual performances, such as the design of works, should not be the object of electronic auctions.

Article 54 of the Public Sector Directive stipulates the framework for the use of electronic auctions. Member States may provide that contracting authorities may use electronic auctions. In open, restricted or negotiated procedures in the case referred to in Article 30(1)(a), the contracting authorities may decide that the award of a public contract must be preceded by an electronic auction when the contract specifications can be established with precision. In the same circumstances, an electronic auction may be held on the reopening of competition among the parties to a framework agreement as provided for in the second indent of the second subparagraph of Article 32(4) and on the opening for competition of contracts to be awarded under the dynamic purchasing system referred to in Article 33. The electronic auction must be based: i) either solely on prices when the contract is awarded to the lowest price, or ii) on prices and/or on the new values of the features of the tenders indicated in the specification when the contract is awarded to the most economically advantageous tender.

Contracting authorities who decide to hold an electronic auction must state that fact in the contract notice. The specifications must include, *inter alia*, the following details:

(a) the features, the values for which will be the subject of electronic auction, provided that such features are quantifiable and can be expressed in figures or percentages;
(b) any limits on the values which may be submitted, as they result from the specifications relating to the subject of the contract;
(c) the information which will be made available to tenderers in the course of the electronic auction and, where appropriate, when it will be made available to them;
(d) the relevant information concerning the electronic auction process;
(e) the conditions under which the tenderers will be able to bid and, in particular, the minimum differences which will, where appropriate, be required when bidding;
(f) the relevant information concerning the electronic equipment used and the arrangements and technical specifications for connection.

Before proceeding with an electronic auction, contracting authorities must make a full initial evaluation of the tenders in accordance with the award criterion/criteria set and with the weighting fixed for them. All tenderers who have submitted admissible tenders must be invited simultaneously by electronic means to submit new prices and/or new values; the invitation must contain all relevant information concerning individual connection to the electronic equipment being used and must state the date and time of the start of the electronic auction. The electronic auction may take place in a number of successive phases. The electronic auction may not start sooner than two working days after the date on which invitations are sent out.

When the contract is to be awarded on the basis of the most economically advantageous tender, the invitation must be accompanied by the outcome of a full evaluation of the relevant tenderer, carried out in accordance with the weighting provided for in the first subparagraph of Article 53(2). The invitation must also state the mathematical formula to be used in the electronic auction to determine automatic re-rankings on the basis of the new prices and/or new values submitted. That formula must incorporate the weighting of all the criteria fixed to determine the most economically advantageous tender, as indicated in the contract notice or in the specifications; for that purpose, any ranges must, however, be reduced beforehand to a specified value. Where variants are authorised, a separate formula must be provided for each variant.

Throughout each phase of an electronic auction, the contracting authorities must instantaneously communicate to all tenderers at least sufficient information to enable them to ascertain their relative rankings at any moment. They may also communicate other information concerning other prices or values submitted, provided that that is stated in the specifications. They may also at any time announce the number of participants in that phase of the auction. In no case, however, may they disclose the identities of the tenderers during any phase of an electronic auction.

Contracting authorities must close an electronic auction in one or more of the following manners:

(a) in the invitation to take part in the auction they must indicate the date and time fixed in advance;
(b) when they receive no more new prices or new values which meet the requirements concerning minimum differences. In that event, the contracting authorities must state in the invitation to

take part in the auction the time which they will allow to elapse after receiving the last submission before they close the electronic auction;
(c) when the number of phases in the auction, fixed in the invitation to take part in the auction, has been completed. When the contracting authorities have decided to close an electronic auction in accordance with subparagraph (c), possibly in combination with the arrangements laid down in subparagraph (b), the invitation to take part in the auction must indicate the timetable for each phase of the auction.

After closing an electronic auction, contracting authorities must award the contract in accordance with Article 53 on the basis of the results of the electronic auction. Contracting authorities may not have improper recourse to electronic auctions nor may they use them in such a way as to prevent, restrict or distort competition or to change the subject-matter of the contract, as put up for tender in the published contract notice and defined in the specification.

The use of electronic signatures

Directive 1999/93/EC of the European Parliament and of the Council of 13 December 1999 on a Community framework for electronic signatures[18] and Directive 2000/31/EC of the European Parliament and of the Council of 8 June 2000 on certain legal aspects of information society services, in particular electronic commerce, in the internal market ('Directive on electronic commerce')[19] should, in the context of the Public Sector Directive, apply to the transmission of information by electronic means. The public procurement procedures and the rules applicable to service contests require a level of security and confidentiality higher than that required by these Directives. Accordingly, the devices for the electronic receipt of offers, requests to participate and plans and projects should comply with specific additional requirements. To this end, use of electronic signatures, in particular advanced electronic signatures, should, as far as possible, be encouraged. Moreover, the existence of voluntary accreditation schemes could constitute a favourable framework for enhancing the level of certification service provision for these devices.

Public procurement and the environment

Under Article 6 of the Treaty, environmental protection requirements are to be integrated into the definition and implementation of the

Community policies and activities referred to in Article 3 of that Treaty, in particular with a view to promoting sustainable development. The Public Sector Directive therefore clarifies how the contracting authorities may contribute to the protection of the environment and the promotion of sustainable development, whilst ensuring the possibility of obtaining the best value for money for their contracts. Nothing in the Public Sector Directive should prevent the imposition or enforcement of measures necessary to protect public policy, public morality, public security, health, human and animal life or the preservation of plant life, in particular with a view to sustainable development, provided that these measures are in conformity with the Treaty.

The technical specifications drawn up by public purchasers need to allow public procurement to be opened up to competition. To this end, it must be possible to submit tenders which reflect the diversity of technical solutions. Accordingly, it must be possible to draw up the technical specifications in terms of functional performance and requirements, and, where reference is made to the European standard or, in the absence thereof, to the national standard, tenders based on equivalent arrangements must be considered by contracting authorities. To demonstrate equivalence, tenderers should be permitted to use any form of evidence. Contracting authorities must be able to provide a reason for any decision that equivalence does not exist in a given case. Contracting authorities that wish to define environmental requirements for the technical specifications of a given contract may lay down the environmental characteristics, such as a given production method, and/or specific environmental effects of product groups or services. They can use, but are not obliged to use appropriate specifications that are defined in ecolabels, such as the European Eco-label, (multi-)national eco-labels or any other eco-label provided the requirements for the label are drawn up and adopted on the basis of scientific information using a procedure in which stakeholders, such as government bodies, consumers, manufacturers, distributors and environmental organisations can participate, and provided the label is accessible and available to all interested parties. Contracting authorities should, whenever possible, lay down technical specifications so as to take into account accessibility criteria for people with disabilities or design for all users. The technical specifications should be clearly indicated, so that all tenderers know what the requirements established by the contracting authority cover.

In appropriate cases, in which the nature of the works and/or services justifies applying environmental management measures or schemes during the performance of a public contract, the application of such measures or schemes may be required. Environmental management schemes, whether or not they are registered under Community instruments such as Regulation (EC) No 761/2001 (EMAS),[20] can demonstrate that the economic operator has the technical capability to perform the contract. Moreover, a description of the measures implemented by the economic operator to ensure the same level of environmental protection should be accepted as an alternative to environmental management registration schemes as a form of evidence.

Article 50 deals with Environmental management standards. It provides that contracting authorities may require the production of certificates drawn up by independent bodies attesting the compliance of the economic operator with certain environmental management standards, and they must refer to the Community Eco-Management and Audit Scheme (EMAS) or to environmental management standards based on the relevant European or international standards certified by bodies conforming to Community law or the relevant European or international standards concerning certification. They must recognise equivalent certificates from bodies established in other Member States. They must also accept other evidence of equivalent environmental management measures from economic operators.

Procurement and employment

Employment and occupation are key elements in guaranteeing equal opportunities for all and contribute to integration in society. In this context, sheltered workshops and sheltered employment programmes contribute efficiently towards the integration or reintegration of people with disabilities in the labour market. However, such workshops might not be able to obtain contracts under normal conditions of competition. Consequently, it is appropriate that Member States may reserve the right to participate in award procedures for public contracts to such workshops or reserve performance of contracts to the context of sheltered employment programmes.

According to Article 19, a specific category of public sector contracts are regarded as reserved contracts. Member States reserve the right to participate in public contract award procedures to sheltered workshops, or provide for such contracts to be performed in the context of sheltered employment programmes where most of the employees concerned are disabled persons who, by reason of the nature or the seriousness of their impairment, cannot carry on occupations under normal conditions. The contract notice must make reference to this provision.

The laws, regulations and collective agreements, at both national and Community level, which are in force in the areas of employment conditions and safety at work apply during performance of a public contract, provided that such rules, and their application, comply with Community law. In cross-border situations, where workers from one Member State provide services in another Member State for the purpose of performing a public contract, Directive 96/71/EC concerning the posting of workers in the framework of the provision of services[21] lays down the minimum conditions which must be observed by the host country in respect of such posted workers. If national law contains provisions to this effect, non-compliance with those obligations may be considered to be grave misconduct or an offence concerning the professional conduct of the economic operator concerned, liable to lead to the exclusion of that economic operator from the procedure for the award of a public contract.

Public procurement and WTO

Council Decision 94/800/EC, which covered the Agreements reached in the Uruguay Round multilateral negotiations[22] (1986 to 1994), approved the WTO Agreement on Government Procurement, the aim of which is to establish a multilateral framework of balanced rights and obligations relating to public contracts with a view to achieving the liberalisation and expansion of world trade. In view of the international rights and commitments devolving on the Community as a result of the acceptance of the Agreement, the arrangements to be applied to tenderers and products from signatory third countries are those defined by the Agreement. This Agreement does not have direct effect. The contracting authorities, covered by the Agreement which comply with the Public Sector Directive and which apply the latter to economic operators of third countries which are signatories to the Agreement, should therefore be in conformity with the Agreement. It is also appropriate that those coordinating provisions should guarantee for Community economic operators' conditions for participation in public procurement which are just as favourable as those reserved for economic operators of third countries which are signatories to the Agreement.

Procurement and culture

The awarding of public contracts for certain audiovisual services in the field of broadcasting should allow aspects of cultural or social significance to be taken into account which render application of procurement rules inappropriate. For these reasons, an exception must therefore be made for public service contracts for the purchase, development, production or co-production of off-the-shelf programmes and other preparatory services, such as those relating to scripts or artistic performances necessary for the production of the programme and contracts concerning broadcasting times. However, this exclusion should not apply to the supply of technical equipment necessary for the production, co-production and broadcasting of such programmes. A broadcast should be defined as transmission and distribution using any form of electronic network.

Procurement, small and medium enterprises and subcontracting

In order to encourage the involvement of small and medium-sized undertakings in the public contracts procurement market, it is advisable to include provisions on subcontracting. According to Article 25, in the contract documents, the contracting authority may ask or may be required by a Member State to ask the tenderer to indicate in his tender any share of the contract he may intend to subcontract to third parties and any proposed subcontractors. This indication must be without prejudice to the question of the principal economic operator's liability. The theme of public procurement and subcontracting originates in the original Works Directives where contracting authorities are allowed to specify to concessionaires a minimum percentage of the works to be subcontracted. Along these lines, Article 60 of the Public Sector Directive provides that the contracting authority may either: (a) require the concessionaire to award contracts representing a minimum of 30 per cent of the total value of the work for which the concession contract is to be awarded, to third parties, at the same time providing the option for candidates to increase this percentage, this minimum percentage being specified in the concession contract, or (b) request the candidates for concession contracts to specify in their tenders the percentage, if any, of the total value of the work for which the concession contract is to be awarded which they intend to assign to third parties.

Contractual performance and public procurement

Contract performance conditions are compatible with the Public Sector Directive provided they are not directly or indirectly discriminatory and are indicated in the contract notice or in the contract documents.

They may, in particular, be intended to favour on-site vocational training, the employment of people experiencing particular difficulty in achieving integration, the fight against unemployment or the protection of the environment. For instance, mention may be made, amongst other things, of the requirements – applicable during performance of the contract – to recruit long-term job-seekers or to implement training measures for the unemployed or young persons, to comply in substance with the provisions of the basic International Labour Organisation (ILO) Conventions, assuming that such provisions have not been implemented in national law, and to recruit more disabled persons than are required under national legislation.

According to Article 26 which stipulates conditions for performance of contracts, contracting authorities may lay down special conditions relating to the performance of a contract, provided that these are compatible with Community law and are indicated in the contract notice or in the specifications. The conditions governing the performance of a contract may, in particular, concern social and environmental considerations.

Procurement and probity

The award of public contracts to economic operators who have participated in a criminal organisation or who have been found guilty of corruption or of fraud to the detriment of the financial interests of the European Communities or of money laundering should be avoided. Where appropriate, the contracting authorities should ask candidates or tenderers to supply relevant documents and, where they have doubts concerning the personal situation of a candidate or tenderer, they may seek the cooperation of the competent authorities of the Member State concerned. The exclusion of such economic operators should take place as soon as the contracting authority has knowledge of a judgement concerning such offences rendered in accordance with national law that has the force of *res judicata*. If national law contains provisions to this effect, non-compliance with environmental legislation or with legislation on unlawful agreements in public contracts, which has been the subject of a final judgement or a decision having equivalent effect, may be considered as a professional or grave misconduct of the economic operator concerned. Non-observance of national provisions implementing the Council Directives 2000/78/EC[23] and 76/207/EEC[24] concerning equal treatment of workers, which has been the subject of a final judgement or a decision having equivalent effect, may be considered an offence concerning the professional conduct of the economic operator concerned or grave misconduct.

Article 45 of the Public Sector Directive deals with the personal situation of the candidate or tenderer. It provides that any candidate or tenderer who has been the subject of a conviction by final judgement of which the contracting authority is aware for one or more of the reasons listed below, must be excluded from participation in a public contract:

(a) participation in a criminal organisation, as defined in Article 2(1) of Council Joint Action 98/733/JHA[25];
(b) corruption, as defined in Article 3 of the Council Act of 26 May 1997[26] and Article 3(1) of Council Joint Action 98/742/JHA[27] respectively;
(c) fraud within the meaning of Article 1 of the Convention relating to the protection of the financial interests of the European Communities[28];
(d) money laundering, as defined in Article 1 of Council Directive 91/308/EEC of 10 June 1991 on prevention of the use of the financial system for the purpose of money laundering.[29]

Member States must specify, in accordance with their national law and having regard for Community law, the implementing conditions for this paragraph. They may provide for derogation from the requirement referred to in the first subparagraph for overriding requirements in the general interest. For the purposes of this paragraph, the contracting authorities must, where appropriate, ask candidates or tenderers to supply the documents referred to in paragraph 3 and may, where they have doubts concerning the personal situation of such candidates or tenderers, also apply to the competent authorities to obtain any information they consider necessary on the personal situation of the candidates or tenderers concerned. Where the information concerns a candidate or tenderer established in a State other than that of the contracting authority, the contracting authority may seek the cooperation of the competent authorities. Having regard for the national laws of the Member State where the candidates or tenderers are established, such requests must relate to legal and/or natural persons, including, if appropriate, company directors and any person having powers of representation, decision or control in respect of the candidate or tenderer.

The award criteria

Contracts should be awarded on the basis of objective criteria which ensure compliance with the principles of transparency, non-discrimination and equal treatment and which guarantee that tenders are assessed in conditions of effective competition. As a result, it is appropriate to allow the application of two award criteria only: "the lowest price" and "the most economically advantageous tender".

To ensure compliance with the principle of equal treatment in the award of contracts, it is appropriate to lay down an obligation – established by case-law – to ensure the necessary transparency to enable all tenderers to be reasonably informed of the criteria and arrangements which will be applied to identify the most economically advantageous tender. It is therefore the responsibility of contracting authorities to indicate the criteria for the award of the contract and the relative weighting given to each of those criteria in sufficient time for tenderers to be aware of them when preparing their tenders. Contracting authorities may derogate from indicating the weighting of the criteria for the award in duly justified cases for which they must be able to give reasons or where the weighting cannot be established in advance, in particular on account of the complexity of the contract. In such cases, they must indicate the descending order of importance of the criteria. Where the contracting authorities choose to award a contract to the most economically advantageous tender, they must assess the tenders in order to determine which one offers the best value for money. In order to do this, they must determine the economic and quality criteria which, taken as a whole, must make it possible to determine the most economically advantageous tender for the contracting authority. The determination of these criteria depends on the object of the contract since they must allow the level of performance offered by each tender to be assessed in the light of the object of the contract, as defined in the technical specifications and the value for money of each tender to be measured. In order to guarantee equal treatment, the criteria for the award of the contract should enable tenders to be compared and assessed objectively. If these conditions are fulfilled, economic and qualitative criteria for the award of the contract, such as meeting environmental requirements, may enable the contracting authority to meet the needs of the public concerned, as expressed in the specifications of the contract. Under the same conditions, a contracting authority may use criteria aiming to meet social requirements in response to the needs of particularly disadvantaged groups. Such requirements must be defined in the specifications of the contract and the disadvantaged groups concerned must be those intended to receive the works, supplies or services which are the object of the contract.

Exclusive rights in the utilities

The scope of existing Utilities Directive 98/38/EEC covers, at present, certain contracts awarded by contracting entities operating in the telecommunications sector. A legislative framework, as mentioned in the Fourth report on the implementation of the telecommunications regulations of 25 November 1998, has been adopted to open this sector. One of its consequences has been the introduction of effective competition, both *de jure* and *de facto,* in this sector. For information purposes, and in the light of this situation, the Commission has published a list of telecommunications services[30] which may already be excluded from the scope of that Directive by virtue of Article 8. Further progress has been confirmed in the Seventh report on the implementation of telecommunications regulations of 26 November 2001. The Commission considers that it is no longer necessary to regulate purchases by entities operating in this sector.

On the other hand, Directive 93/38/EEC excludes from its scope purchases of voice telephony, telex, mobile telephone, paging and satellite services. Those exclusions were introduced to take account of the fact that the services in question could frequently be provided only by one service provider in a given geographical area because of the absence of effective competition and the existence of special or exclusive rights. The introduction of effective competition in the telecommunications sector removes the justification for these exclusions. The Commission has therefore included the procurement of such telecommunications services in the scope of the new Utilities Directive.

The new Utilities Directive provides for an appropriate definition of the concept of special or exclusive rights. As a consequence of the definition, an entity may take advantage of a procedure for the expropriation or use of property or may place network equipment on, under or over the public highway. In particular, for the purposes of constructing networks or port or airport facilities, such activities will not in themselves constitute exclusive or special rights within the meaning of this Directive. Nor does the fact that an entity that supplies drinking water, electricity, gas or heat to a network which is itself operated by an entity enjoying special or exclusive rights granted by a competent authority of the Member State concerned in itself, constitute an exclusive or special right within the meaning of this Directive. Nor may rights granted by a Member State in any form, including by way of acts of concession, to a limited number of undertakings on the basis of objective, proportionate and non-discriminatory criteria that allow any interested party fulfilling those criteria to enjoy those rights, be considered special or exclusive rights.

Postal utilities

Taking into account the further opening up of Community postal services to competition and the fact that such services are provided through a network comprising contracting authorities, public undertakings and other undertakings, the award of contracts by entities providing postal services should be subject to the rules of the new Utilities Directive 2004/18/EC and aim at creating a framework for sound commercial practice which allows for greater flexibility than is offered by the existing Utilities Directive 93/38. For a definition of the activities in question, it is necessary to take into account the definitions of Directive 97/67/EC of the European Parliament and of the Council of 15 December 1997 on common rules for the development of the internal market of Community postal services and the improvement of quality of service.[31]

Irrespective of their legal status, entities providing postal services are not currently subject to the rules set out in Directive 93/38/EEC. The adjustment of contract award procedures to this Directive could therefore take longer to implement for such entities than for entities already subject to those rules which will merely have to adapt their procedures to the amendments made by this Directive.

Competitive markets in utilities

The new Utilities Directive should not apply to markets where the participants pursue an activity which is directly exposed to competition on markets to which access is not limited within the relevant Member State. The new Utilities Directive has therefore introduced a procedure, applicable to all sectors covered by its provisions that will enable the effects of current or future opening up to competition to be taken into account. Such a procedure should provide legal certainty for the entities concerned, as well as an appropriate decision making process, ensuring, within short time limits, uniform application of Community law in this area.

Direct exposure to competition should be assessed on the basis of objective criteria, taking account of the specific characteristics of the sector concerned. The implementation and application of appropriate Community legislation opening a given sector, or a part of it, will be considered to provide sufficient grounds for assuming there is free access to the market in question. Such appropriate legislation should be identified in an annex which can be updated by the Commission. When updating, the Commission takes into particular account the possible adoption of measures entailing a genuine opening up to competition of sectors other than those for which legislation is already mentioned in Annex XI, such as that of railway transports. Where free access to a given market does not result from the implementation of appropriate Community legislation, it should be demonstrated that, *de jure* and *de facto*, such access is free. For this purpose, the application by a Member State of Directive 94/22/EC, which opens up a sector such as the coal sector to competition, is a condition to be taken into account for the purposes of Article 30.

Article 30 of the new Utilities Directive provides for a procedure for establishing whether a given activity is directly exposed to competition. The question of whether an activity is directly exposed to competition shall be decided on the basis of criteria that are in conformity with the Treaty provisions on competition, such as the characteristics of the goods or services concerned, the existence of alternative goods or services, the prices and the actual or potential presence of more than one supplier of the goods or services in question. If free access to a given market cannot be presumed, it must be demonstrated that access to the market in question is free *de facto* and *de jure*.

When a Member State considers that access to the relevant market activity is free, it must notify the Commission and provide all relevant facts, and in particular of any law, regulation, administrative provision or agreement, where appropriate together with the position adopted by an independent national authority that is competent in relation to the regulation of activity concerned. The Commission can issue a Decision which verifies that the relevant activity is provided in a competitive environment. Such verification is also presumed if the Commission has not adopted a Decision concerning the inapplicability of the Utilities Directive within a certain period.[32]

Part 2 Future developments

Public procurement and Public-Private Partnerships

In the context of its Strategy for the internal market 2003–2006[33], the European Commission launched a Green Paper on Public-Private Partnerships (PPPs) and Community law on public procurement and concessions, in order to launch a debate on the best way to ensure that PPPs can develop in a context of effective competition and legal clarity. The publication of the Green Paper is also one of the actions planned under the European Initiative for Growth[34] and responds to certain requests made in the course of the public consultation on the Green Paper on services of general interest.[35]

The Green Paper aims to demonstrate the extent to which Community rules apply to the phase of selection of the private partner and to the subsequent phase, with a view to identifying any uncertainties, and to analyse the extent to which the Community framework is suited to the imperatives and specific characteristics of PPPs. A wide variety of instruments are available to make PPPs more open to competition in a transparent legal environment, i.e. legislative instruments, interpretative communications, actions to improve the coordination of national practice or the exchange of good practices between Member States.

The Green Paper on Public-Private Partnerships and Community Law on Public Contracts and Concessions[36] has introduced the phenomenon of PPPs from the perspective of Community legislation on public contracts and concessions. Community law does not lay down any special rules covering the phenomenon of PPPs. It nonetheless remains true that any act, whether it be contractual or unilateral, whereby a public entity entrusts the provision of an economic activity to a third party must be examined in the light of the rules and principles resulting from the Treaty, particularly as regards the principles of freedom of establishment and freedom to provide services (Articles 43 and 49 of the EC Treaty),[37] which encompass in particular the principles of transparency, equality of treatment, proportionality and mutual recognition.[38] Moreover, detailed provisions apply in the cases covered by the Directives relating to the coordination of procedures for the award of public contracts.[39] These Directives are thus "essentially aimed at protecting the interests of traders established in a Member State who wish to offer goods or services to contracting authorities established in another Member State and, to that end, to avoid both the risk of preference being given to national tenderers or applicants whenever a contract is awarded by the contracting authorities and the possibility that a body governed by public law may choose to be guided by considerations other than economic ones."[40] However, the application of the detailed provisions of these Directives is circumscribed by certain assumptions and mainly concerns the award of contracts.

The rules applicable to the selection of a private partner derive firstly from the definition of the contractual relationship which that party enters into with a contracting body.[41] Under Community secondary legislation, any contract for pecuniary interest concluded in writing between a contracting body and an operator, which have as their object the execution of works, or provision of a service, is designated as a "public works or public services contract".

The concept of "concession" is defined as a contract of the same type as a public contract except for the fact that the consideration for the works to be carried out or the services to be provided consists either solely in the right to exploit the construction or service, or in this right together with payment. The assessment of the elements in these definitions must, in the view of the Court, be made in such a way as to ensure that the Directive is not deprived of practical effect.[42] For example, the formalism attached to the concept of contract under national law cannot be advanced to deprive the Directives of their practical effect. Similarly, the pecuniary nature of the contract in question does not necessarily imply the direct payment of a price by the public partner, but may derive from any other form of economic consideration received by the private partner.

The contracts denoted as public works or public services contracts, defined as having priority,[43] are subject to the detailed provisions of Community Directives. The concessions of so-called "non-priority" works and public services contracts are governed only by some sparse provisions of secondary legislation. Lastly, some projects, and in particular services concessions, fall completely outside the scope of secondary legislation. The same is true of any assignment awarded in the form of a unilateral act.

The legislative framework governing the choice of private partner has thus been the subject of Community coordination at several levels and degrees of intensity, with a wide variety of approaches persisting at national level, even though any project involving the award of tasks to a third party is governed by a minimum base of principles deriving from Articles 43 to 49 of the EC Treaty.

The European Commission has already taken initiatives under public procurement law to deal with the PPP phenomenon. In 2000 it published an Interpretive Communication on concessions and Community public procurement law,[44] in which it defined, on the basis of the rules and principles derived from the Treaty and applicable secondary legislation, the outlines of the concept of concession in Community law and the obligations incumbent on the public authorities when selecting the economic operators to whom the concessions are granted. In addition, the new Directives of the European Parliament and the Council designed to modernise and simplify the Community legislative framework and to establish an innovative award procedure, designed principally to meet the specific features of the award of "particularly complex contracts" and thereby certain forms of PPPs. This new procedure, designated as "competitive dialogue", allows the public authorities to hold discussions with the applicant businesses in order to identify the solutions best suited to their needs.

Although the Green Paper focuses on issues covered by the law on public contracts and concessions, it should be noted that the Commission has already adopted measures, in certain fields, designed to remove barriers to PPPs. Thus, there has already been clarification of the rules on the treatment in the national accounts of contracts entered into by public entities under partnerships with private entities. It is worth noting that the adoption of the statute for a European company will facilitate trans-European PPPs.[45]

Revision of remedies in public procurement

The Remedies Directives 89/665 (review procedures/public supply and public works contracts in traditional sectors) and 92/13 (review procedures/public contracts in the water, energy, transport and telecommunications sectors) were designed to ensure effective implementation of the Directives on public procurement procedures. The opening up of public contracts to Community competition requires considerably stronger guarantees of transparency and non-discrimination, the effectiveness of which depends in particular on effective, rapid remedies at national level in the event of infringement of Community law on public procurement or of national rules transposing that law.

It has emerged, however, that not all public authorities in the Member States are implementing Community law on public procurement procedures in a satisfactory manner. The fact that only a small percentage of calls to tender are published (16.2 per cent for the European Union in 2002) and that the figure varies appreciably from one Member State to another, type of contracting authority and sector of activity, shows that the Directives are not yet fully effective. Clearly, it is not possible in this situation to take full advantage of genuine competition between potential tenderers throughout the Community.

Moreover, initial consultations launched by Commission departments with the Member States, economic operators and their representatives have revealed that the operation of national review procedures does not always make it possible to correct failures to respect Community law on public procurement effectively or quickly. It has also become apparent that the effectiveness of review mechanisms in the public procurement field varies appreciably from one Member State to another, which may discourage some economic operators from tendering for public contracts.

The process of revising the Remedies Directives, which will not be launched until the public procurement package is in force and the process of consulting all the interested parties is complete, will provide an opportunity to reassess and reinforce the effectiveness of the remedies provided for in Directives 89/665 and 92/13, as and where necessary.

At this stage, the Commission feels that any amendments should merely adapt and improve certain provisions of the Remedies Directives, without altering the philosophy and principles which underlie them. For example, the principle of the Member States' procedural autonomy will not be called into question. Member States will, in particular, retain the power to select a court, tribunal or independent authority competent to hear challenges relating to Community law on public procurement in accordance with their national law. However, the unsatisfactory situation brought about mainly by the very heterogeneous operation of Member States' national review procedures, and recent developments in case-law, require clarification of, or greater precision in the existing legislative framework, in order to ensure that there are sanctions which are effective and proportionate and which have a deterrent effect on infringements of Community law on public procurement, especially the most serious infringements (direct award of contracts without prior notification).

Adoption of the legislative package coordinating public procurement procedures will require technical adjustments to the Remedies Directives, namely, references to the new Directives. Essentially, therefore, the proposal to amend the Directives, if adopted by the Commission, should clarify or strengthen the existing provisions.

7
Public-Private Partnerships

Introduction

From a constitutional point of view, the state is under an obligation to provide a range of services to the public in the form of general infrastructure, healthcare, education, housing, transport, energy, defence, social security and policing to name a few. Traditionally, the state, either in its own capacity or through delegated monopolies and publicly controlled enterprises has engaged in market activities in order to serve public interest.

The concept of the state encapsulates an entrepreneurial dimension to the extent that it deploys wealth as policy instrument (*dominium*).[1] However, although entering into transactions with a view to providing goods, services and works to the public, this type of action by the state does not resemble the commercial characteristics of entrepreneurship, in as much as the aim of the state's activities is not the maximisation of profits[2] but the observance of public interest.

Such participation by the state in the relevant market takes place on behalf of the public and the society as a whole,[3] and the whole process has been described as *corporatism*.[4] In fact, *corporatism* has been seen as a market phenomenon which has created a specific forum for the supply and demand sides. This forum is known as *public markets*.[5] Public markets, in contrast to private ones, are the forum where *public interest*[6] substitutes *profit maximisation*.[7] *Corporatism* has also revealed the dimension of the state as a service provider to the public and that notion has always been linked with the procurement and subsequent state-ownership of the relevant assets. As a process of public sector management, corporatism has primarily been delivered through competitive tendering in order to satisfy the needs for accountability and transparency. Alongside the above objectives, competitive tendering has also represented a procedural delivery system for corporatism which has aimed, at least in principle, at introducing a balanced equilibrium in the supply/demand public procurement equation. Thus, the public and private sectors transact through an institutionalised structure which aims at replicating a regime of competition similar to that which exists in private markets.[8] Private markets are generally structured as a result of competitive pressures originating in the buyer/supplier interaction and their configuration can vary from monopoly/oligopoly to perfect competition, whereas public markets reveal a different picture, their structure being based upon a monopsony/oligopsony character.

Due to their different integral nature and structure, private and public markets require different control and regulation. Whereas the weaponry for the control of private markets is dominated by anti-trust law and policy, public markets are *fora* where the structural and behavioural remedial tools of competition law have limited applicability, mainly due to the fact that anti-trust often clashes, *ipso facto*, with the monopolistic structures which exist in public markets. The control of private markets through anti-trust law and policy reveal a set of rules of negative nature; contemporary anti-trust is ill-disposed towards cartels and abuse of dominance, thus undertakings must *restrain* their activities to an acceptable range which is pre-determined[9] by the competent authorities. On the other hand, public markets require a set of regulatory rules that have positive character and the sort of regulation envisaged aims at creating an appropriate environment which would facilitate *market access*.[10]

Irrespective of the different control and regulation private and public markets require, as a result of the difference in their integral nature and structure, the rationale behind the process of regulating public markets can be summarised as the attempt to establish an effectively competitive regime, similar to that envisaged for the operation of private markets.[11] The accomplishment of such an objective could bring about two types of beneficial effects for the supply/demand equation and enhance the image of corporatism. On the one hand, competition in public markets could benefit the supply side of the equation (the industry), by means of optimal allocation of resources, rationalisation of production and supply, promotion of mergers and acquisitions and elimination of sub-optimal firms and creation of genuinely competitive industries. On the other hand, corporatism operating through a genuinely competitive regime has been also deemed to yield substantial purchasing savings for the public sector.[12]

The integration of the public sector management through a liberalised public procurement regime underpins the concept of corporatism. The opening-up of traditional public procurement has envisaged a competitive regime which would instigate the convergence of prices for goods, works and services destined for the public sector. Savings could materialise as a result of the elimination of preferential purchasing patterns and discriminatory procurement decisions which often tend to favour sub-optimal *national champions* at the expense of competitive industries.

From corporatism to contractualised governance

If one accepts the fact that the introduction of elements of competition in public markets through competitive tendering would have desirable effects for corporatism, a question which might arise is to what extent private markets can be entrusted with the delivery of public services, and, as a consequence, if the concept of corporatism is compatible with them. As mentioned previously, private markets operate under the laws of demand and supply and the private sector is profit orientated. A first step from corporatism towards government by contract appears to be the process of privatisation. Privatisation, as a process of transfer of public assets and operations to private hands, on grounds of market efficiency and competition, as well as responsiveness to customer demand and quality considerations is often accompanied by simultaneous regulation by the state, in the form of a legal framework within which privatised industries will pursue public interest functions. It is not entirely clear if the process of privatisation would reclaim public markets and transform them to private ones. One should never underestimate the fact that the control of operations related to public interest remains within the competence of the state in the form of the regulatory regime, thus maintaining strong public market characteristics. The extent to which the market freedom of a privatised entity could be curtailed by regulatory frameworks deserves a complex and thorough analysis, which exceeds by far the remit of this article. However, it could be maintained that through the privatisation process, the previously clear-cut distinction between public and private markets becomes blur, as a new market place emerges. This type of market embraces strong public law elements to the extent that it is regulated by the state with a view to observing public interest in the relevant operations. The economic freedom and the risks associated with such operations are also subject to regulation, a fact which implies that the above regulatory framework incorporates more than mere procedural rules. This market place reveals a transformation from traditional *corporatism* to a public management system where *governance is dispersed through contract* under terms and conditions determined by the state.

Alongside privatisation, the notion of *contracting out* represents a further departure from the premises of traditional corporatism. The notion of *contracting out* is an exercise which aims at achieving potential savings and efficiency gains for contracting authorities, when they *test the market* in an attempt to define whether the provision of works or the delivery of services from a commercial operator could be cheaper than that from the in-house team. Contracting out differs from privatisation to the extent that the former represents a transfer of undertaking only, whereas the latter denotes transfer of ownership. Contracting out depicts a price-discipline exercise by the state, against the principle of *insourcing*, where, the self-sufficient nature of corporatism resulted in budgetary inefficiencies and poor quality of deliverables to the public. Contracting out uses competitive tendering, which is the procedural mechanism for the delivery of corporatism as the trojan horse in an attempt to maximise outsourcing in the delivery of public service.

Both the privatisation and contracting out processes resemble the *principle of outsourcing*, which is often utilised in restructuring exercises in the private sector. Outsourcing introduces elements of contractualisation in the production process, as sub-contracting takes over from the in-house operation in the production chain. Government by contract, along the same lines, introduces the principle of outsourcing in the dispersement of public service, but the *contractualised governance*[13] appears far more stringent than private sector outsourcing by virtue of its regulation. Furthermore, apart from operational savings, outsourcing in the private sector would normally spread the risk factor amongst the operations in the production chain. If the sub-contractor cannot deliver according to the expectations, the main operator can switch to an alternative with no major implications. Outsourcing, therefore, introduces an element of flexibility in the production process. It remains to be seen whether contractualised governance or government by contract conforms with the same parameters (savings, risk sharing, flexibility) as private sector outsourcing.

The integral characteristics of privately financed projects reveal the degree that the state and its organs are prepared to drift away from *traditional corporatism*[14] towards *contractualised governance*. The degree of departure from traditional corporatism also reflects the state's perception *vis-à-vis* its responsibilities towards the public. A shift towards contractualised governance would indicate the departure from the assumption that the state embraces both roles of asset owner and service deliverer. It should also insinuate the shrinkage of the state and its organs and the need to define a range of core activities that are not to be contractualised.[15]

Part 1 The emergence of the Private Finance Initiative

The Private Finance Initiative (PFI) represents a process of public sector management which envisages the utilisation of private finances in the delivery of public services and the provision of public infrastructure. The PFI has arrived in times when the role and the responsibilities of the state are being redefined and also has been seen as part of a process of slimming the state down to a bare minimum of fiscal responsibilities towards the public. The state then assumes a regulatory role in the market place where the private sector is elevated to a service deliverer. The principal benefit from such an exercise could be that the public sector does not have to commit its own, often scarce, capital resources in delivering public services. Other reasons put forward for involving private finances in delivering public services include quality improvement, innovation, management efficiency and effectiveness, elements that are often underlying the private sector entrepreneurship. Consequently, the public sector would receive value-for-money in the delivery of services to the public, whereas it can also be maintained that through this process the state manages in a better way public finances, to the extent that capital resources can be utilised in priority areas.

When the Private Finance Initiative was launched in 1992, it did not receive the envisaged response from either the public or the private sectors. The initial approach to privately financed projects by the public sector represented a disguised tendering for their financing, and as such it revealed a number of procedural and commercial inadequacies in the whole process. Policy makers incorrectly assumed that the mere private financing of projects could enhance their quality and value-for-money, as well as transform the often ill-fated traditional public procurement process into a supply chain system of advanced structure and entrepreneurial flair. The PFI was wrongfully conceived as a *panacea* for the limitations of the traditional public procurement process,[16] which was blamed for inefficiencies and poor value-for-money.[17]

In principle, privately financed projects destined for the public sector have been an option in the UK public procurement process since the eighties, where the government, with great deal of caution, allowed the conclusion of a limited number of contracts. The government applied the so called *Ryrie Rules* in the process of allowing private finances to be used in public projects, subject to two strict conditions. The first one concerned the cost-effective nature of the privately financed delivery in comparison with a publicly funded alternative. To reach such a conclusion, contracting authorities should have established a public sector comparator, whereby the privately financed delivery model could be tested and compared against the traditional publicly funded one. The second condition for the government to give clearance for a privately financed project related to the compulsory substitution of publicly funded schemes with privately funded ones. In other words, private finances were conceived as an exclusive alternative method in delivering public services and not as a complementary one.

Meeting the two conditions of the *Ryrie Rules* was not an easy exercise for public authorities, particularly in attempting to establish the cost-effective nature of a privately financed project versus a publicly funded alternative and its value-for-money. Quite often the rationale behind such comparisons was founded upon unsound grounds. For example, in order to achieve a meaningful comparison, the two delivery models should be benchmarked against a set of *variable parameters* (e.g. technical merit, quality of deliverables, aesthetic reasons, maintenance facilities, warranties, and last but not least, overall price). This was not always the case, as the specifications of the project were firmly predetermined from the outset by the public authority in question and the pricing of the project evolved around them. Hence, the only *variable parameter* to compare the two delivery models unfolded around pricing. The procurement of privately financed projects was a disguised tendering for their financing, and as such it was bound to have very limited impact upon the procurement process. There was little chance that the private sector could beat the privileged position governments enjoy in the financial markets and raise the capital required to finance a service or an infrastructure project in more preferable terms. Furthermore, the private sector would normally require extra levels of capital return for the deferred payment facility that the public sector would use for repayments during the life of the contract. In the light of the above considerations, it is not a surprise that only a handful of privately financed projects were concluded, particularly complex projects of massive scale and of multi-national dimension.

Against this background and bearing in mind the recently imposed restraints on public expenditure, e.g. prudence in Public Sector

Borrowing Requirement (PSBR), EMU convergence criteria, the PFI was given a new lease of life when the 1997 Labour Government committed itself, in principle, to the concept and as a consequence, public authorities in the United Kingdom have been required to explore all potential ways of involving private finances in their public procurement process prior to committing their own funds.

There are two broad categories under which privately financed projects can be classified. The first one covers the so-called *financially free standing ones*, where it is expected that the private sector designs, builds, finances and then operates an asset. The recovery of its costs is guaranteed by direct charges on the users of the service which the particular asset provides. These projects are often described as *concession contracts*, where the successful contractor is granted an exclusive right over a period of time to exploit the asset that it has financed, designed and built. The state and its authorities may also contribute, in financial terms, to the repayments in order to render the project viable or the service charge to the end users acceptable. The second category of privately financed projects embraces projects which have as their object the provision of services by the private sector to the public, in conjunction with and subject to the relevant investment in assets that are necessary to deliver the required service to the public. In such cases, the private sector provider is reimbursed by a series of future payments by the contracting authority, payments which depend upon the successful delivery of those services in accordance with certain specified quality standards.

Privately financed projects have two constituent elements which are prerequisites for their completion: i) a genuine allocation of contractual risk and ii) value-for-money for the public sector. The first element represents the integral balance of contractual relationships. Under traditional public procurement transactions, a widespread assumption indicates that contractual relationships are based upon a disproportionate risk allocation amongst the parties. Although in traditional public procurement systems, the demand side appears the dominant part in the equation, when it comes to risk allocation, the roles appear reversed.[18] Risk allocation is a much misunderstood concept in contractual relationships in general, but particularly in public purchasing transactions it has never been properly addressed.[19] Risk allocation is the result of negotiations between the parties and is normally expected to reflect the pricing element of contractual arrangements between them. Thus, risk and pricing operate in an analogous relation within a contract. The more risk a party assumes, the higher the price to be paid by the other party, and *vice versa*.

In traditional public procurement transactions the demand side inevitably undertakes too much risk, as a result of its practices.[20] The award of publicly funded contracts takes place predominately by reference to *the lowest price*, which constitutes one of the two permissible award criteria under the procurement rules (the other being the criterion of *the most economically advantageous offer*). When contracting authorities award their contracts by reference to pricing, this would normally reflect the amount of risk they are prepared to resume.[21]

There is not any golden rule as to what represents an acceptable risk transfer in a contract, the latter being private or public, for risk allocation primarily reflects the parties' perception of a transaction with reference to their own criteria. These criteria are often influenced by a range of parameters such as speculation, fear, certainty, as well as by a number of qualitative attributes of the parties, e.g. sound forecast and planning, market intelligence.

On the other hand, value-for-money as the second constituent element of a privately financed project should reflect a benchmarked comparison between public and privately financed models of service delivery. The comparison should not only take into account factors such as quality or technical merit, but mainly aspects of sound supply chain management reflecting efficiency gains, in the sense that the conclusion of a privately financed project would resemble to a large extent a contractual arrangement between private parties. Value-for-money as an element in a PFI deal is a precursor of best purchasing practice by contracting authorities and also reflects the underlying competitive elements which are necessary in order to meet the accountability and transparency standards and principles.[22]

The intellectual origins of the Private Finance Initiative

The origins of the PFI can be traced in the attempts to moderate the widespread dissatisfaction from traditional public procurement methods. The nexus of contractual relations between public authorities and the private sector has been often criticised for not giving the best value-for-money. The criticism has been primarily directed towards three elements of the process: i) adversarial contractual relations as a result of compulsory competitive tendering, ii) inefficient risk allocation, and iii) poor contractual performances resulting in delayed and over-budgeted completions.

Competitive tendering in public procurement has been reproached for creating a confrontational environment, where the antagonising relations which emanate from the tendering and contract award processes are often reflected in the performance stage of the contract. Public procurement procedures which are based upon a win-to-win process have been deemed to deprive significant elements one can expect in the delivery of public services. For example, competitive tendering has been dissociated with innovation and quality. Also, as a result of inefficiently written specifications upon which the tender should be constructed, the deliverables often differ dramatically from contractual expectations.

On the other hand, risk allocation is probably the most crucial element in contractual relations that affects pricing as well as the overall contractual framework. Risk represents the level of financial exposure of a party prior to, after the conclusion of a contract or during its performance. In traditional public procurement, the risk allocation tends to favour the supply side, which mainly assumes the risks related to the tendering process. During the performance stage of the contract and up to its completion, the demand side could, usually, shift a considerable amount of risk by requesting from the supply side performance or defects bonds or other means of financial guarantees.

Finally, traditional procurement methods have often revealed a picture of poor contracts management as a result of inefficient control systems operated by public authorities. Poor contracts management has resulted in abysmally out-of-control contractual performances with all the financial consequences attributed to the delayed completion of the projects.

Competitive tendering, amongst other things, has been deemed responsible for cyclical demand structures in public purchasing, a situation where the supply side (the industry) responds to the demand side (public authorities) through cycles of institutionalised bureaucracy (tender submission, selection, evaluation and contract award processes). The demand side has institutionalised the procurement process, by imposing a disciplinarian compartmentalisation of the relevant processes (advertisement, expression of interest, selection, qualification, tender, and contract award).

The institutionalisation of the procurement process intends to facilitate the main objectives of the European public procurement rules: the establishment of the principles of transparency and competitiveness in the award of public contracts and the achievement of savings for the public sector. The bureaucratic system which supports traditional public procurement uses the effects of transparency as leverage for value-for-money results. The fact that more suppliers are aware of a forthcoming public contract and the fact that interesting suppliers are aware that their rivals are informed about it, indicates two distinctive parameters which are relevant to savings and value-for-money. The first parameter focuses on value-for-money for the demand side and reveals the possibility for contracting authorities to compare prices and quality. The second parameter has an effect on the supply side of the equation (the suppliers) which amongst other things cannot longer rely on lack of price comparisons when serving the public sector. Openness in public procurement, by definition, results in price competition and the benefits for contracting authorities appear achievable. The institutionalised nature of the public procurement process also reflects the relative balance of powers in the demand/supply equation.

However, the traditional public procurement process often suffers from unnecessarily repetitive functions (in particularly the advertisement, selection and qualification processes) which can be cost ineffective and pose a considerable financial burden on the demand side. In addition, the institutionalised process of public procurement may pose a question over long-term savings and value for money considerations. Price competition, as a result of the awareness of forthcoming public contracts, represents a rather static effect in the value for money process. The fact that more and more interested suppliers are aware and do submit tenders, in the long run, appears rather as a burden. If transparency and the resulting price competitiveness are based on a *win-to-win* process, the potential benefits for contracting authorities could easily be counterbalanced by the administrative costs in tender evaluation and replies to unsuccessful tenderers. Furthermore, the risk management factor is much higher in a win-to-win purchasing scenario. Price competitiveness represents also some threats for contracting authorities, to the extent that quality of deliverables as well as the delivery process itself could be jeopardised, if contracting authorities deal with different and unknown contractors. It could thus be argued here that price competitiveness, as a trade effect potentially beneficial for the demand side of the public purchasing equation, has a static character. It seems that it does not take into account medium or long-term purchasing patterns, as well as counter effects of competition. Two elements deserve further analysis here:

The first raises questions over the aggregate loss of the economy through transparent competitive purchasing patterns. For example, if a large number of interested suppliers submit their offer to a particular contracting authority, two types of costs should be examined. Firstly, the cost which is attributed to the response and tendering stage of the procurement process. Human and capital resources are directed by the suppliers towards the preparation of documents and the submission of the offers. If one of these suppliers wins the contract, the remaining would have suffered an unrecoverable loss. If that aggregate loss exceeds the benefit/saving accomplished by the contracting authority by following transparent and competitive purchasing patterns, value for money has not been achieved. Secondly, along the same lines, the evaluation and selection process during tendering represents a considerable administrative cost for the contracting authorities. If the principle of transparency complements the principle of equal treatment, contracting authorities should give the same attention to all interested suppliers that have submitted a response. Downsizing the list through evaluation and assessment based on stipulated criteria is by no means an inexpensive exercise. Human and capital resources have to be directed by contracting authorities towards meeting that cost. If the latter exceeds the potential savings achieved through the competitive tendering route, then value for money is unaccomplished.

The second element that deserves attention relates to the definition of price competitiveness in public purchasing, as well as its interrelation with anti-trust law and policy. A question which arises in price competitive tendering patterns is *what would be the lowest offer contracting authorities can accept*. If the maximisation of savings is the only achievable objective in the public procurement process, the transparent/competitive pattern cannot guarantee and evaluate safeguards in relation to underpriced offers. If the supply side responds to the perpetuated competitive purchasing pattern by lowering prices, contracting authorities could face a dilemma: where to stop. It should be mentioned here that the European rules provide for an automatic disqualification of an "abnormally low offer". The term has not been interpreted in detail by the judiciary at European and domestic levels and serves rather as a "lower bottom limit".[23] Also, when an offer appears low, contracting authorities may request clarification from the tenderer in question. Contracting authorities face a dilemma in evaluating and assessing low offers other than abnormal ones. It is difficult for them to identify dumping or predatory pricing disguised behind a low offer for a public contract. In addition, even if there is an indication of anti-competitive price fixing, the European public procurement rules do not provide for any kind of procedure. The suspension of the award procedures (or even the suspension of the conclusion of the contract itself) would be unlikely without a thorough and exhaustive investigation by the competent anti-trust authorities.

Against this background, the PFI was originally construed as the process that could bring the public and private sectors closer and break the mistrust which has surrounded traditional public procurement. The PFI should not be conceived as a capital facility to the state and its organs in the process of delivering public services. It should not be seen as a borrowing exercise by the public sector, as the latter can acquire capital in much more preferential terms than any private person. The PFI should be rather conceived as a process of involving the private sector in the delivery of public services. As such, the PFI attempts to introduce a contractual element in the delivery of public services, to the extent that the private sector, as a contractual party undertakes the responsibility to provide not only an asset but to deliver its associated functions to the public. Therefore, the PFI has contributed in changing the traditionally acquisitorial nature of public sector contracts by inserting a service delivery element.

One of the most important attractions of the PFI has been the ability of public authorities to classify the relevant transactions as exempted from the Public Sector Borrowing Requirement (PSBR), thus by-passing centrally controlled budgetary allocations and cash limits in the public sector spending. In such a way, the PFI represented a viable solution to cash-stranded public authorities, which could, independently, proceed and strike deals that otherwise would not have materialised. Furthermore, the public spending relating to the repayments of the privately financed transactions would not appear as public debt. By taking privately financed transactions out of the PSBR balance sheet, the government may implicitly have attempted to liberalise public purchasing from budgetary constraints and public spending capping. It could be also argued that such an attempt could indicate the beginning of the end to the institutionalised decision making process and control of public procurement imposed under the European (and domestic) public procurement regime.

The paramount implication of not classifying privately financed projects as public debt could be that such purchasing would not fall under the annual comprehensive spending review of the government. In fact, non-inclusion of PFI deals in the PSBR could transform the structure of public markets[24] by reversing the roles and the relative importance of the demand and supply sides. Indeed, it was originally suggested[25] that the private sector should initiate demand by exploring the overall potential and delivery options and then introduce the plan to the relevant public authority. Such a scenario could also mean dismantling of public markets and the elevation of private markets[26] as the forum for the pursuit of public interest. However, the practice not to include PFI projects in the PSBR balance sheet and the assumption that the relevant spending does not represent public debt were often described as legal and policy acrobatisms.[27]

The procedural delivery of the Private Finance Initiative

The PFI is proclaimed[28] to represent an evolution in the public sector management and a step forward in achieving real value-for-money in public purchasing. Numerous guidance notes have been issued by government departments[29] in an attempt to provide a framework for smooth procedural delivery process. However, a number of difficult issues arise when a privately financed contract is examined under the spectrum of the European Public Procurement Directives.[30] Notwithstanding the fact that a PFI project is privately financed, it will be paid by public funds, thus compliance with the European public procurement rules is of paramount importance. It would be naive for contracting authorities to ignore the spirit and the wording of the Directives. It could also be embarrassing for them if litigation before domestic courts or the European Court of Justice concerning the award procedures of a privately financed project is initiated. Clearly, there is a great deal of uncertainty in relation to the compatibility of the European public procurement rules and the PFI. The situation has not yet been clarified by the European Commission, which seems to sit in the background waiting for the domestic government to determine issues of compatibility.

It appears that two major issues in a privately financed project may cause considerable friction between the European Commission and contracting authorities. The first one relates to the contractual nature of the privately financed transaction, when viewed through the spectrum of the European Public Procurement Directives. The second issue is concerned with the process of contract award, and in particular the type of procedures that contracting authorities may use in order to conclude a private financed project.

The contractual nature of a PFI project

A privately financed project can be classified as a "public services contract" or as a "public works contract" depending upon the nature of the deliverables. It could also be considered as a "mixed contract", where both services and construction work are part of the project. Finally, it can be characterised as a "concession contract". The contractual nature of a PFI project is crucial in its procedural delivery and detrimental in complying with the relevant European procurement rules, as it triggers the applicability of different Directives and requirements stipulated therein.

The services/works dilemma

In order to classify a PFI project as public works or public services contract, three significant factors should be taken into account.

i) the intention of the contracting authority
ii) the description of the contract's specification and standardisation
iii) the issue of ownership of the asset to be privately financed

The intention of the contracting authority to procure a privately financed project is the starting point in deciding whether the relevant contract is a public works or services one. In many cases, contracting authorities perceive a PFI project as the vehicle for the provision of a service to the public. However, they do not distinguish between the facilities provision and the provision of the necessary infrastructure. Clearly, prior to any procedural steps towards the procurement process, the contracting authority should have in place a plan of action (establish business needs, appraise options, create business case and project reference, evaluate market soundings, create project team)[31] which will determine whether the project is a works or a services contract. To facilitate the contracting authority's decision on the subject, reference to the definitions of works or services contracts according to the relevant European Directives is crucial.[32] It is, therefore, up to the contracting authority to identify the generic contractual nature of the project.

The extent to which the description of the contract's specification and standardisation requirements emerge from the contracting authority's intention to procure a privately financed project reflects the disposition of the contracting authority towards the classification of the project as a works or a services contract. Contracting authorities must provide an accurate description of the contractual specifications using non-discriminatory standards. The contractual specifications are the competitive benchmark amongst the private sector candidates/tenderers. Underspecification, which is normally the case in PFI projects, raises serious questions over the contractual nature of a privately financed project. Furthermore, apart form their competitive benchmark use, specifications are the core part of the contract itself. Underspecified PFI projects tend to appear as services contracts, as the service element of the contract takes the predominant part in the equation.[33] Underspecification at the preliminary level of the procurement process of a PFI project is usually rectified by negotiating the specifications with the preferred bidder prior to the conclusion of the contract. This sort of practice appears questionable in terms of its legality[34] and the value-for-money aspect for the contracting authority.[35]

The question of ownership of the asset to be privately financed also plays a crucial role in determining the contractual nature of the project. If the asset remains in the ownership of the contracting authority, the objective of the contract is to finance, design, and build the asset. This contractual nexus reveals in a large number of cases a works contract. In cases where a service element (maintenance or operation) is part of the contract, it represents an ancillary component which should be looked at separately if it exceeds certain thresholds. On the other hand, if the ownership of the asset which will be privately financed is retained by the contractor, the objective of the contract is to finance, design, build and operate the asset for a given period, with or without an option to transfer it to the contracting authority at the end of the contract. Such contractual arrangement often reveals a services contract.

The consequences of the classification of a PFI project as a "public services contract" or as a "public works contract" are reflected in the advertisement and publicity requirements and the award procedures. The financial threshold for advertisement and publicity requirements in the OJEC for services contracts is considerably lower (200,000 EURO) than the threshold of works contracts (5 million EURO). However, certain public services contracts need not to be advertised Community-wide.[36] With reference to the award procedures, the utilisation of negotiated procedures appears more flexible in public services contracts, where their specification requirements cannot be set by the contracting authority in advance.[37] Nevertheless, this option is not available for public works contracts.

The case of mixed contracts

Special attention is required in cases of "mixed contracts", where works and services are part of the project. The distinguishing factor here is the "incidental purpose test", where works or services are considered incidental to the main objective of the contract.[38] The concept of incidental purpose was developed by the European Court of Justice in the absence of specific and explicit rules in the Public Works Directive regarding public projects where works and services form an integral part of the contract.

However, in many PFI projects, both works and services are often indistinguishable elements of the contract, in the sense that they form a contractual package which cannot be split in a commercially viable way. In such cases, the incidental purpose test provides little help. The very fact that a public project is privately financed reveals an element of a service to be provided to the contracting authority from the outset. The majority of privately financed contracts envisage management and operational services in addition to the procurement of construction works. They are obviously a "mixed type" of public contracts; however, their classification as public services or public works contracts requires further elaboration. It appears rather difficult to decide the incidental purpose of the works or the services involved in a PFI project. Unfortunately, the ECJ did not clarify the constituencies of the term "incidental", so the contractual nature of a "mixed type" public contract could be assessed. It has been suggested by the Court[39] that the value of the works or the services could be used as the decisive criterion in describing a mixed public contract as a public services or public works contract. However, in PFI projects the contractual elements of works and services are closely interdependent and their pricing is mutually affected. Their potential split would result in an artificial outcome, as the value of the works element without the service element would not reflect commercially realistic figures.

The danger in classifying a mixed contract as a services contract appears to be the potential contravention of the Public Works Directive. Even if the services contract is properly advertised and awarded according to the relevant European Directive, its award could be linked with the award of a works contract outside the framework of the Works Directives. In many PFI projects the services element tends to be overstressed. It then emerges that a privately financed public service contract is a disguised public works contract. This appears as an unsatisfactory outcome and such course of action by contracting authorities is legally questionable before domestic courts or the ECJ.

In deciding the contractual nature of a PFI mixed type project, the threshold test represents the safest option for contracting authorities, when a realistic split of the contractual elements can be achieved. In cases where the ownership of an asset is vested with the contractor, the value of the operation and management element of the contract should be counterbalanced with the residual value of the asset after a certain period of time, when an option to transfer the asset to the contracting authority is exercised. If the operation and management (services) element exceeds the residual value of the asset (which represents the construction costs minus depreciation), there is a strong indication that the project is a public services contract. On the other hand, when ownership of an asset remains with the contracting authority, the value of the operation and management element of the contract during its life should be compared with the construction costs, when these are completed. Again, if the services element exceeds in value the works element, the project is a services contract.

The case of concession contracts

The classification of a PFI project as a concession contract depends very much upon the repayment method to the contractor by the contracting authority. The definition of a *public works concession* contract under the EU Procurement Directives covers an agreement between a contractor and a contracting authority concerning either the execution or both the execution and design of a work and for which remunerative considerations consist, at least partly, in the right of the *concessionaire* to exploit exclusively the finished construction works for a period of time.[40] Public works concessions which are privately financed are often *financially free standing* projects, where the contractor finances, designs, builds and then operates an asset, and recovers its costs by direct charges on the users of the service which the asset provides. There is usually an option to transfer the asset to the contracting authority by the end of the concession period or at break points during the life of the concession.

The Public Works Directive has adopted a special, mitigated regime for the award of concession contracts.[41] The provisions of the Directive only apply to concession contracts when the value is at least 5 million EURO. There are no rules given as to the way in which the contract value must be calculated. For the award of concession contracts, contracting authorities must apply similar rules on advertising as the advertising rules concerning open and restricted procedures for the award of every works contract. Also, the provisions on technical standards and on criteria for qualitative selection of candidates and tenderers do apply to the award of concession contracts. The Directive does not prescribe the use of specific award procedures for concession contracts. The Directive presupposes that concession contracts should be awarded in two rounds, such as in the case of restricted procedures or negotiated procedures for ordinary works contracts. Nothing, however, prevents contracting authorities from applying a one-round open procedure. The Directive contains no rules on the minimum number of candidates which have to be invited to negotiate or to submit a tender. It would seem that a contracting authority may limit itself to selecting only one single candidate, provided the intention to award a concession contract has been adequately published. A contracting authority may under no circumstances refrain from publicising a notice to the Official Journal indicating its intention to proceed with the award of a concession works contract.[42]

Contracting authorities awarding the principal concession contract may impose contractual obligations upon the concessionaire to subcontract at least 30 per cent of the total work provided for by the principal contract to third parties. Such sub-contracting arrangements by the concessionaire, even if they are not contracting authorities themselves, should be pursued in accordance with the advertisement, selection and qualification criteria and award procedures of public works contracts, if their value exceeds 5 million EURO. Exceptions to this requirement apply in a limited number of cases where negotiated procedures without prior advertisement are allowed,[43] and in the case of sub-contracting works to affiliated undertakings[44] of the concessionaire.

Interestingly, public service concessions, although included in the draft Public Services Directive,[45] have been excluded from its final and as a consequence, their award falls outside the thrust of EU Public Procurement rules. The exclusion of service concessions falls short of the aspirations to regulate concession contracts for the public sector under the Works Directive and breaks the consistency in the two legal instruments. The reasons for the exclusion of service concessions from the regulatory regime of public procurement could be attributed to the different legal requirements in Member States to delegate powers to services *concessionaires*. The delegation of services by public authorities to private undertakings in some Member States runs contrary to their constitutional provisions regarding state monopolies, public security and defence matters.[46]

Concession contracts under European public procurement law represent a grey area. Their regulation appears, *prima facie*, to be incompatible with the main principles of the liberalisation of public procurement, but eventually the requirement imposed on concessionaires to sub-contract principal contracts to third parties, at least up to 30 per cent of their total value, attempts to bring the whole regime in conformity with the Community's policy on the opening up of the public sector contracts. However, the relaxed language of their regulation cannot guarantee legal certainty. It is rather unfortunate that private undertakings whose construction projects are subsidised from the state by more than 50 per cent must comply with the Public Procurement Directives,[47] whereas concessionaires cannot be forced to avoid discrimination on grounds of nationality when they contract out construction work to third parties.

The award procedures for PFI

Public contracts can be awarded by virtue of three types of procedures: open, negotiated or restricted procedures. Open procedures are those where every interested supplier, contractor or service provider may submit an offer. Restricted procedures are those procedures for the award of public contracts whereby only those contractors invited by the contracting authority may submit tenders. The selection of the winning tender usually takes place in two rounds. In the first round, all interested contractors may submit their interest and the contracting authority selects, from the candidates, those who will be invited to tender. In principle, the minimum number of candidates to be selected is five. In the second round, bids are submitted and the successful tender is selected. Negotiated procedures are procedures for the award of public contracts whereby contracting authorities consult contractors of their choice and negotiate the terms of the contract with one or more of them. There are two types of negotiated procedures: i) negotiated procedures with prior notification and ii) negotiated procedures without prior notification. Negotiated procedures with prior notification provide for selection of candidates in two rounds. In the first round, all interested contractors may submit their tenders and the contracting authority selects from the candidates, those who will be invited to negotiate. In the second round, negotiations with various candidates take place and the successful tender is selected. In principle, the minimum number of candidates to be selected is three, provided that there are a sufficient number of suitable candidates. Negotiated procedures without prior notification may be conducted in one single round. Contracting authorities are allowed to choose whichever contractor they want, begin negotiations directly with this contractor and award the contract to him. These procedures should be used only in exceptional situations.

The Public Procurement Directives stipulate that open procedures, where possible should constitute the norm. Although contracting authorities can freely opt for open or restricted procedures, the latter should be justified by reference to the nature of the products or services to be procured and the balance between contract value and administrative costs associated with tender evaluation. A more rigorous set of conditions apply for the use of negotiated procedures. When negotiated procedures with prior notification are used, they must be justified on grounds of irregular or unacceptable tenders received as a result of a previous call. Negotiated procedures without prior notification are restrictively permitted in absence of tenders, when the procurement involves manufactured products or construction works purely for research and development, when for technical or artistic reasons or reasons connected with the protection of exclusive rights a particular supplier or contractor is selected, in cases of extreme urgency brought by unforeseeable events not attributable to the contracting authorities, when additional deliveries and supplies or works would cause disproportionate technical operational and maintenance difficulties.

All negotiations with candidates or tenderers on fundamental aspects of contracts, in particular on prices, are prohibited in open and restricted procedures; discussions with candidates or tenderers may be held, but only for the purpose of clarifying or supplementing the content of their tenders or the requirements of the contracting authorities and provided this does not involve discriminatory practices.[48] The need for such a prohibition is clear, since the possibility to negotiate may allow the contracting authority to introduce subjective appraisal criteria. The European Court of Justice has condemned post tender negotiations[49] and a Declaration on the above subject has been made by the European Council and the Commission of the European Communities.[50] It should be also clear that the selection process must be completely distinguished from the award process. Quite often, contracting authorities appear to fuse the two basic processes of the award of public procurement contracts. This runs contrary to legal precedence of the European Court of Justice.[51]

In contrast with the above background, when contracting authorities award PFI projects classified as public works or public services contracts, they have been urged to have recourse to negotiated procedures.[52] The official line adopted is that a privately financed project could meet all the conditions imposed by the European public procurement rules for allowing the negotiated procedures to be used in contract awards and form a sort of precedence for future projects. Negotiated procedures for public works and services contracts with prior notification shall be used in the following cases: in the event of irregular tenders as a result of open or restricted procedures; in cases that the works are carried out purely for the purpose of research and development; in exceptional cases where the nature of the service does not permit overall pricing; in cases where the contract specification of the services to be procured is not possible. On the other hand, negotiated procedures without prior notification can be used in the following cases: in the absence of tenders responding to open or restricted procedures; when for technical or artistic reasons or reasons connected with the protection of exclusive rights the services could only be procured by a particular contractor or service provider; in cases of extreme urgency brought about by events unforeseeable by the contracting authority; when design contests are awarded provided the contracting authority negotiates with all participants; when additional services have to be awarded to a prior contract which had not been foreseen at the time of its award and cannot be separated from the main contract without great inconvenience to the contracting authority and the additional works or services must not exceed 50 per cent of the value of main contract; when repetitive or similar services to a main contract are awarded within three years of its award and subject to the main contract being awarded through either open or restricted procedures.

It should be maintained here that the European Institutions never looked favourably at the use of negotiated procedures by contracting authorities. The European Court of Justice has always been very reluctant in accepting the use of negotiated procedures, particularly without prior advertisement.[53] In a number of notable cases[54] before it relating to improper use of the award procedures, the Court has maintained the exceptional character of negotiated procedures and the extremely onerous obligation of contracting authorities to justify them. In fact, in every case relating to the justification of the negotiated procedures, the Court has condemned the relevant authorities for breaching the European Procurement Directives. It might be construed from the case-law of the Court of Justice that the particular procedure stipulated by the rules requires some sort of clearance prior to its utilisation. This is not however the case, as the only form of official notification by contracting authorities when they use negotiated procedures is a notice containing the reasons for having recourse to such procedures and is communicated to the European Commission after the award of the contract in question. This rather reinforces the exceptional character of the negotiated procedures rather than their prohibitive nature.

Publicity requirements

The European Public Procurement Directives have established a regime which *inter alia* provides a mechanism for all the information needed to the relevant parties or the public in relation to the award of public contracts. Contracting authorities are under explicit obligation to furnish timely a range of information on their own initiative[55] or upon request.[56] This obligation is, in principle, extended to all PFI projects that are awarded under the procurement rules. However, practice has shown that very little information concerning the award of a PFI contract sees the light of publicity, often being described as *"commercially confidential"*. The onus is on the public authority to meet these publicity requirements, although the private sector appears extremely reluctant in allowing vital information regarding contractual structures, financial arrangements, technical specifications, pricing to be in the public domain. Given the fact that a PFI project is substantially more complicated than a conventional public procurement equivalent, the argument of essential or confidential information being made public appears a valid one.

The Freedom of Information Act in the United Kingdom has implications for the publicity of PFI contracts, implications which mirror the obligations of contracting authorities stipulated in the Public Procurement Directives. In particular, a statutory obligation to make public certain information is proposed. This obligation covers information relating to reasons for rejection or disqualification and pricing. The appropriate publicity requirements will be included in the individual contracts between public authorities and contractors. The above obligation is intended to apply to all government departments, local authorities, the National Health Service, and all other public bodies, while it will also be extended to the privatised utilities and private organisations which perform public interest functions under contractual arrangements with the state. An exemption for confidentially commercial information will apply, provided *substantial harm* to a party can be demonstrated.

Part 2 The development of public-private partnerships at European level

The term public-private partnership is not defined at European Union level. Public-private partnerships denote a contractual format between public authorities and private sector undertakings. Such relations aim at delivering infrastructure projects, as well as many other schemes in areas covering transport, public health, education, public safety, and waste management and water distribution and have the following characteristics: the relatively long duration of the relationship; the funding source for the project; the strategic role of the private sector in the sense that it is expected to provide input into different stages of the project such as design, completion, implementation, and funding and finally the distribution of risks between the public and private sectors and the expectation that the private sector will assume substantial risk

Public authorities in the Member States often have recourse to public-private partnership arrangements to facilitate mainly infrastructure projects. Budget constraints confronting national governments and the widespread assumption that private sector know-how will benefit the delivery of public services appear as the main policy drivers[57] for selecting a public-private partnership route. Also, the accounting treatment of public-private partnership contracts benefits national governments as the assets involved in a public-private partnership should be classified as non-government assets, and therefore recorded off balance sheet for public accountancy purposes,[58] subject to two conditions: i) that the private partner bears the construction risk, and ii) that the private partner bears at least one of either availability or demand risk. However, it is necessary to assess whether a public-private partnership option offers real value added compared with the conclusion of traditional public contracts.[59]

At European level, as part of the Initiative for Growth, the Council has approved a series of measures designed to increase investment in the infrastructure of the trans-European transport networks and also in the areas of research, innovation and development,[60] as well as the delivery of services of general interest.[61] European Community law does not lay down any special rules covering the award or the contractual interface of public-private partnerships. Nevertheless, such arrangements must be examined in the light of the rules and principles resulting from the European Treaties, particularly as regards the principles of freedom of establishment and freedom to provide services (Articles 43 and 49 of the EC Treaty),[62] which encompass in particular the principles of transparency, equality of treatment, proportionality and mutual recognition[63] and the Public Procurement Directives.[64] The Commission has already taken initiatives under public procurement law to deal with the award of public-private partnerships. In 2000 it published an Interpretive Communication on concessions and Community public procurement law,[65] in which it defined, on the basis of the rules and principles derived from the

Treaty and applicable secondary legislation, the outlines of the concept of concession in Community law and the obligations incumbent on the public authorities when selecting the economic operators to whom the concessions are granted.

The Green Paper on Public-Private Partnerships distinguishes two major formats of public-private partnerships: the contractual formant, also described as the concession model, and the institutional format which is often described as the "joint-venture model".

The contractual public-private partnership

The contractual model of a public-private partnership reflects on a relation between public and private sectors based solely on contractual links. It involves different interfaces where tasks and responsibilities can be assigned to the private partner, including the design, funding, execution, renovation or exploitation of a work or service. In this category, concession contracts and arrangements such as the private finance initiative or arrangements of similar contractual nexus create the link between public and private sectors.

There are few provisions of secondary legislation which coordinate the procedures for the award of contracts designated as concession contracts in Community law. In the case of works concessions, there are only certain advertising obligations, intended to ensure prior competition by interested operators, and an obligation regarding the minimum time-limit for the receipt of applications.[66] The contracting authorities are free to decide how to select the private partner, although in so doing they must nonetheless guarantee full compliance with the principles and rules resulting from the Treaty. The rules governing the award of services concessions apply only by reference to the principles resulting from Articles 43 and 49 of the Treaty, in particular the principles of transparency, equality of treatment, proportionality and mutual recognition.[67]

The Community law applicable to the award of concessions is derived primarily from general obligations which involve no coordination of the legislation of Member States. In addition, and although the Member States are free to do so, very few have opted to adopt national laws to lay down general and detailed rules governing the award of works or services concessions.[68] Thus, the rules applicable to the selection of a concessionaire by a contracting body are, for the most part, drawn up on a case-by-case basis. This situation may present problems for Community operators. The lack of coordination of national legislation could in fact be an obstacle to the genuine opening up of such projects in the Community, particularly when they are organised at transnational level. The legal uncertainty linked to the absence of clear and coordinated rules might in addition lead to an increase in the costs of awarding such projects. Moreover, it could be argued that the objectives of the internal market might not be achieved in certain situations, owing to a lack of effective competition on the market.

On the other hand, the rules applicable to the award of public-private partnerships in the format of a public works contracts or public services contracts[69] are contained in the Public Sector Directives,[70] where a contracting authority must normally have recourse to the open or restricted procedure to choose its private partner. By way of exception, and under certain conditions, recourse to the negotiated procedure is sometimes possible. In this context, the Commission has pointed out that the derogation under Article 7(2) of Directive 93/37/EEC, which provides for recourse to negotiated procedure in the case of a contract when "the nature of the works or the risks attaching thereto do not permit prior overall pricing", is of limited scope. This derogation is to cover solely the exceptional situations in which there is uncertainty *a priori* regarding the nature or scope of the work to be carried out, but is not to cover situations in which the uncertainties result from other causes, such as the difficulty of prior pricing owing to the complexity of the legal and financial package put in place.[71]

Since the adoption of Directive 2004/18/EC, a new procedure known as "competitive dialogue" may apply when awarding particularly complex contracts.[72] The competitive dialogue procedure is launched in cases where the contracting body is objectively unable to define the technical means that would best satisfy its needs and objectives or in cases where it is objectively unable to define the legal and/or financial form of a project. This new procedure will allow the contracting bodies to open a dialogue with the candidates for the purpose of identifying solutions capable of meeting these needs. At the end of this dialogue, the candidates will be invited to submit their final tender on the basis of the solution or solutions identified in the course of the dialogue. These tenders must contain all the elements required and necessary for the performance of the project. The contracting authorities must assess the tenders on the basis of the pre-stated award criteria. The tenderer who has submitted the most economically advantageous tender may be asked to clarify aspects of it or confirm commitments featured therein, provided this will not have the effect of altering fundamental elements in the tender or invitation to tender, or falsifying competition or of leading to discrimination.

The competitive dialogue procedure should provide the necessary flexibility in the discussions with the candidates on all aspects of the contract during the set-up phase, while ensuring that these discussions are conducted in compliance with the principles of transparency and equality of treatment, and do not endanger the rights which the Treaty confers on economic operators. It is underpinned by the belief that structured selection methods should be protected in all circumstances, as these contribute to the objectivity and integrity of the procedure leading to the selection of an operator. This in turn guarantees the sound use of public funds and reduces the risk of practices that lack transparency and strengthens the legal certainty necessary for such projects. In addition, the new Directives make clear the benefit to contracting authorities of formulating the technical specifications in terms of either performance or functional requirements. New provisions will thus give the contracting bodies more scope to take account of innovative solutions during the award phase, irrespective of the procedure adopted.[73]

The institutional public-private partnership

The joint venture model of public-private partnerships involves the establishment of an entity held jointly by the public partner and the private partner.[74] The joint entity thus has the task of ensuring the delivery of a work or service for the benefit of the public. Direct interface between the public partner and the private partner in a forum with a legal personality allows the public partner, through its presence in the body of shareholders and in the decision-making bodies of the joint entity, to retain a relatively high degree of control over the development of the projects, which it can adapt over time in the light of circumstances. It also allows the public partner to develop its own experience of running the service in question, while having recourse to the support of a private partner. An institutional public-private partnership can be put in place, either by creating an entity held jointly by the public sector and the private sector, or by the private sector taking control of an existing public undertaking.

The law on public contracts and concessions does not of itself apply to the transaction creating a mixed-capital entity. However, when such a transaction is accompanied by the award of tasks through an act which can be designated as a public contract, or even a concession, it is important that there be compliance with the rules and principles arising from this law (the general principles of the Treaty or, in certain cases, the provisions of the Directives).[75] The selection of a private partner called on to undertake such tasks while functioning as part of a mixed entity can therefore not be based exclusively on the quality of its capital contribution or its experience, but should also take account of the characteristics of its offer – the most economically advantageous – in terms of the specific services to be provided. Thus, in the absence of clear and objective criteria allowing the contracting authority to select the most economically advantageous offer, the capital transaction could constitute a breach of the law on public contracts and concessions.

In this context, the transaction involving the creation of such an entity does not generally present a problem in terms of the applicable Community law when it constitutes a means of executing the task entrusted under a contract to a private partner. However, the conditions governing the creation of the entity must be clearly laid down when issuing the call for competition for the tasks which one wishes to entrust to the private partner. Also, these conditions must not discriminate against or constitute an unjustified barrier to the freedom to provide services or to freedom of establishment, or be disproportionate to the desired objective.

However, in certain Member States, national legislation allows the mixed entities, in which the participation by the public sector involves the contracting body, to participate in a procedure for the award of a public contract or concession even when these entities are only in the course of being incorporated. In this scenario, the entity will be definitively incorporated only after the contract has actually been awarded to it. In other Member States, a practice has developed which tends to confuse the phase of incorporating the entity and the phase of allocating the tasks. Thus the purpose of the procedure launched by the contracting authority is to create a mixed entity to which certain tasks are entrusted.

Such a solution does not appear to offer satisfactory answers in terms of the provisions applicable to public contracts and concessions.[76] In the first case, there is a risk that the effective competition will be distorted by a privileged position of the company being incorporated, and consequently of the private partner participating in this company. In the second case, the specific procedure for selecting the private partner also poses many problems. The contracting authorities encounter certain difficulties in defining the subject-matter of the contract or concession in a sufficiently clear and precise manner in this context, as they are obliged to do. The Commission has frequently noted that the tasks entrusted to the partnership structure are not clearly defined and that, in certain cases, they even fall outside any contractual framework.

This in turn raises problems not only with regard to the principles of transparency and equality of treatment, but even risks prejudicing the general interest objectives which the public authority wishes to attain. It is also evident that the lifetime of the created entity does not generally coincide with the duration of the contract or concession awarded, and this appears to encourage the extension of the task entrusted to this entity without a true competition at the time of this renewal. In addition, it should be pointed out that the joint creation of such entities must respect the principle of non-discrimination in respect of nationality in general and the free circulation of capital in particular.[77] Thus, for example, the public authorities cannot normally make their position as shareholder in such an entity contingent on excessive privileges which do not derive from a normal application of company law.[78]

On the other hand, the creation of an institutional public-private partnership may also lead to a change in the body of shareholders of a public entity. In this context, it should first be emphasised that the changeover of a company from the public sector to the private sector is an economic and political decision which, as such, falls within the sole competence of the Member States.[79] Community law on public contracts is not as such intended to apply to transactions involving simple capital injections by an investor in an enterprise, whether this latter be in the public or the private sector. Such transactions fall under the scope of the provisions of the Treaty on the free movement of capital,[80] implying in particular that the national measures regulating them must not constitute barriers to investment from other Member States.[81] Nevertheless, the provisions on freedom of establishment within the meaning of Article 43 of the Treaty must be applied when a public authority decides, by means of a capital transaction, to cede to a third party a holding conferring a definite influence in a public entity providing economic services normally falling within the responsibility of the State.[82]

When public authorities grant an economic operator a definite influence in a business under a transaction involving a capital transfer, and when this transaction has the effect of entrusting to this operator tasks falling within the scope of the law on public contracts which had been previously exercised, directly or indirectly, by the public authorities, the provisions on freedom of establishment require compliance with the principles of transparency and equality of treatment, in order to ensure that every potential operator has equal access to performing those activities which had hitherto been reserved.

The phenomenon of public-private partnerships represents a genuine attempt to introduce the concept of contractualised governance in the delivery of public services. Although the public sector has always depended upon traditional corporatism to disperse public services, there is mounting evidence that the role and the involvement of the state in the above process is under constant review. The private finance initiative can be described as an institutionalised mechanism in engaging the private sector in the delivery of public services, not only through the financing but mainly through the operation of assets. The private sector assumes a direct responsibility in serving the public interest, as part of its contractual obligations *vis-à-vis* the public sector. The motive and the intention behind such an approach focus on the benefits which would follow as a result of the private sector's involvement in the delivery of public services. Efficiency gains, qualitative improvement, innovation, value-for-money and flexibility appear as the most important ones, whereas an overall better allocation of public capital resources sums up the advantages of privately financed projects.

Both the private finance initiative and the phenomenon of public-private partnerships do not alter the character of the contractual relationship between the private and public sectors, for such a character is predominately determined by other factors attributed to the legal order in question. The contractual relationship between the private and public sectors is not merely determined by the fact that one party to the agreement is a public authority, but mainly by reference to the appropriate forum for access to justice, or the relevant remedial availability.[83] Under both traditional corporatism and contractualised governance, the contractual nexus between the private and public sectors maintains the same characteristics which are influenced by the disposition of the relevant legal and judicial system. What the PFI does change is the thrust of that contractual relationship. The integral nature of corporatism evolves around the notion of public ownership of assets destined to serve public interest. The PFI brings an end to the notion of public ownership and instead introduces the concept of service delivery in the relevant contractual relationship between private and public sectors. The private sector is no longer a supplier to the public sector but rather a partner through a concession. It seems that there is a quasi-agency relationship between the private and public sectors, in the sense that the former provides the relevant infrastructure and in fact delivers public services on behalf of the latter. Where corporatism was always delivered under considerable budgetary constraints, a fact that reflects not only the relative balance of power between the demand and supply sides and the risk allocation factor in their contractual arrangements but mainly the adversarial environment and the compromised quality of the deliverables, contractualised governance appears to prioritise the value-for-money principle, which has primarily qualitative attributes.

Both corporatism and contractualised governance should be delivered through a system that guarantees accountability, openness and competitiveness. Such a system for the delivery of public services is encapsulated in the European public procurement regime, which is expected to be the most appropriate delivery process for public-private partnerships. Contractual award arrangements are entirely covered by the Public Procurement Directives, which provide for a disciplined, transparent and relatively swift system for the award of public procurement contracts.[84] What remains is the development of comprehensive guidelines for the deployment of private finances in the delivery of public services[85] and the embedment of relevant legislation[86] that empowers public authorities to contractualise their governance. The public-private partnership regime needs to benefit from a simplification and standardisation process, so a kind of routine similar to that reigning the award of traditional public procurement contracts can assist the demand and supply sides in delivering more privately financed deals. However, the relative volume of public-private partnerships projects is not the critical factor in determining its success. It is rather the value-for-money element that is expected to crop up through the involvement of private entrepreneurship in the delivery of public services.

Public-private partnerships as a concept-tool of public sector management have, in theory, a promising future. In reality, they should be benchmarked against traditional publicly funded systems, both in qualitative and quantitative terms. Only then one can assess with reasonable confidence their merits and impact upon the delivery of public services.

8
The Procurement of Services of General Interest

Introduction

The jurisprudence of the European Court of Justice has indicated on numerous occasions that public procurement has a multi-faceted dimension in assisting the process of the common market. In particular, the Court has demonstrated the pivotal position of public procurement in the process of determining the parameters under which public subsidies and state financing of public services constitute state aids. In the centre of the debate regarding the relation between state aids and the financing of services of general interest, within the broader remit of the interplay of subsidies and public services, public procurement has emerged as an essential component of state aids regulation.[1] The European Court of Justice has inferred that the existence of public procurement, as a legal system and a procedural framework, verifies conceptual links, creates compatibility safeguards and authenticates established principles applicable in state aids regulation. Public procurement in the common market not only does represent the procedural framework for the contractual interface between public and private sectors,[2] it also reflects on the character and nature of activities of the state and its organs in pursuit of public interest.[3] Public procurement regulation has acquired legal, economic and policy dimensions, as market integration and the fulfilment of treaty principles are balanced with policy choices.[4]

The implications of the debate are important, not only because of the necessity for a coherent application of state aids regulation in the common market[5] but also because of the need for a legal and policy framework regarding the financing of services of general interest and public service obligations by Member States. The significance of the topic is reflected in the attempts of the European Council[6] to provide for a policy framework of greater predictability and increased legal certainty in the application of the State aid rules to the funding of services of general interest. The present article intends to define the connection between public procurement and services of general interest and to ascertain the parameters of interplay between public procurement and state financing of public services within the regulatory regime of state aids.

Part 1 The services of general interest under EU law

The EU Treaty does not include as a Community objective the provision or the organisation or the financing of services of general interest and therefore does not assign specific and explicit powers to the Community in the area of services of general interest. Except for a sector-specific reference in the area of transport,[7] services of general economic interest are referred to in Articles 16 and Article 86(2) of the EC Treaty. Furthermore, according to the Charter of Fundamental Rights of the European Union, the Union recognises and respects access to services of general economic interest, in order to promote the social and territorial cohesion of the Union.[8]

Although Article 16 EC confers responsibility upon the Community and the Member States to ensure, each within their respective sphere of competencies, that their policies enable services of general economic interest to fulfil their missions, it does not provide the Community with specific means of action. On the other hand, Article 86(2) EC implicitly recognises the right of the Member States to assign specific public service obligations to economic operators. It manifests a fundamental principle ensuring that services of general economic interest can continue to be provided and developed in the common market. Providers of services of general interest are exempted from application of the Treaty rules only to the extent that any exemption is strictly necessary to allow them to fulfil their mission to pursue activities of general interest. Thus, such deviation from the Treaty rules is subject to the principles of neutrality, freedom to define and proportionality.[9] Therefore, in the event of conflict, the fulfilment of a public service mission can effectively prevail over the application of Community rules, including internal market and competition rules, subject to the conditions foreseen in Article 86(2) EC. Consequently, the Treaty protects the effective performance of a general interest task but not necessarily the provider as such.

The concept of *services of general interest* is a surrogate notion of the term services of general economic interest found in Articles 16 and 86(2) of the EC Treaty. However, its remit is broader and covers both market and non-market services which the public authorities regard as being of general interest and subject them to specific public service obligations. Within Community law and practice, the concept of services of general interest refers to services of an economic nature[10] which the Member States or the Community subject to specific public service obligations in order to serve the general interest of the public. It thus covers certain services provided by the big network industries such as transport, postal services, energy and communications, but it also extends to any other economic activity which is subjected to public service obligations. The term *public service obligations* denotes specific requirements that are imposed by public authorities on the provider of the service in order to ensure that certain public interest objectives are met, for instance, in the matter of air, rail and road transport and energy. The application of such obligations can be at Community, national or regional level.

The economic nature of services of general interest is reflected in the Community's attempts to achieve a gradual opening of the markets for large network industries such as telecommunications, postal services, electricity, gas and transport in which services of general economic interest can be provided. The Community has adopted a comprehensive regulatory framework for these services which specifies public service obligations at European level and includes aspects such as universal service, consumer and user rights and health and safety concerns. These industries have a clear Community-wide dimension and present a strong case for developing a concept of European general interest, as well as a concept of services which pursue Community-wide public interest. This debate is also reflected and explicitly recognised in Title XV of the EU Treaty, which gives the Community specific responsibility for trans-European networks in the areas of transport, telecommunications and energy infrastructure, with the dual objective of improving the smooth functioning of the internal market and strengthening social and economic cohesion. However, there are services of general interests which are not subject to a comprehensive regulatory regime at Community level, such as waste management, water supply and public service broadcasting. The provision of these services of general interest is subject to the internal market, competition and State aid rules, provided that these services can affect trade between Member States, and also *lex specialis* regimes.[11]

The services of general interest through public procurement

The application of public procurement rules, apart from the objective to integrate intra-community public sector trade, has served as a yardstick to determine the nature of an undertaking in its contractual interface when delivering public services. Public procurement regulation has prompted the recognition of a distinctive category of markets within the common market, often described as public markets.[12] Public markets are such *fora* where the state and its organs would enter in pursuit of public interest.[13] Their respective activity does not resemble the commercial characteristics of private entrepreneurship, in as much as the aim of the public sector is not the maximisation of profits but the serving of public interest.[14] This substitution of public interest for profit maximisation is the fundamental factor for the creation of *public markets*.[15]

There are further variances that distinguish public from private markets. These focus on structural elements of the market place, competitiveness, demand conditions, supply conditions, the production process, and finally pricing and risk. These variances also indicate different methods and approaches employed in the regulation of public markets.[16] Public markets tend to have monopsony structures (the state and its organs often appear as the sole outlet for an industry's output) and function differently from private markets. In terms of its origins, demand in public markets is institutionalised and operates mainly under budgetary considerations rather than price mechanisms. It is also based on fulfilment of tasks (pursuit of public interest) and it is single for many products. Supply also has limited origins. Close ties exist between the public sector and its industries supplying its needs and there is often a limited product range. Products are rarely innovative and technologically advanced and pricing is determined through tendering and negotiations. The purchasing decision is primarily based upon the life-time cycle, reliability, price and political considerations. Purchasing patterns follow tendering and negotiations and often purchases are dictated by policy rather than price/quality considerations.

Within the remit of public markets, the funding of services of general interest by the state may emerge through different formats, such as the payment of remuneration for services under a public contract, the payment of annual subsidies, preferential fiscal treatment or lower social contributions. However, the most common format is the existence of a contractual relation between the state and the undertaking charged to deliver public services. The above contractual relation should, under normal circumstances emerge through the public procurement framework, not only as an indication of market competitiveness but mainly as a demonstration of the nature of the deliverable services as services of "general interest having non industrial or commercial character". The latter description appears as a necessary condition for the applicability of the public procurement regime.

The non-commercial character of services of general interest have

For the public procurement regime to apply in a contractual interface between public and private sectors, the contracting authority must be the state or an emanation of the state, and in particular, a *body governed by public law*. The above category is subject to a set of cumulative criteria,[17] *inter alia* "it must be established for the specific purpose of meeting needs in the general public interest not having an industrial or commercial character".

The criterion of specific establishment of an entity to meet needs in the general interest having non-commercial or industrial character has been the subject of the Court's attention in some landmark cases.[18] In order to define the term *needs in the general interest,* the Court drew its experience from jurisprudence in the public undertakings field as well as case-law relating to public order.[19] The Court approached the above concept by a direct analogy to the concept of "general economic interest", as defined in Article 90(2) EC.[20] The concept "general interest", under the public procurement regime denotes the requirements of a community (local or national) in its entirety, which should not overlap with the specific or exclusive interest of a clearly determined person or group of persons.[21] Moreover, the requirement of the *specificity* of the establishment of the body in question was approached by reference to the reasons and the objectives behind its establishment. Specificity of the purpose of an establishment does not mean exclusivity, in the sense that other types of activities may also be carried out without the entity escaping classification as a body governed by public law.[22]

On the other hand, the requirement of non-commercial or industrial character of needs in the general interest has raised some difficulties. The Court interpreting the meaning of non-commercial or industrial undertakings had recourse to case-law relating to public undertakings, where the nature of industrial and commercial activities of private or public undertakings was defined.[23] The industrial or commercial character of an organisation depends much upon a number of criteria that reveal the thrust behind the organisation's participation in the relevant market. The state and its organs may act either by exercising public powers or by carrying out economic activities of an industrial or commercial nature by offering goods and services on the market. The key factor appears in the organisation's intention to achieve profitability and pursue its objectives through a spectrum of commercially motivated decisions. The distinction between the range of activities which relate to public authority and those which, although carried out by public persons, fall within the private domain is drawn most clearly from case-law and judicial precedence of the Court concerning the applicability of competition rules of the Treaty to the given activities.[24]

The non-commercial or industrial character of an activity is a strong indication of the existence of a general interest activity. The Court in *BFI*[25] had the opportunity to consider the relationship between bodies governed by public law and the pursuit of activities of general interest having non-industrial or commercial nature. The non-commercial or industrial character is a criterion intended to clarify the term needs in the general interest. In fact, it is regarded as a category of needs of general interest. The Court recognised that there might be needs of general interest, that have an industrial and commercial character and also that private undertakings can meet needs of general interest that do not have industrial and commercial character. However, the acid test for needs in the general interest not having an industrial or commercial character is that, the state or other contracting authorities choose themselves to meet these needs or to have a decisive influence over their provision.

If an activity which meets general needs is pursued in a competitive environment, there is a strong indication that the pursuing entity it is not a body governed by public law.[26] In the *Agora* case the Court indicated that the relationship between competitiveness and commerciality has significant implications on the relevant activity which meets needs of general interest. Market forces reveal the commercial or industrial character of an activity, irrespective of whether the latter meets the needs of general interest. However, market competitiveness as well as profitability cannot be absolute determining factors for the commercial or the industrial nature of an activity, as they are not sufficient to exclude the possibility that a body governed by public law may choose to be guided by considerations other than economic ones. The absence of competition is not a condition necessarily to be taken into account in order to define a body governed by public law, although the existence of significant competition in the market place may be indicative of the absence of a need in the general interest which does not carry commercial or industrial elements. The Court reached this conclusion by analysing the nature of the bodies governed by public law contained in Annex 1 of the Works Directive 93/37 and verifying that the intention of the state in establishing such bodies has been to retain decisive influence over the provision of the needs in question.

Commerciality and its relationship with needs in the general interest is perhaps the most important theme that has emerged from the Court's jurisprudence and is highly relevant to the debate concerning the relationship between services of general interest and the organisations which pursue them. In fact the above theme sets out to explore the interface between profit-making and public interest, as features that underpin the activities of bodies governed by public law. Certain activities, which by their nature fall within the fundamental tasks of the public authorities, cannot be subject to a requirement of profitability and therefore are not meant to generate profits. It is possible, therefore, to attribute the distinction between bodies whose activity is subject to the public procurement legislation and other bodies, to the fact that the criterion of "needs in the general interest not having an industrial or commercial character" indicates the lack of competitive forces in the relevant marketplace. Although the state as entrepreneur enters into transactions with a view to providing goods, services and works for the public, to the extent that it exercises *dominium*, these activities do not resemble the characteristics of entrepreneurship, in as much as the aim of the state's activities is not the maximisation of profits but the observance of public interest. Public markets are the *fora* where *public interest* substitutes *profit maximisation*.[27]

Services of general interest and contracting authorities

The dual capacity of an entity as a public service provider and a commercial undertaking, and the weighting of the relevant activity in relation to the proportion of its output, should be the decisive factor in determining whether an entity is a body governed by public law for the purposes of the public procurement regime. This argument appeared for the first time before the Court in the *Strohal*[28] case. Its was suggested that only if the activities in pursuit of the "public services obligations" of an entity supersede its commercial thrust, the latter could be considered as a body covered by public law and a contracting authority.[29]

In practice, the argument put forward implied a selective application of the Public Procurement Directives in the event of dual capacity entities. This sort of application is not entirely unjustified as, on a number of occasions,[30] the Public Procurement Directives themselves utilise thresholds or proportions considerations in order to include or exclude certain contracts from their ambit. However, the Court ruled out a selective application of the Directives in the case of dual capacity contracting authorities, based on the principle of legal certainty. It substantiated its position with the fact that only the purpose for which an entity is established is relevant in order to classify it as body governed by public law and not the division between public and private activities. The pursuit of commercial activities by contracting authorities blends in compatibly with their aims and objectives to pursue public interest, without the need for any weighting attached to such activities in order to determine the nature of the contracting authorities. Thus, contracts awarded in pursuit of commercial purposes fall under the remit of the Public Procurement Directives. The Court recognised the fact that by extending the application of public procurement rules to activities of a purely industrial or commercial character, an onerous constraint would probably be imposed upon the relevant contracting authorities. This may also seem unjustified on the grounds that public procurement law, in principle, does not apply to private bodies, which carry out identical activities.[31] The above situation represents a considerable disadvantage in delineating the distinction between private and public sector activities and their regulation, if the only factor appears to be the nature of the organisation in question. The Court suggested that that disadvantage could be avoided by selecting the appropriate legal instrument for the objectives pursued by public authorities. As the reasons for the creation of a body governed by public law would determine the legal framework which would apply to its contractual relations, those responsible for establishing it must restrict its thrust in order to avoid the undesirable effects of that legal framework on activities outside its scope.

The Court in *Strohal* established dualism, to the extent that it specifically implied that contracting authorities may pursue a dual range of activities; to procure goods, works and services destined for the public, as well as participate in commercial activities. Thus they can clearly pursue other activities in addition to those which meet needs of general interest not having an industrial and commercial character. The proportion of activities pursued by an entity which aims to meet needs of general interest not having an industrial or commercial character and commercial activities is irrelevant for the characterisation of that entity as a body governed by public law. What is relevant is the intention of establishment of the entity in question, which reflects on the "specificity" requirement of meeting needs of general interest. Also, specificity does not mean exclusivity of purpose. Instead, specificity indicates the intention of establishment to meet general needs. Along these lines, ownership or financing of an entity by a contracting authority does not guarantee the condition of establishment of that entity to meet needs of general interest not having industrial and commercial character.

The dual capacity of contracting authorities is irrelevant to the applicability of public procurement rules. If an entity is a contracting authority, it must apply public procurement rules irrespective of the pursuit of general interest needs or the pursuit of commercial activities. Also, if a contracting authority assigns the rights and obligations of a public contract to an entity, which is not a contracting authority, that entity must follow public procurement rules. The contrary would be acceptable only if the contract fell within the remit of the entity, which is not a contracting authority, and the contract was entered into on its behalf by a contracting authority.

Links between contracting authorities and private undertakings

Contractual and legal or regulatory links between the state and contracting authorities and also between the state and private undertakings expose the inadequacy of the public procurement framework. Such links dilute the concept of contracting authorities, which is essential to the applicability of the public procurement framework, to a degree that the provisions could not apply. Under the domestic laws of the Member States of the European Union, there are few restrictions which could prevent contracting authorities from acquiring private undertakings in an attempt to participate in market activities. The Public Procurement Directives have not envisaged such a scenario, where the avoidance of the rules could be justified on the fact that the entities which award the relevant contracts cannot be classified as contracting authorities within the meaning of the Directives. As a consequence, there is a considerable risk in circumventing the Public Procurement Directives if contracting authorities award their public contracts via private undertakings under their control, which cannot be covered by the framework of the Directives.

The Court, prior to the *Strohal* case, did not have the opportunity to examine such corporate relationships between the public and private sectors and the effect that public procurement law has upon them. Even in *Strohal*, the Court did not rule directly on the subject, but instead it provided the necessary inferences for national courts, in order to ascertain whether such relations between public and private undertakings have the aim or the result of avoiding the application of the Public Procurement Directives. Indeed, national courts of the Member States, when confronted with relevant litigation, must establish *in concreto* whether a contracting authority has established an undertaking in order to enter into contracts for the sole purpose of avoiding the requirements specified in public procurement law. Such conclusions must be beyond doubt based on the examination of the actual purpose for which the undertaking in question has been established. The rule of thumb appears to be the connection between the nature of a project and the aims and objectives of the undertaking which awards it. If the realisation of a project does not contribute to the aims and objectives of an undertaking, then it is assumed that the project in question is awarded "on behalf" of another undertaking, and if the latter beneficiary is a contracting authority under the framework of public procurement law, then the relevant Directives should apply.

The Court applied the *Strohal* principles to *Teckal*,[32] where it concluded that the exercise, by a contracting authority, of control over the management of an entity similar to that exercised over the management of its own departments prevents the applicability of the Directives. The *Teckal* judgement revealed also the importance of the *dependency test* between contracting authorities and private undertakings. Dependency, in terms of overall control of an entity by the state or another contracting authority presupposes a control similar to that which the state or another contracting authority exercises over its own departments. The "similarity" of control denotes lack of independence with regard to decision-making.

One of the criteria stipulated in the Public Procurement Directives for the existence of bodies governed by public law as contracting authorities is that they must be financed, for the most part, by either the state, regional or local authorities, or other bodies governed by public law; or subject to management supervision by these bodies, or having an administrative or supervisory board, more than half of whose members are appointed by the state, regional or local authorities or by other bodies governed by public law. To assess the existence of the above criterion of bodies governed by public law, the Court assumed that there is a close dependency of these bodies on the State, in terms of corporate governance, management supervision and financing.[33] These dependency features are alternative (in contrast to being cumulative), thus the existence of one satisfies the criterion. The Court held in *OPAC*[34] that management supervision by the state or other contracting authorities entails not only administrative verification of legality or appropriate use of funds or exceptional control measures, but the conferring of significant influence over management policy, such as the narrowly circumscribed remit of activities, the supervision of compliance, as well as the overall administrative supervision. Of interest and high relevance is the Court's analysis and argumentation relating to the requirements of management supervision by the state and other public bodies, where it maintained that entities entrusted to provide social housing in France are deemed to be bodies governed by public law, thus covered by the Public Procurement Directives. The Court (and the Advocate General) drew an analogy amongst the dependency features of bodies governed by public law on the state. Although the corporate governance and financing feature are quantitative (the state must appoint more than half of the members of the managerial or supervisory board or it must finance for the most part the entity in question), the exercise of management supervision is a qualitative one. The Court held that management supervision by the state denotes dependency ties similar to the financing or governance control of the entity concerned.

Receiving public funds from the state or a contracting authority is an indication that an entity could be a body governed by public law. However, this indication is not an absolute one. The Court, in the *University of Cambridge* case[35] was asked whether i) awards or grants paid by one or more contracting authorities for the support of research work; ii) consideration paid by one or more contracting authorities for the supply of services comprising research work; iii) consideration paid by one or more contracting authorities for the supply of other services, such as consultancy or the organisation of conferences; and iv) student grants paid by local education authorities to universities in respect of tuition for named students constitute public financing for the University.

The Court held that only specific payments made to an entity by the state of other public authorities have the effect of creating or reinforcing a specific relationship or subordination and dependency. The funding of an entity within a framework of general considerations indicates that the entity has close dependency links with the state of other contracting authorities. Thus, funding received in the form of grants or awards paid by the state or other contracting authorities, as well as in the form of student grants for tuition fees for named students, constitutes public financing. The rationale for such approach lies in the lack of any contractual consideration between the entity receiving the funding and the state or other contracting authorities which provide it in the context of the entity's public interest activities. The Court drew an analogy of public financing received by an entity with the receipt of subsidies.[36] However, if there is a specific consideration for the state to finance an entity, such as a contractual nexus, the Court suggested that the dependency ties are not sufficiently close to merit the entity financed by the state meeting the third criterion of the term bodies governed by public law. Such a relationship is analogous to the dependency that exists in normal commercial relations formed by reciprocal contracts, which have been negotiated freely between the parties. Therefore, funding received by Cambridge University for the supply of services for research work, or consultancies, or conference organisation cannot be deemed as public financing. The existence of a contract between the parties, apart from the specific considerations for funding, indicates strongly supply substitutability, in the sense that the entity receiving the funding faces competition in the relevant markets. The Court stipulated that the proportion of public finances received by an entity, as one of the alternative features of the *dependency* criterion of the term bodies governed by public law must exceed 50 per cent to enable it meeting that criterion. For assessment purposes of this feature, there must be an annual evaluation of the (financial) status of an entity for the purposes of being regarded as a contracting authority.

Procurement, contractualised governance and services of general interest

The above inferences from the Court, which point out themes that have emerged within the public sector management such as commercialism and public services, dualism and dependency, prompt the start of an important debate relevant to the main thesis of this article: the nature of governance in delivering (and financing) public services. The dramatic change in the relationship between public and private sectors, the perceptions of the public toward the dispersement of public services, as well as new forms of governance emanating through the privatisation process have witnessed an era of contractualised governance in the delivery of public services.

Whereas, *traditional corporatism* mapped the dimension of the state as a service provider and asset owner, with public procurement as the verification process of public law norms[37] such accountability, probity and transparency, it failed to mimic the competitive structure of private markets. Corporatism allowed the creation of *marchés publics*, *sui generis* markets where competitive tendering attempted to satisfy public law norms and introduce a balanced equilibrium in the supply/demand equation.[38] A first step away from corporatism towards government by contract appears to be the process of privatisation.[39] Privatisation, as a process of transfer of public assets and operations to private hands, on grounds of market efficiency and competition, as well as responsiveness to customer demand and quality considerations, is often accompanied by simultaneous regulation. It is not entirely clear whether privatisation has reclaimed public markets and transformed them to private ones. The extent to which the market freedom of a privatised entity could be curtailed by regulatory frameworks deserves a complex and thorough analysis, which exceeds by far the remit of this article. However, it could be maintained that through the privatisation process, the previously clear-cut distinction between public and private markets becomes blur. However, there is strong evidence of public law elements in the relations between public and private sectors, to the extent that regulation is the dominant feature of such relations in order to observe public interest in the relevant operations. The economic freedom and the risks associated with such operations are also subject to regulation, a fact which implies that any regulatory framework incorporates more than procedural rules.

In various jurisdictions within the common market, the socio-economic climate is very much in favour towards public–private sector partnerships, in the form of joint ventures or in the form of private financing of public projects.[40] Member States increasingly use public-private schemes, including design-build-finance-operate contracts, concessions and the creation of mixed-economy companies to ensure the delivery of infrastructure projects or services of general interest. However, it would be difficult, in legal and political terms, to justify the empowerment of the private sector in as much as it could assume the role of service deliverer along the public sector across all Member States of the European Union. Constitutional provisions could nullify such attempts and often a number of socio-economic factors would collide with the idea of private delivery of public services. The evolution of public/private sector relations has arrived in times when the role and the responsibilities of the state are in the process of being redefined.[41] Constitutionally, the state and its organs are under obligation to provide a range of services to the public in the form of healthcare, education, transport, energy, defence, social security, policing. The state and its organs then enter the market place and procure goods, works and services in pursuit of the above objective, on behalf of the public.[42] The state in its own capacity or through delegated or legal monopolies and publicly controlled enterprises has engaged in market activities in order to serve public interest. Traditionally, the function of the state as a public service provider has been linked with ownership of the relevant assets. The integral characteristics of privately financed projects reveal the degree that the state and its organs are prepared to drift away from *traditional corporatism* towards *contractualised governance*. Departure from traditional corporatism also reflects the state's perception *vis-à-vis* its responsibilities towards the public. A shift towards contractualised governance would indicate the departure from the assumption that the state embraces both roles of asset owner and service deliverer. It should also insinuate the shrinkage of the state and its organs and the need to define a range of core activities that are not to be contractualised.[43] Finally, in practical terms, it would be very difficult to prove the intention of a contracting authority to circumvent the public procurement rules and enforce their application on private undertakings.

The "public" nature of public procurement

The remit and thrust of public procurement legislation relies heavily on the connection between contracting authorities and the state. A comprehensive and clear definition of the term *contracting authorities*, a factor that determines the applicability of the relevant rules is probably the most important element of the public procurement legal framework. The structure of the Directives is such as to embrace the purchasing behaviour of all entities, which have a close connection with the state. These entities, although not formally part of the state, disperse public funds in pursuit or on behalf of public interest. The Directives describe as contracting authorities the *state*, which covers central, regional, municipal and local government departments, as well as *bodies governed by public law*. Provision has been also made to cover entities, which receive more than 50 per cent subsidies from the state or other contracting authorities. The enactment of the Utilities Directives[44] brought under the procurement framework entities operating in the water, energy, transport and telecommunications sectors. A wide range of these entities are covered by the term *bodies governed by public law*, which is used by the Utilities Directives for the contracting entities operating in the relevant sectors.[45] Another category of contracting authorities under the Utilities Directives includes *public undertakings*.[46] The term indicates any undertaking over which the state may exercise direct or indirect dominant influence by means of ownership, or by means of financial participation, or laws and regulations which govern the public undertaking's operation. Dominant influence can be exercised in the form of a majority holding of the undertaking's subscribed capital, in the form of majority controlling of the undertaking's issued shares, or, finally in the form of the right to appoint the majority of the undertaking's management board. Public undertakings cover utilities operators, which have been granted exclusive rights of exploitation of a service. Irrespective of their ownership, they are subject to the Utilities Directive in as much as the *exclusivity* of their operation precludes other entities from entering the relevant market under substantially the same competitive conditions. Privatised utilities could be, in principle, excluded from the procurement rules when a genuinely competitive regime[47] within the relevant market structure would rule out purchasing patterns based on non-economic considerations.

Although the term contracting authorities appears rigorous and well-defined, public interest functions are dispersed through a range of organisations which *stricto sensu* could not fall under the ambit of the term contracting authorities, since they are not formally part of the state, nor all criteria for the definition of bodies governed by public law are present.[48] The Court addressed the *lex lacuna* through its landmark case *Beentjes*.[49] The Court diluted the rigorous definition of contracting authorities for the purposes of public procurement law, by introducing a *functional dimension* of the state and its organs. In particular, it considered that a *local land consolidation committee* with no legal personality, but with its functions and compositions specifically governed by legislation as part of the state. The Court interpreted the term contracting authorities in *functional terms*. It regarded the local land consolidation committee as part of the state, even though it was not part of the state administration in *formal terms*,[50] since it depended on the public authorities for the appointment of its members, its operations were subject to public supervision and it had as its main task the financing and award of public works contracts. The Court held that the aim of the public procurement rules, as well as the attainment of freedom of establishment and freedom to provide services would be jeopardised, if the public procurement provisions were to be held inapplicable, solely because entities, which were set up by the state to carry out tasks entrusted to by legislation were not formally part of its administrative organisation.

The Court in two recent cases applied the functionality test when it was requested to determine the nature of entities which could not meet the criteria of bodies governed by public law, but had a distinctive public interest remit. In *Teoranta*,[51] a private company established according to national legislation to carry out the business of forestry and related activities was deemed as falling within the notion of the state. The company was set up by the state and was entrusted with specific tasks of public interest, such as managing national forests and woodland industries, as well as providing recreation, sporting, educational, scientific and cultural facilities. It was also under decisive administrative, financial and management control by the state, although the day-to-day operations were left entirely to its board. The Court accepted that since the state had at least indirect control over the *Teoranta's* policies, in functional terms the latter was part of the state. In the *Vlaamese Raad*,[52] the Flemish parliament of the Belgian federal system was considered part of the "federal" state. The Court held that the definition of the state encompasses all bodies which exercise legislative, executive and judicial powers, at both regional and federal levels. The Raad, as a legislative body of the Belgian state, although under no direct control by it,[53] was held as falling within the definition of the state and thus being regarded as a contracting authority.

The functional dimension of contracting authorities has exposed the Court's departure from the formality test, which has rigidly positioned an entity under state control on *stricto sensu* traditional public law grounds. Functionality, as an ingredient of assessing the relationship between an entity and the state demonstrates, in addition to the elements of management or financial control, the importance of constituent factors such as the intention and purpose of establishment of the entity in question. Functionality depicts a flexible approach in the applicability of the Procurement Directives, in a way that the Court through its precedence established a pragmatic approach as to the nature of the demand side of the public procurement equation.

Part 2 How are public services financed?

Market mechanisms and competitive forces offer insufficient assurances for the provision of services of general interest. The need for specific arrangements appears necessary in order to ensure their universal access, security of continuity or full geographical coverage. Member States have enjoyed a wide range of discretion as to the financing of services of general interest and the calculation of any extra cost attributed to their provision. Legal and policy traditions and the specific nature and characteristics of the services concerned, lead Member States to apply different mechanisms such as direct financial support through the State budget (in the form of subsidies or other financial advantages such as tax reductions), special or exclusive rights (such as a legal monopoly), contributions by market participants (in the form of a universal service fund), tariff averaging (for example a uniform country-wide tariff in spite of considerable differences in the cost of provision of the service) and solidarity-based financing (in the form of social security contributions).

In many instances, public service compensations are used as a funding mechanism of services of general economic interest, with only guidance from State aid rules that over-compensation is prohibited. In some cases, sector-specific legislation lays down specific rules for the financing of the extra cost of public service obligations. For electronic communications, sector specific regulation requires Member States to withdraw all special or exclusive rights, but it provides for the possibility of creating a fund to cover the extra cost of providing a universal service on the basis of contributions from market participants.[54] With reference to postal services, the Postal Directive allows a defined postal monopoly to be maintained and a universal service fund to be created for the purposes of financing the postal service.[55] In the field of air transport, Member States can grant a temporary exclusive license on the basis of an open tender in order to ensure a regular service on certain routes for which the market does not offer adequate service.[56] In public transport, the Community has laid down rules for the calculation of compensation.[57]

The rules governing the function of the internal market, competition law and policy and the application of state aid rules aim to ensure that any financial support granted to providers of services of general economic interest does not distort the competitive equilibrium and functioning of the internal market. Also, the sector-specific legislation in place seeks only to ensure that the financing mechanisms put in place by the Member States are least distortive of competition and facilitate market entry.

The ECJ and its approach to the financing of services of general interest

There are three approaches under which the European judiciary and the Commission have examined the financing of public services: *the state aids approach, the compensation approach and the quid pro quo approach*. The above approaches reflect not only conceptual and procedural differences in the application of state aid control measures within the common market, but also raise imperative and multifaceted questions relevant to the state funding of services of general interest.[58]

The State aids approach[59] examines state funding granted to an undertaking for the performance of obligations of general interest. It thus regards the relevant funding as state aid within the meaning of Article 87(1) EC[60] which may however be justified under Article 86(2) EC,[61] provided that the conditions of that derogation are fulfilled and, in particular, if the funding complies with the principle of proportionality. The state aids approach provides for the most clear and legally certain procedural and conceptual framework to regulate state aids, since it positions the European Commission, in its administrative and executive roles at the centre of that framework.

The compensation approach[62] reflects upon a "compensation" being intended to cover an appropriate remuneration for the services provided or the costs of providing those services. Under that approach State funding of services of general interest amounts to State aid within the meaning of Article 87(1) EC, only if and to the extent that the economic advantage which it provides exceeds such an appropriate remuneration or such additional costs. European jurisprudence considers that state aids exist only if, and to the extent that, the remuneration paid, when the state and its organs procure goods or services, exceeds the market price.

The choice between the state aids approach and the compensation approach does not only reflect upon a theoretical debate; it mainly reveals significant practical ramifications in the application of state aid control within the common market. Whilst it is generally accepted that the pertinent issue of substance is whether the state funding exceeds what is necessary to provide for an appropriate remuneration or to offset the extra costs caused by the general interest obligations, the two approaches have very different procedural implications. Under the compensation approach, state funding which does not constitute state aid escapes the clutches of EU state aid rules and need not be notified to the Commission. More importantly, national courts have jurisdiction to pronounce on the nature of the funding as state aid without the need to wait for an assessment by the Commission of its compatibility with *acquis*. Under the state aid approach the same measure would constitute state aid, which, must be notified in advance to the Commission. Moreover, the derogation in Article 86(2) EC is subject to the same procedural regime as the derogations in Article 87(2) and (3) EC, which means that new aid cannot be implemented until the Commission has declared it compatible with Article 86(2) EC. Measures which infringe that stand-still obligation constitute illegal aid. Another procedural implication from the application of the compensation approach is that national courts must offer to individuals the certain prospect that all the appropriate conclusions will be drawn from the infringement of the last sentence of Article 88(3) EC, as regards the validity of the measures giving effect to the aid, the recovery of financial support granted in disregard of that provision and possible interim measures.

Departing from the rationale of the above approaches, a third approach has been introduced in order to assist in understanding the relationship between the funding of public services and state aids. The *quid pro quo* approach distinguishes between two categories of state funding; in cases where there is a direct and manifest link between the state financing and clearly defined public service obligations, any sums paid by the State would not constitute state aid within the meaning of the Treaty. On the other hand, where there is no such link or the public service obligations were not clearly defined, the sums paid by the public authorities would constitute state aids.

The *quid pro quo* approach[63] positions at the centre of the analysis of state funding of services of general interest a distinction between two different categories; i) the nature of the link between the financing granted and the general interest duties imposed and ii) the degree of clarity in defining those duties. The first category would comprise cases where the financing measures are clearly intended as a *quid pro quo* for clearly defined general interest obligations, or in other words where the link between, on the one hand, the State financing granted and, on the other hand, clearly defined general interest obligations imposed is direct and manifest. The clearest example of such a direct and manifest link between State financing and clearly defined obligations are public service contracts awarded in accordance with public procurement rules. The contract in question should define the obligations of the undertakings entrusted with the services of general interest and the remuneration which they will receive in return. Cases falling into that category should be analysed according to the compensation approach. The second category consists of cases where it is not clear from the outset that the State funding is intended as a *quid pro quo* for clearly defined general interest obligations. In those cases the link between State funding and the general interest obligations imposed is either not direct or not manifest, or the general interest obligations are not clearly defined.

The *quid pro quo* approach appears at first instance consistent with the general case-law on the interpretation of Article 87(1) EC. Also it gives appropriate weight to the importance of services of general interest, within the remit of Article 16 EC and of Article 36 of the EU

Charter of Fundamental Rights. On the other hand, the *quid pro quo* approach presents a major shortcoming: it introduces elements[64] of the nature of public financing into the process of determining the legality of state aids. According to state aids jurisprudence, only the effects of the measure are to be taken into consideration,[65] and as a result of the application of the *quid pro quo* approach legal certainty could be undermined.

Public service obligations

A category of services of general interest is the concept of public service obligations with reference to the Common Transport policy of the Community and the way the Treaty and also secondary legislation regulates their financing and their relationship with state aids. It appears that the financing of public service obligations and its interplay with state aids follows the compensation approach, where the state provides for adequate and fair compensation to undertakings in order to provide the relevant services that have public interest characteristics. However, the regulation of the funding of such services is *lex specialis*, in the sense that Article 84 EC expressly excludes the application of state aids provisions to air transport and therefore, the reimbursement of undertakings costs for fulfilling public service obligation requirements must be assessed on the basis of the general rules of the Treaty, which apply to air transport.[66] The Treaty provides that state aids are compatible with its principles, if they meet the needs of coordination of transport or if they represent reimbursement for the discharge of certain obligations inherent in the concept of public service.[67] In the context of air transport, public service obligation is defined[68] as any obligation imposed upon an air carrier to take, in respect of any route which it is licensed to operate by a Member State, all necessary measures to ensure the provision of a service satisfying pre-determined standards of continuity, regularity, capacity and pricing, which standards the air carrier would not assume if it were solely considering its economic interest.[69] A Member State may thus reimburse the air carrier selected for carrying out the imposed public service obligation[70] by taking into account the costs and revenue (that is the deficit) generated by the service.[71]

The acceptability of the reimbursement shall be considered in the light of state aid principles as interpreted by the Court. In this context it is important that the airline, which has access to a route on which a public service obligation has been imposed, may be compensated only after being selected by public tender. However, Community rules on public procurement contracts do not apply to the awarding by law or contract of exclusive concessions which are entirely regulated by the procedure provided for pursuant to Article 4 (1) of Regulation 2408/92, which has set out uniform and non-discriminatory rules for the distribution of air traffic rights on routes upon which public service obligations have been imposed.

This tendering procedure enables Member States to value the offer for that route, and make their choice by taking into consideration both the consumers interest and cost of the compensation. Furthermore, the criteria for calculation of the compensation have been clearly established. A reimbursement calculated on the basis of the operating deficit incurred on a route cannot involve any overcompensation of the air carrier. Such a system excludes the possibility of state aid elements being included within the reimbursement for public service obligations. A compensation of the mere deficit incurred on a specific route (including a reasonable remuneration for capital employed) by an airline which has been fairly selected following an open bidding procedure, is a neutral commercial operation between the relevant State and the selected airline which cannot be considered as aid. The essence of an aid lies in the benefit for the recipient;[72] a reimbursement limited solely to losses sustained because the operation of a specific route does not bring about any special benefit for the company which has been selected on the basis of objective criteria.

Therefore, the Commission considers that compensation for public service obligations does not involve aid provided that: i) the undertaking has been correctly selected through a call for tender, on the basis of the limitation of access to the route to one single carrier, and ii) the maximum level of compensation does not exceed the amount of deficit as laid down in the bid. However, the fact that the public tender has not been conducted in accordance with the public procurement regime, give rise to certain concerns.

In case there is clear evidence that the Member State has not selected the best offer, the Commission may request information from the Member State in order to be able to verify whether the award includes State aid elements. In fact, such elements are likely to occur where the Member State engages itself to pay more financial compensation to the selected carriers than it would have paid to the carrier which submitted the best (not necessarily the cheapest) offer. Although the public tendering process under Regulation 2408/92 refers to the compensation required as just one of the criteria to be taken into consideration for the selection of submissions, the Commission considers however, that the level of compensation is the main selection criterion.[73] Indeed, other criteria such as adequacy, prices and standards required are generally already included in the public service obligations themselves. Consequently, it is possible that the selected carrier could be other than the one which requires the lowest financial compensation. However, if the Commission considers that the Member State concerned has not selected the best offer it will most likely conclude that the chosen carrier has received aid pursuant to Article 92 EC. Should the Member State not have notified the aid pursuant to Article 93(3) EC, the Commission would consider the aid, in the case that compensation has already been paid, as illegally granted and would open the procedure pursuant to Article 93(2) EC.[74]

The role of public procurement in the assessment of state aids

The application of the state aid approach creates a *lex and a policy lacunae* in the treatment of funding of services of general economic interest and other services, which is filled by the application of the public procurement regime. In fact, it presupposes that the delivery of services of general economic interest emerge and take place in a different market, where the state and its emanations act in a public function. Such markets are not susceptible to the private operator principle[75] which has been relied upon by the Commission and the European Courts[76] to determine the borderline between market behavior and state intervention. The state aids approach runs parallel to the assumption that services of general interest emerge and their delivery takes place within distinctive markets, which bear little resemblance with private markets in terms of competitiveness, demand and supply substitutability, structure and even regulation.

European jurisprudence distinguishes the economic nature of state intervention and the exercise of public powers.[77] The application of the private operator principle is confined to the economic nature of state intervention[78] and is justified by the principle of equal treatment between the public and private sectors,[79] which requires that intervention by the State should not be subject to stricter rules than those applicable to private undertakings. The non-economic character of state intervention[80] renders immaterial the test of private operator, for the reason that profitability, and thus the *raison d'être* of the private investment, is not present. It follows that services of general economic interest cannot be part of the same demand/supply equation, as other normal services the state and its organs procure.[81] Along the above lines, a convergence emerges between public procurement jurisprudence and the state aid approach in the light of the reasoning behind the *BFI*[82] and *Agora*[83] cases. Services of general economic interest are *sui generis*, having as main characteristics the lack of industrial and commercial character, where the absence of profitability and competitiveness are indicative of the relevant market place. As a rule of thumb, the procurement of such services should be subject to the rigour and discipline of public procurement rules and in analogous ratione, classified as state aid, in the absence of the competitive award procedures. In consequence, the application of the public procurement regime reinforces the character of services of general interest as non-commercial or industrial and the existence of *marchés publics*.[84]

Of interest is the latest case *Chronopost*,[85] where the establishment and maintenance of a public postal network such as the one offered by the French *La Poste* to its subsidiary *Chronopost* was not considered as a "market network". The Court arrived at this reasoning by using a market analysis which revealed that under normal conditions it would not have been rational to build up such a network with the considerable fixed costs which are necessary to provide third parties with the assistance that was required in that case. Therefore the determination of a platform under which the normal remuneration a private operator occurs would have constituted an entirely hypothetical exercise. As the universal network offered by *La Poste* was not a "market network" there were no specific and objective references available in order to establish what normal market conditions should be. On the one hand, there was only one single undertaking, i.e. *La Poste* that was capable of offering the services linked to its network and none of the competitors of *Chronopost* had ever sought access to the French Post Office's network. Consequently, objective and verifiable data on the price paid within the framework of a comparable commercial transaction did not exist. The Commission's solution of accepting a price that covered all the additional costs, fixed and variable, specifically incurred by *La Poste* in order to provide the logistical and commercial assistance, and an adequate part of the fixed costs associated with maintaining the public postal network, represented a sound way in order to exclude the existence of State aid within the meaning of Article 87(1) EC. The *Chronopost* ruling disapplied the private investor principle from state aids regulation, by indirectly accepting the state aids approach and therefore the existence of *sui generis markets* within which services of general interest emerge and are delivered and which cannot feasibly be compared with private ones.

The interaction of public procurement with the three approaches of state aids assessment

The compensation approach relies heavily upon the real advantage theory to determine the existence of any advantages conferred to undertakings through state financing.[86] Thus, under the real advantage theory, the advantages which are conferred by the public authorities to undertakings and threaten to distort competition are examined together with the obligations on the recipient of the aid. Public advantages thus constitute aid only if their amount exceeds the value of the commitments the recipient enters into. The compensation approach treats the costs offsetting the provision of services of general interest as the base line over which state aids should be considered. That base line is determined by the market price, which corresponds to the given public/private contractual interface and is demonstrable through the application of public procurement award procedures. The application of the compensation approach reveals a significant insight of the financing of services of general interest. A quantitative distinction emerges, over and above which state aids exist. The compensation approach introduces an applicability threshold of state aids regulation, and that threshold is the perceived market price, terms and conditions for the delivery of the relevant services.

An indication of the application of the compensation approach is reflected in the *Strohal*[87] case, where an undertaking could provide commercial services and services of general interest, without any relevance to the applicability of the public procurement rules. The rationale of the case runs parallel with the real advantage theory, up to the point of recognising the different nature and characteristics of the markets under which normal (commercial) services and services of general interest are provided. The distinction begins where, for the sake of legal certainty and legitimate expectation, the activities of undertakings of dual capacity are equally covered by the public procurement regime and the undertaking in question is considered as *contracting authority* irrespective of any proportion or percentage between the delivery of commercial services and services of general interest. This finding might have a significant implication for the compensation approach in state aids jurisprudence: irrespective of any costs offsetting the costs related to the provision of general interest, the entire state financing could be viewed under the state aids approach.

Nevertheless, the real advantage theory upon which the compensation approach seems to rely runs contrary to the apparent advantage theory which underlines Treaty provisions[88] and the so-called "effects approach"[89] adopted by the Court in determining the existence of state aids. The real advantage theory seems to underpin the *quid pro quo* approach and it also creates some conceptual difficulties in reconciling jurisprudential precedent in state aids regulation.

The *quid pro quo* approach appears to define state aids no longer by reference solely to the effects of the measure, but by reference to criteria of a purely formal or procedural nature. This means that the existence of a procedural or a substantive link between the state and the service in question lifts the threat of state aids regulation, irrespective of any effect the state measure has on competition. However, the Court considers that to determine whether a state measure constitutes aid, only the effects of the measure are to be taken into consideration, whereas other elements[90] typifying a measure are not relevant during the stage of determining the existence of aid, because they are not liable to affect competition. However, the relevance of these elements may appear when an assessment of the compatibility of the aid[91] with the derogating provisions of the Treaty takes place.

The application of the *quid pro quo* approach amounts to introducing such elements into the actual definition of aid. The presence of a direct and manifest link between the state funding and the public service obligations amounts to the existence of a public service contract awarded after a public procurement procedure. In addition, the clear definition of public service obligations amounts to the existence of laws, regulations or contractual provisions which specify the nature and content of the undertaking's obligations. The borderline of the market price, which will form the conceptual base above which state aids would appear, is not always easy to determine, even with the presence of public procurement procedures. The state and its organs as contracting authorities (state emanations and bodies governed by public law) have wide discretion to award public contracts under the public procurement rules.[92] Often, price plays a secondary role in the award criteria. In cases when the public contract is awarded to the lowest price,[93] the element of *market price* under the compensation approach could be determined. However, when the public contract is to be awarded by reference to the most economically advantageous offer,[94] the market price might be totally different than the price the contracting authority wishes to pay for the procurement of the relevant services. The mere existence of public procurement procedures cannot, therefore, reveal the necessary element of the compensation approach: the market price which will determine the "excessive" state intervention and introduce state aids regulation.

Finally, the *quid pro quo* approach relies on the existence of a direct and manifest link between state financing and services of general interest, an existence indicated through the presence of a public contract concluded in accordance with the provisions of the Public Procurement Directives. Apart from the criticism it has received concerning the introduction of elements into the assessment process of state aids, the interface of the *quid pro quo* approach with public procurement appears as the most problematic facet in its application. The procurement of public services does not always reveal a public contract between a contracting authority and an undertaking.

The *quid pro quo* approach appears to define state aids no longer by reference solely to the effects of the measure, but by reference to criteria of a purely formal or procedural nature. This means that the existence of a procedural or a substantive link between the state and the service in question lifts the threat of state aids regulation, irrespective of any effect the state measure has on competition. However, the Court considers that to determine whether a State measure constitutes aid, only the effects of the measure are to be taken into consideration, whereas other elements[95] typifying a measure are not relevant during the stage of determining the existence of aid, because they are not liable to affect competition. However, the relevance of these elements may appear when an assessment of the compatibility of the aid[96] with the derogating provisions of the Treaty takes place. The application of the *quid pro quo* approach amounts to introducing such elements into the actual definition of aid. Its first criterion suggests examining whether there is a direct and manifest link between the State funding and the public service obligations. In practice, this amounts to requiring the existence of a public service contract awarded after a public procurement procedure. Similarly, the second criterion suggests examining whether the public service obligations are clearly defined. In practice, this amounts to verifying that there are laws, regulations or contractual provisions which specify the nature and content of the undertaking's obligations.

Although the public procurement regime embraces activities of the *state*, which covers central, regional, municipal and local government departments, as well as *bodies governed by public law,* and public utilities, in-house contracts are not subject to its coverage. The existence of dependency, in terms of overall control of an entity by the state or another contracting authority renders the public procurement regime inapplicable. Dependency presupposes a control similar to that which the state of another contracting authority exercises over its own departments. The "similarity" of control denotes lack of independence with regard to decision-making. The Court in *Teckal*,[97] regarded a contract between a contracting authority and an entity under its control is not a public contract, irrespective of that entity being a contracting authority or not. The control that the contracting authority exercises over the entity must be similar to that which exercises over its own departments and at the same time the entity must perform the essential part of its activities for the benefit of the contracting authority. The similarity of control as a reflection of dependency reveals another facet of the thrust of contracting authorities: the non-applicability of the public procurement rules for in-house relationships.

Along the same line of arguments, contracts to affiliated undertakings escape the clutches of the Directives. Article 6 of the Services Directive provides for the inapplicability of the Directive to service contracts which are awarded to an entity which is itself a contracting authority within the meaning of the Directive on the basis of an exclusive right which is granted to the contracting authority by a law, regulation or administrative provision of the Member State in question. Article 13 of the Utilities Directive provides for the exclusion of certain contracts between contracting authorities and affiliated undertakings. For the purposes of Article 1(3) of the Utilities Directive, an affiliated undertaking is one the annual accounts of which are consolidated with those of the contracting entity in accordance with the requirements of the seventh company law Directive.[98] These are service contracts, which are awarded to a service-provider, which is affiliated to the contracting entity, and also service contracts, which are awarded, to a service-provider, which is affiliated to a joint venture formed for the purpose of carrying out an activity covered by the Directive.[99]

In addition, the connection between the state and entities which operate in the utilities sector and have been privatised is also weak for the purposes of justifying the presence of a public procurement contract for the delivery of services of general interest. Privatised utilities could be, in principle, excluded from the procurement rules when a genuinely competitive regime[100] within the relevant market structure would rule out purchasing patterns based on non-economic considerations. Under the Tokyo Round GATT Agreement on Government Procurement, the term public authorities confined itself to central governments and their agencies only.[101] The new World Trade Organisation Government Procurement Agreement (GPA) applies in principle to all bodies which are deemed as "contracting authorities" for the purposes of the Public Supplies and Public Works Directives. As far as utilities are concerned, the GPA applies to entities, which carry out one or more of certain listed "utility" activities,[102] where these entities are either "public authorities" or "public undertakings", in the sense of the Utilities Directive. However, the GPA does not cover entities operating in the utilities sector on the basis of *special and exclusive rights*. In many instances, Member States grant special or exclusive rights in order to ensure the financial viability of a provider of a service of general economic interest. The granting of such rights is not *per se* incompatible with the Treaty. The Court of Justice has ruled that Article 86(2) EU permits the Member States to confer on undertakings to which they entrust the operation of services of general economic interest exclusive rights which may hinder the application of the rules of the Treaty on competition insofar as restrictions on competition, or even the exclusion of all competition, by other economic operators are necessary to ensure the performance of the particular tasks assigned to the undertakings possessed of the exclusive rights.[103] However, Member States must ensure that such rights are compatible with internal market rules and do not amount to abuse of a dominant position within the meaning of Article 82 by the operator concerned. Generally speaking, exclusive or special rights may limit competition on certain markets only insofar as they are necessary for performing the particular public service task. In addition, Member States' freedom to grant special or exclusive rights to providers of services of general interest can also be restricted in sector-specific Community legislation.

Part 3 Market forces and services of general interest

The European Court of Justice, as well as the Court of First Instance has approached the subject of financing services of general interest from different perspectives. These perspectives show a degree of inconsistency but they shed light on the demarcation of competitiveness and protection with respect to the financing of public services. Also, the inconsistent precedent has opened a most interesting debate focusing on the role and remit of the state within the common market and its relation with the provision and financing of services of general interest. The conceptual link between public procurement and the financing of services of general interest reveals the policy implications and the interplay of jurisprudence between public procurement and state aids. The three approaches used by the Courts to construct the premises upon which the funding of public service obligations, services of general interest, and services for the public at large could be regarded as state aids, utilise public procurement in different ways. On the one hand, under the state aids and compensation approaches, public procurement sanitises public subsidies as legitimate contributions towards public service obligations and services of general interest. From procedural and substantive viewpoints, the existence of public procurement award procedures, as well as the existence of a public contract between the state and an undertaking reveals the necessary links between the markets where the state intervenes in order to provide services of general interest. In fact, both approaches accept the *sui generis* characteristics of public markets and the role the state and its organs play within such markets. On the other hand, the *quid pro quo* approach relies on public procurement to justify the clearly defined and manifest link between the funding and the delivery of a public service obligation. It assumes that without these procedural and substantive links between public services and their financing, the financing of public services is state aids.

In most cases, public procurement connects the activities of the state with the pursuit of public interest. The subject of public contract and their respective financing relates primarily to services of general interest. Thus, public procurement indicates the necessary link between state financing and services of general interest, a link which takes state aids regulation out of the equation. The existence of public procurement and the subsequent contractual relations ensuing from the procedural interface between the public and private sectors neutralise state aids regulation. In principle, the financing of services of general interest, when channelled through public procurement reflects market value. However, it should be maintained that the safeguards of public procurement reflecting genuine market positions are not robust and the foundations upon which a quantitative application of state aids regulation is based, are not stable. The markets within which the services of general interest have emerged and are being delivered reveal little evidence of similarities with private markets. They also do not render meaningful any comparison with private markets, which present competitiveness and substitutability of demand and supply as key features of their structure. The approach adopted by the European judiciary indicates the presence of *marchés publics*, *sui generis* markets where the state intervenes in pursuit of public interest. State aids regulation could be applied, as a surrogate system of public procurement, to ensure that distortions of competition do not emerge as a result of the inappropriate financing of services.

A new approach

The debate of the delineation between market forces and protection in the financing of public services took a twist. The Court in *Altmark*,[104] followed a hybrid approach between the compensation and the *quid pro quo* approaches. It ruled that where subsidies are regarded as compensation for the services provided by the recipient undertaking in order to discharge public service obligations, they do not constitute state aids. Nevertheless for the purpose of applying that criterion, national courts should ascertain that four conditions are satisfied: first, the recipient undertaking is actually required to discharge public service obligations and those obligations have been clearly defined; second, the parameters on the basis of which the compensation is calculated have been established beforehand in an objective and transparent manner; third, the compensation does not exceed what is necessary to cover all or part of the costs incurred in discharging the public service obligations, taking into account the relevant receipts and a reasonable profit for discharging those obligations; fourth, where the undertaking which is to discharge public service obligations is not chosen in a public procurement procedure, the level of compensation needed has been determined on the basis of an analysis of the costs which a typical undertaking, well-run and adequately provided with appropriate means so as to be able to meet the necessary public service requirements, would have incurred in discharging those obligations, taking into account the relevant receipts and a reasonable profit for discharging the obligations.

The first criterion which requires the existence of a clear definition of the framework within which public service obligations and services of general interest have been entrusted to the beneficiary of compensatory payments runs consistently with Article 86(2) EC jurisprudence, where an express act of the public authority to assign services of general economic interest[105] is required. However, the second criterion which requires the establishment of the parameters on the basis of which the compensation is calculated in an objective and transparent manner departs from existing precedent,[106] as it establishes an *ex post* control mechanism by the Member States and the European Commission. The third criterion that the compensation must not exceed what is necessary to cover the costs incurred in discharging services of general interest or public service obligations is compatible to the proportionality test applied in Article 86(2) EC. However, there is an inconsistency problem, as the European judiciary is rather unclear on the question whether any compensation for public service obligations may comprise a profit element.[107] Finally, the fourth criterion which establishes a comparison of the cost structures of the recipient on the one hand and of a private undertaking, well-run and adequately provided to fulfil the public service tasks, in the absence of a public procurement procedure, inserts elements of subjectivity and uncertainty that will inevitably fuel more controversy.

The four conditions laid down in *Altmark* are ambiguous. In fact they represent the hybrid link between the compensation approach and the *quid pro quo* approach. The Court appears to accept unequivocally the parameters of the compensation approach (*sui generis* markets, remuneration over and above normal market prices for services of general interest), although the link between the services of general interest and their legitimate financing requires the presence of public procurement, as procedural verification of competitiveness and cost authentication of market prices. However, the application of the public procurement regime cannot always depict the true status of the market. Furthermore, the condition relating to the clear definition of an undertaking's character in receipt of subsidies to discharge public services in an objective and transparent manner, in conjunction with the costs attached to the provision of the relevant services could give rise to major arguments across the legal and political systems in the common market. The interface between public and private sectors in relation to the delivery of public services is in an evolutionary state across the common market. Finally, the concept of "reasonable profit" over and above the costs associated with the provision of services of general interest could complicate matters more, since they appear as elements of subjectivity and uncertainty.

The principle of the Member States' autonomy to make policy choices regarding services of general economic interest equally applies with regard to financing their provision. Member States enjoy a wide margin of discretion when deciding whether and how to finance the provision of services of general economic interest. The financing mechanisms applied by Member States include direct financial support through the State budget, special or exclusive rights, and contributions by market participants, tariff averaging and solidarity-based financing. In the absence of Community harmonisation, the main limit to this discretion is the requirement that such financing mechanism must not distort competition within the common market. However, other relevant criteria for selecting a financing mechanism, such as the efficiency of the financial mechanism, its redistributive effects, the long-term investment of providers on services and infrastructure and finally the security of service provision could introduce a new debate platform, from where a *lex specialis* approach or a sector-specific regulation could be adopted.

The relation of public procurement with state aids reveals a symbiotic flexibility embedded in the regime of regulating the award of public contracts. That flexibility conferred to contracting authorities is augmented by a wide margin of discretion available to Member States to introduce public policy considerations in dispersing public services. State aids, as regional development considerations, or as part of a national of EU wide industrial policy are inherently a part of this symbiotic policy approach. This finding removes the often misunderstood justification of public procurement as an economic exercise and places it in the heart of an ordo-liberal interpretation of the European integration process. On the other hand, the conceptual interrelation of public procurement with the financing of services of general interest reveals the policy and jurisprudence links between public procurement and state aids. These links offer a prism of an asymmetric geometry analysis, where the three approaches used to conceptualise the funding of public service obligations, services of general interest, and services for the public at large, utilise public procurement in different ways. The presence of public procurement award procedures, as well as the existence of a public contract between the state and an undertaking verifies the state aid approach and the compensation approach to the extent that they provide the necessary links between the markets where the state intervenes in order to provide services of general interest. On the other hand, the *quid pro quo* approach relies on public procurement to justify the clearly defined and manifest link between the funding and the delivery of a public service obligation. Even the hybrid approach adopted by *Altmark* confirms the delineation between market forces through competitiveness and protection through state aids in the financing of services of general interest. The public procurement framework not only will be used to insert competitiveness and market forces within *marchés publics,* but more importantly, in the author's view, it will be used by the European judiciary and the European Commission as a system to verify conceptual links, create compatibility safeguards and authenticate established principles applicable in state aids regulation.

Conclusions

In the year of the adoption of the European Constitution, the common market and its principles have been assessed by European institutions. Considerable progress has been made in achieving a frontier-less European Union; however, trade obstacles still remain. Public procurement has been re-affirmed as a key parameter for the common market and at the same time as an important policy tool at domestic level.

Public procurement regulation is an essential instrument of the internal market. With the European Union in an expansion mode, European institutions need to provide a hint as to what public procurement stands for. There is a new generation of legal instruments currently through the legislative process which intend to simplify and modernise the regime. In addition, there is strong evidence that the existence of competitive conditions within public markets would disengage the applicability of the relevant Directives. This development indicates the referral of public markets to anti-trust, perhaps as the ultimate regulatory regime.

The regulation of public procurement reflects on two opposite dynamics: one of a community-wide orientation and one of national priorities. The influence of neo-classical economic theory on public procurement regulation has taken the relevant regime through the paces of the liberalisation of public markets within the European Union and with reference to the World Trade Organisation. Anti-trust and its remedies have played a seemingly important role in determining the necessary competitive conditions for the supply side to service the public sector. However, we have seen the emergence of a *sui generis* market place where the mere existence and functioning of anti-trust is not sufficient to achieve the envisaged objectives. Public markets require a positive regulatory approach in order to enhance market access.

Whereas anti-trust and the neo-classical approach to economic integration depend heavily on price competition, public procurement regulation requires a system which primarily safeguards market access. Such regulatory system could be described as public competition law.

The above scenario represents the first departure from the *stricto sensu* neo-classical perspective of public procurement. A policy orientation has emerged mainly through the jurisprudential approach of the regime and the willingness of the Court to expand on the element of flexibility that is inherent in the Public Procurement Directives. The neo-classical versus the ordo approach reflects the frequently rehearsed debate about the origins of anti-trust law and policy *per se*. The European integration has benefited from a system where the neo-classical approach has contributed to the functioning of an environment of workable competition. However, consistently the rigidity of the neo-classical influence has been diluted with policy considerations, often attributed to national policy requirements. The reflection of the above picture is presented in public procurement regulation, although there are certain differences: the Court has allowed for a flexible policy-oriented application of public procurement, where in anti-trust the Commission has eroded the strict neo-classical approach of controlling market power with the plethora of policy considerations. In public procurement regulation, the similarity of balancing an economic exercise with policy choice is remarkable.

As the market structure of the European Community reveals strong tendencies towards industrial concentration through mergers and acquisitions, rationalisation and restructuring of firms, downsizing, outsourcing and optimisation of human and capital resources within the sectors of the European industries, the integration of public markets has threatened to bring about an end to long-standing dependency purchasing patterns which have undoubtedly sustained certain industries in the Member States of the European Union.

The Pubic Procurement Directives introduce a regime that attempts to establish gradually a public market in the European Union. This regime seeks to accomplish unobstructed access to public markets through transparency of public expenditure relating to procurement, improved market information, elimination of technical standards capable of discriminating against potential contractors and uniform application of objective criteria of participation in tendering and award procedures. The Directives have been amended in 2004 and their new remit is based upon two basic premises: *simplification* and *modernisation*. Drawing on the wealth of experience from three previous generations of legal instruments, and the Court's jurisprudential inferences to public procurement regulation, the new Directives are set to achieve what is perhaps the most challenging objective of the internal market: fully integrate its public sector and abolish any remaining non-tariff barriers. The new regime maps also a clear-cut *dichotomy* between the public and the utilities sectors respectively. Although the same fundamental principles underpin the liberalisation of procurement in government and public utilities, their separate regulation reveals a diametrically opposed nature of the contracting authorities/entities under these sectors. Over the past two decades public utilities in the EU Member States have been undergoing a process of transformation. Their change in ownership from public to private has stimulated commercialism and competitiveness and provided for the justification of a more relaxed regime and the acceptance that utilities, in some form or another represent a *sui generis* contracting authorities not in need of a rigorous and detailed regulation of their procurement. The above dichotomy reflects an insight of current market conditions and political priorities across the European Union, as well as an indication that the main emphasis should be placed on attempts to open up the public sector.

The evolution of public-private partnerships represents a genuine attempt to introduce the concept of contractualised governance in the delivery of public services. There is mounting evidence that the role and the involvement of the state in the above process is under constant review. Public-private partnerships reveal an institutionalised mechanism in engaging the private sector in the delivery of public services, not only through the financing but mainly through the operation of assets. Efficiency gains, qualitative improvement, innovation, value-for-money and flexibility appear as the most important ones, whereas an overall better allocation of public capital resources sums up the advantages of privately financed projects.

However, public-private partnerships do not alter the character of the contractual relationship between the private and public sectors, for such character is predominantly determined by other factors attributed to the legal order in question. They, instead, bring an end to the notion of public ownership and introduce the concept of service delivery in the relevant contractual relationship between private and public sectors. The private sector is no longer a supplier to the public sector but rather a partner through a concession or an institutionalised arrangement such as a joint venture between public and private sectors. It seems that there is a quasi-agency relationship between the private and public sectors, in the sense that the former provides the relevant infrastructure and in fact delivers public services on behalf of the latter.

In its jurisprudence, the Court has reflected on the relative importance of public procurement to the fundamental freedoms of the common market, namely the right of establishment and the freedom to provide services. The approach taken by the Court revealed a positive yet restrictive interpretation of the Directives. By conferring the principle of direct effect upon their provisions where appropriate, and inviting national courts to play prominent role in future public procurement litigation, the Court has hinted towards its preference for a decentralised enforcement of the Directives. The Court has also played an important function in delineating key concepts within the public procurement legal framework, such as *contracting authorities* and *award criteria*. This has exposed *flexibility* as a significant characteristic of the Directives. The Court developed a reasoning which recognises discretion in the hands of contracting authorities, discretion which is integral to the legal framework, as well as compatible to the attainment of the fundamental freedoms of the common market and complementary with other policies. The Court's approach acknowledged that the relevant legal framework has to move on with the times, requirements and priorities of the common market.

The relation of public procurement with state aids reveals the symbiotic flexibility embedded in the regime of regulating the award of public contracts. That flexibility conferred to contracting authorities is augmented by a wide margin of discretion available to Member States to introduce public policy considerations in dispersing public services. On the other hand, the conceptual interrelation of public procurement with the financing of services of general interest reveals strong policy and jurisprudence links between public procurement and state aids. These links offer a prism of conceptualising the funding of public service obligations, services of general interest, and services for the public at large, by utilising public procurement in different ways. The presence of public procurement will not only be used to insert competitiveness and market forces within the public markets of the European Union, but more importantly, it will be used by the European judiciary and the European Commission as a system to verify conceptual links, create compatibility safeguards and authenticate established principles applicable in state aids regulation.

Public procurement remains one of the most influential instruments of policy choice in the hands of Member States and the European institutions within the process of European integration. Its complementarity and compatibility with common policies is recognised and accepted by European institutions, including the European Court of Justice and Member States.

Notes

Chapter 1   European Integrtion and Public Procurement

1. See Articles 2 and 3 of the Treaty of Rome (EC).
2. See Articles 48 and 67 EC respectively.
3. The Court of Justice has recognised a fifth freedom, the free movement of payments, which is closely related to the freedom of movement of capital, see cases 286/82 & 26/83 *Luisi & Carbone v. Ministero del Tesoro* [1984] ECR 377, *308/86 Ministere Public v. Lambert* [1988] ECR 478. The Treaty of Rome provides also for the accomplishment of this freedom in Articles 67(2) and 106. The free movement of payments, a complementary principle of the free mobility of capital as a production factor plays an extremely important role in the process of integration of public markets, and in particular in financing public projects either through indirect or direct investment.
4. Article 102a EC.
5. See case 26/62 NV *Algemene Transport-en Expeditie Onderneming Van Gend en Loos v. Nederlandse Administrtie der Belastigen* [1963] ECR 1.
6. The period from the establishment of the European Communities until 31/12/1969. See Art. 8(7) EC.
7. European Commission, *White Paper for the Completion of the Internal Market*, COM (85) 310 fin., 1985.
8. The completion of the internal market required the adoption at Community level and the implementation at national level of some 300 Directives on the subjects specified in the Commission's White Paper. See also the *Third Report of the Commission to the European Parliament on the Implementation of the White Paper*, COM (88) 134 fin.
9. See Lord Cockfield's quotation in the Cechinni Report *1992 The European Challenge, The Benefits of a Single Market*, Aldershot, Wildwood House, 1988.
10. See Commission of the European Communities, *The Cost of Non-Europe, Basic Findings, Vol. 5, Part. A; The Cost of Non-Europe in Public Sector Procurement*, Official Publications of the European Communities, Luxembourg, 1988. Also the Cechinni Report *1992 The European Challenge*, Aldershot, Wildwood House, 1988.
11. The relevant market place is then defined as public markets. See M. L. Harrison, *Corporatism and the Welfare State*, Aldershot, Gower 1984, Chapter 1.
12. See T. Daintith, *The Changing Constitution*, Oxford University Press 1985, pp. 140–212, elaborates on the distinction between *dominium* and *imperium* as functions of a modern state.
13. See P. Konstadacopoulos, *The linked oligopoly concept in the Single European Market*, Public Procurement Law Review, 1995, Vol. 4, p. 213.
14. See C. Bovis, *The Regulation of Public Procurement as an element in the Evolution of European Economic Law*, European Law Journal, Spring 1998.

15. See Denis Swann, *The Retreat of the State*, Harvester-Wheatsheaf 1988, Chapter 1–2.
16. See the response of the European Commission to a Parliamentary Question relating to the powers of a Member State to privatised publicly-controlled entities, OJ 1997 No C72/82.
17. See S. Arrowsmith, *The Legality of Secondary Procurement Policies under the Treaty of Rome and the Works Directive*, Public Procurement Law Review, 1992, Vol. 1. p. 410.
18. See Articles 29(4) and 29(a) of the EC Public Works Directive 71/305; also Art. 26 of EC Public Supplies Directive 77/62.
19. For a thorough analysis see, J. M. Fernadez Martin and O. Stehmann, *Product Market Integration versus Regional Cohesion in the Community*, European Law Review, 1991, Vol. 16, p. 216.
20. European Commission, *Public Procurement: Regional and Social Aspects*, COM (89) 400.
21. Commission of the European Communities, *Statistical Performance for keeping watch over public procurement*, 1992.
22. See case *Cooperative Vereniging "Suiker Unie" UA v. Commission* [1975] ECR 1663, in which the European Court of Justice recognised the adverse effects of concerted practices in tendering procedures on competition in the common market. This case appears to have opened the way for the application of competition law on public procurement in the Community. The applicability of Competition Law provisions of the Treaty (Articles 85, 86) in controlling collusive tendering and anti-competitive behaviour of suppliers, was also the subject of Commission Decision 92/204, OJ 1992 L92/1. It could be argued that competition law and policy applies equally to private as well as public markets, but the explicit provisions of the Directives on consortia participation in tendering procedures might limit the scope of Articles 85, 86 in public procurement.
23. For the constitutional aspects of the application of a Regulation in domestic legal orders see the reservations of the French Government after the adoption of the SEA and in particular Art. 100A EC, which constitutes the legal basis of all Public Procurement Directives after 1986 in Kapteyn and Verloren van Themaat, *Introduction to the Law of the European Communities*, 2nd ed., 1989, Kluwer-Deventer, pp. 470–479.
24. Reference is made here to the first generation of Public Procurement Directives: for Public Supplies, EC Directives 70/32 and 77/62 as amended by Directive 80/767 and 88/295; for Public Works, EC Directives 71/304 and 71/305 as amended by Directive 89/440. See Chapter 3 for more details.
25. See the FIDE Congress on *The Application in the Member States of the Directives on Public Procurement*, Madrid 1990.
26. COM (84) 717 fin.
27. See case 239/85 *Commission v. Belgium* [1986] ECR 1473; also case 300/81 *Commission v. Italy* [1983] ECR 449.
28. See case 102/79 *Commission v. Belgium* [1980] ECR 1489; also case 147/86 *Commission v. Hellenic Republic* [1988] ECR 765.
29. European Commission, *White Paper for the Completion of the Internal Market*, COM (85) 310 fin., 1985.

30. See the European Commission's *Concentration Memorandum*, Competition Series, Study no 3, Brussels 1966: *The problem of Industrial Concentration in the Common market*. For a detailed analysis of industrial concentration in the European Community see C. Bovis, *Business Law in the European Union*, Chapter 2, Sweet and Maxwell, 1997.
31. See Commission of the European Communities, *Statistical Performance for keeping watch over public procurement*, 1992.
32. The Utilities Directive 90/531 (OJ 1900 L297) and the Services 93/50 Directive (OJ 1992 L209/1) have been implemented by Spain, Portugal and Greece at a later stage in relation to the other Member States.
33. The Commission has accomplished a Mid-Term Assessment on the Functioning of Public Procurement in 1996, which has predominately resulted in the publication of the *Green Paper on Public Procurement in the European Union: Exploring the Way Forward*.
34. See C. Bovis, *EC Public Procurement Law*, Longman, European Law Series, 1997. H. Fernandez Martin, *EC Public Procurement Rules: A Critical Analysis*, OUP, 1996. S. Arrowsmith, *The Law of Public and Utilities Procurement*, Sweet & Maxwell, 1996. P. Armin-Trepte, *Public Procurement in the EC*, CCH Europe, 1993. A. Cox, P*ublic Procurement in the European Community: The internal market rules and the enforcement regime after 1992*, Earlsgate Press, 1993. Various authors, *Public Procurement: Legislation and Commentary*, Butterworths European Law Service, 1992. F. Weiss, *Public Procurement in European Community Law*, Athlone Publishers, 1992. P. Lee, *Public Procurement, Current EC Legal Developments*, Butterworths, 1992.

Chapter 2   Public Procurement Regulation

1. Public Supplies contracts: EC Directive 70/32, 77/62 as amended by Directive 80/767 and 88/295 and consolidated by Directive 93/36, OJ 1993, L 199.
2. Public Works contracts: EC Directive 71/304, 71/305 as amended by Directive 89/440, and consolidated by Directive 93/37, OJ 1993, L 199.
3. Public Utilities contracts: EC Directive 90/531, as amended by Directive 93/38, OJ 1993, L 199.
4. Public Services contracts: EC Directive 92/50 of 18/6/92, OJ 1992 L 209.
5. OJ 1977, L 13/1.
6. OJ 1980, L 215/1.
7. OJ 1980, L 71/1.
8. OJ 1980, L 215/1.
9. COM (85) 310 fin.
10. OJ 1988, L 127/1.
11. Article 7(2) of Directive 88/295.
12. Article 1(a) of Directive 88/295.
13. Article 6(1)(c) of Directive 88/295.
14. Article 3(2) (a)(b)(c) of Directive 88/295.
15. Article 9 of Directive 88/295.
16. Article 7 of Directive 88/295. See the White Paper on Completing the Internal Market, paras. 61–79; also Council Resolution of 7 May

1985, OJ 1985, C 136, on a new approach in the field of technical harmonisation and standards.
17. Directive 93/36, OJ 1993, L 199.
18. Directive 93/37, OJ 1993, L 199.
19. Directive 92/50 of 18/6/92, OJ 1992 L 209.
20. Directive 93/38, OJ 1993, L 199.
21. Article 1(a) of Directive 71/305 as amended by Directive 89/440.
22. General Industrial Classification of Economic Activities within the European Communities, see Annex II Directive 71/305.
23. Concession contracts are public works projects under which the consideration for the works consists in a franchise (concession) to operate the completed works or in a franchise plus payment. For more details see the Guide to the Community rules on opening government procurement, OJ 1987, L 358/1 at 28.
24. Article 1(d) of Directive 93/37.
25. Article 3(3) Directive 71/305.
26. OJ 1971, C 82/13.
27. Article 3 of Directive 93/37.
28. This definition resembles the Court's ruling on state controlled enterprises in case 152/84 *Marshall v. Southampton and South West Hampshire Area Health Authority* [1986] ECR 723.
29. Article 3 of Directive 77/62 as amended by Directive 88/295.
30. Article 2 Directive 71/305 as amended by Directive 89/440.
31. See Articles 29(4) and 29(a) of Directive 71/305; also Article 26 of Directive 77/62.
32. See the Commission's Communication on the *Regional and Social Aspects of Public Procurement*, where it gives an overview of the preference schemes still existing in Member States, COM(89) 400 fin.
33. Article 2(1) of Directive 93/37.
34. Article 2(2) of Directive 93/37.
35. Article 4(b) of Directive 93/37.
36. Article 5(a) of Directive 93/37.
37. Article 5(c) of Directive 93/37. Also see the relation between public procurement and Defence Policy in Chapter 7 below.
38. Article 2(4) and Article 8 of the Utilities Directive amended by Directive 93/38.
39. Article 2(5) (a) of the Utilities Directive amended by Directive 93/38.
40. Article 2(5) (b) of the Utilities Directive amended by Directive 93/38.
41. Article 3(1) of the Utilities Directive amended by Directive 93/38.
42. Article 3(2) to (4) of the Utilities Directive amended by Directive 93/38.
43. Article 6(1) of the Utilities Directive amended by Directive 93/38.
44. Article 7(2) of the Utilities Directive amended by Directive 93/38.
45. Article 8(2) of the Utilities Directive amended by Directive 93/38.
46. Article 9(1) (a) of the Utilities Directive amended by Directive 93/38.
47. It has been considered that these exemptions might be the appropriate framework to introduce a common energy policy.
48. In the future sea-ferry operators would be excluded, but their position has been kept under review. Inland water ferry services and river ferry services operated by public authorities were to be brought within the rules.

49. For the concept of origin of goods and their lawful free circulation in the Common Market, see Regulation 802/68, OJ English Special Edition 1968 (1), p. 165.
50. This includes the purchase of, on the one hand, services producing audio-visual works such as films, videos and sound recording, including advertising and, on the other hand broadcasting time (transmission by air, satellite or cable).
51. These have been excluded because they are not part of the Community liberalisation package for the telecommunications services market.
52. This refers to contracts which constitute transactions concerning shares, for example. In the public sector, it will also include within the derogation contracts awarded to financial intermediaries to arrange such transactions because these are specifically excluded from the scope of investment services (Category 6 of annex IA). However, this exclusion does not appear in the Utilities Directive so that contracts for the services of intermediaries who will make the arrangements for such transactions would be subject to the provisions of the Utilities Directive.
53. Article 20(2)(b) of amending Utilities Directive 93/38.
54. See COM (90) 372 fin, SYN 293 and COM (91) 322 fin, SYN 293.
55. This practice resembles the market testing process often employed in the United Kingdom between a contracting authority and an in-house team.
56. An affiliated undertaking, for the purposes of Article 1(3) of the Utilities Directive, is an undertaking the annual accounts of which are consolidated with those of the contracting entity in accordance with the requirements of the seventh Company Law Directive (Council Directive 83/349 (OJ. 1983 L 193/1)).
57. See the explanatory memorandum accompanying the text amending the Utilities Directive (COM (91) 347-SYN 36 1) which states that this provision relates, in particular, to three types of service provision within groups. These categories, which may or may not be distinct, are: the provision of common services such as accounting, recruitment and management; the provision of specialised services embodying the know how of the group; the provision of a specialised service to a joint venture.
58. OJ 1989 L 395.
59. OJ 1992 L 76/7.
60. Directive 92/13, OJ 1992, L 76/7.
61. See Article 7 of EC Directive 92/13.
62. See Case 188/89, *Foster v. British Gas* [1990] ECR-1313, in which the European Court of Justice ruled that a Directive capable of having direct effect could be invoked against a body which is subject to the *control* of the State and has been delegated special powers.
63. This was the view of Advocate General Lenz in case 247/89, *Commission v. Portugal* [1991] ECR I 3659.
64. EC Directive 90/531, as amended by EC Directive 93/38, OJ L 199.
65. Article 1(1) of Directive 93/38.
66. Article 1(2) of Directive 93/38.
67. The determination of a genuinely competitive regime is left to the utilities operators themselves. See case, C 392/93, *The Queen and H.M. Treasury, ex parte British Telecommunications PLC*, OJ 1993, C 287/6. This is perhaps a first step towards self-regulation which could lead to the

disengagement of the relevant contracting authorities from the public procurement regime.
68. Article 9(1) of Directive 93/36; Article 11(1) to (3) of Directive 93/37; Article 22(1)(a) to (c) of Directive 93/38; Article 15(1) of Directive 92/50.
69. See case 272/91R, *Commission v. Italian Republic*, order of June 12, 1992.
70. Article 9(2) of Directive 93/36; Article 11(2) of Directive 93/37; Article 21 of Directive 93/38; Article 15(2) of Directive 92/50.
71. Article 9(3) of Directive 93/36; Article 11(5) of Directive 93/37; Article 24 of Directive 93/38; Article 16(1) of Directive 92/50.
72. Article 3(1) of Directive 93/37; Article 14(c) of Directive 93/38.
73. Article 5(1)(a) of Directive 93/36.
74. Article 5(1)(c) of Directive 93/36.
75. Article 14(b) of Directive 93/38.
76. Article 14(a) of Directive 93/38.
77. Article 7(1) of Directive 92/50.
78. Article 5(2) to (6) of Directive 93/36; Article 6(1) to (5) of Directive 93/37; Article 14(4) to (13) of Directive 93/38; Article 7(2) to (8) of Directive 92/50.
79. Case 76/81, *SA Transporoute et Travaux v. Minister of Public Works* [1982] ECR 457.
80. Article 27 of Directive 93/37 and Article 31 of Directive 93/38.
81. Article 22 of Directive 93/36.
82. Article 20 of Directive 93/36; Article 24 of Directive 93/37; Article 31 of Directive 93/38; Article 29 of Directive 92/50.
83. Article 25 of Directive 71/305.
84. Article 22 of Directive 93/36; Article 26 of Directive 93/37; Article 31(b) of Directive 93/38; Article 31 of Directive 92/50.
85. Article 21 of Directive 71/305 as amended by Directive 89/440 and Article 18 of Directive 77/62 as amended by Directive 88/295. The same regime is followed in the Utilities Directive 90/531, Article 26, and the Services Directive 92/50, Article 26.
86. Articles 20–23 of Directive 77/62; Articles 23 *et seq.* of Directive 71/305; Articles 29 *et seq.* of Directive 90/531; Articles 29 *et seq.* of Directive 92/50.
87. Article 25 of Directive 93/36; Article 29 of Directive 93/37; Article 35 of Directive 92/50.
88. See Article 27 of Directive 93/37, Article 31 of Directive 93/38 and Article 22 of Directive 92/50.
89. Case 76/81, *SA Transporoute et Travaux v. Minister of Public Works* [1982] ECR 457.
90. See case C-27/86, *Constructions et Enterprises Indusrtielles S.A (CEI) v. Association Intercommunale pour les Autoroutes des Ardennes*; case C-28/86, *Ing.A. Bellini & Co. S.p.A. v. Regie de Betiments*; case C-29/86, *Ing.A. Bellini & Co. S.p.A. v. Belgian State* [1987] ECR 3347.
91. See case C-89/92, *Ballast Nedam Groep NV v. Belgische Staat* [1994] 2 CMLR.
92. Case C-5/97, *Ballast Nedam Groep NV v. Belgische Staat*, judgement of 18 December 1997.
93. Case C-176/98, *Holst Italia v. Comune di Cagliari*, judgement of 2 December 1999.

94. Evidence of financial and economic standing may be provided by means of references including: i) appropriate statements from bankers; ii) the presentation of the firm's balance sheets or extracts from the balance sheets where these are published under company law provisions; and iii) a statement of the firm's annual turnover and the turnover on construction works for the three previous financial years.
95. See case C-94/99, *ARGE Gewässerschutzt v. Bundesministerium für Land- und Forstwirtschaft*, paragraph 30, judgement of 7 December 2000.
96. Case 31/87, *Gebroeders Beentjes B.V. v. State of Netherlands* [1988] ECR 4635.
97. See *Bellini* Case 28/86, op.cit.
98. See case C-71/92, *Commission v. Spain*, judgement of June 30, 1993. Also, *Beentjes*, op.cit. at paragraphs 15 and 16, where the simultaneous application of selection of tenderers and award procedures is not precluded, on condition that the two are governed by different rules.
99. Article 1(d) of Directive 93/36; Article 1(e) of Directive 93/37; Article 1(7)(a) of Directive 93/38; Article 1(d) of Directive 92/50.
100. Article 1(f) of Directive 93/36; Article 1(g) of Directive 93/37; Article 1(7)(c) of Directive 93/38; Article 1(c) of Directive 92/50.
101. See the section on framework agreements under *Specific Types of Contracts under the Public Procurement Directives*, op.cit.
102. Article 6(2) of Directive 93/36; Article 7(2) of Directive 93/37; Article 20(1) of Directive 93/38; Article 11(2) of Directive 92/50.
103. Article 6(3) of Directive 93/36; Article 7(3) of Directive 93/37; Article 20(3) of Directive 93/38; Article 11(3) of Directive 92/50.
104. Article 1(e) of Directive 93/36; Article 1(f) of Directive 93/37; Article 1(7)(b) of Directive 93/38; Article 1(d) of Directive 92/50.
105. Article 12 of Directive 93/36; Article 13 of Directive 93/37; Article 26(2) of Directive 93/38; Article 19(4) of Directive 92/50.
106. Article 24 of Directive 93/36.
107. Cases C-199/85, *Commission v. Italy* [1987] ECR 1039; also C-3/88, *Commission v. Italy* [1989] ECR 4035.
108. C-199/85, *Commission v. Italy*, op. cit. C-3/88, *Commission v. Italy*, op. cit. C-24/91, *Commission v. Spain* [1994] CMLR 621; C-107/92, *Commission v. Italy*, judgement of August 2, 1993; C-57/94, *Commission v. Italy*, judgement of May 18, 1995; C-296/92, *Commission v. Italy*, judgement of January 12, 1994.
109. See case C-107/92, *Commission v. Italy*, judgement of August 2, 1993.
110. Article 26(1)(a) of Directive 93/36; Article 30(1)(a) of Directive 93/37; Article 34(1)(b) of Directive 93/38; Article 36(1)(b) of Directive 92/50.
111. Article 26(1)(b) of Directive 93/36; Article 30(1)(b) of Directive 93/37; Article 34(1)(a) of Directive 93/38; Article 36(1)(a) of Directive 92/50.
112. See Article 26 of Directive 93/36, Article 30 of Directive 93/37, Article 34 of Directive 93/38 and Article 36 of Directive 92/50.
113. Case 76/81, *SA Transporoute et Travaux v. Minister of Public Works* [1982] ECR 457.
114. See Case 103/88, *Fratelli Costanzo S.p.A. v. Comune di Milano* [1989] ECR 1839; Case 296/89, *Impresa Dona Alfonso di Dona Alfonso & Figli s.n.c. v. Consorzio per lo Sviluppo Industriale del Comune di Monfalcone*, judgement of June 18, 1991.

115. Case 76/81 *Transporoute* [1982] ECR 417, *op. cit.*
116. Case C-285/99 & 286/99, *Impresa Lombardini SpA v. ANAS*, judgement of 27 November 2001.
117. The Advisory Committee for Public Procurement was set up by Decision 77/63 (OJ 1977 L 13/15) and is composed of representatives of the Member States belonging to the authorities of those States and has as its task to supervise the proper application of Public Procurement Directives by Member States.
118. See case C-94/99, *ARGE Gewässerschutzt*, *op. cit.*
119. In *ARGE* the Court adopted a literal interpretation of the Directives and concluded that if the legislature wanted to preclude subsidised entities from participating in tendering procedures for public contracts, it should have said so explicitly in the relevant Directives. See paragraphs 26 *et seq.* of the Court's judgement. Although the case has relevance in the fields of selection and qualification procedures and award criteria, the Court made no references to previous case-law regarding state aids in public procurement, presumably because the *Dupont de Nemours* precedence is still highly relevant.
120. Case 31/87, *Gebroeders Beentjes v. The Netherlands*, *op. cit.*, paragraph 19.
121. Case C-324/93, *R. v. The Secretary of State for the Home Department, ex parte Evans Medical Ltd and Macfarlan Smith Ltd*, judgement of 28 March 1995, where the national court asked whether factors concerning continuity and reliability as well as security of supplies fall under the framework of the most economically advantageous offer, when the latter is being evaluated.
122. Framework agreements should not be confused with framework contracts, the latter producing binding effects.
123. Article 9 of Directive 93/37.
124. Case 31/87, *Gebroeders Beentjes B.V. v. The Netherlands* [1989] ECR 4365.
125. See *Bellini Case* 28/86 [1987] ECR 3347.
126. See, to that effect, paragraph 31, where the Court stipulated that an award criterion linked to the campaign against unemployment must be expressly mentioned in the contract notice so that contractors may become aware of its existence.
127. Directive 77/62, OJ C 61/26 [1977], as amended by Directive 98/50, OJ L 132 [1998] and consolidated by Directive 2001/23 OJ. L 82/16 [2001].
128. Case C 29/91, *Dr Sophie Redmond Stichting v. Bartol* [1992] IRLR 369.
129. Case C 382/92, *Commission v. United Kingdom* [1994] ECR 1.
130. Case 24/85, *Spijkers v. Gebroders Benedik Abbatoir CV* [1986] ECR 1, 1123. Case C 209/91, *Rask v. ISS Kantinservice* [1993] ECR 1. Case C 392/92, *Schmidt v. Spar und Leihkasse der fruherer Amter Bordersholm, Kiel und Cronshagen* [1994] ECR 1, 1320.
131. Case C 392/92, *Schmidt v. Spar und Leihkasse der fruherer Amter Bordersholm, Kiel und Cronshagen* [1994] ECR 1, 1320.
132. Case C 48/94, *Rygaard v. Stro Molle Akustik*, judgement of September 19, 1995, not yet reported.
133. See case C-324/86, *Tellerup*, judgement of 10 February 1998.
134. See case C-172/99, judgement of 25 January 2001, point 21/22.
135. See also the conclusions of Advocate-General Léger in Case C-172/99, in particular paragraphs 28 to 37; and also paragraph 22 of the judgement in this case.

136. See case C-513/99, *Concordia Bus Filandia v. Helsingin Kaupunki et HKL-Bussiliikenn*, nyr.
137. See the opinion of Advocate General Mischo delivered on 13 December 2001.
138. Clearly the Advocate General wanted to exclude any possibility of environmental considerations being part of selection criteria or disguised as technical specifications, capable of discriminating against tendderes that could not meet them.

Chapter 3 Lessons from Jurisprudence

1. See the recital of Directive 89/440, OJ L 210/1 1989 amending the original Works Directive 71/305 concerning co-ordination of procedures for the award of public works contracts.
2. See European Commission, *White Paper for the Completion of the Internal Market*, COM (85) 310 fin., 1985.
3. See case C-45/87, *Commission v. Ireland* [1988] ECR 4929; also case C-359/93, *Commission v. The Netherlands*, judgement of January 24, 1995.
4. See case C-45/87, *Commission v. Ireland, op. cit.*
5. See case C-359/93, *Commission v. The Netherlands, op. cit.*
6. See Article 27 of Directive 93/37, Article 31 of Directive 93/38 and Article 22 of Directive 92/50.
7. Case 76/81, *SA Transporoute et Travaux v. Minister of Public Works* [1982] ECR 457.
8. See case C-27/86, *Constructions et Enterprises Indusrtielles S.A (CEI) v. Association Intercommunale pour les Autoroutes des Ardennes*; case C-28/86, *Ing.A. Bellini & Co. S.p.A. v. Regie de Betiments*; case C-29/86, *Ing.A. Bellini & Co. S.p.A. v. Belgian State* [1987] ECR 3347.
9. See case C-89/92, *Ballast Nedam Groep NV v. Belgische Staat* [1994] 2 CMLR.
10. Case C-5/97, *Ballast Nedam Groep NV v. Belgische Staat*, judgement of 18 December 1997.
11. Case C-176/98, *Holst Italia v. Comune di Cagliari*, judgement of 2 December 1999.
12. See *Bellini case, op. cit.*
13. See case C-94/99, *ARGE Gewässerschutzt v. Bundesministerium für Land- und Forstwirtschaft*, paragraph 30, judgement of 7 December 2000.
14. Case 31/87, *Gebroeders Beentjes B.V. v. State of Netherlands* [1988] ECR 4635.
15. See *Bellini* Case 28/86, *op. cit.*
16. See case C-71/92, *Commission v. Spain*, judgement of June 30, 1993. Also, *Beentjes, op. cit.* at paragraphs 15 and 16, where the simultaneous application of selection of tenderes and award procedures is not precluded, on condition that the two are governed by different rules.
17. See Bovis, *Public Procurement as an Instrument of Industrial Policy in the European Union* (Chapter 7), in T. Lawton (ed.), Industrial Policy and Competitiveness in Europe, Macmillan Publishers, 1998, pp. 138–160; Fernadez Martin and O. Stehmann, *Product Market Integration versus Regional Cohesion in the Community*, European Law Review, 1991, Vol. 16, p. 216.

18. See European Commission, Public Procurement: Regional and Social Aspects, COM (89) 400.
19. Case 84/86, *Commission v. Hellenic Republic*, not reported.
20. Case C-21/88, *Dupont de Nemours Italiana S.p.A v. Unita Sanitaria Locale No. 2 di Carrara*, judgement of March 20, 1990 [1990] ECR 889.
21. Case C-351/88, *Lavatori Bruneau Slr. v. Unita Sanitaria Locale RM/24 di Monterotondo*, judgement of 11 July 1991.
22. Case C-360/89, *Commission v. Italy* [1992] ECR I 3401.
23. Directives 71/305 and 89/440
24. Articles 23 to 26 of Directive 71/305.
25. CaseC- 362/90, *Commission v. Italy*, judgement of March 31, 1992.
26. See case C-74/76, *Ianelli & Volpi Spa v. Ditta Paola Meroni* [1977] 2 CMLR 688.
27. See case C-18/84, *Commission v. France* [1985] ECR 1339; case 103/84, *Commission v. Italy* [1986] ECR 1759; also, case C-244/81, *Commission v. Ireland* [1982] ECR 4005.
28. Cases C-199/85, *Commission v. Italy* [1987] ECR 1039; also C-3/88, *Commission v. Italy* [1989] ECR 4035.
29. C-199/85, *Commission v. Italy*, op. cit. C-3/88, *Commission v. Italy*, op. cit. C-24/91, *Commission v. Spain* [1994] CMLR 621; C-107/92, *Commission v. Italy*, judgement of August 2, 1993; C-57/94, *Commission v. Italy*, judgement of May 18, 1995; C-296/92, *Commission v. Italy*, judgement of January 12, 1994.
30. See case C-107/92, *Commission v. Italy*, judgement of August 2, 1993.
31. See Article 26 of Directive 93/36, Article 30 of Directive 93/37, Article 34 of Directive 93/38 and Article 36 of Directive 92/50.
32. Case 76/81, *SA Transporoute et Travaux v. Minister of Public Works* [1982] ECR 457.
33. See Case 103/88, *Fratelli Costanzo S.p.A. v. Comune di Milano* [1989] ECR 1839; Case 296/89, *Impresa Dona Alfonso di Dona Alfonso & Figli s.n.c. v. Consorzio per lo Sviluppo Industriale del Comune di Monfalcone*, judgement of June 18, 1991.
34. Case 76/81 *Transporoute* [1982] ECR 417, *op. cit.*
35. Case C-285/99 & 286/99, *Impresa Lombardini SpA v. ANAS*, judgement of 27 November 2001.
36. The Advisory Committee for Public Procurement was set up by Decision 77/63 (OJ 1977 L 13/15) and is composed of representatives of the Member States belonging to the authorities of those States and has as its task to supervise the proper application of Public Procurement Directives by Member States.
37. See case C-94/99, *ARGE Gewässerschutzt*, *op. cit.*
38. See paragraphs 26 *et seq.* of the Court's judgement.
39. Case 31/87, *Gebroeders Beentjes v. The Netherlands*, *op. cit.*, paragraph 19.
40. Case C-324/93, *R. v. The Secretary of State for the Home Department, ex parte Evans Medical Ltd and Macfarlan Smith Ltd*, judgement of 28 March 1995, where the national court asked whether factors concerning continuity and reliability as well as security of supplies fall under the framework of the most economically advantageous offer, when the latter is being evaluated.

41. See paragraph 22 of *Beentjes*.
42. See paragraph 37 of *Beentjes*.
43. See case C-513/99, *Concordia Bus Filandia v. Helsingin Kaupunki et HKL-Bussiliikenne*, pending. The case concerns *inter alia* the permissibility of environmental considerations as part of the award criteria.
44. See Case 24/91, *Commission v. Kingdom of Spain* [1994] CMLR 621; case 247/89, *Commission v. Portugal* [1991] ECR I 3659.
45. See Case 188/89, *Foster v. British Gas* [1990] ECR-1313, in which the European Court of Justice ruled that a Directive capable of having direct effect could be invoked against a body which is subject to the *control* of the State and has been delegated special powers.
46. This was the view of Advocate General Lenz in case 247/89, *Commission v. Portugal* [1991] ECR I 3659.
47. EC Directive 90/531, as amended by EC Directive 93/38, OJ L 199.
48. Article 1(1) of Directive 93/38.
49. Article 1(2) of Directive 93/38.
50. See case, C 392/93, *The Queen and H.M. Treasury, ex parte British Telecommunications PLC*, OJ 1993, C 287/6.
51. Council Decision 87/565, OJ 1987, L 345.
52. See C. Bovis, *Public entities awarding procurement contracts under the framework of EC Public Procurement Directives*, Journal of Business Law, 1993, Vol. 1, pp. 56–78; S. Arrowsmith, *The Law of Public and Utilities Procurement*, Sweet & Maxwell, 1997, pp. 87–88.
53. Case 31/87, *Gebroeders Beentjes B.V. v. State of Netherlands* [1988] ECR 4635.
54. The formality test and the relation between the state and entities under its control was established in cases C-249/81, *Commission v. Ireland* [1982] ECR 4005; C-36/74 *Walrave and Koch v. Association Union Cycliste International et al.* (1974) ECR 1423.
55. See cases C-353/96, *Commission v. Ireland* and C-306/97, *Connemara Machine Turf Co Ltd v. Coillte Teoranta*, judgement of 17 December 1998.
56. See case C-323/96, *Commission v. Kingdom of Belgium*, judgement of 17 September 1998.
57. For a similar approach, see also case C-144/97 *Commission v. France* [1998] ECR 1-613.
58. Article 1(b) of Directive 93/37.
59. This type of dependency resembles the Court's definition in its ruling on state controlled enterprises in case 152/84 *Marshall v. Southampton and South West Hampshire Area Health Authority* [1986] ECR 723.
60. See case C-237/99, *Commission v. France*, judgement of 1 February 2001.
61. See case C-380/98, *The Queen and H.M. Treasury, ex parte University of Cambridge*, judgement of 3 October 2000.
62. See paragraph 25 of the Court's judgement as well as the Opinion of the Advocate General, in paragraph 46.
63. See case C-107/98, *Teckal Slr v. Comune di Viano*, judgement of 18 November 1999.
64. See Council Directive 83/349, OJ 1983 L193/1.
65. See cases C-223/99, *Agora Srl v. Ente Autonomo Fiera Internazionale di Milano*, and C-260/99 *aExcelsior Snc di Pedrotti runa & C v. Ente Autonomo*

Fiera Internazionale di Milano, judgement of 10 May 2001; C-360/96, *Gemeente Arnhem Gemeente Rheden v. BFI Holding BV*, judgement of 10 November 1998. C-44/96, *Mannesmann Anlangenbau Austria AG et al. v. Strohal Rotationsdurck GesmbH*, judgement of 15 January 1998.

66. See the Opinion of Advocate-General Léger, point 65 of the Strohal case.
67. See case C-179/90, *Merci Convenzionali Porto di Gevova* [1991] ECR 1-5889; General economic interest as a concept represents "activities of direct benefit to the public"; point 27 of the Opinion of Advocate-General van Gerven.
68. See P. Valadou, *La notion de pouvoir adjudicateur en matière de marchés de travaux*, Semaine Juridique, 1991, Ed. E, No. 3. p. 33.
69. See case C-44/96, *Mannesmann Anlangenbau Austria*, op. cit.
70. For example see Case 118/85 *Commission v. Italy* [1987] ECR 2599 para 7, where the Court had the opportunity to elaborate on the distinction of activities pursued by public authorities.
71. See Case C-364/92 *SAT Fluggesellschafeten* [1994] ECR 1-43; also Case C-343/95 *Diego Cali et Figli* [1997] ECR 1-1547.
72. See case C-360/96, *Gemeente Arnhem Gemeente Rheden v. BFI Holding BV*, op. cit.
73. See case C-223/99, *Agora Srl v. Ente Autonomo Fiera Internazionale di Milano*, op. cit.
74. M. A. Flamme et P. Flamme, *Enfin l' Europe des Marchés Publics*, Actualité Juridique – Droit Administratif, November 20 1989, p. 653, argue along the same lines.
75. Case C-44/96, *Mannesmann Anlangenbau Austria. v. Strohal Rotationsdurck GesmbH*, op. cit.
76. For a comprehensive analysis of the case, see the annotation by Bovis in 36 CMLR (1999), pp. 205–225.
77. See Article 3(1) of Directive 93/37; Article 5(1) of Directive 93/36; Article 14 of Directive 93/38; Article 7(1) of Directive 92/50; Article 6(5) of Directive 93/37; Article 2(1)(2) of Directive 93/37.
78. See C. Bovis, *The Liberalisation of Public Procurement in the European Union and its Effects on the Common Market*, Ashgate, 1998, Chapter 1, p. 16 et seq.
79. See in particular, *Working Together – Private Finance and Public Money*, Department of Environment, 1993. *Private Opportunity, Public Benefit – Progressing the Private Finance Initiative*, Private Finance Panel and HM Treasury, 1995.
80. Case C-107/98, *Teckal Slr v. Comune di Viano*, op. cit.
81. See the Compliance Directives 89/665 and 92/13, which ensure the availability of remedies to interested parties and aggrieved tenderers, access to justice and sufficient compensation to tenderers that suffered damages because of illegal acts of contracting authorities.
82. See the reasoning of the Court in the cases *BFI*, *Strohal* and *Agora* cases, op. cit.
83. See cases C-380/98, (Cambridge University) at paragraph 17, C-44/96, (Strohal), paragraph 33; C-360/96, (BFI) paragraphs 42 and 43; C-237/99, (OPAC), paragraphs 41 and 42.
84. Case 31/87, *Gebroeders Beentjes B.V. v. The Netherlands* [1989] ECR 4365.

85. See *Bellini Case* 28/86 [1987] ECR 3347.
86. Nord-Pas-de-Calais (Case C-225/98, *Commission v. French Republic* [2000] ECR 7445.
87. See, *Beentjes*, paragraph 29.
88. See, to that effect, paragraph 31, where the Court stipulated that an award criterion linked to the campaign against unemployment must be expressly mentioned in the contract notice so that contractors may become aware of its existence.
89. See paragraphs 14 and 52 of the *Beentjes* and *Nord-pas-de-Calais* judgements respectively.
90. There are a number of legal instruments relevant to social policy at Community level that may apply to public procurement. They include, in particular, Directives on safety and health at work (for example, Council Directive 89/391 on the introduction of measures to encourage improvements in the safety and health of workers at work, and Directive 92/57 on the implementation of minimum safety and health requirements at temporary or mobile construction sites), working conditions and the application of employment law (for example, Directive 96/71/EC of the European Parliament and of the Council concerning the posting of workers in the framework of the provision of services, OJ L 18/1 of 21.1.1997, and Directive 2001/23 on the safeguarding of employees' rights in the event of transfers of undertakings, businesses or parts of undertakings or businesses, OJ L 82/16 of 22.3.2001, codifying Directive 77/187/EEC), Directive 2000/43/EC of 29.6.2000 implementing the principle of equal treatment between persons irrespective of racial or ethnic origin (OJ 2000 L 180/22) and Directive 2000/78/EC of 27.11.2000 establishing a general framework for equal treatment in employment and occupation (OJ 2000 L 303/16).
91. See *General Building and Maintenance v. Greenwich Borough Council* [1993] IRLR 535. Along these lines, see the Commission's Interpretative Communication on the Community law applicable to public procurement and the possibilities for integrating social considerations into public procurement, COM (2001) 566, 15/10/01.
92. Directive 77/62, OJ C 61/26 [1977], as amended by Directive 98/50, OJ L 132 [1998] and consolidated by Directive 2001/23 OJ L 82/16 [2001].
93. Case C 29/91, *Dr Sophie Redmond Stichting v. Bartol* [1992] IRLR 369.
94. Case C 382/92, *Commission v. United Kingdom* [1994] ECR 1.
95. Case 24/85, *Spijkers v. Gebroders Benedik Abbatoir CV* [1986] ECR 1, 1123. Case C 209/91, *Rask v. ISS Kantinservice* [1993] ECR 1. Case C 392/92, *Schmidt v. Spar und Leihkasse der fruherer Amter Bordersholm, Kiel und Cronshagen* [1994] ECR 1, 1320.
96. Case C 392/92, *Schmidt v. Spar und Leihkasse der fruherer Amter Bordersholm, Kiel und Cronshagen* [1994] ECR 1, 1320.
97. Case C 48/94, *Rygaard v. Stro Molle Akustik*, judgement of September 19, 1995, not yet reported.
98. See case C-324/86, *Tellerup*, judgement of 10 February 1998.
99. See the analysis of C. Bovis, *The Compatibility of socio-economic policies with competitive tendering: the case of contract compliance and transfer of*

	undertakings, Chapter 21 in Legal Regulation of the Employment Relations, Collins, Davies and Rideout (ed.) Kluwer 2000.
100.	See case C-172/99, judgement of 25 January 2001, point 21/22.
101.	See also the conclusions of Advocate-General Léger in Case C-172/99, in particular paragraphs 28 to 37; and also paragraph 22 of the judgement in this case.
102.	See case C-513/99, *Concordia Bus Filandia v. Helsingin Kaupunki et HKL-Bussiliikenne*, pending.
103.	See the opinion of Advocate General Mischo delivered on 13 December 2001.
104.	See the debate in this article on selection and qualification and technical standards, pp. 2–5.
105.	See the analysis in the opinion, paragraphs 77 to 123.

Chapter 4   Public Procurement as Economic and Policy Exercise

1. See European Commission, *White Paper for the Completion of the Internal Market*, COM (85) 310 fin., 1985.
2. See Commission of the European Communities, *The Cost of Non-Europe, Basic Findings, Vol. 5, Part A: The Cost of Non-Europe in Public Sector Procurement*, Official Publications of the European Communities, Luxembourg, 1988. Also the Cechinni Report *1992 The European Challenge*, Aldershot, Wildwood House, 1988.
3. The European Commission has claimed that the regulation of public procurement could bring substantial savings of ECU 20 bn or 0.5 per cent of GDP to the (European) public sector. See European Communities, *The Cost of Non-Europe, op. cit.*
4. See Commission of the European Communities, Statistical Performance for keeping watch over public procurement, 1992. Also *The Cost of Non-Europe, Basic Findings, Vol. 5, Part A: The Cost of Non-Europe in Public Sector Procurement, op. cit.*
5. See Bovis, *Recent case law relating to public procurement: A beacon for the integration of public markets*, 39 Common Market Law Review, 2002.
6. The term implies a firm with more than a third of its turnover made in its own country and has enjoyed formal or informal government protection. The term has been defined by Abravanel, and Ernst (1992), *Alliance and acquisition strategies for European national champions*, The McKinsey Quarterly, No. 2, pp. 45–62.
7. See Nicolaides (ed.), *Industrial Policy in the European Community: A Necessary Response to Economic Integration*, Martinus Nijhoff, 1993.
8. See Communication from the European Commission to the Council, the European Parliament, the Economic and Social Committee, and the Committee of the Regions, "Working together to maintain momentum" 2001 Review of the Internal Market Strategy, Brussels, 11 April 2001, COM (2001) 198 final. Also European Commission, Commission Communication, Public procurement in the European Union, Brussels, March 11, 1998, COM (98) 143.

9. The adverse effects of concerted practices in tendering procedures on competition in the common market were recognised by the European Court of Justice in case *Cooperative Vereniging "Suiker Unie" UA v. Commission* [1975] ECR 1663.
10. See the Cechinni Report *1992 The European Challenge*, Aldershot, Wildwood House, 1988.
11. See European Commission, *The Cost of Non-Europe, Basic Findings, Vol. 5, Part A: The Cost of Non-Europe in Public Sector Procurement*, Official Publications of the European Communities, Luxembourg, 1988.
12. *ibid.*
13. See European Commission, *The Opening-up of Public Procurement to Foreign Direct Investment* in the European Community, CC 93/79, 1995.
14. See P. Nicolaides (ed.), *Industrial Policy in the European Community: A Necessary Response to Economic Integration*, Martinus Nijhoff, 1993.
15. EC Regulation 4064/89 [1989] OJ L 391/1.
16. See EC Regulation 1983/83 on exclusive distribution agreements ((OJ 1984 L 173/1); EC Regulation 1984/83 on exclusive purchasing agreements (OJ L 173/5); EC Regulation 2349/84 on patent licence agreements (OJ 1984 L 219); EC Regulation 123/85 on motor vehicle distribution and servicing agreements (OJ 1985 L 15/16); EC Regulation 417/85 on specialisation agreements (OJ 1995 L 53/1); EC Regulation 418/85 on research and development agreements (OJ 1985 L 53/5); EC Regulation 4087/88 on franchising agreements (OJ 1988, L 369/46); EC Regulation 556/89 on know-how licensing agreements (OJ 1989, L 61/1). See also C. Bovis, *Business Law in the European Union*, Chapters 2 and 3, Sweet and Maxwell, 1997.
17. See C. Bovis, *The Regulation Public Procurement as an Instrument of Industrial Policy in the Common Market* in T. Lawton (ed.) *European Industrial Policy and Competitiveness: concepts and instruments*, Macmillan Publishers, 1998.
18. Dunning, J. H. (1979), *Explaining Changing Patterns of International Production: in Defence of the Eclectic Theory*, Oxford Bulletin of Economics and Statistics, Vol. 41, No. 4, pp. 269–295.
19. Dunning, J. H. (1993), *The Globalisation of Business, The Challenge of the 1990s*, Routledge, London and New York.
20. The term tradability of public contracts denotes the effectiveness of the supply side to engage in transactions with public authorities in Member States other than the State of its residence or nationality.
21. McLachlan, D. L. (1985), *Discriminatory Public Procurement, Economic Integration and the Role of Bureaucracy*, Journal of Common Market Studies, Vol. 23, No. 4, pp. 357–372.
22. Porter, M. E. (1990), *The Competitive Advantage of Nations*, Macmillan, London.
23. Prahalad C. K. and Y. Doz (1987), *The Multinational Mission, Balancing Local Demands and Global Vision*, The Free Press.
24. Dunning, J. (1982), *Multinational Enterprises in the 1970's*, in: K. Hopt, *European Merger Contract*, de Fruyter, Berlin.
25. Vandermerwe, S., *A Framework for constructing Euro-networks*, European Management Journal, Vol. 11, No. 1, pp. 55–61.

26. Tirole, J. (1988), *The Theory of Industrial Organization*, The MIT Press, Cambridge.
27. See Valadou, *La notion de pouvoir adjudicateur en matière de marchés de travaux*, Semaine Juridique, 1991, Ed. E, No. 3; Bovis, *La notion et les attributions d'organisme de droit public comme pouvoirs adjudicateurs dans le régime des marchés publics*, Contrats Publics, Septembre 2003.
28. Flamme et Flamme, *Enfin l' Europe des Marchés Publics*, Actualité Juridique – Droit Administratif, 1989.
29. On the issue of public interest and its relation with profit, see cases C-223/99, *Agora Srl v. Ente Autonomo Fiera Internazionale di Milano* and C-260/99 *Excelsior Snc di Pedrotti Runa & C v. Ente Autonomo Fiera Internazionale di Milano* [2001] ECR 3605; C-360/96, *Gemeente Arnhem Gemeente Rheden v. BFI Holding BV* [1998] ECR 6821; C-44/96, *Mannesmann Anlangenbau Austria AG et al. v. Strohal Rotationsdurck GesmbH* [1998] ECR 73.
30. See Bovis, *The Liberalisation of Public Procurement in the European Union and its Effects on the Common Market*, Ashgate, 1998, Chapter 1.
31. Monopsony is the reverse of monopoly power. The state and its organs often appear as the sole outlet for an industry's output.
32. See Article 26(1)(a) of Directive 93/36; Article 30(1)(a) of Directive 93/37; Article 34(1)(b) of Directive 93/38; Article 36(1)(b) of Directive 92/50.
33. The thresholds laid down by the Directives are as follows:
    EURO 5 m for all work and construction projects (Article 3(1) of Directive 93/37; Article 14(c) of Directive 93/38).
    EURO 200,000 for supplies contracts within the European Union (Article 5(1)(a) of Directive 93/36) and
    EURO 136,000 for supplies contracts from third countries (Article 5(1)(c) of Directive 93/36) which participate in the WTO Government Procurement Agreement.
    EURO 600,000 for supplies of telecommunication equipment under the Utilities Directive (Article 14(b) of Directive 93/38) and ECU 400,000 for all other supplies contracts awarded by public utilities (Article 14(a) of Directive 93/38).
    EURO 200,000 for services contracts (Article 7(1) of Directive 92/50).
34. See Bovis, *An Impact Assessment of the European Community's Public Procurement Law and Policy*, Journal of Business Law, Issue 5, 1999.
35. See the recital of Directive 89/440, OJ L 210/1 1989 amending the original Works Directive 71/305 concerning co-ordination of procedures for the award of public works contracts, stating that "it is necessary to improve and extend the safeguards in the Directives that are designed to introduce transparency into the procedures and practices for the award of such contracts, in order to be able to monitor compliance with the prohibition of restrictions more closely and at the same time to reduce disparities in the competitive conditions faced by nationals of different Member States".
36. The demand side often omits risk assessment tests during the evaluation process. The Directives remain vague as to the methods for assessing financial risk, leaving a great deal of discretion in the hands of contracting authorities. Evidence of financial and economic standing may be

provided by means of references including: i) appropriate statements from bankers; ii) the presentation of the firm's balance sheets or extracts from the balance sheets where these are published under company law provisions; and iii) a statement of the firm's annual turnover and the turnover on construction works for the three previous financial years. See case C-27/ 86, *Constructions et Enterprises Indusrtielles S.A (CEI) v. Association Intercommunale pour les Autoroutes des Ardennes*; case C-28/86, *Ing.A. Bellini & Co. S.p.A. v. Regie de Betiments*; case C-29/86, *Ing.A. Bellini & Co. S.p.A. v. Belgian State* [1987] ECR 3347.

37. See Lawton (ed.), *Industrial Policy and Competitiveness in Europe*, Macmillan, 1998.

38. The European rules provide for an automatic disqualification of an "obviously abnormally low offer". The term has not been interpreted in detail by the judiciary at European and domestic levels and serves rather as a "lower bottom limit". The contracting authorities are under duty to seek from the tenderer an explanation for the price submitted or to inform him that his tender appears to be abnormally low and to allow a reasonable time within which to submit further details, before making any decision as to the award of the contract. See Case 76/81, *SA Transporoute et Travaux v. Minister of Public Works* [1982] ECR 457; Case 103/88, *Fratelli Costanzo S.p.A. v. Comune di Milano* [1989] ECR 1839; Case 296/89, *Impresa Dona Alfonso di Dona Alfonso & Figli s.n.c. v. Consorzio per lo Sviluppo Industriale del Comune di Monfalcone* [1991] ECR 2967; Case C-285/99 & 286/99, *Impresa Lombardini SpA v. ANAS* [2001] ECR 9233.

39. See Commission Communication, Public Procurement, September 22 1989, C 311 89.

40. See the Commission's arguments in the *Benjees* (Case Case 31/87, *Gebroeders Beentjes B.V. v. State of Netherlands* [1988] ECR 4635), *Nord-Pas-de-Calais* (Case C-225/98, *Commission v. French Republic* [2000] ECR 7445), and the Concordia C-513/99, *Concordia Bus Filandia v. Helsingin Kaupunki et HKL-Bussiliikenne* [2002] ECR 7213.

41. See Case C-45/87, *Commission v. Ireland* [1988] ECR 4929; Also Case C-359/93, *Commission v. The Netherlands* [1995] ECR 151.

42. Case 76/81, *SA Transporoute et Travaux v. Minister of Public Works* [1982] ECR 457; Case 103/88, *Fratelli Costanzo S.p.A. v. Comune di Milano* [1989] ECR 1839; Case 296/89, *Impresa Dona Alfonso di Dona Alfonso & Figli s.n.c. v. Consorzio per lo Sviluppo Industriale del Comune di Monfalcone* [1991] ECR 2967; Case C-285/99 & 286/99, *Impresa Lombardini SpA v. ANAS* [2001] ECR 9233.

43. See Posner, *Antitrust Law*, 2nd Edition, Chicago, 2000.

44. See Monti, *Article 81 EC and Public Policy*, 39 Common Market Law Review, 2002, where it is argued that public policy considerations balance the legality test of *ab initio* illegal restrictive agreements by virtue of Art 81(1)(2) EC with a set of requirements contained in Art 81(3) EC and also developed by the EC Commission in its jurisdictional capacity to provide individual exemptions.

45. See Bazex, *Le droit public de la concurrence*, RFDA, 1998; Arcelin, *L'enterprise en droit interne et communautaire de la concurrence*, Paris, Litec, 2003;

Guézou, *Droit de la concurrence et droit des marches publics: vers une notion transverale de mise en libre concurrence*, Contrats Publics, Mars 2003.

46. See Jacquemin and de Jong, *European Industrial Organization*, Macmillan, 1997; Möschel, *Competition Law from and Ordo Point of View*, in Peackock and Willgerodt, German Neo-Liberals and the Social Market Economy, Macmillan, 1989.

47. See Commission Interpretative Communication on the Community law applicable to public procurement and the possibilities for integrating social considerations into public procurement, COM (2001) 566, 15 October 2001. Also, Commission Interpretative Communication on the Community law applicable to public procurement and the possibilities for integrating environmental considerations into public procurement, COM (2001) 274, 4 July 2001.

48. See European Commission, Special Sectoral Report no 1, Public Procurement, Brussels, November 1997.

49. See European Commission, *Public Procurement: Regional and Social Aspects*, COM (89) 400.

50. The legislation on public procurement in the early days clearly allowed for "preference schemes" in less favoured regions of the common market which were experiencing industrial decline. See Articles 29(4) and 29(a) of the EC Public Works Directive 71/305; also Art. 26 of EC Public Supplies Directive 77/62. Such schemes required the application of award criteria based on considerations other than the lowest price or the most economically advantageous offer, subject to their compatibility with Community Law in as much as they did not run contrary to the principle of free movement of goods and to competition law considerations with respect to state aids. Since the completion of the Internal market (1992) they have been abolished, as they have been deemed capable in contravening directly or indirectly the basic principle of non-discrimination on grounds of nationality stipulated in the Treaty of Rome.

51. For a thorough analysis see, Fernadez-Martin and Stehmann, *Product Market Integration versus Regional Cohesion in the Community*, European Law Review, Vol. 16, 1991.

52. See Bovis, *The Liberalisation of Public Procurement in the European Union and its Effects on the Common Market, op. cit.*

53. European Commission, *Public Procurement: Regional and Social Aspects*, COM (89) 400.

54. Commission of the European Communities, *Statistical Performance for keeping watch over public procurement*, 1992.

55. See case C-74/76, *Ianelli & Volpi Spa v. Ditta Paola Meroni* [1977] 2 CMLR 688.

56. See case C-18/84, *Commission v. France*, 1985, ECR 1339; case 103/84, *Commission v. Italy*, 1986, ECR 1759; also, case C-244/81, *Commission v. Ireland*, 1982, ECR 4005.

57. See Bovis, *Public Procurement as an Instrument of Industrial Policy in the European Union*, Chapter 7, in T. Lawton (ed.), *Industrial Policy and Competitiveness in Europe*, Macmillan Publishers, 1998; Fernadez Martin and Stehmann, *Product Market Integration versus Regional Cohesion in the Community, op. cit.*

58. Sub-contracting plays a major role in the opening up of public markets as it is the most effective way of small and medium sized enterprises' participation in public procurement. All Directives on Public Procurement, influenced by Commission's Communications on sub-contracting and small and medium enterprises encourage the use of sub-contracting in the award of public contracts. Particularly, in public supplies contracts, the contracting entity in the invitation to tender may ask the tenderers on their intention to sub-contract to third parties part of the contract. In public works contracts, contracting authorities awarding the principal contract to a concessionaire may require the subcontracting to third parties of at least 30 per cent of the total work provided for by the principal contract.

59. An example of such approach is the views of the UK Government in relation to the involvement of the private sector in delivering public services. The so-called *Private Finance Initiative (PFI)*, has been utilised as a procurement and contractual system in order to create a framework between the public and private sectors working together in delivering public services. See in particular, *Working Together – Private Finance and Public Money*, Department of Environment, 1993. *Private Opportunity, Public Benefit – Progressing the Private Finance Initiative*, Private Finance Panel and HM Treasury, 1995.

60. Of interest is the recent case *ARGE* (paragraphs 26 *et seq.* of the Court's judgement), where even the receipt of aid or subsidies incompatible with the Treaty by an entity may be a reason for disqualification from the selection process, as an obligation to repay an illegal aid would threaten the financial stability of the tenderer in question. See Case C-94/99, *ARGE Gewässerschutzt v. Bundesministerium für Land-und Forstwirtschaft*, judgement of 7 December 2000, where the Court concluded that if the legislature wanted to preclude subsidised entities from participating in tendering procedures for public contracts, it should have said so explicitly in the relevant Directives.

61. See Case C-380/98, *The Queen and H.M. Treasury, ex parte University of Cambridge* [2000] ECR 8035 at paragraph 17; Case C-44/96, C-44/96, *Mannesmann Anlangenbau Austria AG et al. v. Strohal Rotationsdurck GesmbH* [1998] ECR 73, paragraph 33; Case C-360/96, *Gemeente Arnhem Gemeente Rheden v. BFI Holding BV* [1998] ECR 6821 at paragraphs 42 and 43; C-237/ 99, *Commission v. France* [2001] ECR 934, at paragraphs 41 and 42.

62. See Bovis, *The Compatibility of Compulsory Tendering with Transfer of Undertakings: the case of Contract Compliance and the Acquired Rights Directive*, Chapter 21, Legal Regulation of the Employment Relations, Collins, Davies and Rideout (ed.) Kluwer, 2000.

63. See ILEA Contract Compliance Equal Opportunities Unit, *Contract Compliance: a brief history*, London, 1990.

64. For a detailed analysis see P. E. Morris, "Legal Regulation of Contract Compliance: an Anglo-American Comparison", (1990) 19 *Anglo-American Law Review*, 87.

65. In particular in the US, see Case 93-1841 *Adarand Constructors v. Pena*, 1995 Annual Volume of US Supreme Court. The United States Supreme Court questioned the constitutionality in the application of contract

compliance as a potential violation of the equal protection component of the Fifth Amendment's Due Process Clause and ordered the Court of Appeal to re-consider the employment of socio-economic policy objectives in the award of federal public procurement contracts.

66. For an overview of the Social Policy in North American systems, see Cnossen and Bovis, *The framework of social policy in federal states: An analysis of the law and policy on industrial relations in USA and Canada*, (1996) 12, *International Journal of Comparative Labour Law and Industrial Relations*.

67. For example, in United Kingdom, every initiative relating to contract compliance has been outlawed by virtue of the Local Government Act 1988. Contract compliance from a public law perspective has been examined by T. Daintith, in 'Regulation by Contract: the new prerogative', (1979) 32 C.L.P, 41. For a comprehensive analysis of the issue of contract compliance in relation to public contracts across the European Community, see McCrudden, *Contract Compliance and Equal Opportunities*, OUP 1997.

68. See case 31/87, *Gebroeders Beenjes B.V. v. The Netherlands* [1989] ECR 4365. Also see case C360/89, *Commission v. Italy* [1992] ECR 3401.

69. There are a number of legal instruments relevant to social policy at Community level, that may apply to public procurement. They include, in particular, Directives on safety and health at work (for example, Council Directive 89/391 on the introduction of measures to encourage improvements in the safety and health of workers at work, and Directive 92/57 on the implementation of minimum safety and health requirements at temporary or mobile construction sites), working conditions and the application of employment law (for example, Directive 96/71/EC of the European Parliament and of the Council concerning the posting of workers in the framework of the provision of services, OJ L 18/1 of 21.1.1997, and Directive 2001/23 on the safeguarding of employees' rights in the event of transfers of undertakings, businesses or parts of undertakings or businesses, OJ L 82/16 of 22.3.2001, codifying Directive 77/187/EEC), Directive 2000/43/EC of 29.6.2000 implementing the principle of equal treatment between persons irrespective of racial or ethnic origin (OJ 2000 L 180/22) and Directive 2000/78/EC of 27.11.2000 establishing a general framework for equal treatment in employment and occupation (OJ 2000 L 303/16).

70. It should be mentioned that adherence to health and safety laws have been considered by a British court as part of the technical requirements specified in the Works Directive for the process of selection of tenderers; see *General Building and Maintenance v. Greenwich Borough Council* [1993] IRLR 535. Along these lines, see the Commission's Interpretative Communication on the Community law applicable to public procurement and the possibilities for integrating social considerations into public procurement, COM (2001) 566, 15/10/01.

71. See Kruger, Nielsen, and Brunn, *European Public Contracts in a Labour Law Perspective* (DJOF Publishing, 1997).

72. See Bovis, *Social Policy Considerations and the European Public Procurement regime*, (1998) 3 *International Journal of Comparative Labour Law and Industrial Relations*.

73. See the application of the rule of reason to the principle of free movement of goods and also the competition law principle prohibiting cartels and collusive behaviour.
74. Case 31/87, *Gebroeders Beentjes v. The Netherlands, op. cit.*, paragraph 19.
75. Case C-324/93, *R. v. The Secretary of State for the Home Department, ex parte Evans Medical Ltd and Macfarlan Smith Ltd* [1995] ECR 563, where the national court asked whether factors concerning continuity and reliability as well as security of supplies fall under the framework of the most economically advantageous offer, when the latter is being evaluated.
76. See paragraph 22 of *Beentjes*.
77. See paragraph 37 of *Beentjes*.
78. See Directive 77/62, OJ C 61/26 [1977], as amended by Directive 98/50, OJ L 132 [1998] and consolidated by Directive 2001/23 OJ L 82/16 [2001]. For a comprehensive analysis of the implications of transfer of undertakings in public procurement see Case C 29/91, *Dr Sophie Redmond Stichting v. Bartol* [1992] ECR 3189; Case C 382/92, *Commission v. United Kingdom* [1994] ECR 2435; Case 24/85, *Spijkers v. Gebroders Benedik Abbatoir CV* [1986] ECR 1123; Case C 209/91, *Rask v. ISS Kantinservice* [1993] ECR 5735; Case C 392/92, *Schmidt v. Spar und Leihkasse der fruherer Amter Bordersholm, Kiel und Cronshagen* [1994] ECR 1320; Case C 392/92, *Schmidt v. Spar und Leihkasse der fruherer Amter Bordersholm, Kiel und Cronshagen* [1994] ECR 1320; Case C 48/94, *Rygaard v. Stro Molle Akustik* [1995] ECR 2745; Case C-324/86, *Tellerup* [1998] ECR 739.
79. See Case C-513/99, *Concordia Bus Filandia Oy Ab v. Helsingin Kaupunki et HKL-Bussiliikenne* [2002] ECR 7213.
80. The applicability of Competition Law and Policy of the Treaty (Articles 85, 86) in controlling collusive tendering and anti-competitive behaviour of suppliers, was the subject of Commission Decision 92/204, OJ 1992 L92/1.
81. See C. Bovis, *Business Law in the European Union*, Chapter 3, Sweet and Maxwell, 1997.
82. Thomsen, S. and Nicolaides P. (1991), *The evolution of Japanese Direct Investment in Europe: Death of a Salesman*, Royal Institute of International Affairs, London.
83. The term implies a firm with more than a third of its turnover made in its own country and has enjoyed formal or informal government protection. The term has been defined by Abravanel, R. and D. Ernst (1992), *Alliance and acquisition strategies for European national champions*, The McKinsey Quarterly, No. 2, pp. 45–62.
84. Abravanel, R. and D. Ernst (1992), *Alliance and acquisition strategies for European national champions*, The McKinsey Quarterly, No. 2, pp. 45–62.
85. Davies, S. and B. Lyons (1993), *The EC Industrial Organization Data Matrix*, Mimeo.
86. See European Commission, *SMEs participation in public procurement in the European Community* (SEC(92) 722). European *Commission Action Programme for SMEs* (COM (86) 445); (b) *Public Procurement: Regional and Social Aspects* (COM (89) 400); (c) *Promoting SME Participation in the Community* (COM (90) 166).

87. See European Commission, *SME TASK FORCE: SMEs and Public Procurement*, Brussels 1988. European Commission, *Pan European Forum on Sub-Contracting in the Community*, Brussels 1993.
88. See Council Decision 80/271, OJ 1979 L 71/1 and Council Decision 87/565, OJ 1987, L 345/24. Also the Agreement on Government Procurement as a result of the negotiations during the GATT Uruguay Round which was signed on April 15, 1996. The new Government Procurement Agreement (GPA), after ratification by its signatories, is in force since January 1, 1996.
89. European Commission, *Statistical Performance for keeping watch over public procurement*, 1992.

Chapter 5 A Critical Assessment of Public Procurement

1. 5 million EURO for all work and construction projects, Article 3(1) of Directive 93/37; Article 14(c) of Directive 93/38.
   200,000 EURO for supplies contracts within the European Union [Article 5(1)(a) of Directive 93/36] and
   136,000 EURO for supplies contracts from third countries [Article 5(1)(c) of Directive 93/36]
   600,000 EURO for supplies of telecommunication equipment under the Utilities Directive [Article 14(b) of Directive 93/38] and ECU 400,000 for all other supplies contracts awarded by public utilities [Article 14(a) of Directive 93/38]
   200,000 EURO for services contracts [Article 7(1) of Directive 92/50].
2. Articles 17 and 20 of the Public Supplies (93/36) and Public Works (93/37) Directives respectively.
3. Article 29(5) of Directive 71/305 as amended by Directive 89/440.
4. Case 76/81, *SA Transporoute et Travaux v. Minister of Public Works* [1982] ECR 457; Case No 104/75, *SA SHV Belgium v. La Maison Ideale et Societe Nationale du Longement*, before the Belgian Conseil d'Etat, judgement of 24/6/86 of the Belgian Conseil d'Etat.
5. Article 1(d) of Directive 93/36; Article 1(e) of Directive 93/37; Article 1(7)(a) of Directive 93/38; Article 1(d) of Directive 92/50.
6. Article 1(f) of Directive 93/36; Article 1(g) of Directive 93/37; Article 1(7)(c) of Directive 93/38; Article 1(c) of Directive 92/50.
7. Article 1(e) of Directive 93/36; Article 1(f) of Directive 93/37; Article 1(7)(b) of Directive 93/38; Article 1(d) of Directive 92/50.
8. Article 1(5) of Directive 93/38.
9. Article 20(2)(i) of Directive 93/38.
10. Article 1(f) of Directive 93/36; Article 1(g) of Directive 93/37; Article 1(7)(c) of Directive 93/38; Article 1(c) of Directive 92/50.
11. Article 6(2) of Directive 93/36; Article 7(2) of Directive 93/37; Article 20(1) of Directive 93/38; Article 11(2) of Directive 92/50.
12. Article 6(3) of Directive 93/36; Article 7(3) of Directive 93/37; Article 20(3) of Directive 93/38; Article 11(3) of Directive 92/50.
13. Article 12 of Directive 93/36; Article 13 of Directive 93/37; Article 26(2) of Directive 93/38; Article 19(4) of Directive 92/50.
14. Utilities were first regulated in their procurement by virtue of EC Directive 90/531, OJ 1990, L 297.

15. See Articles 37 and 90 EC.
16. Article 7 of Directive 88/295. See the White Paper on Completing the Internal Market, paras. 61–79; also Council Resolution of 7 May 1985, OJ 1985, C 136, on a new approach in the field of technical harmonisation and standards.
17. See the Documents of the Advisory Committee for the Opening up of Public Procurement, *Policy Guidelines on the Obligation to refer to European Standards*, CCO/91/67 final.
18. See the report of the Advisory Committee for the Opening up of Public Procurement, *Standards for Procurement*, CCO/92/02.
19. Commission of the European Communities, *The Use of Negotiated Procedures as a Non-Tariff Barrier in Public Procurement*, Brussels, 1995. The industries/sectors investigated included Chemicals & Pharmaceuticals, Heavy Steel Structures, Mechanical Engineering, Office Machinery & Electronic Data Processing Equipment, Electrical Engineering, Instrument Engineering, Motor Vehicles, Aerospace, Railway Rolling-Stock, and Food Processing.
20. See the Green Paper on Public Procurement in the European Union: Exploring the way forward, European Commission 1996.

Chapter 6 The New Public Procurement Regime

1. The current Public Procurement Directives have been recently amended by Directive 2004/18, OJ L 134, 30.4.2004 on the coordination of procedures for the award of public works contracts, public supply contracts and public service contracts and Directive 2004/17, OJ L 134, 30.4.2004 coordinating the procurement procedures of entities operating in the water, energy, transport and postal services sectors.
2. See the proposal from the European Commission OJ C 29 E, 30.1.2001, p. 11 and OJ C 203 E, 27.8.2002, p. 210; the opinion of the Economic and Social Committee OJ C 193, 10.7.2001, p. 7; the opinion of the Committee of the Regions OJ C 144, 16.5.2001, p. 23; the opinion of the European Parliament of 17 January 2002 (OJ C 271 E, 7.11.2002, p. 176), Council Common Position of 20 March 2003 (OJ C 147 E, 24.6.2003, p. 1) and Position of the European Parliament of 2 July 2003 (not yet published in the Official Journal). See also the Legislative Resolution of the European Parliament of 29 January 2004 and Decision of the Council of 2 February 2004.
3. See the Green Paper on Public Procurement in the European Union: Exploring the way forward, European Commission 1996.
4. See Article 80 of Directive 2004/18, regarding implementation, where Member States are obliged to bring into force the laws, regulations and administrative provisions necessary to comply with the Public Sector Directive no later than 31 January 2006 and by that deadline to inform the European Commission on the measures they intend to introduce in order to incorporate the Directive's provisions into national laws.
5. The current Public Procurement regime includes the Public Supplies Directive 93/36/EEC, OJ L 199, 9.8.1993 as amended by Directive 97/52/EC OJ L 328, 28.11.1997; The Public Works Directive 93/37/EEC, OJ L 199, 9.8.1993 as amended by Directive 97/52/EC OJ L 328, 28.11.1997;

The Utilities Directives 93/38/EEC OJ L 199, 9.8.1993 as amended by Directive 98/4/EC OJ L 101, 1.4.1998; The Public Services Directive 92/50/EEC, OJ L 209, 24.7.1992 as last amended by Directive 97/52/EC OJ L 328, 28.11.1997; The Remedies Utilities Directive 92/13/EEC OJ L 076, 23.03.1992; The Public Remedies Directive 89/665/EEC OJ L 395, 30.12.1989.

6. The co-ordination of national procedures is the ratione behind all public procurement legal instruments.
7. See Bovis, *Public Procurement and the Internal Market of the 21st Century: Economic Exercise versus Policy Choice*, Chapter 17 in EU Law for the 21st Century: Rethinking the New Legal Order, O'Keeffe and Tridimas (eds), Hart Publishing 2005.
8. See Directives 92/50/EEC of 18 June 1992 relating to the coordination of procedures for the award of public service contracts OJ L 209, 24.7.1992, p. 1, as last amended by Directive 2001/78/EC (OJ L 285, 29.10.2001, p. 1).
9. See Directive 93/36/EEC of 14 June 1993 coordinating procedures for the award of public supply contracts OJ L 199, 9.8.1993, p. 1, as last amended by Directive 2001/78/EC.
10. See Directive 93/37/EEC of 14 June 1993 concerning the coordination of procedures for the award of public works contracts OJ L 199, 9.8.1993, p. 54, as last amended by Directive 2001/78/EC.
11. For a comprehensive analysis of the public procurement case-law, see Bovis, *Recent case law relating to public procurement: A beacon for the integration of public markets*, 39 CMLRev, 2002.
12. See Communication from the European Commission to the Council, the European Parliament, the Economic and Social Committee, and the Committee of the Regions, "Working together to maintain momentum" 2001 Review of the Internal Market Strategy, Brussels, 11 April 2001, COM (2001) 198 final. Also, European Commission, Commission Communication, Public procurement in the European Union, Brussels, March 11, 1998, COM (98) 143. See Commission Interpretative Communication on the Community law applicable to public procurement and the possibilities for integrating social considerations into public procurement, COM (2001) 566, 15 October 2001. Also, Commission Interpretative Communication on the Community law applicable to public procurement and the possibilities for integrating environmental considerations into public procurement, COM (2001) 274, 4 July 2001.
13. See case C-94/99, *ARGE Gewässerschutz v. Bundesministerium für Land- und Forstwirtschaft*, paragraph 30, judgement of 7 December 2000, where the Court stated that ruled that directly or indirectly subsidised tenders by the state or other contracting authorities or even by the contracting authority itself can be legitimately part of the evaluation process.
14. See OJ L 193, 18.7.1983, p. 1, as last amended by Directive 2001/65/EC (OJ L 283, 27.10.2001, p. 28).
15. See case C-76/81, *SA Transporoute et Travaux v. Minister of Public Works* [1982] ECR 457; case C-27/86, *Constructions et Enterprises Indusrtielles S.A (CEI) v. Association Intercommunale pour les Autoroutes des Ardennes*; case C-28/86, *Ing.A. Bellini & Co. S.p.A. v. Regie de Betiments*; case C-29/86,

Ing.A. Bellini & Co. S.p.A. v. Belgian State [1987] ECR 3347; case C-89/92, *Ballast Nedam Groep NV v. Belgische Staat* [1994] 2 CMLR; case C-5/97, *Ballast Nedam Groep NV v. Belgische Staat*, judgement of 18 December 1997; case C-176/98, *Holst Italia v. Comune di Cagliari*, judgement of 2 December 1999.

16. Articles 44 to 46 govern the conduct of the procedure for Verification of the suitability and choice of participants and award of contracts, Criteria for qualitative selection, and Suitability to pursue a professional activity.
17. Article 53 refers to the award criteria being the most economically advantageous offer or the lowest price. When the award is made to the tender most economically advantageous from the point of view of the contracting authority, various criteria linked to the subject-matter of the public contract in question, for example, quality, price, technical merit, aesthetic and functional characteristics, environmental characteristics, running costs, cost-effectiveness, after-sales service and technical assistance, delivery date and delivery period or period of completion. When the award criterion refers to the lowest price only, no other factors should play a part.
18. See OJ L 13, 19.1.2000, p. 12.
19. See OJ L 178, 17.7.2000, p. 1.
20. See Regulation (EC) No 761/2001 of the European Parliament and of the Council of 19 March 2001 allowing a voluntary participation by organisations in a Community eco-management and audit scheme (EMAS) (OJ L 114, 24.4.2001, p. 1).
21. See OJ L 18, 12.1.97, p. 1.
22. See OJ L 336, 23.12.1994, p. 1.
23. See Council Directive 2000/78/EC of 27 November 2000 establishing a general framework for equal treatment in employment and occupation (OJ L 303, 2.12.2000, p. 16).
24. See Council Directive 76/207/EEC of 9 February 1976 on the implementation of the principle of equal treatment for men and women as regards access to employment, vocational training and promotion, and working conditions (OJ L 39, 14.2.1976, p. 40). Directive amended by Directive 2002/73/EC of the European Parliament and of the Council (OJ L 269, 5.10.2002, p. 15).
25. See OJ L 351, 29.12.1998, p. 1.
26. See OJ C 195, 25.6.1997, p. 1.
27. See OJ L 358, 31.12.1998, p. 2.
28. See OJ C 316, 27.11.1995, p. 48.
29. See OJ L 166, 28.6.1991, p. 77. Directive as amended by Directive 2001/97/EC of the European Parliament and of the Council of 4 December 2001 (OJ L 344, 28.12.2001, p. 76).
30. See OJ L 336, 23.12.1994, p. 1.
31. See OJ L 15, 21.1.1998, p. 14. Directive as last amended by Regulation (EC) No 1882/2003 (OJ L 284, 31.10.2003, p. 1).
32. According to Article 68(2), for the adoption of a Decision the Commission shall be allowed a period of three months commencing on the first working day following the date on which it receives the notification or the request. However, this period may be extended once

by a maximum of three months in duly justified cases, in particular if the information contained in the notification or the request or in the documents annexed thereto is incomplete.

33. Strategy for the internal market, Priorities 2003–2006, COM (2003) 238 final.
34. Communication from the Commission "A European initiative for growth: Investing in networks and knowledge for growth and jobs", COM (2003) 690 final, 11 November 2003. This report was approved by the Brussels European Council on 12 December 2003.
35. See Report on the results of the consultation on the Green Paper on general interest services.
36. COM (2004) 237 fin.
37. The rules on the internal market, including the rules and principles governing public contracts and concessions, apply to any economic activity, i.e. any activity which consists in providing services, goods, or carrying out works in a market, even if these services, goods or works are intended to provide a "public service", as defined by a Member State.
38. See Interpretive Communication of the Commission on concessions in Community law, OJ C 121, 29 April 2000.
39. See Directives 92/50/EEC, 93/36/EEC, 93/37/EEC, 93/38/EEC, relating to the coordination of procedures for the award respectively of public service contracts, public supply contracts, public works contracts, and contracts in the water, energy, transport and telecommunications sectors. These Directives will be replaced by Directive 2004/18/EC of the European Parliament and of Council of 31 March 2004 relating to the coordination of procedures for the award of public works, supply and services contracts, and Directive 2004/17/EC of the European Parliament and of the Council of 31 March 2004 relating to the coordination of procedures for the award of contracts in the water, energy, transport and postal services sectors. Moreover, in certain sectors, and particularly the transport sector, the organisation of a PPP may be subject to specific sectoral legislation. See Regulation (EEC) No 2408/92 of the Council on access of Community air carriers to intra-Community air routes, Council Regulation (EEC) No 3577/92 applying the principle of freedom to provide services to maritime transport within Member States, Council Regulation (EEC) No 1191/69 on action by Member States concerning the obligations inherent in the concept of a public service in transport by rail, road and inland waterway, as amended by Regulation (EEC) No 1893/91, and the amended proposal for a Regulation of the European Parliament and of the Council on action by Member States concerning public service requirements and the award of public service contracts in passenger transport by rail, road and inland waterway (COM (2002) 107 final).
40. See Joint cases C-285/99 and C-286/99, *Impresa Lombardini v. ANAS*, Judgement of 27 November 2001, paragraph 36 and, to that effect case C-380/98, *University of Cambridge*, ECR I-8035 and case C-19/00, *SIAC construction*, ECR I-7725.
41. In PPPs, the public partners are primarily national, regional or local authorities. They may also be public law bodies created to fulfil general

interest tasks under State control, or certain network system operators. To simplify matters, the term "contracting body" will be used in this document to designate all of these agencies. Thus this term covers "contracting authorities" within the meaning of Directives 92/50/EEC, 93/36/EEC, 93/37/EEC and 2004/18/EC and the contracting entities of the type "public authorities" and "public undertakings" within the meaning of Directives 93/38/EEC and 2004/17/EC.

42. Judgement of the Court of 12 July 2001, Case C-399/98, *Scala*, ECR I-5409, see in particular points 53 to 55.
43. i.e. those listed in Annex IA of Directive 92/50/EEC or Annex XVIA of Directive 93/38/EEC.
44. Interpretative Communication on concessions under Community law, OJ C 121, 29 April 2000.
45. Council Regulation (EC) No 2157/2001, 8 October 2001.

Chapter 7   Public-Private Partnerships

1. See T. Daintith, *The Executive Power Today: Bargaining and Economic Control* in *The Changing Constitution*, J. Jowell and D. Oliver (eds), Oxford University Press, 1985, where reference is made to the distinction between *dominium* and *imperium* (the use of force by way of regulatory or criminal law) as two ways of policy implementation by the state.
2. The industrial or commercial character of an organisation depends much upon a number of criteria that reveal the thrust behind the organisation's participation in the relevant market. The state and its organs may act either by exercising public powers or by carrying economic activities of an industrial or commercial nature by offering goods and services on the market. See for example, case 118/85 *Commission v. Italy* [1987] ECR 2599 para 7, where the European Court of Justice had the opportunity to elaborate on the distinction of activities pursued by public authorities and activities of commercially oriented undertakings. The key issue is the organisation's intention to achieve profitability and pursue its objectives through a spectrum of commercially motivated decisions. The distinction between the range of activities which relate to public authority and those which, although carried out by public persons, fall within the private domain is drawn most clearly from case-law and judicial precedence of the ECJ concerning the applicability of competition rules of the Treaty to the given activities. See cases C-364/92 *SAT Fluggesellschaften* [1994] ECR I-43 and C-343/95 *Diego Cali et Figli* [1997] ECR I-1547).
3. The origins of such activities can be found in J. J. Rousseau, *The Social Contract*, where a core range of obligations is undertaken by the state on behalf of its subjects. This is perhaps the first attempt to contractualised the state/society relationship.
4. See M. L. Harrison, *Corporatism and the Welfare State*, Chapter 1, Aldershot, Gower 1984.
5. See M. A. Flamme et P. Flamme, *Enfin l' Europe des Marchés Publics*, Actualité Juridique – Droit Administratif, November 20 1989, p. 653.

6. The concept "public interest" denotes the requirements of a community (local or national) in its entirety which should not overlap with the specific or exclusive interest of a clearly determined person or group of persons. See P. Valadou, *La notion de pouvoir adjudicateur en matière de marchés de travaux*, Semaine Juridique, 1991, Ed. E, No. 3. p. 33. Also, the European Court of Justice has approached the above concept of public interest by a direct analogy of the concept "general economic interest", as defined in Article 90(2) EC, which refers to public undertakings). See case C-179/90, *Merci Convenzionali Porto di Gevova* [1991] ECR 1-5889, where the notion general economic interest as a concept represents "activities of direct benefit to the public".
7. Apart from the above fundamental differentiating factor, a number of striking variances distinguish private from public markets. These variances focus on structural elements of the relevant market place, competitiveness, demand conditions, supply conditions, the production process, and finally pricing and risk. They also provide for an indication as to the different methods and approaches employed in their regulation. See, C. Bovis, *The Liberalisation of Public Procurement and its Impact on the Common Market*, Ashgate – Dartmouth Publishing International, 1998, pp. 5–11.
8. Corporatism has been deemed as an important instrument of industrial policy of a state, in particular where procurement systems have been utilised with a view to promoting structural adjustment policies and favour *national champions*. See C. Bovis, *The Choice of Policies and the Regulation Public Procurement in the European Community* in T. Lawton (ed.) *European Industrial Policy and Competitiveness: concepts and instruments*, Macmillan Publishers, 1998.
9. Although anti-trust rules are of negative nature, by no means they can be deemed static. Perceptions concerning cartels and abusive dominant behaviour change in line with contemporary socio-economic parameters.
10. See C. Bovis, *The Regulation of Public Procurement as an element in the Evolution of European Economic Law*, European Law Journal, Vol. 4. issue 2, p. 220 *et seq*. June 1998.
11. The adverse effects of concerted practices in tendering procedures on competition in the common market were recognised by the the European Court of Justice in case *Cooperative Vereniging "Suiker Unie" UA v. Commission* [1975] ECR 1663.
12. See European Commission, *The Cost of Non-Europe, Basic Findings, Vol. 5, Part A: The Cost of Non-Europe in Public Sector Procurement*, Official Publications of the European Communities, Luxembourg, 1988. The European Commission has claimed that the regulation of public procurement through the newly established regime and the resulting elimination of non-tariff barriers arising from discriminatory and preferential purchasing patterns of Member Sates could bring about substantial savings of 20 billion EURO or 0.5 per cent of GDP to the (European) public sector.
13. For an analysis of the concept, see C. Bovis, *The Liberalisation of Public Procurement and its Impact on the Common Market*, pp. 4–20, *op. cit*.

14. See P. J. Birkinshaw, *Corporatism and Accountability in Corporatism and the Corporate State*, N. O'Sullivan and A. Cox (eds), Edward Elgar, 1988.
15. For example, defence, policing or other essential or core elements of governance. It is maintained here that activities related to *imperium* (the use of force by way of regulatory or criminal law) could not be the subject of contractualised governance. A useful analysis for such argument is provided in case C-44/96, *Mannesmann Anlangenbau Austria AG et al. v. Strohal Rotationsdurck GesmbH*, (judgement of January 15, 1998), where the notions of public security and safety are used to described a range of activities by the state which possess the characteristic of "public service obligations". For a commentary of the case, see C. Bovis, *Redefining Contracting Authorities under the EC Public Procurement Directives: An Analysis of the case C-44/96, Mannesmann Anlangenbau Austria AG et al. v. Strohal Rotationsdurck GesmbH*, Common Market Law Review, Autumn 1998.
16. See, R. Thomas, *Private Finance Initiative – Government by Contract*, European Public Law, Vol. 3, issue 4, p. 519 *et seq*. December 1997.
17. A number of reasons which have been put forward include *inter alia* poor specification design, wrong contractual risk allocation, poor control systems for contractual performance and bad planning and delivery processes.
18. The structure of public markets reveals that in the supply/demand equation, the dominant part appears to be the demand side (the state and its organs as purchasers), which initialises demand through an institutionalised purchasing system, whereas the supply side (the industry) fights for access to the relevant markets. Although this is normally the case, one should not exclude the possibility of market oligopolisation and the potential manipulation of the demand side. These advanced market structures can occur more often in the future, as a result of the well established trends of industrial concentration. See C. Bovis, *The Liberalisation of Public Procurement and its Impact on the Common Market, op. cit.* p. 7; Also, P. Konstadacopoulos, *The linked oligopoly concept in the Single European Market*, Public Procurement Law Review, 1995, Vol. 4, p. 213.
19. Normally in a public contract risk assessment includes contractual elements which are associated with the design or construction of a project, the required investment and financing, planning and operational matters, maintenance, residualisation, obsolescence, political/legal aspects, industrial relations, usage volumes and finally currency transactions.
20. A number of impact assessment studies of the procurement regime upon the demand and supply sides have revealed the disproportionate risk allocation amongst the parties. See, European Commission, *The Use of Negotiated Procedures as a Non-Tariff Barrier in Public Procurement*, Brussels, CC 9364, 1995. In this study, the author investigated on behalf of the European Commission the award patterns of public contracts in six EC Member States. The results showed the overall preference of contracting authorities towards *the lowest price* award criterion. Even in cases where *the most economically advantageous offer* was used for the award of a public contract, contracting authorities prioritised the price given by

tenderers amongst the other parameters (technical reasons, aesthetic reasons, quality of deliverables, after sales service or maintenance).
21. In another impact assessment study undertaken on behalf of the European Commission, (*The Opening-up of Public Procurement to Foreign Direct Investment* in the European Community, Brussels, CC 93/79, 1995) the author examined the impact of the public procurement regime upon foreign direct investment. Investment patterns towards industries doing business with the public sector showed a considerable link between the "low risk" assessments of the public contracts of these industries.
22. In its policy statement *Public Sector Comparators and Value for Money*, February 1998, the HM Treasury Taskforce has set out the role of comparators in public procurement, stressing the importance of the value-for-money principle. The comparators are indices which help to distinguish between the lowest cost and the best value for money for public authorities and also their use as an exercise of financial management and a means of demonstrating savings to public authorities.
23. Case 76/81, *SA Transporoute et Travaux v. Minister of Public Works* [1982] ECR 457; Case No 104/75, *SA SHV Belgium v. La Maison Ideale et Societe Nationale du Longement*, before the Belgian Conseil d'Etat, judgement of 24/6/86 of the Belgian Conseil d'Etat.
24. The structure of public markets often reveals a monopsony/oligopsony character. In terms of its origins, demand in public markets is institutionalised and operates mainly under budgetary considerations rather than price mechanisms. It is also based on fulfilment of tasks (pursuit of public interest) and it is single for many products. Supply also has limited origins, in terms of the establishment of close ties between the public sector and industries supplying it and there is often a limited product range. Products are rarely innovative and technologically advanced and pricing is determined through tendering and negotiations. The purchasing decision is primarily based upon the life-time cycle, reliability, price and political considerations. Purchasing patterns follow tendering and negotiations and often purchases are dictated by policy rather than price/quality considerations.
25. See *Working Together – Private Finance and Public Money*, Department of the Environment, 1993.
26. Private markets are generally structured as a result of competitive pressures originating in the buyer/supplier interaction and their configuration can vary from monopoly/oligopoly to perfect competition. Demand arises from heterogeneous buyers with a variety of specific needs. It is based on expectations and is multiple for each product. Supply, on the other hand, is offered through various product ranges, where products are standardised using known technology, but constantly improved through research and development processes. The production process is based on mass-production patterns and the product range represents a large choice including substitutes, whereas the critical production factor is cost level. The development cycle appears to be short to medium-term and finally, the technology of products destined for the private markets is evolutionary. Purchases are made when an acceptable balance between price and quality is achieved. Purchase orders are multitude and at

27. The *Public Accounts Parliamentary Committee* and the *Accounting Standards Board* (ASB) took different views with the HM Treasury over the issue of excluding PFI deals from the Public Sector Borrowing Requirement. In its December 1997 report, the *Accounting Standards Board* came out in favour of including PFI projects in the PSBR, although the Treasury, backed by the National Audit Office and the Audit Commission had issue guidelines to the contrary.
28. A number of government documents have eulogised the Private Finance Initiative. See in particular, *Working Together – Private Finance and Public Money*, Department of Environment, 1993. *Private Opportunity, Public Benefit – Progressing the Private Finance Initiative*, Private Finance Panel and HM Treasury, 1995.
29. See the *Guidelines for Smoothing the Procurement Process*, Private Finance Panel and HM Treasury, 1996. Also *A Step by Step Guide to PFI*, HM Treasury, 1997
30. The European Public Procurement Directives include the Supplies Directive 93/36 (OJ 1993 L199/1), the Works Directive 93/37 (OJ 1993 L 199/54), the Utilities Directive 93/38 (OJ 1993 L199/84), and finally the Services Directive 92/50 (OJ 1992 L 209/1).
31. These stages represent the necessary steps that a contracting authority should take before publicising its intention to procure a PFI project. See *A Step-by-Step Guide to the PFI Procurement Process*, Private Finance Executive Panel, 1997.
32. According to Article 1(a) of the Works Directive 93/37, a works contract refers to the execution, by whatever means, of a work corresponding to the requirements specified by the contracting authority. According to Article 1(a) of Services Directive 92/50, a services contract refers to the provision of a service by a service provider to a contracting authority.
33. Interestingly, the Services Directive 92/50 allows the use of negotiated procedures in cases where specifications of a contract cannot be drawn [Article 11(2)(c)].
34. If the contract specifications were negotiated with a sole contractor, other tenderes/candidates are discriminated against. Contract specifications cannot be part of any award procedures, particularly the negotiated ones. See C. Bovis, *EC Public Procurement Law*, Longman, European Law Series, 1997, pp. 63–66.
35. Contract specifications affect essentially the price of the contract. There is no real element of competition in the process, when the contracting authority cannot compare other offers with the offer of the preferred bidder.
36. Services which are included in Part B of the Services Directive 92/50: hotel and restaurant services, rail transport services, water transport services, supporting and auxiliary transport services, legal services, personnel placement and supply services, investigation and security services, education and vocational education services, health and social services, recreational, cultural and sporting services.

37. See Article 11(2)(c) of the Services Directive 92/50.
38. See case C-331/92, *Gestion Hotelera Internacional SA v. Communidad Autonoma de Canarias* [1994] ECR 1-1329.
39. This line of argumentation was forwarded by the European Commission in its submissions in the *Gestion Hotelera* case.
40. Article 1(d) of the Works Directive 93/37.
41. Article 3 of the Works Directive 93/37.
42. See C. Bovis, *EC Public Procurement Law*, Longman, op. cit., pp. 67–68.
43. See Article 7(3) of the Works Directive 93/37.
44. See Article 3(4) of the Works Directive 93/37. An affiliated undertaking is one over which the concessionaire exercises dominant influence directly or indirectly or vice versa or both the concessionaire and its affiliated undertaking are part of another undertaking which exercises directly or indirectly dominant influence over them.
45. See COM (90) 372 fin, SYN 293 and COM (91) 322 fin, SYN 293.
46. See C. Bovis, *The Liberalisation of Public Procurement and its Impact on the Common Market*, op. cit., pp. 71–77.
47. See Article 2 of the Works Directive 93/37.
48. See for example Article 24 of the Supplies Directive 93/36.
49. Case 243/89, *Commission v. Denmark*, judgement of 22 June 1993.
50. See European Commission, *Declaration on the use of post-tender negotiations*, OJ [1994] L 111/114.
51. See case 31/87 *Gebroeders Beentjes v. Netherlands* [1988] ECR 4635. Also case C-71/92, *Commission v. Spain*, judgement of June 30, 1993.
52. See Private Finance Panel, *Private Opportunity, Public Benefit*, 1995.
53. See the analysis of the relevant case-law in C. Bovis, *EC Public Procurement Law*, op. cit., pp. 77–103.
54. Case 199/85, *Commission v. Italy* [1987] ECR 1039; case 31/87, *Gebroeders Beenjes v. The Netherlands* [1988] ECR 4635; case 3/88, *Commission v. Italy* [1989] ECR 4035; case 24/91, *Commission v. Kingdom of Spain* [1994] CMLR 621; case 107/92, *Commission v. Italy*, judgement of August 2, 1993; case C 324/93, *R. v. The Secretary of State for the Home Department, ex parte. Evans Medical Ltd and Macfarlan Smith Ltd*, judgement of March 28, 1995; case C-57/94, *Commission v. Italy*, judgement of May 18, 1995; case 296/92, *Commission v. Italy*, judgement of January 12, 1994.
55. After a contract award, contracting authorities are obliged to publish a Contract Award Notice (CAN) in the OJEC. This is a form of formal notification of the award of the contract, of the successful tenderer and the price of its offer, as well as the reasons for its selection.
56. Any eliminated candidate from the selection process has the right to ask the contracting authority for the reasons for his rejection, and any tenderer whose bid has been rejected has the right to ask for the reasons and for the name of the successful tenderer. The contracting authority must provide the information requested within fifteen days of receiving the request. Contracting authorities must also inform candidates or tenderers who so request of the grounds for their decision to cancel an award procedure.
57. See Communication from the Commission of 23 April 2003 "Developing the trans-European transport network: innovative funding solutions

– interoperability of electronic toll collection systems", COM (2003) 132, and the Report of the high-level group on the trans-European transport network of 27 June 2003.
58. See Eurostat, (Statistical Office of the European Communities), press release STAT/04/18 of the 11th of February 2004.
59. See Communication from the Commission to the Council and to the Parliament "Public finances in EMU 2003", published in the European Economy No 3/2003 (COM (2003) 283 final).
60. Conclusions of the Presidency, Brussels European Council, 12 December 2003.
61. COM (2003) 270 final.
62. The rules on the internal market, including the rules and principles governing public contracts and concessions, apply to any economic activity, i.e. any activity which consists in providing services, goods, or carrying out works in a market, even if these services, goods or works are intended to provide a "public service', as defined by a Member State.
63. See Interpretive Communication of the Commission on concessions in Community law, OJ C 121, 29 April 2000.
64. i.e. Directives 92/50/EEC, 93/36/EEC, 93/37/EEC, 93/38/EEC, relating to the coordination of procedures for the award respectively of public service contracts, public supply contracts, public works contracts, and contracts in the water, energy, transport and telecommunications sectors. These Directives will be replaced by Directive 2004/18/EC of the European Parliament and of Council of 31 March 2004 relating to the coordination of procedures for the award of public works, supply and services contracts, and Directive 2004/17/EC of the European Parliament and of the Council of 31 March 2004 relating to the coordination of procedures for the award of contracts in the water, energy, transport and postal services sectors, which will be published in the near future in the OJ. Moreover, in certain sectors, and particularly the transport sector, the organisation of a PPP may be subject to specific sectoral legislation. See Regulation (EEC) No 2408/92 of the Council on access of Community air carriers to intra-Community air routes, Council Regulation (EEC) No 3577/92 applying the principle of freedom to provide services to maritime transport within Member States, Council Regulation (EEC) No 1191/69 on action by Member States concerning the obligations inherent in the concept of a public service in transport by rail, road and inland waterway, as amended by Regulation (EEC) No 1893/91, and the amended proposal for a Regulation of the European Parliament and of the Council on action by Member States concerning public service requirements and the award of public service contracts in passenger transport by rail, road and inland waterway (COM (2002) 107 final).
65. Interpretative Communication on concessions under Community law, OJ C 121, 29 April 2000.
66. See Article 3(1) of Directive 93/37/EEC, and Articles 56 to 59 of Directive 2004/18/EC.
67. Although the Commission had proposed that services concessions be included in Directive 92/50/EEC, in the course of the legislative process the Council decided to exclude them from the scope of that Directive. In

the *Telaustria* case, the Court stated that *"[the] obligation of transparency which is imposed on the contracting authority consists in ensuring, for the benefit of any potential tenderer, a degree of advertising sufficient to enable the services market to be opened up to competition and the impartiality of procurement procedures to be reviewed"*. See Case C-324/98. See also ruling of 30 May 2002, also Case C-358/00, *Deutsche Bibliothek*, ECR I-4685. These principles are also applicable to other State acts entrusting an economic service to a third party, as for example the contracts excluded from the scope of the Directives owing to the fact that they have a value below the threshold values laid down in the secondary legislation (Order of the Court of 3 December 2001, Case C-59/00, *Vestergaard*, ECR I-9505), or so-called non-priority services.

68. Spain (law of 23 May 2003 on works concessions), Italy (Merloni law of 1994, as amended) and France (Sapin law of 1993) have nonetheless adopted such legislation.
69. i.e. those listed in Annex IA of Directive 92/50/EEC and Annex XVIA of Directive 93/38/EEC.
70. i.e. Directives 93/37/EEC, 92/50/EEC and 2004/18/EC.
71. For example, it may apply when the works are to be carried out in a geologically unstable or archaeological terrain and for this reason the extent of the necessary work is not known when launching the tender procedure. A similar derogation is provided for in Article 11(2) of Directive 92/50, and in Article 30(1)(b) of Directive 2004/18/EC.
72. Article 29 of Directive 2004/18/EC.
73. Article 23 of Directive 2004/18/EC and Article 34 of Directive 2004/17/EC.
74. The Member States use different terminology and schemes in this context (for example, the Kooperationsmodell, joint PPPs, Joint Ventures).
75. Note that the principles governing the law on public contracts and concessions apply also when a task is awarded in the form of a unilateral act (e.g. a legislative or regulatory act).
76. When planning and arranging such transactions, the test involving the use of the standard forms – which include the elements indispensable for a well-informed competition, – also demonstrate how difficult it can be to find an adequate form of advertising to award tasks falling within the scope of the law on public contracts or concessions.
77. Participation in a new undertaking with a view to establishing lasting economic links is covered by the provisions of Article 56 relating to the free movement of capital. See Annex I of Directive 88/361/EEC, adopted in the context of the former Article 67, which lists the types of operations which must be considered as movements of capital.
78. See Judgements of the Court of 4 June 2002, Case C-367/98, *Commission v. Portugal*, ECR I-4731; Case C-483/99, *Commission v. France*, ECR I-4781; and Judgements of 13 May 2003, Case C-463/00, *Commission v. Spain*, ECR. I-4581; Case C-98/01, *Commission v. United Kingdom*, Rec. I-4641. On the possible justifications in this framework, see Judgement of the Court of 4 June 2002, Case C-503/99, *Commission v. Belgium*, ECR I-4809.

79. This follows from the neutrality principle of the Treaty in relation to ownership rules, recognised by Article 295 of the Treaty.
80. Article 56 ff. of the EC Treaty.
81. See Communication of the Commission on certain legal aspects concerning intra-EU investment OJ No C 220, 19 July 1997, p. 15.
82. See, on these lines, the Judgement of the Court of 13 April 2000, Case C-251/98, *Baars*, ECR I-2787.
83. See the FIDE Congress on *The Application in the Member States of the Directives on Public Procurement*, Madrid 1990.
84. One the most notorious features of the existing PFI process is the abysmally lengthy negotiation stage and the prolonged pre-contractual arrangements. This represents a considerable (recoverable) cost which would be reflected in the final deal. See *Financial Times*, 24/07/98, where its was reported that lengthy negotiations due to the lack of clear guidelines and standard contractual forms presented a serious deterrent factor in concluding PFI contracts. The average PFI gestation period is 18 months compared with 2 months in traditional public procurement contracts.
85. A serious set back for the Private Finance Initiative in the United Kingdom was the report of the Accounting Standards Board *(The Tweedie Report – September 1998)* which criticised the practice of the HM Treasury not to include PFI deals in the Public Sector Borrowing Requirement (PSBR) balance sheet. The report condemned such practices and urged the government, for the sake of legal certainty and good public sector management and accounting to issue new guidelines for future PFI projects and treat them in the same way as traditional public procurement spending.
86. Prior to 1997, there was considerable uncertainty as to the legal position of the parties to a privately financed project. The relevant legislation did not provide *in concreto* for the rights and obligations of the private sector and threatened with *ultra vires* agreements concluded between certain public authorities (local authorities and health trusts) and the private sector. It was unclear whether these authorities had explicit or implied powers to enter into such contracts, a situation which left privately financed transactions *in limbo*. As a consequence, the *National Health Service (Private Finance) Act 1997* and the *Local Government Act (Contracts) 1997* have been enacted in order to clear all legal obstacles. Both acts have introduced a "clearance system" where the relevant authorities must certified a prospective PFI deal with the government, checking not only its *vires* but the whole commercial viability and procedural delivery mechanism of a privately financed contract.

Chapter 8 The Procurement of Services of General Interest

1. See the Commission Communication on services of general interest in Europe, OJ C 17, 19.1.2001; the Green Paper on services of general interest, COM (2003) 270, 21.5.2003, the White Paper on Services of general interest, COM (2004), 12.5.2004.

2. The Public Procurement regime includes the Public Supplies Directive 93/36/EEC, OJ L 199, 9.8.1993 as amended by Directive 97/52/EC OJ L 328, 28.11.1997; The Public Works Directive 93/37/EEC, OJ L 199, 9.8.1993 as amended by Directive 97/52/EC OJ L 328, 28.11.1997; The Utilities Directives 93/38/EEC OJ L 199, 9.8.1993 as amended by Directive 98/4/EC OJ L 101, 1.4.1998; The Public Services Directive 92/50/EEC, OJ L 209, 24.7.1992 as last amended by Directive 97/52/EC OJ L 328, 28.11.1997; The Remedies Utilities Directive 92/13/EEC OJ L 076, 23.03.1992; The Public Remedies Directive 89/665/EEC OJ L 395, 30.12.1989. The Public Procurement Directives have been recently amended by Directive 2004/18, OJ L 134, 30.4.2004 on the coordination of procedures for the award of public works contracts, public supply contracts and public service contracts and Directive 2004/17, OJ L 134, 30.4.2004 coordinating the procurement procedures of entities operating in the water, energy, transport and postal services sectors.
3. See Bovis, *La notion et les attributions d'organisme de droit public comme pouvoirs adjudicateurs dans le régime des marchés publics*, Contrats Publics, Septembre 2003.
4. See Bovis, *Public Procurement and the Internal Market of the 21st Century: Economic Exercise versus Policy Choice*, Chapter 17 in EU Law for the 21st Century: Rethinking the New Legal Order, O'Keeffe and Tridimas (eds), Hart Publishing 2005. Also Communication from the European Commission to the Council, the European Parliament, the Economic and Social Committee, and the Committee of the Regions, "Working together to maintain momentum" 2001 Review of the Internal Market Strategy, Brussels, 11 April 2001, COM (2001) 198 final. Also, European Commission, Commission Communication, Public procurement in the European Union, Brussels, March 11, 1998, COM (98) 143. See Commission Interpretative Communication on the Community law applicable to public procurement and the possibilities for integrating social considerations into public procurement, COM (2001) 566, 15 October 2001. Also, Commission Interpretative Communication on the Community law applicable to public procurement and the possibilities for integrating environmental considerations into public procurement, COM (2001) 274, 4 July 2001.
5. See Bartosch, The relationship of Public Procurement and State Aid Surveillance – The Toughest Standard Applies? Common Market Law Review, 35, 2002 and the case-law provided in the analysis.
6. See the Conclusions of the European Council of 14 and 15 December 2001, paragraph 26; Conclusions of the Internal Market, Consumer Affairs and Tourism Council meeting of 26 November 2001 on services of general interest; Commission Report to the Laeken European Council on Services of General Interest of 17 October 2001, COM (2001) 598; Communication from the Commission on the application of the State aid rules to public service broadcasting, OJ 2001 C 320, p. 5; see also the two general Commission Communications on Services of General Interest of 1996 and 2000 in OJ 1996 C 281, p. 3 and OJ 2001 C 17, p. 4.
7. See Article 73 EU Treaty.
8. See Article 36 of the Charter of Fundamental Rights.

9. See Commission Communication on services of general interest, COM (2000) 553.
10. See cases C-180-184/98 *Pavel Pavlov and Others v. Stichting Pensioenfonds Medische Specialisten* [2000] ECR I-6451. The Court pronounced that any activity consisting in offering goods and services on a given market is an economic activity. Thus, economic and non-economic services can co-exist within the same sector and sometimes even be provided by the same organisation.
11. For example, specific Community rules on environmental legislation such as Directive 75/442, OJ L 194, 25.7.1975, on waste, and Regulation 259/93 OJ L 30, 6.2.1993, on shipment of waste have establish the *principle of proximity*, which overrides other fundamental community principles. According to this principle, waste should be disposed of as near as possible to the place it was generated. For television broadcasting, the importance of public service broadcasting for the democratic, social and cultural needs of each society a specific Protocol on the systems of public broadcasting in the Member States has been annexed to the Amsterdam Treaty. See also the so-called Television without Frontiers Directive 89/552 on the co-ordination of certain provisions laid down by law, regulation or administrative action in Member States concerning the pursuit of television broadcasting activities, OJ L 298, 17.10.1989.
12. See Bovis, *Public Procurement within the framework of European Economic Law*, European Law Journal, 4.2.1998.
13. See Valadou, *La notion de pouvoir adjudicateur en matière de marchés de travaux*, Semaine Juridique, 1991, Ed. E, No. 3.
14. See Flamme et Flamme, *Enfin l' Europe des Marchés Publics*, Actualité Juridique – Droit Administratif, 1989.
15. On the issue of public interest and its relation with profit, see cases C-223/99, *Agora Srl v. Ente Autonomo Fiera Internazionale di Milano* and C-260/99 *Excelsior Snc di Pedrotti Runa & C v. Ente Autonomo Fiera Internazionale di Milano* [2001] ECR 3605; C-360/96, *Gemeente Arnhem Gemeente Rheden v. BFI Holding BV* [1998] ECR 6821; C-44/96, *Mannesmann Anlangenbau Austria AG et al. v. Strohal Rotationsdurck GesmbH* [1998] ECR 73.
16. See Bovis, *The Liberalisation of Public Procurement in the European Union and its Effects on the Common Market*, Chapter 1, Ashgate Dartmouth, 1998.
17. See Article 1(b) of Directive 93/37. The criteria for bodies governed by public law to be considered as a contracting authority for the purposes of the EU Public Procurement Directives are: i) they must be established for the specific purpose of meeting needs in the general public interest not having an industrial or commercial character; ii) they must have legal personality; and iii) they must be financed, for the most part, by either the state, or regional or local authorities, or other bodies governed by public law; or subject to management supervision by these bodies, or having an administrative or supervisory board, more than half of whose members are appointed by the state, regional or local authorities or by other bodies governed by public law. There is a list of such bodies in Annex I of Directive 93/37 which is not an exhaustive one, in the sense

that Member States are under an obligation to notify the Commission of any changes to that list.

18. See cases C-223/99, *Agora Srl v. Ente Autonomo Fiera Internazionale di Milano* and C-260/99 *Excelsior Snc di Pedrotti Runa & C v. Ente Autonomo Fiera Internazionale di Milano* [2001] ECR 3605; C-360/96, *Gemeente Arnhem Gemeente Rheden v. BFI Holding BV* [1998] ECR 6821; C-44/96, *Mannesmann Anlangenbau Austria AG et al. v. Strohal Rotationsdurck GesmbH* [1998] ECR 73.
19. See the Opinion of Advocate-General Léger, point 65 of the Strohal case.
20. See case C-179/90, *Merci Convenzionali Porto di Gevova* [1991] ECR 1-5889; General economic interest as a concept represents "activities of direct benefit to the public"; point 27 of the Opinion of Advocate-General van Gerven.
21. See Valadou, *La notion de pouvoir adjudicateur en matière de marchés de travaux*, Semaine Juridique, 1991, Ed. E, No. 3. p. 33.
22. See case C-44/96, *Mannesmann Anlangenbau Austria, op. cit.* footnote 12.
23. For example see Case 118/85 *Commission v. Italy* [1987] ECR 2599 para 7, where the Court had the opportunity to elaborate on the distinction of activities pursued by public authorities and those pursued by commercial undertakings. For a detailed analysis, see Bovis, *Recent case law relating to public procurement: A beacon for the integration of public markets*, 39 Common Market Law Review, 2002.
24. See Case C-364/92 *SAT Fluggesellschafeten* [1994] ECR 1-43; also Case C-343/95 *Diego Cali et Figli* [1997] ECR 1-1547.
25. See case C-360/96, *Gemeente Arnhem Gemeente Rheden v. BFI Holding BV* [1998] ECR 6821.
26. See case C-223/99, *Agora Srl v. Ente Autonomo Fiera Internazionale di Milano* and C-260/99 *Excelsior Snc di Pedrotti Runa & C v. Ente Autonomo Fiera Internazionale di Milano* [2001] ECR 3605C-223/99.
27. See Flamme et Flamme, *Enfin l' Europe des Marchés Publics*, Actualité Juridique – Droit Administratif, November 20 1989, p. 653, argue along the same lines.
28. See case C-44/96, *Mannesmann Anlangenbau Austria AG et al. v. Strohal Rotationsdurck GesmbH* [1998] ECR 73.
29. In support of its argument that the relevant entity (*Österreichische Staatsdruckerei*) is not a body governed by public law, the Austrian Government maintained that the proportion of public interest activities represents no more than 15–20 per cent of its overall activities. For a comprehensive analysis of the case and an insight to the concept of contracting authorities for the purposes of public procurement, see the annotation by Bovis in 36 Common Market Law Review, 1999, pp. 205–225.
30. For example, the relevant provisions stipulating the thresholds for the applicability of the Public Procurement Directives [Article 3(1) of Directive 93/37; Article 5(1) of Directive 93/36; Article 14 of Directive 93/38; Article 7(1) of Directive 92/50]; the provisions relating to the so-called "mixed contracts" [Article 6(5) of Directive 93/37], where the proportion of the value of the works or the supplies element in a public contract determines the applicability of the relevant Directive;

and finally the relevant provisions which embrace the award of works contracts subsidised *directly* by more than 50 per cent by the state within the scope of the Directive [Article 2(1)(2) of Directive 93/37].

31. See Bovis, *The Liberalisation of Public Procurement in the European Union and its Effects on the Common Market*, Chapter 1, *op. cit.* footnote 10.
32. See case C-107/98, *Teckal Slr. v. Commune di Viano* [1999] ECR I-8121.
33. This type of dependency resembles the Court's definition in its ruling on state controlled enterprises in case 152/84 *Marshall v. Southampton and South West Hampshire Area Health Authority* [1986] ECR 723.
34. C-237/99, *Commission v. France* [2001] ECR 934.
35. See case C-380/98, *The Queen and H.M. Treasury, ex parte University of Cambridge* [2000] ECR 8035.
36. See paragraph 25 of the Court's judgement as well as the Opinion of the Advocate General, paragraph 46.
37. See Freeman, *Extending Public Law Norms through Privatization*, 116 Harvard Law Review, 2003, p. 1285 *et seq*. Freeman argues that privatisation does not curtail the remit of the state. On the contrary it enacts a process of "publicisation", where through the extension of public law norms to private undertakings entrusted with the delivery of public services the state maintains a dominant position in the dispersement of governance. Also, along the same lines see Frug, *New Forms of Governance, Getting Public Power to Private Actors*, 49 UCLA Review 2002, p. 1687.
38. Corporatism has been deemed as an important instrument of industrial policy of a state, in particular where procurement systems have been utilised with a view to promoting structural adjustment policies and favour *national champions*. See Bovis, *The Choice of Policies and the Regulation Public Procurement in the European Community* in T. Lawton (ed.) *European Industrial Policy and Competitiveness: concepts and instruments*, Macmillan Publishers, 1998.
39. Alongside privatisation, the notion of contracting out represents a further departure from the premises of traditional corporatism. The notion of contracting out is an exercise which aims at achieving potential savings and efficiency gains for contracting authorities, when they test the market in an attempt to define whether the provision of works or the delivery of services from a commercial operator could be cheaper than that from the in-house team. Contracting out differs from privatisation to the extent that the former represents a transfer of undertaking only, whereas the latter denotes transfer of ownership. Contracting out depicts a price-discipline exercise by the state, against the principle of insourcing, where, the self-sufficient nature of corporatism resulted in budgetary inefficiencies and poor quality of deliverables to the public. See Domberger and Jensen, *Contracting Out by the Public Sector: Theory, Evidence, Prospects*, Oxford Review of Economic Policy, Winter 1997.
40. Classic example of such approach is the views of the UK Government in relation to the involvement of the private sector in delivering public services through the so-called *Private Finance Initiative (PFI)*, which attempts to create a framework between the public and private sectors working together in delivering public services. See in particular, *Working Together*

– *Private Finance and Public Money*, Department of Environment, 1993. *Private Opportunity, Public Benefit – Progressing the Private Finance Initiative*, Private Finance Panel and HM Treasury, 1995.

41. See Freeman, *The Private Role in Public Governance*, 75 NYUL Rev, 2000, p. 534 *et seq*. Also, Bovis, *Understanding Public Private Partnerships*, 2002 Alexander Maxwell Law Scholarship Trust.
42. See the ratione of the Court in the cases *BFI*, *Strohal* and *Agora* cases, *op. cit.* footnotes 9 and 12.
43. For example, defence, policing or other essential or core elements of public governance. It is maintained here that activities related to *imperium* (the use of force by way of regulatory or criminal law) could not be the subject of contractualised governance. A useful analysis for such argument is provided in case C-44/96, *Mannesmann Anlangenbau Austria AG et al. v. Strohal Rotationsdurck GesmbH* [1998] ECR 73, where the notions of public security and safety are used to described a range of activities by the state which possess the characteristic of "public service obligations". For a commentary of the case, see Bovis, *Redefining Contracting Authorities under the EC Public Procurement Directives: An Analysis of the case C-44/96, Mannesmann Anlangenbau Austria AG et al. v. Strohal Rotationsdurck GesmbH*, 36 Common Market Law Review, 1998.
44. EC Directive 90/531, as amended by EC Directive 93/38, OJ L 199.
45. Article 1(1) of Directive 93/38.
46. Article 1(2) of Directive 93/38.
47. The determination of a genuinely competitive regime is left to the utilities operators themselves. See case, C 392/93, *The Queen and H.M. Treasury, ex parte British Telecommunications* [1996] ECR I-1631. This is perhaps a first step towards self-regulation which could lead to the disengagement of the relevant contracting authorities from the public procurement regime.
48. This is particularly the case of non-governmental organisations (NGOs) which operate under the auspices of the central or local government and are responsible for public interest functions. See Bovis, *Public entities awarding procurement contracts under the framework of EC Public Procurement Directives*, Journal of Business Law, 1993, Vol. 1, pp. 56–78; Arrowsmith, *The Law of Public and Utilities Procurement*, Sweet & Maxwell, 1997, pp. 87–88.
49. Case 31/87, *Gebroeders Beentjes B.V. v. State of Netherlands* [1988] ECR 4635.
50. The formality test and the relation between the state and entities under its control was established in cases C-249/81, *Commission v. Ireland* [1982] ECR 4005; C-36/74 *Walrave and Koch v. Association Union Cycliste International et al.* (1974) ECR 1423.
51. See cases C-353/96, *Commission v. Ireland* and C-306/97, *Connemara Machine Turf Co Ltd v. Coillte Teoranta* [1998] ECR I-8565.
52. See case C-323/96, *Commission v. Kingdom of Belgium* [1998] ECR I-5063.
53. The fact that the Belgian Government did not, at the time, exercise any direct or indirect control relating to procurement policies over the Vlaamese Raad was considered immaterial on the grounds that a state cannot rely on its own legal system to justify non-compliance with EC law and particular Directives. For these comments, see also case C-144/97 *Commission v. France* [1998] ECR 1-613.

54. See Article 13 of Directive 2002/22/EC, OJ L 108, 24.4.2002, on universal service and users' rights relating to electronic communications networks and services (Universal Service Directive).
55. See Articles 7 and 9(4) of Directive 97/67/EC, OJ L 15, 21.1.1998, on common rules for the development of the internal market of Community postal services and the improvement of quality of service, as amended by Directive 2002/39/EC, OJ L 176, 5.7.2002.
56. See Article 4 of Regulation 2408/92, OJ L 240, 24.8.1992, on access for Community air carriers to intra-Community air routes.
57. See Regulation 1169/69, OJ L 156, 28.6.1969, on action by the Member States concerning the obligations inherent in the concept of a public service in transport by rail, road and inland waterway, as last amended by Regulation 1893/91, OJ L 169, 29.6.1991.
58. See Alexis, *Services publics et aides d'Etat*, Revue du droit de l'Union Européenne, 2002, p. 63; Grespan, *An example of the application of State aid rules in the utilities sector in Italy*, Competition Policy Newsletter, No. 3, October 2002, p. 17; Gundel, *Staatliche Ausgleichszahlungen für Dienstleistungen von allgemeinem wirtschaftlichem Interesse: Zum Verhältnis zwischen Artikel 86 Absatz 2 EGV und dem EG-Beihilfenrecht*, Recht der Internationalen Wirtschaft, 3/2002, p. 222; Nettesheim, *Europäische Beihilfeaufsicht und mitgliedstaatliche Daseinsvorsorge*, Europäisches Wirtschafts und Steuerrecht, 6/2002, p. 253; Nicolaides, *Distortive effects of compensatory aid measures: a note on the economics of the Ferring judgement*, European Competition Law Review, 2002, p. 313; Nicolaides, *The new frontier in State aid control. An economic assessment of measures that compensate enterprises*, Intereconomics, Vol. 37, No. 4, 2002, p. 190; Rizza, *The financial assistance granted by Member States to undertakings entrusted with the operation of a service of general economic interest: the implications of the forthcoming Altmark judgement for future State aid control policy*, Columbia Journal of European Law, 2003; Bovis, *Public procurement, state aids and the financing of public services: between symbiotic correlation and asymmetric geometry*, European State Aids Law Quarterly, November 2003, pp. 563–577.
59. See Case C-387/92 [1994] ECR I-877; Case T-106/95 *FFSA and Others v. Commission* [1997] ECR II-229; Case C-174/97 P [1998] ECR I-1303; Case T-46/97 [2000] ECR II-2125.
60. Article 87(1) EC defines State aid as "any aid granted by a Member State or through State resources in any form whatsoever which distorts or threatens to distort competition by favoring certain undertakings or the production of certain goods ..., in so far as it affects trade between Member States".
61. Article 86(2) EC stipulates that... "Undertakings entrusted with the operation of services of general economic interest ... shall be subject to the rules contained in this Treaty, in particular to the rules on competition, insofar as the application of such rules does not obstruct the performance, in law or in fact, of the particular tasks assigned to them. The development of trade must not be affected to such an extent as would be contrary to the interests of the Community".
62. See Case 240/83, *Procureur de la République v. ADBHU* [1985] ECR 531; Case C-53/00, *Ferring SA v. Agence centrale des organismes de sıcuritı sociale*

(ACOSS) [2001] ECR I-09067. Case Case C-280/00, *Altmark Trans GmbH and Regierungsprāsidium Magdeburg v. Nahverkehrsgesellschaft Altmark GmbH and Oberbundesanwalt beim Bundesverwaltungsgericht* [2003] ECR 1432.

63. See Opinion of Advocate General Jacobs in Case C-126/01, *Ministre de l'economie, des finances et de l'industrie v. GEMO SA* [2003] ECR 3454.
64. For example the form in which the aid is granted (See cases C-323/82 *Intermills v. Commission* [1984] ECR 3809, paragraph 31; Case C-142/87 *Belgium v. Commission*, cited in note 18, paragraph 13; and Case 40/85 *Belgium v. Commission* [1986] ECR I-2321, paragraph 120, the legal status of the measure in national law (See Commission Decision 93/349/EEC of 9 March 1993 concerning aid provided by the United Kingdom Government to British Aerospace for its purchase of Rover Group Holdings over and above those authorised in Commission Decision 89/58/EEC authorising a maximum aid to this operation subject to certain conditions (OJ 1993 L 143, p. 7, point IX), the fact that the measure is part of an aid scheme (Case T-16/96, *Cityflyer Express v. Commission* [1998] ECR II-757), the reasons for the measure and the objectives of the measure ((case C-173/73 *Italy v. Commission* [1974] ECR 709; *Deufil v. Commission* [1987] ECR 901; Case C-56/93 *Belgium v. Commission* [1996] ECR I-723; Case C-241/94 *France v. Commission* [1996] ECR I-4551; Case C-5/01 *Belgium v. Commission* [2002] ECR I-3452) and the intentions of the public authorities and the recipient undertaking (Commission Decision 92/11/EEC of 31 July 1991 concerning aid provided by the Derbyshire County Council to Toyota Motor Corporation, an undertaking producing motor vehicles (OJ 1992 L 6, p. 36, point V.).
65. See case C-173/73 *Italy v. Commission* [1974] ECR 709, paragraph 27; *Deufil v. Commission* [1987] ECR 901; Case C-56/93 *Belgium v. Commission* [1996] ECR I-723 paragraph 79; Case C-241/94 *France v. Commission* [1996] ECR I-4551, paragraph 20; and Case C-5/01 *Belgium v. Commission* [2002] ECR I-3452, paragraphs 45 and 46.
66. See Case 156/77, *Commission v. Belgium* [1978] ECR 1881.
67. A similar approach is followed for maritime transport. See The European Commission's Guidelines on State aid to maritime transport, OJ 1997 C 205.
68. See Article 2 of Regulation 2408/92.
69. Such public service obligations may be imposed on scheduled air services to an airport serving peripheral or development regions in its territory or on a thin route to any regional airport in its territory provided that any such route is considered vital for the economic development of the region in which the airport is located.
70. See Article 4 (1) (h) of Regulation 2408/92 OJ L 240 1992 on access for air carriers to intra-Community air routes.
71. The development and the implementation of these schemes must be transparent. The Commission would expect the selected company to have an analytical accounting system sophisticated enough to apportion the relevant costs (including fixed costs) and revenues.
72. See Case 173/73, *Italian Government v. Commission* [1974] ECR 709.
73. See Cases C301/87 *France v. Commission* [1990] ECR I-307; Case C142/87 *Belgium v. Commission* [1990] ECR I-959.

74. Article 5 of Regulation 2408/92 allows for exclusive concessions on domestic routes granted by law or contract, to remain in force, under certain conditions, until their expiry or for three years, whichever deadline comes first. Possible reimbursement given to the carriers benefiting from these exclusive concessions may well involve aid elements, particularly as the carriers have not been selected by an open tender (as foreseen in the case of Article 4 (1) of Regulation 2408/92).
75. See the Communication of the Commission to the Member States concerning public authorities' holdings in company capital (*Bulletin EC* 9-1984, point 3.5.1). The Commission considers that such an investment is not aid where the public authorities effect it under the same conditions as a private investor operating under normal market economy conditions. See also Commission Communication to the Member States on the application of Articles 92 and 93 of the EEC Treaty and of Article 5 of Commission Directive 80/723/EEC to public undertakings in the manufacturing sector (OJ 1993 C 307, p. 3, point 11).
76. See in particular Case 234/84 *Belgium v. Commission* [1986] ECR 2263, paragraph 14; Case C-142/87 *Belgium v. Commission* (*"Tubemeuse"*) [1990] ECR I-959, paragraph 26; and Case C-305/89 *Italy v. Commission* (*"Alfa Romeo"*) [1991] ECR I-1603, paragraph 19.
77. See Joined Cases C-278/92 to C-280/92 *Spain v. Commission* [1994] ECR I-4103.
78. For example where the public authorities contribute capital to an undertaking (Case 234/84 *Belgium v. Commission* [1986] ECR 2263; Case C-142/87 *Belgium v. Commission* [1990] ECR I-959; Case C-305/89 *Italy v. Commission* [1991] ECR I-1603), grant a loan to certain undertakings (Case C-301/87 *France v. Commission* [1990] ECR I-307; Case T-16/96 *Cityflyer Express v. Commission* [1998] ECR II-757), provide a state guarantee (Joined Cases T-204/97 and T-270/97 *EPAC v. Commission* [2000] ECR II-2267), sell goods or services on the market (Joined Cases 67/85, 68/85 and 70/85 *Van der Kooy and Others v. Commission* [1988] ECR 219; Case C-56/93 *Belgium v. Commission* [1996] ECR I-723; Case C-39/94 *SFEI and Others* [1996] ECR I-3547), or grant facilities for the payment of social security contributions (Case C-256/97 *DM Transport* [1999] ECR I-3913), or the repayment of wages Case C-342/96 *Spain v. Commission* [1999] ECR I-2459).
79. See Case C-303/88 *Italy v. Commission* [1991] ECR I-1433, paragraph 20; Case C-261/89 *Italy v. Commission* [1991] ECR I-4437, paragraph 15; and Case T-358/94 *Air France v. Commission* [1996] ECR II-2109, paragraph 70.
80. For example where the public authorities pay a subsidy directly to an undertaking (Case 310/85 *Deufil v. Commission* [1987] ECR 901), grant an exemption from tax (Case C-387/92 *Banco Exterior* [1994] ECR I-877; Case C-6/97 *Italy v. Commission* [1999] ECR I-2981; Case C-156/98 *Germany v. Commission* [2000] ECR I-6857) or agree to a reduction in social security contributions (Case C-75/97 *Belgium v. Commission* [1999] ECR I-3671; Case T-67/94 *Ladbroke Racing v. Commission* [1998] ECR II-1)
81. See the analysis in the Joined Cases C-278/92 to C-280/92 *Spain v. Commission* [1994] ECR I-4103.

82. See Case C-360/96, *Gemeente Arnhem Gemeente Rheden v. BFI Holding BV*, op. cit.
83. Cases C-223/99, *Agora Srl v. Ente Autonomo Fiera Internazionale di Milano* and C-260/99 *Excelsior Snc di Pedrotti Runa & C v. Ente Autonomo Fiera Internazionale di Milano*, op. cit.
84. See Bazex, *Le droit public de la concurrence*, RFDA, 1998; Arcelin, *L'enterprise en droit interne et communautaire de la concurrence*, Paris, Litec, 2003; Guézou, *Droit de la concurrence et droit des marchés publics: vers une notion transverale de mise en libre concurrence*, Contrats Publics, Mars 2003.
85. See Joined Cases C-83/01 P, C-93/01 P and C-94/01 *Chronopost and Others* [2003], not yet reported; see also the earlier judgement of the CFI Case T-613/97 *Ufex and Others v. Commission* [2000] ECR II-4055.
86. See Evans, *European Community Law of State Aid*, Clarendon Press, Oxford, 1997.
87. C-44/96, *Mannesmann Anlangenbau Austria AG et al. v. Strohal Rotationsdurck GesmbH*, op. cit. footnote 9. See also the analysis of the case by Bovis, in 36 CMLR (1999), pp. 205–225.
88. According to Advocate General Léger in his Opinion on the *Altmark* case, the apparent advantage theory occurs in several provisions of the Treaty, in particular in Article 92(2) and (3), and in Article 77 of the EC Treaty (now Article 73 EC). Article 92(3) of the Treaty provides that aid may be regarded as compatible with the common market if it pursues certain objectives such as the strengthening of economic and social cohesion, the promotion of research and the protection of the environment.
89. See case C-173/73 *Italy v. Commission* [1974] ECR 709; *Deufil v. Commission* [1987] ECR 901; Case C-56/93 *Belgium v. Commission* [1996] ECR I-723; Case C-241/94 *France v. Commission* [1996] ECR I-4551; Case C-5/01 *Belgium v. Commission* [2002] ECR I-3452.
90. For example the form in which the aid is granted, the legal status of the measure in national law, the fact that the measure is part of an aid scheme, the reasons for the measure, the objectives of the measure and the intentions of the public authorities and the recipient undertaking.
91. For example certain categories of aid are compatible with the common market on condition that they are employed through a specific format. See Commission notice 97/C 238/02 on Community guidelines on State aid for rescuing and restructuring firms in difficulty, OJ 1997 C 283.
92. According to Article 26 of Directive 93/36, Article 30 of Directive 93/37, Article 34 of Directive 93/38 and Article 36 of Directive 92/50, two criteria provide the conditions under which contracting authorities award public contracts: *the lowest price* or the *most economically advantageous offer*. The first criterion indicates that, subject to the qualitative criteria and financial and economic standing, contracting authorities do not rely on any other factor than the price quoted to complete the contract. The Directives provide for an automatic disqualification of an "obviously abnormally low offer". The term has not been interpreted in detail by the Court and serves rather as an indication of a "lower bottom limit" of contracting authorities accepting offers from the private sector tenderers See Case 76/81, *SA Transporoute et Travaux v. Minister of Public Works* [1982] ECR 457; Case 103/88, *Fratelli Costanzo S.p.A. v. Comune di*

Notes 285

Milano [1989] ECR 1839; Case 295/89, *Impresa Dona Alfonso di Dona Alfonso & Figli s.n.c. v. Consorzio per lo Sviluppo Industriale del Comune di Monfalcone* [1991] ECR 2967.

93. An interesting view of the lowest price representing market value benchmarking is provided by the case C-94/99, *ARGE Gewässerschutz, op. cit.* footnote 9, *where* the Court ruled that directly or indirectly subsidised tenders by the state or other contracting authorities or even by the contracting authority itself can be legitimately part of the evaluation process, although it did not elaborate on the possibility of rejection of an offer, which is appreciably lower than those of unsubsidised tenderers by reference to the of abnormally low disqualification ground.

94. The meaning of the most economically advantageous offer includes a series of factors chosen by the contracting authority, including price, delivery or completion date, running costs, cost-effectiveness, profitability, technical merit, product or work quality, aesthetic and functional characteristics, after-sales service and technical assistance, commitments with regard to spare parts and components and maintenance costs, security of supplies. The above list is not exhaustive.

95. For example the form in which the aid is granted, the legal status of the measure in national law, the fact that the measure is part of an aid scheme, the reasons for the measure, the objectives of the measure and the intentions of the public authorities and the recipient undertaking.

96. For example certain categories of aid are compatible with the common market on condition that they are employed through a specific format. See Commission notice 97/C 238/02, OJ 1997 C 283 on Community guidelines on State aid for rescuing and restructuring firms in difficulty.

97. See case C-107/98, *Teckal Slr v. Comune di Viano* [1999] ECR I-8121.

98. See Council Directive 83/349, OJ 1983 L193/1.

99. The explanatory memorandum accompanying the text amending the Utilities Directive (COM (91) 347-SYN 36 1) states that this provision relates, in particular, to three types of service provision within groups. These categories, which may not or may not be distinct, are: the provision of common services such as accounting, recruitment and management; the provision of specialised services embodying the know how of the group; the provision of a specialised service to a joint venture. The exclusion from the provisions of the Directive is subject, however, to two conditions: the service-provider must be an undertaking affiliated to the contracting authority and, at least 80 per cent of its average turnover arising within the European Community for the preceding three years, derives from the provision of the same or similar services to undertakings with which it is affiliated. The Commission is empowered to monitor the application of this Article and require the notification of the names of the undertakings concerned and the nature and value of the service contracts involved.

100. The determination of a genuinely competitive regime is left to the utilities operators themselves. See case, C 392/93, *The Queen and H.M. Treasury, ex parte British Telecommunications PLC* [1996] ECR I-1631. This approach by the Court is reflected into the current proposals of the Public Procurement Directives to disengage from the relevant

regime genuinely competitive entities and replace public procurement regulation with a sort of sectoral/industry self-regulation.
101. See Council Decision 87/565, OJ 1987, L 345.
102. The listed utility activities which are covered under the new GPA include (i) activities connected with the provision of water through fixed networks; (ii) activities concerned with the provision of electricity through fixed networks; (iii) the provision of terminal facilities to carriers by sea or inland waterway; and (iv) the operation of public services in the field of transport by automated systems, tramway, trolley bus, or cable bus.
103. See case C-320/91, Corbeau, *v.* Commission , ECR [1993] I-2533 point 14.
104. See Case C-280/00, *Altmark Trans GmbH, Regierungsprösidium Magdeburg et Nahverkehrsgesellschaft Altmark GmbH, Oberbundesanwalt beim Bundesverwaltungsgericht*, (third party), judgement of 24 July 2003.
105. See Case 127/73 *BRT v. SABAM* [1974] ECR 313, para. 20; Case 66/86 *Ahmed Saeed Flugreisen v. Commission* [1989] ECR 803, paragraph 55.
106. The standard assessment criterion applied under Article 86(2) EC only requires for the application of Article 87(1) EC to frustrate the performance of the particular public service task, allowing for the examination being conducted on an *ex post facto* basis. See also the ratione behind the so-called "electricity judgements" of the ECJ of 23 October 1997; Case C-157/94 *Commission v. Netherlands* [1997] ECR I-5699; Case C-158/94 *Commission v. Italy* [1997] ECR I-5789; Case C-159/94 *Commission v. France* [1997] ECR I-5815 and C-160/94 *Commission v. Spain* [1997] ECR I-5851; a great deal of controversy exists as to whether the material standard of the frustration of a public service task under Article 86(2) EC had lost its strictness. See Magiera, *Gefährdung der öffentlichen Daseinsvorsorge durch das EG-Beihilfenrecht?*, FS für Dietrich Rauschning 2000.
107. See Opinion of Advocate General Lenz, delivered on 22 November 1984 in Case 240/83 *Procureur de la République v. ADBHU* [1985] ECR 531 (536). Advocate-General Lenz in his opinion held that the indemnities granted must not exceed annual uncovered costs actually recorded by the undertaking, taking into account a reasonable profit. However, the Court In the *ADBHU* case did not allow for the permissibility of taking into account such a profit element. Interestingly, the approach of the Court of First Instance on Article 86(2) EC has never allowed any profit element to be taken into account, but instead focused on whether without the compensation at issue being provided the fulfilment of the specific public service tasks would have been jeopardised.

Index

abnormally low tenders 54, 79, 149
affiliated undertakings 49, 65
Agreement on Government
  Procurement 46, 163
attestation 45
authorities, *see* contracting authorities
award of damages 45, 137
abuse of award procedures 106, 107, 130
anti-trust 3, 14, 18, 111
award criteria 61, 79, 95, 99, 117
  lowest offer 62, 79
  most economically advantageous 63, 80, 81
award procedures 58, 78, 130, 150
  open 58
  restricted 59
  negotiated 60
  accelerated procedures 60
  competitive dialogue 150

bodies governed by public law 49, 50, 85, 148

call for competition 17, 50, 51
Common Product Classification 54
concession contracts 66
  public works concessions 66
  public service concessions 39, 40
conciliation 43, 44
construction projects under
  international agreements 36, 37, 38
contract notice 50
contracts, *see* public contracts
codification 147
codified public supplies, works and
  services directive 146
commerciality and needs in the
  general interest 88
common market 1, 3, 5, 14, 17
competitive dialogue 150
competitive markets in utilities 169

compliance 45
concession contracts 66, 191
connection of contracting authorities
  with private undertakings 92
contract compliance 115
contracting authorities 49, 83, 84
contracts to affiliated undertakings 65
contractual public private
  partnerships 198
contractual performance 164
contractualised governance 17, 88, 92, 179, 216
contractualised governance and
  services of general interest 216
corporatism 177, 180, 181
culture 164

damages 45, 137
defence 10
dependency test 88
design contests 65
dimensionality of public procurement 125
dual capacity of contracting
  authorities 91

economic exercise 5, 6, 100, 101, 102
effects of the principle of
  transparency 128
electronic auctions 157
electronic procurement 155
electronic signatures 160
eligibility of bodies governed by
  public law to tender 148
eligibility requirements 55
employee protection 98
employment 98, 115, 116
enforcement 67, 68, 95, 98
environment 69, 99, 166, 167
environmental considerations as
  award criteria 69, 99, 160

287

estimation of contract value   52, 53
excluded sectors   23
exclusion of contractors   54, 55, 56
exclusive rights   65, 168
extra-territorial effects   47, 48

financial and economic standing
   54, 72, 73
framework agreements   64, 153
framework procurement   153, 154
freedom of establishment   4, 5
freedom of information   196
freedom to provide services   3, 4, 14, 15
functional dimension of contracting
   authorities   83, 84

GATT   46
GPA see Government Procurement
   Agreement   46, 163

impact assessment   124, 139, 141
industrial policy   9, 139
in-house contracts   65
institutional public private
   partnerships   200
intellectual origins of PFI   182, 183, 184

joint and centralised procurement   149
joint venture public private
   partnerships   199

links of contracting authorities with
   private undertakings   95, 96, 213, 214
list of recognised contractors   56, 73, 74, 149, 150

market access   1, 14, 106, 107
mandatory advertisement   50, 125, 128
mixed contracts   189
monetary applicability   52, 53, 54

national treatment   46, 163
nomenclature: NACE   34, 36, 42

non-tariff barriers (NTBs)   3, 14
non-discrimination   72
neo-classical theories   106
non-commercial character   88, 209

Official Journal   50
ordo-liberal theories   112

post-tender negotiations   60
principles of the directives   23
public authorities, see contracting
   authorities
public contracts   33, 35, 38, 42
public service contract   206, 207, 208
public undertakings   39, 40
postal utilities   169
preference purchasing schemes   76, 95, 112, 113
private finance initiative   179, 180, 181, 185, 187, 193
probity   165
procedural delivery of PFI   167
procurement as a policy instrument
   5, 9, 95, 113, 117
public housing schemes   66
public markets   1, 2, 3, 106
public monopolies   134
public nature of public procurement
   82, 208, 209
public policy   5, 95, 112, 113, 115
public private partnerships   175
public procurement regulation   17, 23, 33
public service obligations   224
publication   50, 125, 128
publicity requirements   50, 51

qualification criteria   54
   financial   54, 76, 77
   technical   55
   economic   56, 76, 77
   professional   56
qualitative selection   55
quantitative restrictions   14, 15
qualification criteria   54, 56, 73
qualification of contractors, legal
   requirements   56, 73, 149, 150

recognised contractors   56, 73, 74, 149, 150
regional development   6
remedies   45, 137, 138
regionalism   6, 76, 77
reluctance in initiating litigation   137
rule of reason   117

secret public works contracts   36, 37
selection criteria   55, 56, 76, 77
service providers   43
services contracts   42
   priority   44
   non-priority   44
setting aside procurement awards   47
Single European Act (SEA)   2, 15
small and medium enterprises (SMEs)   6, 7, 164
social policy   67, 68, 95, 96, 113, 115
state monopolies, *see* monopolies
sub-contracting   6, 7, 164
subsidiarity   2, 3, 14, 15
subsidised works contracts   36, 37, 91, 92
selection and qualification   54
selection criteria   54, 55, 73, 74
services   42
services of general interest   208
small and medium enterprises   66, 164
social considerations as award criteria   95, 115, 166

socio-economic considerations   67
standardisation and specification   136
state aids   9, 76, 226, 228, 233
subcontracting   6, 66, 164
supplies   33
sustainability of industries   139

technical capacity   54
technical specifications   72, 73, 136
telecommunications   38, 39, 168, 169
tendering procedures, *see* award procedures
tenders electronic daily (TED)   50, 51
technical standards   72
tendering procedures   58
the principle of non-discrimination   72, 124, 125
the principle of objectivity   78
transfer of undertakings   68, 98, 115, 117
threshold values   53
   Directive on Public Services   53
   Directive on Public Supplies   54
   Directive on Public Utilities   54
   Directive on Public Works   54
transparency, *see* principles of directives

utilities   38, 168, 169

works   35
WTO   46, 163